Reflective Planning, Teaching, and Evaluation: K–12

Reflective Planning, Teaching, and Evaluation: K–12

Judy W. Eby
with
Edward Kujawa
University of San Diego

Prentice Hall, Upper Saddle River, New Jersey 07458

Library of Congress Cataloging-in-Publication Data
Eby, Judy W.
  Reflective planning, teaching, and evaluation: K-12 /
Judy W. Eby, Edward Kujawa.
    p. cm.
  Includes bibliographical references and indexes.
  ISBN 0-02-331331-5
  1. Teaching. 2. Thought and thinking. 3. Educational
tests and measurements. 4. Educational planning. I. Kujawa,
Edward. II. Title.
LB1029.3.E295   1994   93-3985
371.1'02—dc20   CIP

Editor: Debbie Stollenwerk
Production Supervisor: Kelly Ricci/Spectrum Publisher Services
Production Manager: Francesca Drago
Cover Designer: Curtis Tow

This book was set in Caledonia by Carlisle Communications, Ltd.

©1994 by Prentice-Hall, Inc.
A Simon & Schuster Company
Upper Saddle River, New Jersey 07458

Printed in the United States of America
10 9 8 7 6 5

ISBN 0-02-331331-5

Prentice-Hall International (UK) Limited, *London*
Prentice-Hall of Australia Pty. Limited, *Sydney*
Prentice-Hall Canada Inc., *Toronto*
Prentice-Hall Hispanoamericana, S.A., *Mexico*
Prentice-Hall of India Private Limited, *New Delhi*
Prentice-Hall of Japan, Inc., *Tokyo*
Prentice-Hall of Southeast Asia Pte. Ltd., *Singapore*
Editora Prentice-Hall do Brasil, Ltda., *Rio de Janeiro*

This book is dedicated with love and appreciation
to
Richard, Peter, Alex, and Lisa Eby

Preface

THIS BOOK IS intended to initiate a journey of self-discovery for beginning teachers and those who are committed to improving their performances as elementary, middle school, or secondary classroom teachers.

The journey begins with an analysis of how teachers process information about school events. Our goal is to encourage you to reflect on your personal moral principles and recognize how your values and beliefs are likely to be translated into actions that affect your students' accomplishments and satisfaction with school.

PLANNING

No journey is likely to reach a satisfying destination without careful planning. In chapters 2 and 3, you will learn how to diagnose students' needs in order to create a healthy classroom environment that will increase students' intrinsic motivation and prevent discipline problems in your classroom.

In this exciting time of educational change—as schools restructure decision making—teachers have the opportunity to take more responsibility for creating the curricula that they teach. In chapters 4, 5, and 6, you will learn how to reflect on and articulate valuable educational goals and outcomes in the affective, cognitive, and psychomotor domains. You will learn how to create interdisciplinary thematic units and lesson plans that will engage your students in active, hands-on learning.

Throughout the book, award-winning teachers share some of their exciting lessons and unit plans. We are hopeful that you will enjoy reading them and perhaps modifying them for your own classroom use.

TEACHING

In order to present your lessons with enthusiasm and clarity, chapters 7 through 10 provide a variety of current teaching strategies that you can use to structure your classroom experiences. With these you can develop a repertoire of methods that will meet the needs of students with a variety of backgrounds and learning styles.

You will learn effective direct instruction techniques and will be introduced to a variety of teaching skills that promote higher-order thinking, through cooperative learning, role playing, simulation, and other models of teaching. We also present stories told by practicing classroom teachers who share with you how they actually use these strategies. We encourage you to experiment, be creative, and be open to innovation when you begin to teach.

EVALUATION

We believe that evaluation is a critical component of all aspects of teaching and learning. We highlight new assessment techniques that promote success, rather than failure, among learners.

You will learn how your own values and curriculum orientations affect the types of tests you write and the way you assign grades. In chapters 11 and 12, we encourage you to make evaluation a formative experience by including your students in the evaluation process. You will learn how to assist your students as they create portfolios of their academic work, including writing samples, tests, daily work, and creative projects.

You will also learn that the importance of feedback to students in the evaluation process cannot be underestimated. With careful planning and sufficient time and assistance, we believe that most students can and do reach the standards of achievement expected by teachers.

For reflective teachers, there is no final destination on this journey of self-discovery. The process of planning, teaching, evaluating, and reflecting on the process is a continuous one, and most agree that the journey itself is one of the most rewarding and satisfying reasons for being a teacher.

J.E.
E.K.

Acknowledgments

We would like to express our appreciation to the reviewers of this book: Leigh Chiarelott, Bowling Green State University; Donna J. Merkley, Iowa State University; Frances B. Barhydt, Lyndon State College; and Elizabeth Simons, Kansas State University.

Brief Contents

Contents

▼ **CHAPTER 3**

▼ **CHAPTER 4**

▼ **CHAPTER 5**

Planning Motivating Curriculum Units   *115*

▼ **CHAPTER 6**

Sequencing Objectives in Lesson Plans   *137*

▼ **CHAPTER 7**

Reflective Classroom Instruction   *167*

▼ **CHAPTER 8**

Discussion and Questioning Strategies to Promote Cognitive Engagement   *189*

Figures

▼ **CHAPTER 13**

How Reflective Teachers Think

FROM THE MOMENT they walk into the school building in the morning, teachers face a continual stream of questions that need immediate responses, decisions that affect the well-being of their students, value judgments that may conflict with others' points of view, and complex problems that need elegant solutions.

Lori Shoults began her teaching career in the early 1990s at Seth Paine Elementary School in Lake Zurich, Illinois. To illustrate the complexity of the beginning teacher's role and responsibilities, here is a brief account of some of the issues she faced during her first 3 months in the classroom.

When I first walked into my empty classroom in August, I was greeted by a big box of textbooks. I had been hired by this school district because of my interest in and enthusiasm for the whole language approach to teaching reading and writing. So I had the freedom to create my own curriculum rather than rely on the texts. With that freedom came a lot of hard work.

It was very hard to plan before knowing my students, especially the first year, when I didn't even know what second graders were like. I wanted the curriculum in my classroom to be fully integrated. I wanted science and social studies to be a part of reading and writing. What I did was examine all the textbooks in great detail. I made lists of skills that were taught in the English, phonics, and spelling books. From the science, social studies, and reading basals, I looked for topics. I divided the year into 2- to 3-week integrated units on topics such as plants, weather, light, magnets, dinosaurs, animals, and safety.

Within these units, I taught my reading and English skills every morning in a new poem that was related to the unit's theme. I distributed a poem to the students, and they glued it in their folders. We read the poem once just to enjoy its ideas and sounds. Then each day, I asked the students to look for examples of phonics rules, word structures, types of sentences, and punctuation. I focused on two or three new skills each day.

Because I used the whole language approach, the students chose their own reading materials from the books in our room or in the library. To encourage them to read, I decided to use a reading incentive program, which gave credit or rewards for the number of books each student read. But when I considered this idea, it had a lot of drawbacks. Children who read short, easy books would appear to get more credit than those who read long, challenging books. I talked to other teachers to find out what they had tried. One teacher told me about a system of having students keep track of the number of minutes they read rather than the number of books. When I considered this approach, I concluded that it was more productive than focusing on the number of books read because my goal was for the students to read longer stories and books rather than just counting books. It also seemed more fair because students at different achievement levels read books of different lengths. This system gave equivalent credit to each student for time spent reading, at every reading level.

The social studies textbook focused on the concepts of community and geography. I decided to have an overall theme of community, which I implemented by establishing a simulated community in the classroom. We had a teacher, a sheriff, a mayor, a meteorologist, a banker, and a gardener. Students signed up for the jobs they wanted and rotated every week. The learning stations in the class were community sites, such as a post office (letter-writing center), a greenhouse (science center), a newspaper stand (writing center), a telephone company (listening center), a library (reading center), a toy store (learning games), and a computer lab.

My organizational problems were growing more difficult each day. At the beginning of the year, I tried to do it all at once. In addition to my regular reading, writing, and math programs, I set up five rotating math enrichment stations, the community stations, a geography program, and literature circles where students discussed books they were reading on their own. I wasn't able to get to all of these things as I had planned. I kept running out of time during the day. The students were confused. They were always asking when we were going to do different things.

So I sat down and planned for one special activity each day. On Tuesdays we would do community stations, on Wednesdays we had literature circles, and on Fridays we had math enrichment stations. I thought it would be better to have a consistent schedule. The students wanted to know what to expect, and I felt better knowing when to plan for each activity.

For mathematics, I examined the basal text and believed that I could cover the skills in more interesting ways. I wanted to teach with more hands-on activities and use fewer math pages. I decided to use the Everyday Mathematics program (Bell, 1990) for teaching concepts and to use the textbook for practice and review. I also gave the tests from the math book. After using this approach for several months, I found that the students were able to do the textbook tests successfully. More important to me, they were enthusiastic about math. Even my lowest-achieving students felt confident participating in math activities.

After 3 months of teaching, I believed that I was beginning to think like a teacher. At the beginning of the year, my schema for teaching and learning was rudimentary, leading me to make most decisions by trial and error. But later, I thought that I had expanded my knowledge and experience base to the point that, when I reflected on a decision, I had a much better understanding of the consequences of my actions.

REFLECTIVE THINKING

As Lori's account shows, teachers are faced with a multitude of complex issues and judgments. Each decision point requires a thoughtful response. But *thought* is an abstract and multifaceted concept, and *thinking* is a relatively mysterious process. In order to clarify the mystery of thinking, many cognitive psychologists have proposed a theoretical framework known as *information processing* to help us understand how we think.

Processing Information

According to cognitive psychologists, thinking is, first, a perceptual process. As shown in Figure 1–1, each new bit of knowledge from the environment enters the consciousness of an individual through one or more of the five senses. For example, a new fact stated by a teacher is taken in by an individual's sense of hearing. A new idea read in a book enters through the sense of sight, and a new skill such as operating the clutch and stick shift on an automobile enters the consciousness through the sense of touch. The senses register these new bits of knowledge in one-quarter of a second, and within that instant, an executive function of the brain selects some bits of knowledge for retention in its *working memory* and discards other bits of knowledge entirely. This process, known as *selective perception*, is extremely important to the thinking and learning

FIGURE 1–1
Model of How the Brain Processes Information

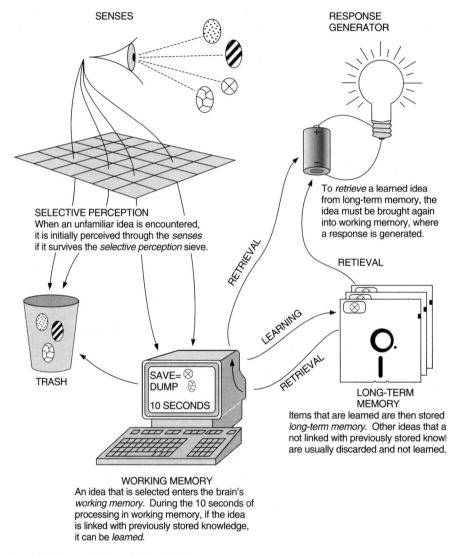

SENSES

RESPONSE GENERATOR

SELECTIVE PERCEPTION
When an unfamiliar idea is encountered, it is initially perceived through the *senses* if it survives the *selective perception* sieve.

RETRIEVAL

To *retrieve* a learned idea from long-term memory, the idea must be brought again into working memory, where a response is generated.

RETIEVAL

LEARNING

RETRIEVAL

TRASH

SAVE= ⊗
DUMP ⊗
10 SECONDS

LONG-TERM MEMORY
Items that are learned are then stored *long-term memory.* Other ideas that a not linked with previously stored knowl are usually discarded and not learned.

WORKING MEMORY
An idea that is selected enters the brain's *working memory.* During the 10 seconds of processing in working memory, if the idea is linked with previously stored knowledge, it can be *learned.*

Reprinted by permission of Peter R. Eby.

processes. We experience it simply as an initial awareness of a new fact, term, idea, or other sensation.

Why are some bits discarded, while others are sent to the working memory? That question is too complex to be answered fully here, but you can certainly recognize that we reject some stimuli when too many bombard us at one time, and we reject other stimuli because they are so foreign to our experience that we think of them as unintelligible.

A thought, fact, or skill that reaches the working memory stays there for less than 10 seconds. According to Gagné (1985), "Working memory is the 'place' where conscious mental work is done" (p. 10). The obvious analogy of working memory is the computer. In fact, the term *information processing* was originally coined in the field of computer technology, but it is currently used to describe human thinking as well. Cognitive psychologists also use the term *cognitive processing* to describe the concept of the human mind's perceiving, sorting, organizing, storing, and recalling knowledge and information.

The stream of new information that is acted on in the working memory is again directed by an executive function of the brain into the *long-term memory* or is rejected and forgotten. A statement made by a teacher, a fact read in a book, or a process such as adding two numbers either is selected for retention in the long-term memory because it is perceived as important, useful, and comprehensible, or is discarded as unimportant, useless, or incomprehensible. Another possibility is that the material is discarded simply because the working memory has a small capacity and cannot process many bits of knowledge at the same time.

What we call *learning* occurs after the information is processed. It refers to the retention of knowledge in the long-term memory in such a way that it can be retrieved at will. This retention process is analogous to storing the information on a computer disk by using the "save" command.

Another part of the thinking process occurs during the *retrieval* of information that is stored in the long-term memory. When we call up a fact or an idea from the long-term memory, it moves back into working memory for further processing and then moves to a *response generator*, where the individual considers an array of possible responses and selects the one that seems to be most suitable in the given situation. The selected response is then performed.

The information processing model is applicable to all kinds of thinking. Students use it when they learn new facts and skills in the classroom. Teachers use it when they assess their students' needs and consider how best to explain the new skill they are teaching.

Teachers who understand the process of acquiring and processing information can apply this knowledge in countless ways to the benefit of their students. They can reduce external stimuli so that the important bits of knowledge are perceived by their students' short-term memories. They can pace the delivery of new information to give students sufficient time to process one bit of knowledge in working memory before introducing another. They can phrase questions in such a way that the questions provide the appropriate cue to retrieve the stored information from long-term memory.

How Teachers' Thinking Affects Student's Learning

The information processing model implies that all human beings think alike—that one brain is as much like another as two computer terminals are. Of course, we know that this is not true. Human personalities, values, and philosophies must be taken into account to fully understand the thinking process.

As a beginning teacher, you are undoubtedly interested in how teachers think, and you are probably even more interested in beginning to assess your own thinking attributes. Are you a systematic and deliberate thinker? A meditative ponderer? A quick, dynamic speculator? A moderate, calm calculator? A creative, original hypothesizer?

Before answering, you may want to know just which of these styles of thinking is best suited to the teaching profession. But, alas, there is no research or data to support an accurate response to this question. Successful and effective teachers come in both genders and in all shapes, sizes, ages, and races, and display a variety of temperaments, personalities, and teaching styles.

However, a growing body of knowledge supports the point of view expressed in this book: that successful and effective teachers tend to reflect actively and productively about the important things in their careers, including their educational goals, the classroom environment, and their own professional abilities.

How will you recognize whether you are a reflective thinker with the potential of becoming a reflective teacher? This book is designed to assist you in making that assessment. You will be confronted with many dilemmas and ambiguous situations that will require you to use your thinking processes. You can monitor your own responses and processes to gain a better understanding of your capacity for reflection. You will also be provided with a model of reflective thinking that may aid you in developing your reflective thinking abilities.

The guiding assumption of this book is that reflective teachers deserve the opportunity to select from a repertoire of ideas rather than to accept and duplicate a single pattern. Therefore, this book provides you with a wide-ranging repertoire of curriculum planning ideas, teaching strategies, and evaluation methods that can be applied in school classrooms.

That does not mean that all of the elements presented here are in agreement with one another. Because this book emphasizes the right and the responsibility of the teacher to make informed decisions, conflicting and competing theories and ideas are frequently presented in this text so that you may reflect on them and make your own judgments. Underlying the ideas presented in this text is the high value placed on encouraging you, the beginning teacher, to use reflective thinking as you consider the alternative modes and methods of teaching.

Definitions of Reflective Thinking and Action

In *How We Think: A Restatement of the Relation of Reflective Thinking to the Educative Process*, John Dewey (1933) defined reflective thinking as the "active, persistent and careful consideration of any belief or supposed form of knowledge in light of the grounds that support it" (p. 9). An analysis of this carefully worded statement creates a powerful verbal image of the reflective thinker and correlates very well with the notion of a reflective teacher.

The first descriptive adjective, *active*, indicates one who voluntarily and willingly takes responsibility for considering personal actions. The reflective teacher is one who actively engages in an energetic search for information and solutions to problems that arise in the classroom. In contrast, many passive teachers fail to consider issues that confront them and their students.

Dewey's use of the word *persistent* implies a commitment to thinking through difficult issues in depth, continuing to consider matters even though it may be uncomfortable or tiring to do so. Although some teachers may begin to seek knowledge and information, they may be satisfied with easy answers and simple solutions. The reflective teacher is rarely satisfied but continually and persistently seeks more knowledge and better ways to teach and manage the classroom.

The *careful* thinker is one who has concern for both self and others. Reflective teachers care deeply about ways to improve their classroom performance and how to bring the greatest possible benefit to the lives of their students. Caring teachers create positive, nurturing classroom environments that promote high self-esteem and concern for each other among their students. Less careful teachers are likely to consider their own needs and feelings to be of greater importance than those of their students. Because they do not reason with care, they may make unreasonable demands on their students.

Dewey's phrase, "belief or supposed form of knowledge," implies that little is known for sure in the teaching profession. The reflective thinker maintains a healthy skepticism about educational theories and practices. While a less reflective teacher might be persuaded that there is only one right way to teach, the reflective teacher observes that individual students may need different conditions for learning and a variety of incentives in order to be successful. A less reflective teacher might adopt each new educational innovation without questioning its value; the reflective teacher greets each of these new ideas with an open but questioning mind, considering whether it is valuable and how it can be adapted to fit the needs of the class.

The final phrase in Dewey's definition, "in light of the grounds that support it," directly relates to the reflective thinker's practice of using evidence and criteria in making a judgment. While less reflective teachers may jump to conclusions very quickly based on initial observations or prior cases, the reflective teacher gathers as much information as possible about any given problem, weighs the value of the evidence against suitable criteria, and then draws a conclusion and makes a judgment. After a decision is made, the less reflective teacher may stick to it rigidly, but the reflective teacher will reconsider decisions and judgments whenever new evidence or information becomes available.

But reflective thinking, even when it is persistent and careful, does not automatically lead to change and improvement. Dewey also acknowledged the importance of *translating thought into action* and specified that attitudes of open-mindedness, responsibility, and "whole-heartedness" are needed for teachers to translate their thoughts into reflective actions.

How does a novice teacher learn to be reflective about personal decisions and actions? The process must begin in courses, which prepare teachers to teach, such as the one you are taking now. Cruickshank (1987) notes, "Literally, to reflect is to think. However, reflection is more than merely bringing something to mind. Once one brings something to mind, one must consider it" (p. 3). Drawing on Dewey's work, Cruickshank suggests, "Rather than behaving purely according to impulse, tradition, and authority, teachers can be reflective—they can deliberate on their actions with open-mindedness, wholeheartedness [*sic*], and intellectual responsibility" (p. 8).

This means that as teachers make any choice or take any action in the classroom, they reflect on how their choices and actions affect their students. For example, at the end of a history lesson, the teacher may begin to tell the students to "read chapter 6 and write an essay summarizing the main idea." But as the teacher is speaking, an inner voice may recall that for the last few days, students had not completed their homework. When asked to produce it, several students claimed that they had not heard the homework assignment given in class. The teacher reflects that some learners need visual reminders while others need to actually write the assignment in their assignment books in order to recall what to do that evening. So, as a reflective action, the teacher follows the spoken words by writing the assignment on the chalkboard, perhaps giving more detail about what the essay should contain. The teacher then walks around the room and reminds students to write the assignment in their assignment books before they leave the classroom. The goals of this reflective thinking and action are to meet the varied needs of the students and to enhance the likelihood that the students can be successful in the assigned classroom task.

Donald Schon (1987) concurs with Dewey's emphasis on action as an essential aspect of the reflective process. He defines the reflective practitioner as one who engages in "reflection-in-action," an interior observation and criticism of personal actions:

> Reflection gives rise to on-the-spot experiment. We think up and try out new actions, . . . test our tentative understandings of them, or affirm the moves we have invented to change things for the better. . . . On-the-spot experiment may work, . . . or it may produce surprises that call for further reflection and experiment. (pp. 28–29)

A Moral and an Ethical Basis for Reflective Thinking

Although reflective thinking and reflection-in-action may appear to be quite valuable and defensible concepts, several researchers raise a serious question about the value of reflective thinking unless it is done according to a set of moral and ethical principles. Strike (1990) notes that two important factors concerning teachers' ethics are that they work with a particularly vulnerable clientele and that the teaching profession has no clear set of ethical principles or standards. Strike recommends that the ethical concepts that are most central to teachers' activities are honesty, respect for diversity, fairness and due process in matters such as discipline and grading, and equity in the distribution of educational resources such as their time.

Furthermore, it is well known that teachers are important models of moral and ethical behavior for the students they teach. As Ryan (1986) notes,

> . . . research has now confirmed what humankind long ago recognized intuitively: People with power and prestige are imitated by those around them. And, although some teachers may not think of themselves as people with power and prestige, the children they teach certainly see them as such. Children watch their teachers to find out how grown-ups act. Therefore, teachers need to be constantly aware of the powerful influence that their actions in the classroom have on students. (p. 231)

Tom (1984) proposes a vision of teaching as a "moral craft," in which the decisions made by teachers are based on moral criteria. Bullough (1989) agrees that, taken by itself, reflectivity is an unfinished concept. "For example, one might carefully weigh a number of alternative forms of punishment and choose to paddle a student because it 'gets results' and never ask the question of whether or not paddling is an ethical action" (p. 16).

Kohlberg (1987) describes *moral judgments* as decisions that are based on what an individual values rather than facts. In his studies of the development of moral reasoning, Kohlberg found that each individual has a set of beliefs about what people ought to do in various situations and what each of us considers to be right and wrong. The teacher who paddles a student may value compliance with authority over respect for students' feelings of self-esteem.

Kohlberg made the study of moral reasoning and development his life's work. His well-respected theory focuses on the concept of *justice,* which includes how people view rules, authority, fairness, and the social contract that binds individuals to society. Kohlberg organized his comprehensive description of three levels (encompassing six stages) of development that an individual may achieve during a lifetime. See Figure 1–2.

FIGURE 1–2
Kohlberg's Six Stages of Moral Development

Level 1 (preconventional)	*Stage 1*	Egocentric—Doesn't consider the needs or interests of others. Follows rules to avoid punishment.
	Stage 2	Individualistic—Acts to meet own needs and interests but recognizes that others have different needs. Follows rules that are in one's own immediate interests.
Level 2 (conventional)	*Stage 3*	Golden Rule—Recognizes the needs and interests of others as well as one's own. Follows the Golden Rule and complies with society's laws.
	Stage 4	Member of Society—Recognizes that society benefits when individuals comply with its rules and laws.
Level 3 (postconventional)	*Stage 5*	Principled—Has a set of moral principles. Recognizes that these may vary from society's rules. Usually chooses to obey laws that are part of the social contract.
	Stage 6	Universal Ethical Principles—Holds principles that respect the worth and dignity of all humanity. May choose not to comply with laws that conflict with own principles.

One way of understanding the three levels is to think of them as three different types of relationships between self and society's moral rules and expectations. From this point of view, Level 1 (preconventional) is a perspective from which rules and social expectations come from some external source and are followed in order to avoid punishment. In Level 2 (conventional), rules and expectations have been internalized by the self and are followed because the individual recognizes the value of a social order that is governed by rules. At Level 3 (postconventional), the individual recognizes the value of society's rules and expectations and at the same time upholds a distinctive set of self-selected ethical principles.

As you consider your own view of rules, expectations, and what you view as justice, where do you fit on Kohlberg's scale? Consider also how teachers' thoughts, judgments, and actions in the classroom are influenced by their own moral development.

Imagine the types of decisions and actions that are likely to be made by classroom teachers who operate at a preconventional stage of moral development. They are likely to consider all classroom events only from their own point of view, disregarding the needs and feelings of their students. They are likely to act impulsively and inconsistently from minute to minute, depending on their own self-centered and immediate interests.

Teachers at the conventional level of moral development are likely to employ consistent rules and expectations based on the principle of mutual benefit and gain. They are likely to set a model for their students of following society's rules and expectations so that the individual can get ahead and so that the societies of the classroom and the nation can flourish. If it is your goal to operate at a conventional level of moral development, you may begin by clarifying for yourself which of society's rules are most important to you and then establish classroom procedures modeled on these rules.

One example of a moral principle that a conventional teacher may value highly and want to include is the notion of developing a sense of community or democracy in the classroom. To do this, each choice you make in the classroom must enhance communication and develop a shared sense of purpose. Throughout the day, there will be many decision points regarding whether students must work alone or can work together on projects and regarding whether to take time to listen to students' interests and concerns or to keep working to finish a chapter by the end of the week. The reflective teacher who chooses to base judgments on the principle of building a sense of community will consistently consider that value in these and many other decision points throughout the day.

If your set of principles includes a high priority on the development of academic excellence, each time you plan a unit of study or assign an academic task, you will want to make sure that it is as challenging as possible. Instead of assigning all students to do the same page in the same textbook or workbook, you will consider what academic task is appropriate for various students in the class. You may assign an exploratory, hands-on task to students who need concrete experiences to develop the concept you are teaching and a more challenging and abstract task to students who have mastered the fundamentals but need to apply what they have learned to other situations.

Teachers who operate at the postconventional level of moral development are likely to have a highly personal and unique set of principles that guide their decisions regarding right and wrong, justice, fairness, and human rights. From time to time, highly principled teachers may find that their values conflict with the rules and expectations imposed on them by the school administration or the larger society.

If your goal is to become a highly principled teacher, you will begin to analyze many relative and conflicting values in order to select and clarify the ones that matter most deeply to you. You must be willing to act on these values even if your actions result in conflicts with others who hold a different set of values.

An example of a value held by a highly principled teacher might be to encourage and support students' creativity, even when students' creative efforts or ideas differ from the norms of society. If you hold this view, you will want to reflect on how to plan lessons that encourage divergent responses. If you value independence and initiative over compliance with authority, you will want to consider how to schedule time and plan learning experiences that call on students to work independently and be responsible for much of their own learning.

In *In A Different Voice*, Gilligan (1982) accepts Kohlberg's conception of justice as one important basis for moral reasoning but asserts that it represents a predominantly male view of moral development. She proposes that the feminine concepts of caring and responsibility are also essential elements of moral development. Noddings (1984) expresses the need for ethical caring in schools because schools are places where human beings interact. She proposes that caring is the basis of the Golden Rule.

These are just a few of the many important moral principles and values that reflective teachers may hold. Because many are important, it is vital for you to clarify the principles that you hold and then consider these priorities when you must make a choice about an issue that may bring more than one principle or value into conflict. For example, in the choice between academic excellence and developing a sense of community, there are likely to be many decision points on whether to push students toward accomplishing challenging academic tasks or to listen to their fears and frustrations about a task's level of difficulty. At this point, the reflective teacher considers which of these priorities is most important in this case and takes the appropriate action as a result.

A book such as this is greatly influenced by the moral principles and values of the author. This work is no exception. In it, you will find a strong commitment to the moral principles of developing a sense of community in the classroom and of developing planning, teaching, and evaluation strategies that promote success rather than failure among students of all achievement levels. Our principles about community building and organizing for success are the guiding criteria that we used to select the classroom management strategies, discipline models, teaching methods, examples of classroom materials, and experiences and methods of evaluation for this book.

Translated into action, this book presents a model of reflective planning, teaching, and evaluation based on a set of clarified moral principles in the hope that education students will view reflection and clarification of their moral principles as one of the first and most important steps in becoming teachers. Accepting this challenge will not be easy. It represents an enormous responsibility with very important consequences. As Schon (1987) suggests, many teaching actions lead to surprising outcomes, some that are successful and others that produce negative or unpleasant results. Reflective teachers are able to reflect on both positive and negative classroom experiences productively, considering what they can learn from each event, gathering information to make better judgments, considering how their actions reflect their moral priorities, and then selecting and implementing the best possible strategy under the circumstances.

Presented throughout this text are situations similar to those that teachers confront every day in their classrooms. You are asked to consider these situations and ask yourself how you would react and what you would decide or choose to do in each case. By writing journal entries regarding topics described in this book, you will examine your beliefs and defend your point of view. You are asked to observe and analyze classroom events, hypothesize cause-and-effect relationships, and look for evidence to test your hypotheses. You are asked to debate and argue educational issues with your classmates, take a stand on complex questions, and propose solutions to multifaceted problems. You are asked to make decisions and predict their consequences or to take actions and examine the consequences, looking for ways to improve the outcomes. By taking an active, persistent, open-minded, and intellectually responsible role in your present educational experiences, you can become a reflective teacher, a lifelong learner, and an agent for positive growth and change in your educational community.

A MODEL OF REFLECTIVE TEACHING

Reflective thinking may occur spontaneously. Faced with a classroom dilemma, such as a student who refuses to turn in classwork or a class that challenges the teacher's grading of a test, most teachers are likely to reflect on the conditions that brought about this trouble and to consider possible actions to take to improve the situation. Faced with a student who refuses to turn in classwork, the teacher may think that the contributing factors to this problem stem from the student's home environment, previous school experiences, or lack of readiness to learn the new material. The teacher may decide to talk to the student's parents about the problem or to have the student tested by the school psychologist. Confronted by a class of angry students who disagree with the grades they received on a recent test, the teacher who values honest feedback is likely to reflect on the quality of the teaching and the amount of preparation students had prior to the test. The teacher who values student success may also reconsider the suitability of the test items and the system used for determining grades. After thinking about these matters, the teacher may decide to allow students to retake the exam, to rescore the present test, or to stand firm on the grades as given.

In these examples, teachers are reflecting, making decisions, considering moral principles, and taking actions as a result. But is spontaneous reflection adequate in the face of the hundreds of important dilemmas and decisions teachers must make every day? Are the teachers' personal observations and insights adequate to make informed judgments, or is there a need to gather information from other informed sources?

We believe that the process of considering cause and effect can be improved by a more systematic inquiry. In this book, we propose a model of reflective teaching that is made up of a series of skills that teachers can learn to improve their own reflection-in-action.

We begin with a useful model of reflective teaching based on the work of John Dewey. Pollard and Tann (1987) analyzed Dewey's work and identified four essential characteristics of systematic reflective teaching:

1. Reflective teaching implies an active concern with aims and consequences, as well as with means and technical efficiency.
2. Reflective teaching combines enquiry and implementation skills with attitudes of open-mindedness, responsibility, and wholeheartedness.
3. Reflective teaching is applied in a cyclical or spiraling process, in which teachers continually monitor, evaluate, and revise their own practice.
4. Reflective teaching is based on teacher judgment, informed partly by self-reflection and partly by insights from educational disciplines.
(pp. 4–5)

In their analysis of these four characteristics, Pollard and Tann identified six reflective enquiry skills that teachers can learn to apply to almost any classroom situation:

Empirical Skills. These relate to the essential issue of knowing what is going on in a classroom or a school. They are concerned with collecting data and with describing situations, processes, and causes and effects with care and accuracy. Two sorts of data are particularly relevant. Objective data—such as what people actually do, their behavior—are important; but so are subjective data, which describe how people feel and think—their perceptions. The collection of both types of data calls for considerable skill on the part of the investigators, particularly when they may be enquiring into their own classroom practice.

Analytical Skills. These skills are needed to interpret descriptive data. Such "facts" are not meaningful until they are placed in a framework which enables a reflective teacher to relate them, one with the other, and to begin to theorize about them.

Evaluative Skills. Evaluative skills are used to make judgements about the educational consequences of the results of the practical enquiry. Evaluation, in the light of aims and values, enables the results of an enquiry to be applied to future policy and practice.

Strategic Skills. Strategic skills take us directly into the realm of planning for action and anticipating its implementation, following the analysis which a reflective teacher carries out.

Practical Skills. Here we are directly concerned with the skills which are involved in action itself. A reflective teacher is one who is able to link analysis and practice and ends and means to good effect. To be highly analytical but ineffectual in practical matters is not a satisfactory balance, any more than the reverse situation would be.

Communication Skills. Communication skills are necessary because reflective teachers are concerned about aims and consequences as well as means. They are likely to need and to want to communicate and discuss their ideas extensively with others. They are likely to need to establish their legitimacy and to gain the support of others in the processes of development in which they engage. Thus, they should be effective communicators. (p. 7)

Figure 1–3 provides a graphic representation of this model of reflective teaching that illustrates the cyclical or spiraling process in which teachers continually monitor, evaluate, and revise their own practice.

To show the contrast between a teacher who actively uses this reflective teaching model and one who does not, let us consider a classroom event in which the teacher must make a judgment about whether or not a student is cheating. The scene is familiar to all of us. The teacher asks students to put everything away except for a

FIGURE 1–3
A Model of Reflective Teaching

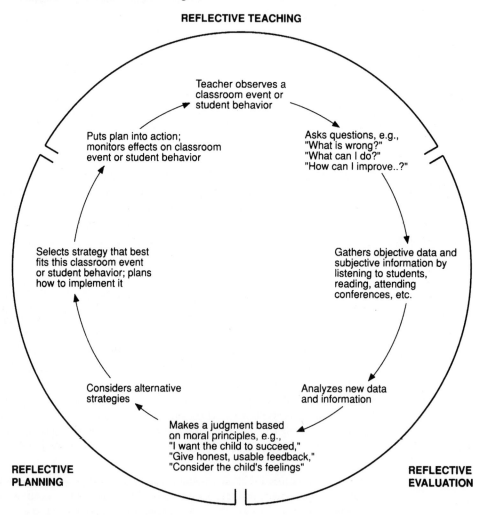

REFLECTIVE TEACHING

Teacher observes a classroom event or student behavior

Puts plan into action; monitors effects on classroom event or student behavior

Asks questions, e.g., "What is wrong?" "What can I do?" "How can I improve..?"

Selects strategy that best fits this classroom event or student behavior; plans how to implement it

Gathers objective data and subjective information by listening to students, reading, attending conferences, etc.

Considers alternative strategies

Analyzes new data and information

Makes a judgment based on moral principles, e.g., "I want the child to succeed," "Give honest, usable feedback," "Consider the child's feelings"

REFLECTIVE PLANNING

REFLECTIVE EVALUATION

Reprinted by permission of Judy W. Eby.

sharpened pencil as she distributes a two-page vocabulary test. On this exam, students must write the definitions of 20 words and use each word correctly in a sentence. The classroom is hushed as the students begin working. The teacher walks around to see that everyone is starting the exam and then sits down at the desk to correct the morning's math papers. After a few moments, a rustling sound calls the teacher's attention to the back of the room. The sound is made by a student unfolding and looking at a piece of notebook paper and then writing on the test paper.

Teachers will vary greatly in response to this situation. One teacher might deal with this classroom event almost reflexively, giving little or no thought to the appropriate response. Such a teacher might immediately walk to the student's desk and tear up the exam, saying in a harsh voice, "You'll take an F on this test for cheating." In this case, the teacher has moved from considering a classroom event to putting a plan into action without using any of the intervening, reflective thinking steps of the model.

A more reflective teacher might ask the student to bring the notebook paper and the exam to the teacher's desk. After examining the notebook paper and finding that it contains a list of the vocabulary words and their definitions, the teacher might make a judgment that the student is cheating. The teacher might then consider two or three strategies for dealing with the matter, including tearing up the paper, giving the student a failing grade, and calling the student's parents to discuss the event. If the teacher highly values the principle of building self-esteem among the students, the teacher is likely to choose the alternative of calling the parents and will quietly tell the student to expect the call that evening.

In the second example, the teacher is applying elements of the reflective teaching model. By asking to see the notebook paper and comparing it to the test, the teacher is gathering information before making a judgment. In this case, the teacher considers several strategies and applies the criterion of developing self-esteem in selecting a strategy. When the teacher puts this plan into action later in the day, there will be more opportunities to gather information from the parents about the student's home life, feelings about school, expectations of success and failure, and other factors that might have contributed to the observed event.

A third, even more highly reflective teacher experiencing the same event might generate a much more in-depth response. On seeing the student with the notebook paper, the teacher might take the student outside the classroom to discuss the observed event. Asking the student the purpose of the paper might result in conflicting information. Perhaps the student replies that the paper was on the floor, but the teacher recognizes that the handwriting is the same as that on the exam paper. The reflective teacher might try to investigate several issues embedded in the observed event by asking the student questions about motives, fears, and needs.

Reflective teachers do not make hasty decisions. In this case, the teacher may decide that there is not enough information to make any judgment about the situation. Perhaps the vocabulary words were too difficult for this student, who, rather than fail, cheated to save face. The teacher may review the student's past performance, give a nongraded placement test to evaluate the student's present achievement level, or telephone the parents to gain information they may have to offer before making a judgment. After discussing the case with others, the teacher may consider a dozen different strategies before creating a plan and putting it into action.

When reflective teachers observe nonproductive behavior in students, it often causes them to examine their own classroom practices. In this case, the reflective teacher might consider strategies that could be employed to prevent the need for such cheating in the future. The teacher might use the moral principle of enhancing self-esteem and building self-discipline in students and might decide that prior to the next vocabulary test, students will be allowed to select words they do not know from the books they are reading for literature, science, and social studies. In this way, all students have an opportunity to select words appropriate to their present level of achievement and be successful in learning how to incorporate these words into their vocabularies.

Of course, this new classroom strategy may generate new difficulties and issues. When the next test occurs, the reflective teacher will actively consider the effects of allowing students to choose their own words and compare the results from the previous tests as a means of gathering data about the new practice. The spiral of observation, reflection, gathering data, considering moral principles, making a judgment, considering strategies, and putting a plan into action continues without end in a reflective teacher's classroom.

An Example of How a Reflective Teacher Thinks and Acts

An interview with Mary Catherine Swanson illustrates the thinking processes of a highly reflective teacher (see the following Reflection). At the time of these events, Mary Catherine was a classroom teacher at Clairemont High School in San Diego, California. At present, Mary Catherine Swanson directs a nationwide program for training other teachers to teach using the AVID curriculum and support systems that she initiated as a classroom teacher in 1980. In 1991, Mary Catherine received the Charles A. Dana Award for Pioneering Achievement in Education. It was the first time such an award was given to a K–12 educator.

Mary Catherine would like teachers to know that if you are willing to do the work that must be done, teaching is the most fulfilling job in the world. But to ensure success for yourselves and for your students, you need to collaborate with other teachers to make schools places where all students can feel successful. It is critical that students experience success in school. That is the key to everything. You must be willing to be introspective about your own teaching so that you are constantly modifying what you are doing to give each student the opportunity to feel successful.

In return, Mary Catherine believes that you will find that students will do anything for teachers who are on their side. After they believe that the teacher cares, even the most difficult students will begin to believe in themselves. "When I think about my teaching career," Mary Catherine says, "I am most proud when I remember many individual students who did not believe in themselves or the 'system.' Given that attitude, they did not stand a chance for success in their lives, but through the AVID program, they learned to believe in themselves and gained the problem-solving skills that allow them to be in control of their own lives."

Lori Shoults, Mary Catherine Swanson, and several other experienced teachers whose ideas and methods you will encounter as you read this book exemplify the growing number of teachers who show a strong commitment to searching for answers and solutions to difficult school-related problems through reflective thinking and action. But commitment alone does not shape a reflective teacher. The amount of support received from colleagues and school administrators can help or hinder the development of a reflective teacher.

School Climates that Nurture Reflective Teachers

Virginia Bailey, known as Ginny to her friends, teaches first grade at Woodland School in Carpentersville, Illinois. She has grown and developed into a highly reflective teacher because of her strong personal commitment to meet the needs of her students. She has also continued to grow professionally by taking graduate-level courses and workshops as a means of updating her fund of information about teaching and learning processes. Ginny also gives credit to her school principal, Herb Price, for supporting her development as a reflective teacher.

As a principal, Mr. Price allows and encourages the teachers on his staff to take risks and to try new strategies if they can demonstrate that the new strategies are developmentally sound for young students. Since Ginny's first interest in experimenting with new reading methods, Mr. Price has fully supported her investigations into the language experience and whole language approach because he believes that these strategies are beneficial to both the affective and cognitive development of students.

"I label my administrative style the three '-ates,'" states Mr. Price. "I facilit*ate,* particip*ate* and celebr*ate* with the teachers and the students in my school over the accomplishments they are able to make. I also encourage teachers when they need it. For example, Ginny had many moments of wondering whether she was doing the right thing during her transition from using the basal reader to the whole language approach. I encouraged her to keep trying because we were both convinced that the whole language approach was developmentally sound."

Educational decisions and judgments such as this one, which was made by a teacher and supported by the principal, are examples of school reform in action. Many educational researchers now believe that the school is the basic unit for change and improvement. School districts in many parts of the country are being restructured to shift responsibility for decision making from central office administrators to the school faculty with support and guidance from the local school community.

What effects do schools have on their students? This is a major question that researchers are now debating. While some believe that the school cannot overcome the effects of poverty and other debilitating home and community influences, Shulman and Sykes (1983) believe that schools can make a difference and that the type of school attended is "enormously consequential," especially for less able students (p. 4).

But consequential in what ways? Some of the possible beneficial effects being studied are increased scholastic achievement, attentive classroom behavior, positive attitudes toward learning, lower rates of absenteeism, continued education, higher employment rates after leaving school, and lower rates of delinquency. Although no studies yet exist that demonstrate a one-to-one correlation between a school characteristic and a beneficial effect, most researchers agree that a school is a unit of

Mary Catherine Swanson
AVID Program Director, San Diego County Office of Education

It's not enough to do our best; we must do what must be done.
—Winston Churchill

Classroom (School) Event

These words by Winston Churchill have inspired my decisions and actions as a teacher. In 1980, I was teaching English at Clairemont High School in San Diego, California. Because of federal integration requirements, the population of African-American and Latino students in our school increased dramatically. When this occurred, I realized that I was going to have to do what must be done to meet the needs of a new type of student in our school.

Asking Questions

In the months before the new students arrived, I asked myself questions: What will the newly transferred students feel as they enter their new school? What prior experiences do they bring that I can build on? How would the new students react if they were given sincere respect and taught with very high expectations?

Gathering Information

From these questions, I began to envision a program that would both challenge and support the incoming students. I called the program AVID, which stands for Advancement Via Individual Determination and is from the Latin root *avidus,* which means eager for knowledge.

I collaborated with two other educators to brainstorm answers to my questions. One educator was the head of student outreach programs at the University of California at San Diego (UCSD); the other was the head of the gifted seminar program at our school. Together we had 48 years of experience to bring to this new program. The three of us met in the spring before the program to share our experiences and discuss intervention plans that would meet the needs of our new students and establish the purpose of the AVID program.

Analyzing the Information and the Situation

My analysis focused on the academic and motivational needs of students from non-English-speaking homes or from families that do not understand how to support their students academically. My colleagues and I agreed that these students could be academically successful if we provided them with a challenge and a valuable incentive and simultaneously gave them extensive academic and affective support.

Making a Judgment Based on Principles

Throughout my teaching career, I have strongly believed that all students can learn and achieve in school. I believe that it is the teacher's responsibility to discover what each student needs (academically and motivationally) in order to learn and to provide that for the student. I also believe that every student in the public schools has a right to the best and most academically challenging courses that are offered in the curriculum.

organization with a particular "ethos" or "culture" and that some of these cultures are clearly more beneficial than others.

Set in the heart of Miami's Liberty City, where crack, drug-related violence and poverty are a fact of life, Charles Drew Elementary School is an oasis. Given every excuse to fail, Drew students instead earn high marks on achievement tests, study-

Based on these principles and beliefs, I made the basic judgment that three pedagogies would best support our students:

1. writing to learn
2. inquiry
3. collaboration.

My colleagues and I believed this to be true for students as well as teachers.

Considering Alternative Strategies

I had observed other intervention programs that provided students with support outside the regular school day. Usually these were staffed by tutors or teachers who were not members of the school faculty. These programs did not work because the school faculty did not understand that the needs of underachieving students must be a central issue in the school, not an after-school tutoring program. I believed then and I do now that the school has to change to meet the needs of all students.

Selecting the Best Strategy

But, the strategy that seemed most important to me was to communicate my high expectations for the AVID students by asking them to take the most rigorous courses available in the school. These included college preparation courses such as biology and algebra instead of basic courses such as general science and practical math. In return, I promised them the support they would need to be successful in these courses.

Putting the Plan into Action

That fall, I began the AVID program with 30 ninth-grade students. All of the students signed a contract with me at the outset. The contract stated that they would select the rigorous college preparation courses and that they would work hard to achieve success in those courses. Students also registered for one class period per day called the *AVID class*. Tutors from UCSD assisted the AVID students in collaborative tutoring groups. Each AVID student carried a notebook to classes to take detailed notes during courses. As homework, they developed questions based on these notes. These questions then became the focus of their subject-specific tutoring groups. From the students' questions, and the collaborative nature of the tutoring groups, they learned to develop and ultimately rely on their own critical-thinking and problem-solving skills.

Parents were involved from the outset; they were invited to quarterly meetings and an end-of-the-year celebration. At these meetings, we helped parents understand the reality of what would happen if their children went to college.

Results

Each year another class of 30 freshmen was added to the program. At the same time, we continued to support the students who were moving up the ranks toward graduation. In 1984, our first class graduated. Twenty-eight of the students were admitted to 4-year colleges and two were admitted to community colleges. Many received financial aid and scholarships. Now, in the early 1990s, 92% of AVID students go to college.

ing everything from basics to ballet. Every Saturday, nearly 200 students troop in for extra help or enrichment.

Thanks to Drew's participation in one of Dade County's two school-based management/shared decision making (SBM/SDM) pilot projects, teachers there help make decisions such as the one that created Saturday classes. (O'Neil, 1990, p. 4)

Sergiovanni (1984) observes that it is difficult to define excellence in schooling, but that it is readily recognized when seen. In excellent schools, "a sense of purpose rallies people to a common cause; work has meaning and life is significant; teachers and students work together and with spirit; and accomplishments are readily recognized" (p. 4).

Many of those who are currently studying school *effectiveness* have limited the definition to "basic skill learning," according to Sergiovanni. He believes that we should expand our vision of effectiveness and study schools that do much more than develop fundamental academic competence. We should include "developing a love of learning, critical thinking and problem-solving skills, aesthetic appreciation, curiosity and creativity" (pp. 4–5).

Sergiovanni observes that important and recognizable differences exist among incompetent, competent, and excellent school leaders. Incompetent principals don't get the job done. Their schools are characterized by malaise, conflict, inefficiency, low achievement, and high absenteeism. Competent principals get the job done in a satisfactory way. Excellent principals exceed expectations by providing a sense of vision and purpose for the entire school community. The result is that "students in excellent schools accomplish far more and teachers work much harder than can ordinarily be expected" (p. 7).

In California, the curriculum is being restructured. In the late 1980s, state-wide committees made up of teachers, administrators, and subject area specialists created new curriculum frameworks that describe literacy in the subject and define the student performance expectations that will lead to literacy (Kierstead & Mentor, 1989).

Although many curriculum documents are seen as finished products, to be implemented by teachers without question, the California curriculum frameworks encourage teachers and principals to translate the general framework and standards into a specific local vision with local plans and goals. Through this dynamic process of curriculum shaping at the school level, teachers are encouraged to use reflective thinking and see themselves as valued members of a team effort.

In the following *Reflection*, Dr. Joe Kopec, principal of San Marcos High School in San Marcos, Texas, reflects on the processes he uses to encourage teachers to develop habits of reflectiveness and to take responsibility for making improvements in the way their school operates so that it meets the needs of the students it serves. A highly motivating principal like Joe Kopec and a stimulating environment like San Marcos High School have a beneficial effect on its students and its teachers. Dr. Kopec expects a great deal of hard work and effort from his teachers and in return he gives them a great deal of support and respect. Within the established mission statement, he encourages their creativity and grants them the autonomy that professionals deserve.

But is teaching a profession? In many ways, the answer to this question is up to you.

The potential for teaching to become a profession has never been stronger than now. Linda Darling-Hammond (1988), director of the Education and Human Resources Program at the RAND Corporation's Center for the Study of Teaching, contends that professionalization of an occupation occurs if and only if those who enter the field have an adequate understanding of the current knowledge base and continue to grow in experience throughout their careers.

At present, you are in the midst of gaining an understanding of the knowledge base on human development and learning, teaching methods, and classroom management strategies. It is likely that your teacher education program itself has recently undergone curricular reform to upgrade its expectations of student teachers. The teacher certification standards you must pass are becoming more rigorous each year.

School restructuring is providing a variety of increased opportunities for collegiality, shared decision making, and active leadership roles for teachers, and these new roles are transforming teaching into a more professional role. Teachers' unions and organizations, including the National Education Association (NEA), the American Federation of Teachers (AFT), the Association of Supervison and Curriculum Development (ASCD), and many smaller groups of subject matter specialists are redefining the job descriptions of teachers to include greater responsibility and accountability.

Reflective teachers are responding to these opportunities by thinking and acting with professionalism. They recognize the value of the service they perform in educating our nation's young people. Through continuing education, they increase their knowledge and skills in teaching and learning throughout their careers. They reflect on the decisons they make and take responsibility for the consequences of their actions. They work with their teachers' associations or school committees to develop standards for professional competency and growth.

This is an exciting time to be a teacher. As a career, teaching offers individuals the opportunity to fulfill their own needs for achievement, recognition, and meaningful contribution as they meet the needs of the students they teach. Teaching is also among the most creative of all careers. Teachers create new learning experiences, materials, organizational systems, and interactions every day of the school year. This book is designed to assist you in the development of your own reflectiveness and your repertoire of teaching strategies and to enhance your professional growth so that you can, in turn, take an active and professional role in every aspect of your school community.

Dr. Joe Kopec

Principal, San Marcos High School, San Marcos, Texas

School Event

When I was hired to be the principal of San Marcos High School, I found that the school had too many failing students and too many students in courses that were not even at the high school level. Many of the students were in remedial courses covering material that should have been learned in junior high school. At the time, most of the teachers didn't seem to recognize that this was an issue; they seemed to accept things as they were, without questioning the low performance of the students. Even the community had come to accept that San Marcos High School was a low-performing school.

Asking Questions

I asked myself how I could change the teachers' expectations of themselves and their students. With support from my district superintendent and the school board, I began to ask the teachers questions to provoke them into reflecting on the way things were and the way things could be. We began to ask ourselves, "What are we about? What's our purpose? Do we really see our school as it is? What does the school we want to be look like?"

Gathering Information

First, I gathered data on student performance, including grades and standardized test scores on the Texas Assessment of Academic Skills (TAAS). I presented this data to the faculty and asked them to describe how well our students performed compared with other similar high schools in the state. Then we analyzed the scores and grades earned by racial and ethnic groups so that we could determine the performance levels of students from different ethnic backgrounds. The scores showed that our students were low, compared with similar schools. Our Hispanic students (about 60% of the student population) had especially low scores.

Analyzing the Information and the Situation

When I presented this data to our faculty, they were stunned by the information. At first they reacted very defensively, asking me, "What do you mean? Are you telling us we're not good teachers?" But, as the instructional leader of the school, I clearly stated to the faculty that these scores were not acceptable. I told the faculty that not only were we going to have to work harder, but we were going to have to work smarter. The first thing we did was review the research on effective schools. The faculty was familiar with this research, and they knew that schools should use data to make decisions. But, when I arrived, what they knew was not being translated into practice.

Making a Judgment

One of the critical elements of the before and after story I am describing is that before I became principal, the teachers had no common belief system. They had never described a set of exit outcomes—what kids need to look like when they graduate and what teachers can do to make sure that students meet these outcomes. For a year, we discussed and argued about the mission and vision of our school.

We wrestled with big ideas until we could embrace them together. At the end of the year, we had agreed on three important beliefs:

1. *All students can learn.* The first idea we focused on was whether all kids can learn. In some of the most heated faculty meetings I've ever had, teachers discussed this very honestly. At first they offered excuses such as, "All kids could learn, but . . . many come from broken homes or they don't learn responsibility at home, . . ."

2. *Success builds success.* This was also very difficult for us because we had to admit that we were not being successful at the time. Gradually faculty began to recognize that our current practices were coercive and punitive rather than encouraging and rewarding. They began to realize that their instructional practices such as accepting failing grades and work from students sent a message that failure was expected. During our discussions, we came to believe that the old adage that kids are free to fail is a whole lot of hogwash. If kids are free to fail, many of them will.

3. *Schools control the conditions for success.* Finally, we began to reflect honestly on our excuses about why students fail. We came to recognize that we, as a faculty, control the environment of the school. We don't control all of the conditions that affect kids' lives, but we control enough. We determine how we're going to teach, who we're going to teach, when we're going to teach, and how many times we're going to teach something.

Considering Alternative Strategies

As we examined our old instructional practices and explored new ones, we considered what we wanted to save and what we wanted to add. To build success, we needed new strategies. Lecture doesn't do the job. Mastery learning doesn't do it all. Cooperative learning appeared to meet many of our requirements. It's the most important new strategy that we initiated.

Selecting the Best Strategies

We began to articulate very specifically what kids need to be like in order to be successful after they leave high school. We used a U.S. Department of Labor report on what employers want (Carnevale, 1989) as a major resource on this task. Our faculty identified a number of exit outcomes—that our students will be creative problem-solvers, communicate effectively with other people, learn how to learn, and have a healthy self-esteem with genuine caring and concern for other people. Our exit outcomes are based on the beliefs that in adult life in our society, that all jobs require updating and that learning is a life-long process.

Putting the Plan into Action

We redesigned many of our school programs using cooperative learning and problem-solving experiences in which students have to be creative, communicate with others, and improve their self-esteem as part of a successful team effort. The teachers in my school have been significantly empowered by the process we underwent together. Now they all know that they are free to be creative and to initiate new ideas to improve their teaching and curricula. But they accept that all the decisions they make must be passed through the screen of our common belief system, identified research base, exit outcomes, and shared vision of what we want our school to be.

OPPORTUNITIES FOR REFLECTION

▼ Reflective Teaching Activity:

In class, choose a newspaper article about a current event. Plan a brief (3–6 minute) lesson on the topic for students in the age group you want to teach. As you plan your lesson, include an introduction that gets your students' attention, a way to teach the main idea of the article, and a brief discussion of the topic so that you can assess what your students learned. Teach the lesson to your classmates and then ask them for feedback on what they experienced during your introduction, the lesson, and the discussion. Use this information to write the following essay.

▼ Reflective Essay: Reflecting on My Own Teaching

Write about the lesson you taught in class. Using the model of reflective teaching in Figure 1–3, discuss what you observed as you were teaching and what you learned from the feedback you received from your classmates. List the questions you are asking yourself and what you would like to do to improve your teaching if you were to teach the lesson again.

▼ Alternate Reflective Essay: My Own Reflective Thinking

Consider the teachers you had in your own school experiences. Describe one who was a reflective thinker. Give an example of a classroom event in which the teacher used reflective thinking. How did the teacher demonstrate this thinking? What decision or action resulted? What was the outcome or result?

Describe an incident in which you used reflective thinking to solve a problem or to confront a puzzling issue. How did you gather information? Describe whether you were then able to translate your thinking into action. What was the result?

What is your assessment of your own reflective thinking at this time? What are the moral principles that guide your judgments? What do you need to work on and develop in order to become a more reflective thinker?

▼ Classroom Visit: Reflective Observation

Observe and describe how the teacher uses space in the classroom. How are the students' desks arranged? Where is the teacher's desk? Does the room feel crowded or spacious? Are there activity spaces? If so, for what purpose are they used?

Observe and describe the use of light, color, and decorations. What feelings do you have when you walk into this classroom? Would you like to be a student in this room? Why or why not?

Draw a map of the classroom. Draw another, showing how you would prefer to arrange the desks and spaces if it were your classroom.

REFERENCES

BELL, M. (1990). *Everyday mathematics first grade teachers' manual.* Evanston, IL: Everyday Learning Corp.

BULLOUGH, R. (1989). Teacher education and teacher reflectivity. *Journal of Teacher Education, 40*(2), 15–21.

CARNEVALE, A. (1989). *Workplace basics: The skills employers want.* Washington, DC: U.S. Department of Labor.

CRUICKSHANK, D. (1987). *Reflective teaching.* Reston, VA: Association of Teacher Educators.

DARLING-HAMMOND, L. (1988). The futures of teaching. *Educational Leadership, 46*(3), pp. 4–10.

DEWEY, J. (1933). *How we think: A restatement of the relation of reflective thinking to the educative process* (rev. ed.). Lexington, MA: D.C. Heath.

GAGNE, E. (1985). *The cognitive psychology of school learning.* Boston: Little, Brown.

GILLIGAN, C. (1982). *In a different voice.* Cambridge, MA: Harvard University Press.

KIERSTEAD, J., & MENTOR, S. (1989). Translating the vision into reality in California schools. *Educational Leadership, 46*(2), 35–40.

KOHLBERG, L. (1987). *The measurement of moral judgment: Vol. 1. Theoretical foundations and research validation.* London: Cambridge University Press.

NODDINGS, N. (1984). *Caring: A feminine approach to ethics and moral education.* Berkeley: University of California Press.

O'NEILL, J. (1990). Piecing together the restructuring puzzle. *Educational Leadership, 47*(7), 4–10.

POLLARD, A., & TANN, S. (1987). *Reflective teaching in the primary school.* London: Cassell.

RYAN, K. (1986). The new moral education. *Phi Delta Kappan, 67,* 228–233.

SCHON, D. (1987). *Educating the reflective practitioner.* San Francisco: Jossey-Bass.

SERGIOVANNI, T. (1984). Leadership and excellence in schooling. *Educational Leadership, 41*(5), 4–13.

SHULMAN, L., & SYKES, G. (Eds.). (1983). *Handbook of teaching and policy.* New York: Longman.

STRIKE, K. (1990). The legal and moral responsibility of teachers. In J. Goodlad, R. Soder, & K. Sirotnik (Eds.), *The moral dimensions of teaching.* San Francisco: Jossey-Bass. (pp. 188–223)

TOM, A. (1984). *Teaching as a moral craft.* New York: Longman.

2

Planning for a Healthy Classroom Environment

WHEN YOU WALK into a classroom, you can sense a particular climate or environment within a few moments. A multitude of sensory images enters your consciousness: sights, sounds, and smells for the most part. The way the room is arranged, the messiness or neatness, the wall decorations, the movements and noises made by the students, and the smell of chalk dust or an animal cage all combine into a unique flavor or climate in the classroom. The behavior, body language and facial expressions of the teacher and students give you the most important clues about what life is like in this classroom. You may sense healthy elements such as excitement, energy, joy, cooperation, and pride, or you may sense debilitating elements such as fear, aimlessness, frustration, and tension. These are all components of the classroom environment, which is largely established by the teacher during the first days and weeks of the school year.

This chapter describes in some detail what reflective teachers think about and how they make decisions to promote a healthy classroom climate that is supportive of student achievement and satisfaction. It also describes how reflective teachers think about the psychosocial environment of their classrooms and how they carefully structure classroom expectations and incentives to promote enduring patterns of achievement and interest in school.

A GOOD BEGINNING FOR THE SCHOOL YEAR

Studies show that it is the teacher who establishes the particular climate of each classroom (Emmer, Evertson, & Anderson, 1980). Given identical classrooms in the same school, identical materials and resources, and the same clientele, each teacher creates a unique learning environment based on a unique set of expectations, beliefs, attitudes, knowledge, effort, and repertoire of teaching strategies and skills. You have experienced the power of the teacher for many years as a student. It is likely that you still enter every classroom on the first day of a new course hoping that the teacher will be interesting, fair, knowledgeable, and caring.

Many people think that inner-city schools serving lower socioeconomic students are deadly and sterile, while suburban schools serving middle-class students are vital and stimulating. But, in reality, within each school there is a great variety of classroom environments. Talented, caring, and reflective teachers in inner-city schools can and do make learning a joyful experience, and their classrooms shine with good will, understanding, wit, and creativity. There are, however, just as many careless, nonreflective teachers in rural areas and in the suburbs as there are in the inner cities. In any environment, such teachers give little thought to their job or to their classrooms, which are dull with anxiety, disorder, anger, and despair.

Unfortunately, great social and economic disparities exist in the world. Children, who have not created these differences, are their victims. Historically, school has been the great equalizer, the means to rising out of poverty, the chance to make the most of one's potential. Reflective, caring, and creative teachers know that they can make a significant difference in students' lives, and they work especially hard at creating a positive, healthy classroom environment to counteract the effects of poverty, discrimination, and neglect.

Organizing the Physical Environment

The classroom appearance makes a statement about the extent to which the teacher cares for the environment in which the class lives and works. It may be untidy, neat, colorful, drab, filled with objects, plants, animals, and children's art, or left undecorated and unkempt. No two classrooms are alike; each has its unique environment. However, some classrooms (and their occupants) bloom with health, vitality, and strength, while others appear sickly, listless, and debilitated.

Studies of teacher planning (Brophy, 1983; Clark, 1983) show that during the days immediately preceding the school year, teachers are primarily concerned with setting up the physical environment of the classroom. Reflective teachers come to school several days before their contracts call for them to be there. They hang posters, decorate bulletin boards, and consider carefully ways to arrange the students' desks, tables, bookcases, and other furniture to fit their curriculum plans and the needs of their students. Less reflective teachers are likely to show up on the first day of the school year and use the classroom as it was left by the custodial staff after the summer cleaning. We know from the many years we spent in classrooms as students that a bright, colorful, cheerful, and stimulating classroom causes us to expect that school is interesting and that this teacher celebrates life and learning. We also know that drab, undecorated spaces cause us to expect dullness and boredom from school.

How to arrange the desks is a complex issue. Often there are many more desks than the room was designed to hold comfortably. The number of students in a classroom may vary from 15 to 35, and the precise number of students is not known until the last minute, making preplanning difficult. But, generally, teachers know approximately how many students they will have in their classrooms, and they set about arranging the desks in a way that uses space economically and strategically. Their plans are governed by an image of themselves and their students in teaching and learning experiences. While arranging the classroom, teachers envision the "activity flow" of the classroom throughout the coming school year (Joyce, 1978–1979). Teachers envision themselves teaching and can see an image of how the classroom will look filled with students. This imaging helps teachers decide how to arrange the furniture in the room.

Such decisions are not easy to make because each possible arrangement has advantages and disadvantages. Desks can be arranged in rows, circles, semicircles, and small groups. Each arrangement has an effect on how students work and how they perceive their environment. Rows of desks provide an advantage in keeping order but leave little space for activities (Figure 2–1). A large circle of desks can be used if the teacher envisions teaching and learning experiences taking place in the center of the circle, but it will be difficult for all students to see the chalkboard (Figure 2–2).

Doyle (1986) reports that open (nonrow) arrangements result in students' spending "more time working together, initiating their own tasks, and working without teacher attention than students in traditional rooms" (pp. 402–403). Clusters of four desks are used by teachers who value cooperative group learning experiences over teacher-centered learning experiences (Figure 2–3).

Jones (1987) recommends organizing the classroom in shallow concentric circles, no more than three rows deep (Figure 2–4). In this setting, the teacher can

FIGURE 2–1
Classroom Arrangement: Rows of Desks

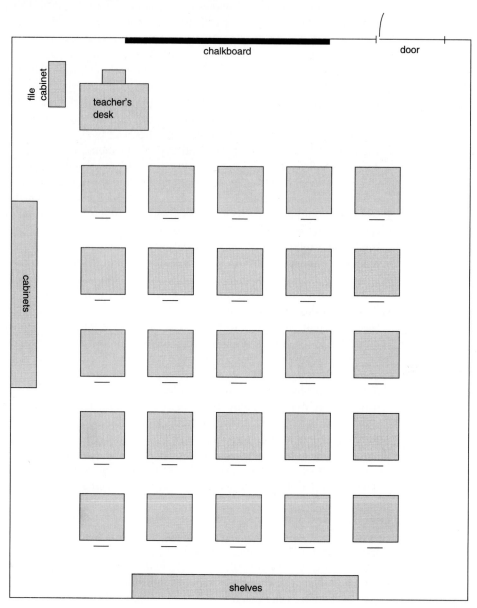

FIGURE 2–2
Classroom Arrangement: Circle of Desks

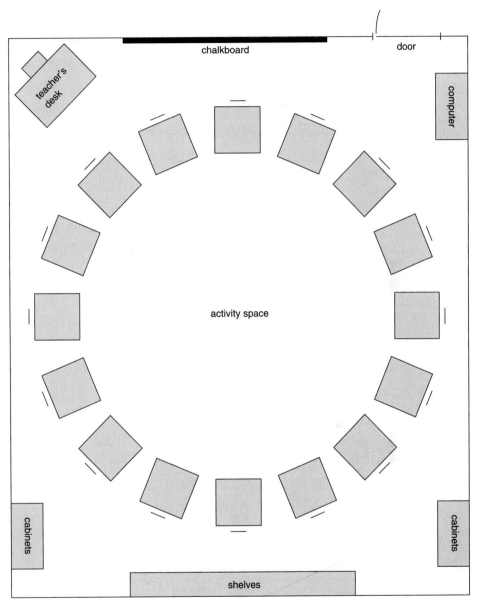

FIGURE 2–3
Classroom Arrangement: Clusters of Desks

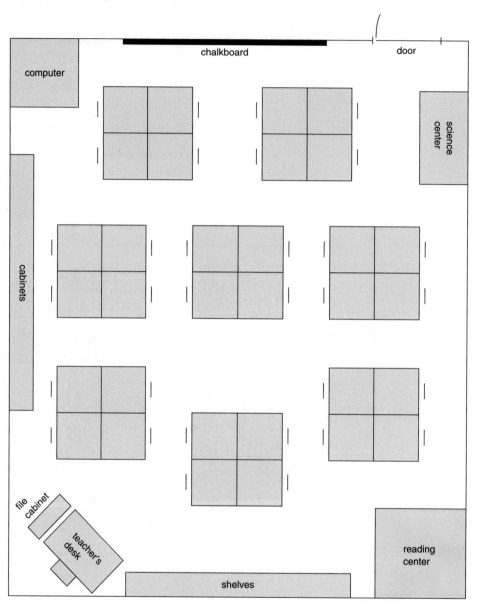

FIGURE 2–4
Classroom Arrangement: Concentric Semicircles

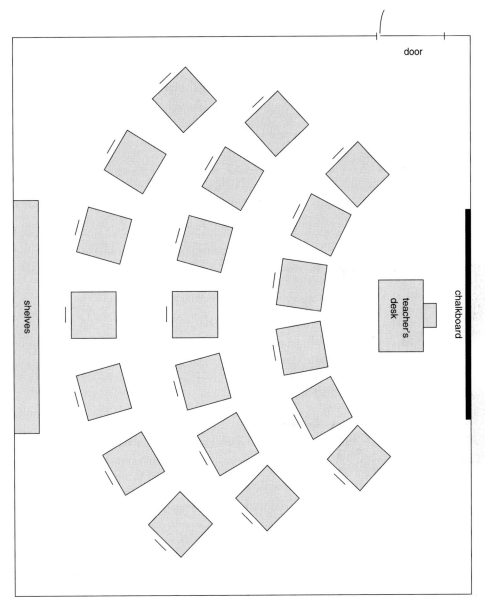

maintain eye contact with all students and is able to move quickly to the side of any student who needs assistance or a reminder to pay attention. Physical proximity is thereby increased and facilitated, and the teacher can circulate more easily to provide individual help.

Activity and work spaces can be arranged by using bookcases and room dividers or simply by arranging tables and chairs in the corners of the room. Some teachers bring in comfortable furniture and rugs to design a space just for quiet reading. Others may create space for science projects and experiments. Computer spaces are appearing in more classrooms. Room arrangement and the use of space are highly individualized decisions. Each teacher makes these decisions to fit a personal image of what a classroom should be, as well as the curriculum and grade level of the class.

Reflective teachers also consider the effects the physical arrangement of the room will have in developing a healthy classroom environment. Rows of desks connote order and efficiency, but do little to build a sense of community. Clusters of desks promote cooperation and communication among groups of students. Large circle or concentric circle arrangements encourage communication and sharing among the entire class. Many reflective teachers change their room arrangements, depending on the goals of a particular learning experience, and thus create a variety of classroom environments to fit a variety of purposes.

The First Day of School

The physical environment and schedule of the classroom may lead students to expect certain things about the way teaching and learning will occur during the school year. These expectations are reinforced even more strongly during the first few minutes of the first day of school. For example, consider the experience of the students on their first day of school in four hypothetical elementary classrooms and the two high school classrooms portrayed in the following two Scenarios.

You can probably recognize the teachers in these opening day scenarios and can give them different names and faces from your own experiences in school. You have been exposed to a variety of teaching styles, methods, attitudes, and philosophies as consumers of education. Now you will soon become teachers yourselves. What style will you have? How will your students perceive you? How will they respond to you? How will they feel when they walk into your classroom on the first day of school?

Each scenario depicts a variation of what is termed *teaching style*. A teaching style is a highly individualized and complex concept made up of personality, philosophy, values, physical and emotional health, past experiences, and current knowledge about the effects of a teacher's behavior on the classroom environment.

Perhaps you may be considering the important question, "Is it possible to control and decide on my teaching style, or is it simply a function of my personality?" The more information you can gather about how teachers create healthy climates for learning, the more power you have to gain self-understanding and control over this and other important matters pertaining to teaching and learning. Evertson (1989) has demonstrated that when teachers develop effective classroom management methods, they can learn to examine their own practices and behaviors. They can learn to use the more productive and positive classroom practices and discontinue the use of less effective methods.

To identify the most effective classroom management strategies, Emmer et al. (1980) conducted a study about how teachers begin the school year and establish their expectations with students. They were especially interested to learn how teachers who are effective classroom managers begin the school year. They hoped to discover some basic principles of effective classroom management that could be taught to beginning teachers. They selected 27 third-grade classrooms in eight elementary schools for their study. Observers were present in each of these classrooms during the first few weeks of school. Using criteria for effective management developed by the team of observers, the 27 teachers were classified into two categories: more effective and less effective classroom managers.

Both groups of teachers had rules and procedures planned for their classes. What distinguished the more effective managers from the others was that they spent a major part of the first day and much time during the next 3 weeks helping their students adjust to their expectations and learn to understand the rules and procedures established for the class. Like Miss Adams and Mr. Catlin, "as soon as most students had arrived, the teachers began describing rules and procedures. In some cases, but not always, pupils were asked to suggest rules. The rules and selected procedures were explained clearly, with examples and reasons" (p. 225).

More effective managers did not rely simply on a discussion of the rules. They spent a considerable amount of time during the first week of school explaining and reminding students of the rules. Many had students rehearse how to follow the procedures, such as how to line up. Most of the teachers taught students to respond to specific signals, such as a bell or another method of calling students to attention. Emmer et al. (1980) observed, "In summary, the more effective managers clearly established themselves as the classroom leaders. They worked on rules and procedures until the students learned them. Teaching content was important for these teachers, but they stressed, initially, socialization into the classroom system. By the end of the first 3 weeks, these classes were ready for the rest of the year" (p. 225).

The reflective teacher, guided by moral principles, also recognizes that it is not simply a matter of establishing leadership that is important; the style of leadership counts as well. Miss Adams, Mr. Catlin, and Mr. Evans quickly established that they were the classroom leaders, but Mr. Catlin's style of leadership best exhibited the underlying moral principles of caring, consideration, and honesty as he interacted with his students. The result is that students in such an environment return the caring, consideration, and honesty to the teacher and exhibit it in their interactions with one another.

In contrast, less effective managers (exemplified by Mr. Baron and Mr. Green) did not have well-thought-out procedures. Although most of them had rules, the rules were somewhat vague and the teachers tended to tell the class the rules and procedures quickly without spending time discussing and internalizing what they really meant. Like Mrs. Destry, the less effective managers in the study moved quickly to academic matters. They seemed to expect the students to be able to comprehend and retain the rules from a single, brief presentation. They did not teach the class routines and procedures.

The First Day at an Elementary School

The scene is an elementary school. It is the first day of the new school year. In one corridor, several classroom doors are open. We see and hear four teachers greet the students in their classes.

Room 101

Miss Adams is standing at the doorway. As children walk in, she says, in a calm, even-toned voice, to each of them, "You'll find your name on a desk," as she gestures toward six clusters of desks. "Sit in that desk and wait quietly." The children obey, and the room is quiet. When all the children have entered, Miss Adams goes into her classroom and quietly shuts the door behind her. The beginning bell rings at precisely that moment.

Room 102

Mr. Baron is nowhere to be seen. Children enter the classroom looking for him, but when they don't see him, they begin to talk and walk around the room. The desks are arranged haphazardly in ragged rows. Two boys try to sit in the same desk, and a scuffle breaks out. The beginning bell rings. Suddenly Mr. Baron comes running down the hall, enters the room yelling, "All right, you guys, sit down and be quiet. What do you think this place is? A zoo?"

Room 103

Mr. Catlin is standing at the door wearing a big smile. As each child enters, he gives the child a sticker with his or her name on it. "Put this sticker on a desk that you like and sit in it," he says. The children enter and quickly claim desks, which are arranged in four concentric arcs facing the front of the room. They talk with each other in the classroom. When the bell rings, Mr. Catlin enters, leaving the door ajar for latecomers.

Room 104

Mrs. Destry is sitting at her desk when the children enter. Without standing up, she tells the children to line up along the side of the room. They comply. When the bell rings, she tells a student to shut the door.

If we were able to enter the classrooms with the students, this is what we might see, hear, and experience after the beginning bell ceased.

Room 101

Miss Adams stands in front of the class. She has excellent posture and a level gaze. As she waits quietly for the children to find their seats, she looks at each child eye to eye. They settle down quickly. When the classroom is perfectly quiet, she begins to talk.

"I see that you have all found your desks. Good. Now we can begin. I like the way you have quieted down. That tells me that you know how to behave in school. Let's review some of the important rules of our classroom."

Pointing to a chart entitled "Class Rules," she reads each aloud and tells the children its significance. "Rule 1: Students will pay attention when the teacher is speaking. This is important because we are here to learn, and there can be no learning if you do not hear what the teacher is saying. Rule 2: Students will use quiet voices when talking in the classroom. This rule is important because a quiet, orderly classroom is conducive to learning. Rule 3: No fighting, arguing, or name calling is allowed. . . ."

The children listen attentively to all items. They do not ask questions or comment on the rules. After the rules are read, Miss Adams assigns helpers for class jobs. The newly appointed monitors pass out the reading books, and the children begin to read the first story in their books. Miss Adams walks quietly from desk to desk to see that each child is reading.

Room 102

Mr. Baron rushes in and slams some books and papers on the desk. Some of them land on the floor nearby. Stooping to pick them up, he says, "Sit down, sit down, or I'll find cages for you instead of desks." The children sit down, but the noise level remains high.

"Enough! Do you want to begin the school year by going to the principal's office? Don't you care about school? Don't you want to learn something?" Gradually, the noise diminishes, but children's voices continue to interrupt from time to time with remarks to their teacher or to fellow classmates.

Mr. Baron calls roll from an attendance book. He does not even look up when a child says "Here" but stares intently at the book. He has several children pass out books at one time, resulting in more confusion about whether children received all the necessary books. Finally, he tells them to begin reading the first story in their reading books. Some do so; others do not. Mr. Baron begins looking through his file cabinet, ignoring the noise.

Room 103

Mr. Catlin walks throughout the room as he talks to the class. From time to time, he stops near a child and puts his hand on the child's shoulder, especially a child who appears restless or insecure. This action seems to help the child settle down and pay attention.

"Welcome back to school! This year should be a good one for all of us. I've got some great new ideas for our math and social studies programs, and we'll be using paperback novels to supplement our reading series. But first, let's establish the rules for our classroom. Why are we here?"

A student raises her hand. Mr. Catlin reads the name tag sticker on her desk and calls on her by name. "To learn," she says timidly.

"Exactly!" Mr. Catlin agrees. "And, what rules can help us to learn the most we've ever learned in a single year?"

Several children begin to call out responses at the same time.

"Wait a moment, class. Can we learn anything like this?"

A chorus of "No's" is heard.

"Then what rule do we need to solve this problem?"

A child raises his hand, is called on, and says, "We need to raise our hands before we talk."

"What a fine rule," Mr. Catlin says with a broad smile. "How many agree?" The hands of most children go up. Mr. Catlin spots one child whose hand is not raised. He walks over to that child, kneels next to the child's desk and says, "Do you agree that this rule will help you learn this year?" "Yes," says the child, and his hand goes up.

After the class has established and agreed on several other class rules, Mr. Catlin talks about the reading program. He offers the children a choice among five paperback novels, distributes them, and tells the children to begin reading. As they read, he circulates around the room, stopping from time to time to ask questions or make comments about the stories to individual children.

Room 104

Mrs. Destry regards the children in their line with an unfriendly gaze. When a child moves or talks, she gives that child a withering stare. From a class list, she begins to read the students' names in alphabetical order, indicating which seat they are to take. The students sit down meekly. No one says a word or makes a sound.

"Now, class, you will find your books in your desks. Take out your reading books and turn to the first page." Going down the rows, each child reads a paragraph aloud while the other children sit silently and listlessly, following along in their books.

The First Day at a High School

Room 205

Mr. Evans is waiting at the front door, welcoming his students. The students enter the classroom and can be heard saying, "Hello, Mr. E." Mr. Evans says hello and that he's glad to have each student in class. He tells them to locate their seats by looking at the overhead in the front of the room. He has a seating chart shown on the overhead. The students begin to sit down and talk about their summer experiences.

After the bell rings, Mr. Evans walks to the center of the room and waits for quiet. The students look up and begin to prepare themselves for Mr. Evans's beginning remarks. One bulletin board in the front of the room is completed in the school colors and includes a picture of the school mascot, a pennant, and words from the fight song. The other bulletin board is filled with mathematical symbols and sayings by famous mathematicians. Along the top of the chalkboard is a set of very colorful geometric designs.

A set of rules is posted conspicuously on one of the walls of the room:

> Rule 1: Respect each other.
> Rule 2: Participate in class.
> Rule 3: Help one another.
> Rule 4: Everyone tries 100%.

Mr. Evans begins by saying, "Welcome to the best high school in the city. I hope each student has found his or her seat using the chart on the overhead. I believe that it is important that you know how to use such items as charts and graphs. I like to take every opportunity to use mathematics in my classroom. In addition, I would like to review the rules of this classroom. If you have any questions related to the rules, we should discuss them immediately.

If you have suggestions for any additional rules, we may want to include them in the initial set of rules I've listed."

Room 206

Mr. Green leaves the teacher's lounge about 30 seconds before class starts. When he arrives at his classroom, the bell rings. Some students are still outside talking with friends. Mr. Green yells at the students to "get inside or I'll begin writing detention slips on the first day." The students begin to take seats or lean against the side shelves.

As you look around the classroom, there is nothing on any of the bulletin boards. Student books are stacked on the side shelves. They are obviously ready to be distributed to the class.

Mr. Green tells the students to "shut up" so that he can call the roll and tell students where their seats are going to be. He stands behind a podium and begins to call names and assign seats. As students go to their seats, they continue talking among themselves. Frequently, Mr. Green calls for silence, but the noise level does not diminish much.

After the students are seated, Mr. Green complains that this is a bad beginning to the school year and warns the students again that he is not afraid to send students to detention if they don't know how to behave. He has used this in the past and he will use it with this class if necessary.

With no discussion of goals, rules, or expectations, Mr. Green appoints some of the boys to pass out the textbooks and writes, "Read Chapter 1" on the chalkboard. Some students begin to read, while others continue to talk with each other. Mr. Green gets out his detention slips and begins to write names on them.

The second major finding of the Emmer et al. study concentrated on the way the two groups of teachers monitored the behavior of their students. Less effective managers did not actively monitor the students' behavior. Instead, they busied themselves with clerical tasks or worked with a single student on a task while ignoring the rest of the class. The study concluded that the consequence of the combination of vague and untaught rules and poor monitoring was that "the children were frequently left without enough information to guide their behavior" (p. 226).

PREVENTIVE DISCIPLINE STRATEGIES
Withitness

Jacob Kounin (1977) also set out to study the differences between well-functioning and poorly functioning classrooms. He videotaped classrooms in action so that the characteristics of each could be analyzed. Although he expected to find that smoothly functioning classrooms were correlated with discipline strategies, he found no such relationship. Instead, he found that the most smoothly functioning classrooms were those characterized by a high degree of student involvement in work and by a teacher style characterized by a high degree of withitness and the ability to pay attention to two things at the same time.

Kounin labeled the most important teacher characteristic that distinguished good classroom managers from poor ones *withitness*. The good managers he observed knew what was going on in their classrooms at all times. They were aware of who was working and who was not. They were also able to *overlap* their instruction with their monitoring of student behavior. As a result, they were able to alter a presentation at the first sign of restlessness or boredom. If a minor disruption occurred between students, the teacher perceived it immediately and was likely to move a student or otherwise prevent the disruption from growing.

Withitness is expressed more through teacher behavior than through words. Eye contact, facial expressions, proximity, gestures, and actions such as stopping an activity demonstrate teacher withitness to students. These teachers are able to continue teaching a lesson while gesturing to a group or standing next to an overactive student who needs to refocus on the lesson. These are examples of the concept of overlapping, in which the teacher is able to deal with both the behavior and the lesson at the same time.

Kounin also studied what he calls the *ripple effect*, a preventive discipline strategy that he found to be particularly useful in elementary classrooms. Kounin observed a student in his own college class reading a newspaper during the lecture. When Kounin reprimanded the student, he observed that his remarks caused changes in behavior among the other members of the class as well. "Side glances to others ceased, whispers stopped, eyes went from windows or the instructor to notebooks on the desk" (1977, p. 1). In subsequent observations in kindergarten classrooms, Kounin found that when teachers spoke firmly but kindly to a student, asking that student to desist from misbehavior, the other students in the class were also likely to desist from that behavior as well. When teachers spoke with roughness, however, the ripple effect was not as strong. "Children who witnessed a teacher desist another child with anger or punitiveness did not conform more nor misbehave less than those witnessing a teacher desist another without anger or punitiveness" (p. 10).

Teacher withitness is an essential attribute of reflective teaching. The model of reflective teaching presented in this book begins with observing conditions and gathering information to make good judgments. Withitness raises the quality and level of reflective thinking because it raises the accuracy of teachers' observations and results in more complete collection of information about classroom conditions. Reflective teachers are always monitoring students' reactions to classroom events and are ready to respond when students show confusion or boredom. Reflective teachers actively monitor students during group activities and independent seat work, looking for signs that students need clarification of the task or the teacher's expectations.

A question of interest to beginning teachers and educational researchers is whether teacher withitness can be learned. Is this quality an inborn trait or personality characteristic that some teachers have and others do not? There is no evidence to answer this question at the present time; however, principals and supervising teachers often note that withitness grows with experience. Few first-year teachers exhibit consistent and accurate withitness. It is gradually developed by teachers as they actively reflect on the effects of their actions and decisions on their students' behavior.

For example, a first-year teacher may gradually become aware that the lessons are too long for the students' attention spans and, from that time on, can perceive when a lesson is moving too slowly or lasting too long. Another teacher may begin to notice that whenever a student is made to establish eye contact, the student ceases to misbehave; this teacher thus develops the active use of eye contact as a part of a repertoire of classroom management skills. The teacher may also become aware that eye contact is ignored in some cultures as a sign of respect. A third teacher may notice that using a strong, confident voice causes the students to pay attention, whereas using a tentative, meek voice causes their attention to wander. Active self-reflection is the first step toward developing withitness.

Teachers' Leadership Styles

Leadership style is not a reflection on the teacher's ability to teach; teachers using any style may or may not be effective in teaching the academic subjects they are employed to teach. But leadership style does significantly affect the way students feel about school and, to a great extent, how students feel about themselves and one another.

Although all teachers have styles unique to their personalities, behaviors, attitudes, and beliefs, Dreikurs and Cassel (1972) identified one type of leadership style that they labeled *autocratic*. Others have used the term *authoritarian* to denote a similar style. Authoritarian teachers believe that it is their responsibility to plan furniture arrangements to maintain order in the classroom and to plan schedules that seldom vary. In this view, it is the teacher's responsibility to make all class rules and establish consequences for misbehavior. They believe that the teacher has the knowledge of subject matter and the responsibility to convey it to students through teacher-centered lectures, discussions, and assignments. It is the student's role to obey the rules and do all assigned work satisfactorily.

In the opening day scenarios, Miss Adams represented a moderately authoritarian teacher, while Mrs. Destry and Mr. Green were quite autocratic. Teachers using these leadership styles are attempting to create a classroom climate that is quiet and orderly. There is often little positive social interaction in the class. Individuals compete for grades and the teacher's attention. Some students attempt to please the teacher by any means possible, while others revolt and undermine the teacher's efforts to control students' behaviors. There is rarely a positive sense of community in a classroom led by an autocratic teacher; the only sense of community that may develop is a shared sense of rebellion in extreme cases.

Dreikurs and Cassel label a second type of leadership *permissive,* although others have used the term *laissez-faire.* Teachers such as Mr. Baron who employ a permissive style appear tentative and powerless. They make few rules and are inconsistent in establishing or delivering the consequences for misbehavior. They accept excuses and seem unable to assert authority over academic work or student behavior. The classroom climate created by such a permissive teacher is characterized primarily by confusion. Students don't know what is expected or how they can succeed. Limits are fuzzy, leading to a constant testing of how much the students can get away with. Little sense of community can develop in a permissive classroom because students often learn to play one against the other to get their way.

The third type of leadership described by Dreikurs and Cassel is the *democratic* style. Democratic teachers, such as Mr. Catlin and Mr. Evans, are neither permissive nor autocratic. They are firm and reasonably consistent about their expectations for academic achievement and student behavior. They discuss the need for rules with their students and involve them in establishing the specific rules and consequences for the class. From time to time, they may initiate a reevaluation of certain rules to update them and make them more usable and meaningful. Democratic teachers assert their power to make decisions but are willing to listen to their students' reactions, needs, and desires. The result is that the sense of power and ownership is distributed among students and the teacher in the same way that it is distributed in a healthy community.

Establishing Rules and Consequences

In a healthy democratic community, the citizens understand and accept the laws that govern their behavior. They also understand and accept that if they break the laws, certain consequences will follow. Healthy democratic classrooms also have laws that govern behavior, although they are usually called *rules.* In the most smoothly managed classrooms, the students also learn to understand and accept the consequences for breaking a rule from the very first week.

In the first day scenarios, each teacher varied in the way rules and consequences were established for the classroom. Miss Adams had established a set of rules beforehand. She read them to the class and explained why each was important. Mr. Baron, Mr. Green, and Mrs. Destry did not present a set of rules. Their actions indicated that they expected the students to discover the rules of the classroom. These are likely to be quite consistent in Mrs. Destry's classroom, but in the cases of Mr. Baron and Mr. Green, we suspect that the rules may change from day to day. Mr. Catlin had planned an entire process for establishing rules. His process involved the students in helping to establish the class rules based on shared expectations and consequences.

Dreikurs and Cassel (1972) described two different types of consequences that are used to guide or shape student behavior. *Natural consequences* are those that follow directly from a student's behavior or action. For example, if a student gets so frustrated while working on an assignment that he rips the paper in half, the natural consequence is that the work will have to be redone from the beginning. If another student wakes up late, the natural consequence is that she misses the bus and has to walk to school, arrives late, and suffers the embarrassment of coming to class tardy. In these cases, there was no intervention on the part of an adult; the consequence grows directly from the student's behavior.

Logical consequences are those that are arranged by the teacher to fit the actions of the students, with the intention of causing students to change their behavior. For example, a teacher may decide that the logical consequence of not turning in a paper on time is that the student must stay in for recess or miss another activity period to finish the paper. When the paper is turned in, the logical consequence then follows that the student may go out to recess.

The difference between a punishment and a consequence is that a consequence is not arbitrary, and it is not dispensed with anger or any other strong emotion. To work effectively, logical consequences must be understood fully by the students. The teacher must describe them and explain the connections between the action and the consequence so that students understand the justification of the consequence. They must be applied consistently to all students who exhibit the behavior.

In many classrooms, teachers write a set of rules on a large piece of posterboard with the consequences for breaking each rule clearly displayed for all students to see. For example, in the elementary school

Rule	Consequence
Wait in line courteously.	Go to the end of the line.
Turn in assignments on time.	Finish late work at recess.
Work quietly.	Take a time-out (3, 5, or 10 minutes).
Do not hurt others.	Take a time-out (15 or 30 minutes).

At the middle or high school level, the posted rules and consequences may resemble these:

Rule	Consequence
Work quietly in study hall.	Study in dean's office.
Use appropriate language.	Write an essay on swearing.
Maintain school property.	Clean and/or repaint.
Turn in assignments on time.	Take a reduced grade.

The Consequence Called Time-Out

A discipline strategy known as *time-out* is frequently used as a consequence for students whose behavior is disruptive to others in the classroom. The student who acts with aggression by fighting or using loud or unacceptable language to gain attention from the teacher or the class is a candidate for this strategy. It requires a quiet, isolated spot in the classroom, perhaps created by arranging large file cabinets or cupboards to block out an area large enough for a single desk and chair. The teacher must describe this entire procedure to the class so that every student knows what it represents. The teacher must describe it as a consequence rather than as a punishment and must explain that a time-out is simply an opportunity for the student to go to a quiet area and get back the self-control that was temporarily lost.

When a student breaks the rule, the teacher quietly but firmly tells the student that the consequence for breaking the rule is to go to the time-out area and stay for the specified number of minutes. When a rule is broken more than once by the same student, the number of minutes increases each time, as shown in the preceding example.

The student is expected to stay in the time-out area, without causing any noise or disruption, for a specified length of time. Rimm (1986) suggests that the teacher use a timer and set it only when the student has calmed down and is quietly sitting in the time-out area. When the timer signals that the time has elapsed, the student may quietly return to the group and resume working.

When used with caution and respect for the feelings of the student, this technique can be a powerful way to modify disruptive behavior. It is a strategy, however, that can be very difficult to apply fairly. If the teacher's voice or body language shows anger and vindictiveness when the teacher tells the student to take the time-out, the student might feel embarrassed and lose, rather than gain, self-control.

In secondary schools, time-out usually means going to another room. An adult supervisor is in charge of monitoring the classroom. Students may do their homework or just sit. They are generally not allowed to talk with one another. If students continue to be disruptive, a more serious consequence may be taken by the faculty and administration. Students are allowed to return to the classroom when they are no longer disruptive. Generally, a student remains in the time-out room until the end of the period and returns to the regular classroom the next day.

Grandma's Rule

Jones (1987) focuses on preventing discipline problems by helping students to develop self-control. One way to assist students in developing self-control is through the use of positive consequences or incentives for learning and behaving cooperatively. To this end, Jones has examined familiar and widely used teacher practices and has recommended ways to refine these practices to make them more effective and to eliminate negative side effects. For example, he examined the familiar incentive systems of grades, gold stars, and being dismissed first and discovered that these systems appear to benefit only the top achievers; they are not genuine incentives for students who cannot realistically meet the established criteria.

Jones also noted that if teachers offer incentives that are not particularly attractive to many students, they will not positively affect student behavior or achievement. He uses the term *genuine incentives* to distinguish those that students perceive as both valuable and realistic for them to earn from those that students perceive to be of little benefit or impossible to achieve.

Jones uses the phrase *Grandma's Rule* to describe a familiar teaching practice: "First, eat your dinner; then you can have dessert." This rule is based on a principle of behavior modification that a behavior that occurs at a naturally high rate of frequency may be used to reinforce behavior that occurs at a naturally low rate. Applied to the classroom, this rule requires that students first do what the teacher expects; then they can do something that they genuinely want to do. Examples of genuine incentives that many students prize are computer activities; films or free time in which students can choose and play games in small groups; and learning experiences in art, drama, and music.

If students are to continue to perceive these favored activities as genuine incentives, they must be delivered as promised. Some teachers promise the incentive but run out of time and do not deliver on their promises. Another counterproductive practice is to continually threaten to reduce or eliminate the incentive if students do not cooperate. Still others deliver the reward even when the work is not done acceptably. When this occurs, the students learn that they can have dessert even if they do not eat their dinner (i.e., they can get the reward without doing their work). This practice can destroy the trust between student and teacher, so that when incentives are established by the teacher, the students do not believe that they will be delivered as promised.

When delivered as promised and as earned, genuine incentives can promote increased achievement among individuals and groups and can cause peer pressure to encourage good behavior. Caring, reflective teachers attempt to understand the real needs and desires of their students and to provide incentives that meet these needs.

Teachers' Body Language

Jones (1987) also found that effective classroom management and control of student behavior depend primarily on the teacher's body language. Strong, effective teachers are able to communicate many important things with eye contact, physical proximity, bodily carriage, gestures, and facial expression.

These teachers do not have to be 6 feet 5 inches tall and weigh 230 pounds. It is fascinating to observe teachers who are small in stature control classrooms with a glance or by standing next to a student who is disturbing the classroom.

Consider the eye contact of the teachers in the first day scenario. Miss Adams had a level gaze and met the students' eyes as she looked at each of them at their first meeting. She communicated that she was aware and in control, in a positive, nonthreatening manner. Mr. Evans made immediate eye contact with each student in a positive way and demonstrated an excitement for the school where he teaches and the students learn. Mrs. Destry gave the students "withering stares" that probably caused them to feel anxious and fearful about the year ahead. Mr. Baron and Mr. Green never met the eyes of their students at all, communicating their lack of preparedness and confidence to manage the classroom.

Mr. Catlin used *physical proximity* as well as eye contact to put his students at ease and to communicate that he was in charge. Jones (1987) recommends the concentric circle desk arrangement that Mr. Catlin used because it causes students to focus their attention on the teacher and enables the teacher to provide help efficiently by moving quickly to the side of any student who is having difficulty. By moving close to the restless student and placing a hand on the student's shoulder, he can help allay fears and turn the focus to the classroom activity. Room arrangement can help or hinder a teacher's ability to control children's behavior. To use physical proximity effectively, the teacher must be able to step quickly to the side of the misbehaving student, as Mr. Catlin did.

The strong, straight posture of Miss Adams reinforced the students' perception that she was an authority worthy of their respect. Good posture and confident *bodily carriage* convey strong leadership, while a drooping posture and lethargic movements convey weakness, resignation, or fearfulness (Jones, 1987).

Gestures are also a form of body language that can communicate positive expectations and prevent problems. Teachers can use gestures to mean "stop," "continue," or "quiet, please" without interrupting the verbal instruction. When used with positive eye contact, physical proximity, bodily carriage, or facial expression, gestures can prevent small disruptions from growing into major behavior problems.

Facial expressions vary greatly among teachers. They can show enthusiasm, seriousness, enjoyment, and appreciation, all of which encourage good behavior; or they can reveal boredom, annoyance, and resignation, which may encourage misbehavior (Jones, 1987). Facial expressions that display warmth, joy, and a sense of humor are those that students themselves report to be the most meaningful. Candidates training to be teachers may even want to look in the mirror at their own expressions to discover how students would see them when they are happy, angry, feeling good about themselves, or upset.

Humor in the Classroom

Csikszentmihalyi and McCormack (1986) recognized the importance of enjoyment in the learning process in a study they conducted on the influence of teachers on their students. When they asked students to tell them who or what influenced them to become the kinds of people they are, 58% mentioned one or more teachers, with descriptions such as these:

> Mrs. A. was influential because her (English) class was a lot of fun. . . . After all these years, I found out for the first time that I really liked English—it was really fun—and I've kept up my interest even though I'm not doing as well as other kids. (p. 419)

Csikszentmihalyi and McCormack believe that teacher enthusiasm, a sense of humor, and the ability to make learning enjoyable are vitally important in the classroom because they are connected with trust and meaningfulness. "How can young people believe that the information they are receiving is worth having, when their teachers seem bored, detached, or indifferent?" they ask (p. 419).

Some teachers use a bit of drama to begin a lesson. They may pose a question or describe a condition that will interest their students. Richard Klein, a teacher at the Ericson School on the west side of Chicago, begins teaching a unit on aviation by asking students what they know about the Wright brothers. The students' replies are seldom very enthusiastic, so he unexpectedly asks them, "Then what do you know about the

Wrong Brothers?" They show a bit more interest but are still unable to provide many informed responses. So Mr. Klein turns off the lights and turns on a videotape of the Three Stooges in a skit called "The Wrong Brothers." Afterward, partly in appreciation of Mr. Klein's humor, the students show a greater willingness to learn about the real historical events.

Likewise, Pam Patterson, a student teacher in Theresa Boone's fifth-grade classroom at Beasley School on Chicago's South Side, discovered that a humorous approach can frequently alleviate discipline problems. In class discussions, she was frustrated when many students tried to speak at the same time, calling out responses without being asked to speak. Although the students knew that they were supposed to raise their hands and be called on before speaking, they would raise their hands and begin speaking at the same time. One day, during a disruptive discussion, Pam quietly raised her hand and stood quietly in front of the noisy class. The noise subsided, and students asked Pam why her hand was raised. Pam told them that she was raising her hand because she wanted to say something. A student responded, "Okay, Miss Patterson, we call on you!" Everyone laughed at the situation. From that time on, whenever the class got noisy during a discussion, Pam simply raised her hand and the students would say, "We call on you," and settle down quietly.

At the secondary level, there may be a great deal of tension in a classroom. Students may appear to have conflicts because of gang-related activity. There may be clashes because the students may not understand cultures different from their own. Students may be struggling with their self-identities or worrying about whether they are going to have dates for the prom. Teachers need cultural sensitivity as well as an awareness that the society in which adolescents dwell is changing. In the midst of this change, teachers need to maintain an environment that has some laughter and joy. Not all problems can be addressed with a set of rules and consequences. Many of the best teachers are remembered for their uncanny ability to diffuse tense situations or boring lessons with humor.

INCREASING INTRINSIC MOTIVATION
The Enhancing Effects of Success

All individuals want to win or succeed. Virtually all students who walk into a classroom on the first day of school hope that this year will be *the year,* that this grade will be *the grade,* and this teacher will be *the teacher* who will make it possible for them to succeed. Some enter secure in the knowledge that they've succeeded before, but they are still anxious to determine whether they can duplicate that success in this new situation. Others enter with a history of failure and harbor only a dim, hidden hope that maybe they could succeed, if only. . . .

Winning and success are the most powerful motivations for future effort and achievement that we know of. As Glasser (1969) noted

> As a psychiatrist, I have worked many years with people who are failing. I have struggled with them as they try to find a way to a more successful life. . . .
> From these struggles I have discovered an important fact: regardless of his back-

ground, his culture, his color, or his economic level, *he will not succeed in general until he can in some way first experience success in one important part of his life.* Given the first success to build upon, the negative factors . . . mean little. (p. 5).

It is possible to restate Glasser's message as a significant principle of teaching and learning: When an individual experiences success in one important part of life, that person can succeed in life regardless of background, culture, color, or economic level. Glasser (1969) further states that the home and the school are the only two places for students to gain a successful sense of self-worth.

Glasser's work may have caused a significant change in the way schools are managed and the way the curriculum is taught. Although change takes place slowly, his landmark book, *Schools Without Failure,* has caused researchers and practitioners to reflect on the fundamental goals of education and to reexamine what students need from the school environment in order to succeed.

Raths (1972) also identified eight emotional needs that people strive to satisfy: the need for love, achievement, belonging, self-respect, freedom from guilt, freedom from fear, economic security, and self-understanding. Raths believes that children whose needs are not satisfied exhibit negative and self-defeating behaviors such as aggressiveness, withdrawal, submissiveness, regressiveness, or psychosomatic illness.

Raths recognizes that teachers cannot expect to satisfy the many unmet needs experienced by all the students in their classrooms. However, he does believe that "children cannot check their emotions at the door and we should not expect them to. . . . If unmet needs are getting in the way of a child's growth and development, his learning and his maturing, I insist that it is your obligation *to try* to meet his needs" (p. 141). His book *Meeting the Needs of Children* contains many pages of specific suggestions about what teachers can do to help meet children's emotional needs so that they are free to learn.

Meeting Students' Affective Needs

In *Motivation and Personality,* Abraham Maslow (1954) first described the human being's *hierarchy of needs.* Maslow recognized that human beings have basic physical and emotional needs that must be satisfied before the individual can attend to the higher needs for achievement and recognition. If the lower needs are not satisfied, the individual is preoccupied by trying to meet them and other, higher level, needs become nonexistent or are pushed into the background. This explains why hungry or tired students cannot learn efficiently. All their capacities are focused on satisfying their need for food or sleep. To satisfy the real hunger needs experienced by many students, some schools provide breakfast, snacks, or milk so that students can pay attention to school tasks.

But what happens when the student has plenty of food and adequate shelter and is well rested? Then "at once other (and 'higher') needs emerge" (p. 375), and these become dominant. The needs for safety and security follow basic physiological needs, and the needs for love and belonging follow safety needs. Imagine two classrooms, one that is led by an autocratic or permissive teacher, in which students feel threatened, insecure, and isolated, and the other, led by a democratic teacher, in which students feel safe, secure, cared for, and connected with other members of the class-community. In the latter setting students are more likely to have their needs met and therefore be ready and able to achieve greater success in academic work.

The work of Glasser (1969, 1986), Raths (1972), and Maslow (1954) on recognizing and meeting children's needs has served, in many ways, as the basis of this chapter, which attempts to describe ways that classrooms can be organized and managed so that students' basic needs for safety, security, love, and belonging are well satisfied. If *and only if* these needs are satisfied, students are able to concentrate a significant portion of their energy and drive on achieving success in school subjects. Maslow's work shows us that intrinsic motivation is something that can be set free and enhanced in school settings. The intrinsic motivation for achievement and recognition for achievement can be released and nurtured by teachers who carefully design a healthy, supportive sense of community in their classrooms.

Community Building

The true story of teacher Jaime Escalante and his students in Watts, Los Angeles, California, which was made into the movie, *Stand and Deliver,* shows the motivational effects of a community. Escalante refused to believe that learning is predicted by past tests or to act on the commonly held expectations that students from Watts could not learn calculus. He knew that they could learn calculus if he could provide them with the necessary knowledge, skills, and motivation to do so. He also recognized that he had the power and the responsibility to teach them. Escalante worked with his students in such a way that the class became a community devoted to a shared sense of purpose rather than a collection of individuals competing for scarce resources or grades.

How does a class of strangers or competitive individuals develop into a community? As with all the other important classroom effects discussed in this chapter, the teacher has the power to create a positive, healthy, mutually supportive, and productive classroom environment from the first day of school. Through furniture arrangement, schedules, the teacher's body language, words of welcome, rules, consequences, and interaction with the class, the teacher demonstrates a unique leadership or teaching style to the students. A sense of community is also achieved through honest and open communication of needs and feelings among students and their teachers.

Laurie Mednick, a fifth-grade teacher at Kellogg School in Chula Vista, California, teaches fourth-, fifth-, and sixth-grade students the communication skills they need to resolve conflicts peacefully. Based on the belief that conflict is inevitable and can even be healthy if dealt with in an honest and caring manner, Laurie sponsors the Peace Patrol program at her school. She describes this program in the following Reflection.

Effective communication between teacher and student is based on mutual trust that grows from the basic moral principles of caring, consideration, and honesty. Reflective teachers who are guided by these moral principles express them in the classroom by listening empathetically, or as in the case of the Peace Patrol in Laurie's class, by teaching students to listen empathetically. Listening is one of the most important ways of gathering subjective information about students' needs to make informed judgments about why students behave the way they do.

Discussions between teacher and student must be guided by consideration for the child's feelings and fragile, developing self-concept. There is also a great need for honest, open exchanges of feelings and information among all members of a classroom. A sense of community and shared purpose grows from a realistic understanding of each other's perceptions and needs.

In a recent report by the California Department of Education entitled, *Second to None: A Vision of the California High School,* it is recommended that secondary schools be restructured in a way that allows students to feel connected academically, socially, and emotionally to other students and adults. Teachers work in clusters of four or five, and they have responsibility beyond teaching the subject matter. They provide support to a group of students and work in an organized fashion to improve the quality of the school. While working in these clusters, teachers and students get to know and understand each other better.

Classroom Meetings

One method often employed by democratic teachers to build mutual caring, consideration, and an honest expression of opinions and perceptions is to hold classroom meetings to discuss problems confronting the class. The classroom meeting was first described by Glasser (1969) in *Schools Without Failure.* Some teachers keep scheduled classroom meetings each week; others schedule them only when necessary. One of the most important effects of a classroom meeting is the sense of community that is created when the students and teacher sit down to solve problems together.

For a detailed account on how to initiate and lead a class meeting, refer to Glasser's books (1969, 1986). An abbreviated description is all that can be included in this chapter. The seating arrangement for a class meeting is a single circle of chairs, so that each member of the class can see the teacher and all other members of the class. The teacher has the responsibility of establishing rules and consequences for the meeting. These usually consist of a rule about one person speaking at a time and accepting the ideas and opinions of others without criticism or laughter. It is very important that, as the leader of the meeting, the teacher be nonjudgmental. When expressing anger or other feelings, class members are encouraged to use *I-statements.*

The meeting may be divided into several parts. For example, the teacher may choose to open with an unfinished statement such as, "I sometimes wonder why . . ." or "I am proud of . . ." or "I am concerned about. . . ." Going once around the circle, every member of the class is encouraged to respond to this opening statement, which has been chosen by the teacher to encourage communication from every member of the group. Although members are encouraged to respond, the teacher makes it clear that any individual can simply say, "Pass." Opening the class meeting in this way has the advantage of allowing everyone to speak at least once during the meeting and may bring out important issues that need discussion.

Laurie Mednick

Fifth Grade Teacher, Kellogg Elementary School, Chula Vista, California

Classroom (School) Event

I was very troubled by the apparent lack of concern my students felt for other people. Instead of treating one another with respect, many of my students were involved in behaviors such as fighting, tattling, putting each other down, and interrupting when others were talking.

Asking Questions

As I observed these behaviors, I asked myself: "How can I help these children to understand that people are different and have different ideas and perceptions, but that they are still very important? How can I help them learn to resolve their own conflicts? How can I teach them to make better choices for themselves?"

Gathering Information

I went to see mentor teachers in my district who were investigating a new Peace Education curriculum and asked them what programs or methods were helpful in building self-esteem. I gained an enormous amount of insight and information from these people as well as an enthusiasm to continue my search.

Analyzing the Information and the Situation

I did a literature search at a university library on the topic of Peace Education and found from the articles that I read that this topic is a major concern to teachers across the country and that a number of programs are designed to address this issue. This search took about 2 months. I became so interested in the topic that I wrote my master's thesis on the subject as well.

Making a Judgment Based on Principles

I decided that instead of trying to solve this problem for my own classroom, that my whole school could really benefit from a conflict management program. This decision was a direct reflection of my values because I believe that each individual is important and must be shown respect and value, even if you don't agree with them. I also believe that there are alternatives to violence and that we need to teach these alternatives to our students.

The second part of the meeting can be devoted to students' concerns. The teacher opens this discussion by asking who has a concern. When a problem is expressed, the teacher moderates discussion on that issue alone until it is resolved. Issues are seldom resolved easily in one meeting, but a problem can be raised, different ideas and opinions can be expressed, and then solutions can be offered by class members. When a reasonable solution is worked out, the teacher's role is to restate the solution and suggest that the class try it for a week and discuss how it worked at the next classroom meeting. Other student concerns can then be expressed.

The third part of the class meeting can address the teacher's concerns. The teacher can bring up a problem by expressing personal feelings or stating expectations for future work. Students' responses can be brought out and discussed and solutions proposed. The sense of community that develops from expressing needs and opinions, hearing other perspectives, and solving problems together is translated into all aspects of life in the classroom. When an argument occurs during recess or when something is perceived by students as unfair, they know that they can discuss it openly and freely in

Considering Alternative Strategies

I considered teaching my students to be more attentive listeners and how to solve problems among themselves without telling the teacher. We also began to practice sharing our feelings using *I* messages, (e.g., "It hurts my feelings when you call me that name. I don't like it").

Selecting the Best Strategy

The Peace Education program that I decided to use teaches students both effective listening and conflict management skills.

Putting the Plan into Action

At first, I used role-playing three to four times a week to involve my students in sharing feelings and practicing conflict resolution by listening to each other with respect. The students were very receptive to the curriculum. They loved being treated with respect by their peers. The class as a whole became very cohesive and helpful toward one another.

Results

After implementing these strategies in my class-room, I selected 30 other fourth, fifth, and sixth graders from other classes to become part of a Peace Patrol program for the entire school. I taught them the same communication and conflict management skills that I had used in my classroom. I meet with the Peace Patrol twice a month for continued training. Each day they wear their blue jackets out on the play-ground and assist other students to resolve their conflicts peacefully.

When a conflict occurs between students, a Conflict Manager takes the students involved in the conflict to a quiet corner or passageway to discuss the event. The patroller listens to each student and then asks them to suggest solutions. If a solution can be found by the children themselves, the Conflict Manager writes a brief report about the conflict and the solution. Copies of the report are given to the students, their teachers, and the principal. As a faculty, we have agreed that whenever we receive a Peace Patrol report, we show our respect for these successful conflict management encounters by congratulating the students for resolving their conflicts peacefully.

a class meeting. When the teacher needs more cooperation or wants higher-quality work, this issue can be brought up in a class meeting. Mutual understanding, tolerance for opposing views, and a way to resolve conflicts results in a strong sense of ownership and commitment to the academic, social, and emotional goals of the class as a whole. The classroom meeting is also a powerful vehicle for developing ownership of class rules, as Tim Curbo describes in the next Reflection.

The classroom meeting satisfies a student's need for belonging, power, freedom, self-understanding, and self-respect and can diminish students' feelings of fear and guilt. Fun and enjoyment can also be planned so that students and teachers can celebrate and enjoy school life together.

The Self-Fulfilling Prophecy

Children are extremely perceptive beings. They understand and react to subtle differences in adult expectations. As Good and Brophy (1987) have shown in their

Tim Curbo

First-Grade Teacher, Hawthorne School, San Francisco, California

Establishing Public Policies in Classroom Meetings

Discipline begins even before the first child enters the classroom. Two weeks before school starts, I begin setting up my classroom. I've found that the physical environment directly affects student behavior. I group children's desks into three large units because I want my students to interact. I believe that this interaction fosters cooperation, problem-solving, and peer teaching and learning.

On the first day of school, we begin with the first of our daily classroom meetings. I do not present a list of rules on the first day. Instead, most of our rules come from a class discussion of problems that arise in the classroom. A fight over a game generates a discussion about sharing, and we develop a common understanding of what we all expect of one another regarding the sharing of classroom materials. I do this because I believe that young children learn best from concrete personal experiences.

Our meetings cause the children to generalize a shared value from a concrete example.

Whenever a problem is discussed, I also try to think about how I can modify the environment or my own teaching to facilitate more constructive behavior. In the example of the fight over the game, I may think about how I could place the game somewhere else to make it more accessible or could make a sign telling how many students can play this game. I may think about whether we need more games of this sort so that all the students can enjoy the participation.

Not all rules can be established in the first week of school. We hold our classroom meeting every day directly after lunch. The meeting serves as a forum for setting "public policies" (rules and procedures) and is a time to model and develop problem-solving skills. We place a chair at the front of the room. Each day six children are allowed to share something that they think is important. The number 6 is arbi-

research, teachers' behaviors communicate to students what the teachers expect of themselves, of the class as a whole, and of individual students.

This effect has come to be known as the *self-fulfilling prophecy* (Brophy, 1983; Good & Brophy, 1987; Rosenthal & Jacobsen, 1968). The process appears to work like this: (1) the teacher makes a decision about the behavior and achievement to be expected from a certain student; (2) the teacher treats students differently depending on the expectations for each one; (3) this treatment communicates to the student what the teacher expects and affects the student's self-concept, achievement motivation, and aspirations, either positively or negatively; (4) if the treatment is consistent over time, it may permanently shape the child's achievement and behavior. "High-expectation students will be led to achieve at higher levels, whereas the achievement of low-expectation students will decline" (Brophy, 1983, p. 54).

Many studies of how teachers' behaviors display their expectations have been done and replicated to confirm original findings. Brophy (1983) found that some teachers treat low achievers this way:

trary, but it works out to about a 15-minute meeting, which is a realistic amount of time for first graders.

When a student shares a problem, we discuss feelings about the problem. I try to draw in the whole class as much as possible, asking, for example, "How did you feel when you were excluded from the game?" or "How would the rest of you feel?" After dealing with feelings, we discuss solutions to the problem. Too often, our discussion of solutions degenerates into blaming and fault finding. I, as the teacher, try to stress that Billy is not the problem, *hitting* is. We need to decide how we feel about hitting so that our school will be a positive place. Billy is a friend who needs our help in learning another way to address his problems. In discussing our feelings, we establish that hitting is not a good solution to the conflict. Then we move on to what would be a good solution, one that is acceptable to all involved. Out of this process emerges our public policies—*in other words, our class rules.*

My philosophy about discipline is to accentuate the positive. I want to give lots of positive reinforcement to those kids who are modeling good discipline. Sometimes in our class meetings, a student will report a positive interaction. Then we discuss the good feelings that were experienced and heap appropriate praise on our friend who is helping make our school a better place.

As a teacher, I am in the position of enforcing the public policies that are established. Consistency is very important. If we generate a class rule, it must be fairly and evenly applied. We must all be aware of the rule, believe in it, and be committed to enforcing it. I've seen idle teacher threats and uneven application of rules erode classroom discipline.

Clarity is also very important. Many children seem to be crying out for help through their misbehavior. They need a caring adult to help them structure their chaotic lives. I've found that the best way to address the needs of these children is to provide them with clear and consistent limits, positive reinforcement, and an opportunity to discuss their feelings and learn new ways of handling their angry feelings.

▼ seat them far away from the teacher
▼ call on them less often
▼ wait less time for them to answer questions
▼ criticize them more frequently
▼ praise them less frequently
▼ provide them with less detailed feedback
▼ demand less work and effort from them. (Brophy, p. 55)

Kerman and Martin (1980) have designed a series of teacher inservices known as Teacher Expectations and Student Achievement (TESA) Workshops that are designed to aid teachers in recognizing their own expectations and how these are communicated to their students. In these workshops, teachers are trained to become more observant of the equity and the quality of their responses to various students in their classrooms.

When teachers use the TESA program, wonderful results have been achieved in getting low-achieving students to respond in the classroom. The success of low-achieving students or nonverbal students giving a few answers to the teacher creates an environment in which students who would not have volunteered to respond become more active in classroom discussions. A teacher who previously may have been actively engaged with a small number of high-achieving, verbal students becomes engaged with the entire class.

Most teachers enjoy working with high-achieving students, but few are as enthusiastic about interacting with lower-achieving students. Reflective teachers realize that teaching is more than telling. They are willing to restate and reexplain concepts and processes to students who do not understand the material the first time. This is one of the most significant challenges of teaching and can be one of the most satisfying and rewarding aspects of the career. If you view teaching lower-achieving students as a challenge rather than an ordeal, you will be less likely to communicate low expectations. Reflective teachers often ponder how they can use this knowledge of the self-fulfilling prophecy to their own and their students' advantages.

SCHEDULING TIME FOR ACTIVE LEARNING
How Time Is Spent in Classrooms

To bring out the best in our students, adequate time must be spent on active learning and teachers must have adequate time to plan. Time is the most important and the scarcest resource in many aspects of our lives. The Beginning Teacher Evaluation Study (BTES) gathered data on the way time is planned and used in elementary classrooms. The research revealed that on the average, "about 58% of the school day is allocated to academic activities, about 23% to nonacademic activities, and about 19% to noninstructional activities such as transitions and class business" (Rosenshine, 1980, p. 123).

The BTES also investigated the amount of time a student spends on teacher-led activities and the time spent on seat work. The average amount of time spent on teacher-led activities (both academic and nonacademic) was only 30% of the school day, or approximately 2 of the 6 hours spent in school. The remaining 70% of the school day was spent on independent seat work in the observed classrooms.

The BTES researchers were especially interested in differentiating between the time allocated for learning by the teacher and the time students were actually engaged in academic learning. *Allocated time* refers to the minutes scheduled for a class subject, but within that period, students may or may not engage in academic work. They may daydream, doodle, read a recreational book, sit idly, or cause mischief rather than work. The study showed that "engagement was higher in teacher-led settings (about 84% of the allocated time) than in seat work settings (about 70%)" (Rosenshine, 1980, p. 124).

It is important to recognize that these numbers are statistical averages. That means that some teachers spend more time and some spend less on any one element of the curriculum. The researchers found that when teachers spent more than the average amount of time on teacher-led, academic lessons, both student engagement and achievement exceeded the average as well. "Teachers with the highest allocated time also had the highest engagement rates" (Rosenshine, 1980, p. 123).

Because seat work took up so much of the school day, the researchers concentrated their efforts on discovering how student achievement could be improved during this time. They found that engaged time during independent seat work was raised when teachers (a) gave substantial explanations, responded to students' questions, and gave feedback before the independent work began and (b) actively monitored what the students were doing during the seat work activities. These two teacher behaviors seemed to create a sense of purposefulness and accountability that students then applied to their seat work, (Rosenshine, 1980, p. 124).

Daily and Weekly Schedules

Teachers at all levels believe that they cannot fit everything they want to teach into the school day. Charles (1983) cites "dealing with the trivial" as one of the teacher's greatest time robbers (p. 243). When teachers simply try to fit everything into the day, they are as likely to include trivial matters as important ones. A reflective teacher weighs the relative importance of each element of the school program and allocates time accordingly. This may mean eliminating certain items entirely and carefully scheduling the minutes of the day to meet the most important needs of the students.

Schedules differ from grade to grade, depending on the relative importance of the subject at that grade level and the way the school is structured and organized. The most frequently used structure in elementary schools is to place students into grade-level *self-contained classrooms* in which one teacher has the responsibility for teaching all the academic subjects. In other cases, students may have a homeroom, but their academic subjects are *departmentalized*, meaning that teachers specialize in one academic area and students move from class to class during the day.

For example, the primary grades are usually structured as self-contained classrooms, and primary teachers often schedule reading and language arts activities for up to one-half of the school day. The intermediate grades may be self-contained or departmentalized, but in either case, math, science, and social studies activities are usually given more time than they are at the primary grades. In junior high school, the schedules are likely to be departmentalized, meaning that each teacher specializes in one subject and teaches it to several classes of students during the day.

No two schedules are alike. Teachers in self-contained classrooms are usually allowed great discretion in how they allocate time. Typically, state requirements mandate how many minutes per week are to be allocated to each of several subjects, but teachers make varied plans within those prescriptions. For example, the state may require a minimum of 150 minutes of math per week. Teacher A may schedule 30 minutes per day; teacher B may schedule 40 minutes for 4 days; and teacher C may schedule 45 minutes on Mondays, Wednesdays, and Fridays with brief review periods on other days.

Elementary class schedules may be rigid or flexible. They may be the same every day or vary greatly. They may be governed by bells or by the teacher's own inner clock. Charles (1983) recommends that however it may be determined, "the daily classroom schedule should be explained in such a manner that students know what activities are to occur at each part of the day and how they are to work and behave during those activities" (p. 10). When students know the schedule, they can learn to manage their own time more efficiently. A teacher who uses a consistent schedule may create a permanent display of the schedule on a bulletin board; a teacher who varies the schedule from day to day can write the current schedule on the chalkboard each morning.

The conventional wisdom of teachers is that the most difficult subjects should be scheduled early in the day, when students are most likely to be attentive. Reading or language arts is quite frequently the first subject of the day in a self-contained classroom, followed by math. Science, social studies, art, and music compose the afternoons. This may be the preferred schedule, but often school constraints make it difficult to achieve. Physical education, art, and music may be taught by other teachers in separate classrooms. The schedule for these special classes may affect the classroom teacher's schedule. Some classes must be scheduled for special classes in the morning, causing classroom teachers to adjust their plans.

Planning Time

Teachers may be annoyed when special classes interrupt their scheduled lessons, but they appreciate one important side effect: When the class leaves for art, music, or physical education, the classroom teacher has a planning period. Planning time is usually required by the teacher's contract and is designed to provide opportunities for individual or collegial planning. Teachers of self-contained classrooms have complete discretion over their planning time, but departmentalized teachers frequently hold meetings during their planning time to discuss how they will plan and deliver their shared curricula.

Teachers use planning time in various ways, some productive and others less so. Charles (1983) recommends that teachers use this time as efficiently as possible by "prioritizing tasks, giving attention to those that are absolutely necessary, such as planning, scoring papers, preparing for conferences, and preparing instructional materials and activities. Also high on the list should come those tasks that are difficult or boring, leaving for later those that are most enjoyable" (p. 244). Less efficient teachers may use the time for socializing, complaining, smoking, eating, reading magazines, or making personal telephone calls. Later they complain that the school day is too short and that they have too much work to do at home.

Charles (1983) states that routine tasks such as watering plants, cleaning the room, feeding animals, and distributing materials should not be done during planning time or by the teacher at all. The teacher who is an efficient time manager delegates as many of these routine tasks as possible to student helpers. This has two effects that contribute to a healthy classroom environment: (a) it reduces the stress teachers feel about time and (b) it provides a sense of responsibility and meaningful accomplishment for the student helpers.

Conclusions

A healthy classroom environment takes an enormous amount of planning. Teachers must consider how to manage and use space, time, and other resources efficiently and effectively.

To prepare yourself for a good first year of teaching, focus especially on the first day and the first 3 weeks of the school year. Formulate a set of rules and procedures that will lead to productive and cooperative student behavior. Then consider how to introduce these rules effectively. Consider the body language and voice quality you want to use to project your self-image as the classroom leader and to convey that you expect your students to view you that way as well.

Allow sufficient time on the first day of school to teach your students what the rules are, the reasons for each, and what they mean. Rehearse your cues and routines with the students so that they internalize how to carry them out. During the next week or two, take time to remind students of the rules and expectations. Do not resort to anger if they need to be reminded. The more effective managers in the Emmer et al. (1980) study also had to use reminders many times during the first 3 weeks of school. The good managers demonstrated their withitness while monitoring the students' behavior during that time, and dealt with inattentive or disruptive behavior consistently.

After being guided through the rules and procedures of the class for 3 weeks, students tend to accept them. They come to understand that these rules and procedures are simply the way life is in this classroom, and for the most part, they adapt their behavior to fit the teacher's expectations.

The overriding concern of reflective teachers is to create a classroom in which students can meet their basic human needs for belonging and achievement. To accomplish this, they consider every aspect of the environment as it relates to children's needs. They arrange the furniture in order to meet students' needs for a sense of belonging; they create rules and schedule time to meet students' needs for security; they provide opportunities for students to write about and discuss their other feelings and needs. They do this because they want to create a nurturing sense of community in their classroom as a means of enhancing successful achievement.

The curriculum and evaluation procedures are also critical factors in creating a healthy classroom environment. Glasser (1986) describes classrooms that provide a sense of belonging, allow students to make choices, and contain a variety of interesting learning activities. Classrooms such as these satisfy the needs of most students and encourage them to learn for the satisfaction of learning. The remaining chapters in this book are designed to assist you in developing learning experiences that promote success, develop cooperation, and enhance intrinsic motivation.

OPPORTUNITIES FOR REFLECTION

▼ Classroom Visit: How Time Is Used In Classrooms

Observe how time is used in the classroom you visit. Is a schedule posted? If so, is it followed rigidly or flexibly? If not, how is the schedule determined? Keep a record of how much time is spent on academic, nonacademic, and classroom management concerns. Create a schedule that you would use if this were your classroom.

▼ Reflective Essay: Exploring My Creativity

Teaching is a very creative career. Some of the creative talents that teachers use include art, music, interior design, drama, photography, and cartooning. What are some of your creative talents that you can use to create a unique and welcoming classroom environment for your future students?

REFERENCES

BROPHY, J. (1983). Classroom organization and management. In D. Smith (Ed.). *Essential knowledge for beginning educators* (pp. 42–59). Washington, DC: American Association of Colleges for Teacher Education.

CHARLES, C. (1983). *Elementary classroom management.* New York: Longman.

CLARK, C. (1983). Research on teacher planning: An inventory of the knowledge base. In D. Smith (Ed.), *Essential Knowledge for beginning educators.* Washington, DC: American Association of Colleges for Teacher Education.

CSIKSZENTMIHALYI, M., & McCORMACK, J. (1986). The influence of teachers. *Phi Delta Kappan, 67*(6), 415–419.

DOYLE, W. (1986). Classroom organization and management. In M. Wittrock (Ed.), *Handbook of research on teaching* (3rd ed., pp. 392–431). New York: Macmillan.

DREIKURS, R. & CASSEL, P. (1972). *Discipline without tears.* New York: Hawthorn.

EMMER, E., EVERTSON, C., & ANDERSON, L. (1980). Effective classroom management at the beginning of the school year. *Elementary School Journal, 80*(5), 219–231.

EVERTSON, C. (1989). Improving elementary classroom management: A school-based training program for beginning the year. *Journal of Educational Research, 83*(2), 82–90.

GLASSER, W. (1969). *Schools without failure.* New York: Harper & Row.

GLASSER, W. (1986). *Control theory in the classroom.* New York: Harper & Row.

GOOD, T., & BROPHY, J. (1987). *Looking in classrooms,* 4th ed. New York: Harper & Row.

JONES, F. (1987). *Positive classroom discipline.* New York: McGraw-Hill.

JOYCE, B. (1978–1979). Toward a theory of information processing in teaching. *Educational Research Quarterly, 3*(4), 66–77.

KERMAN, S., & MARTIN, M. (1980). *Teacher expectations and student achievement: Teacher handbook.* Bloomington, IN: Phi Delta Kappa.

KOUNIN, J. (1977). *Discipline and group management in classrooms.* New York: Holt, Rinehart and Winston.

MASLOW, A. (1954). *Motivation and personality.* New York: Harper & Row.

RATHS, L. (1972). *Meeting the needs of children.* Columbus, OH: Merrill.

RIMM, S. (1986). *Underachievement syndrome: Causes and cures.* Watertown, WI: Apple Publishing.

ROSENSHINE, B. (1980). How time is spent in elementary classrooms. In C. Denham & A. Lieberman (Eds.), *Time to learn* (pp. 107–126). Washington, DC: U.S. Department of Education.

ROSENTHAL, R. (1974). *On the social psychology of the self-fulfilling prophecy: Further evidence for Pygmalion effects and their mediating mechanisms.* New York: MSS Modular Publications.

ROSENTHAL, R. & JACOBSEN, L. (1968). *Pygmalian in the classroom.* New York: Holt, Rinehart and Winston.

Second to none: A vision of the new California high school. (1992). Sacramento: California Department of Education.

3

Diagnosing Students' Needs

IN LATE SUMMER, many teachers make plans and decisions for the coming school year. They may arrange classroom furniture, establish schedules, choose textbooks, consider rules and consequences, and outline major units of study before school begins. But most teachers are aware that these initial plans may need to be modified when the classroom is filled with real students.

Students have a way of disrupting the most carefully considered plans. They walk in, and suddenly the teacher may see that the desks are much too close together or that some of the larger students don't even fit in their chairs. When the books are distributed, it may become evident that some students will have great difficulty reading and understanding the texts at this grade level. When the rules and consequences are discussed, it may become apparent that some of the rules must be spelled out in greater detail and that some of the consequences must be strengthened, at least for some students.

The first day of school can be a humbling and disheartening experience for teachers who have invested a great deal of energy and care in their initial plans. Both experienced and novice teachers report that when they meet their students on the first day of school, they often experience feelings of disappointment and frustration. The actual students seem so much bigger (or smaller), quicker (or slower), more active (or passive) than expected. For experienced teachers who taught the same grade level the year before, part of the jolt comes from their memories of how much more mature and able the class was last year. But, when they consider this more fully, most teachers realize that their memories are based on what their students were able to accomplish at the *end of the year*, when the students were 9 months older and had become adjusted to life in that teacher's classroom.

GATHERING INFORMATION FOR A DIAGNOSIS

There may be no adequate way to prevent this first day letdown. It occurs primarily because a class is made up of unique individuals with widely varied backgrounds, personalities, and needs. In the first weeks of school, some students reveal their needs to teachers who care enough to look for them. Quiet, orderly students may reveal great deficiencies in math or reading skills. Loud, boisterous students may reveal a deep longing for approval. Shy, withdrawn students may be observed to have great unmet needs for being accepted by peers, adults, or both. Some students may simply need breakfast. Others may have language deficiencies that prevent them from learning.

It appears that the number of students with special needs is growing. Recent studies show that "teaching and learning proceed nicely for about half of the students in our schools. For the other half, there are difficulties" (Reynolds, 1989, p. 129). These students have many varied needs. Some have been identified as physically, mentally, or emotionally challenged; they may receive special services or classes through the growing special education systems that have been created to address their needs. Others may be thought of as economically disadvantaged but have never been formally diagnosed or serviced by special education. Still others may have come from homes in which English is the second language or from migrant families who move frequently, resulting in educational disruption.

Can a single teacher, in a single school year, fill all these needs, combat all these inequities, and right all these wrongs? No. But can a reflective, caring teacher fill some of these needs, combat some of these inequities, and right some of these wrongs for some students? Yes. Teachers who are willing to diagnose needs and search for solutions to difficult problems can assist some students in getting their needs met and can make significant and positive differences in the lives of some of the students placed in their classrooms. Moreover, if teachers are able to work with the special education teachers and other professionals in the school system or the community, they can assist students and their families to meet their needs more effectively.

Teachers' Conceptions of How Students Learn

How teachers diagnose their students' needs depends to a large extent on their conception of how students learn. Through experience and research, teachers construct personal theories of learning that then affect their perceptions and reasoning about what students are able to do and what they need. Anderson (1989) has identified two basic conceptions of learning that she terms the *receptive-accrual (R-A)* view and the *cognitive-mediational (C-M)* view (p. 86).

The R-A conception is a view that has been held by many teachers. It is based on the assumption that some students have greater ability than others and that those with greater ability are able to receive and accrue knowledge better and faster than those with less ability. Teachers with this point of view often diagnose students by categorizing them into groups by what the teacher perceives to be variations in ability—highs, middles, and lows.

A growing number of reflective teachers are questioning the R-A view of teaching and learning. They hold the C-M view, which assumes that learning is a function of processing information and that some students have learned from experience how to process information more quickly and accurately than others. Teachers who hold this view do not diagnose students as having a fixed amount of ability. They reflect on the background experiences of each student they meet and seek information to help them discover what the student needs from the school environment to process information more skillfully. The student may need enriched life experiences or training in selecting and applying the appropriate cognitive strategy in order to mediate and improve achievement in school.

Teachers with an R-A conception of learning may diagnose their students' needs before meeting them face to face. This is because they use data such as achievement test scores or ability group placements from the previous year to make their decisions about what students are capable of learning. Teachers with a C-M view of learning are likely to wait until they get to know students well before they diagnose the students' needs.

Interpreting Data from Students' Cumulative Files

A record of information, called the *cumulative file* (often referred to as a *cume file*), is kept for each student in a school. Each year, the classroom teacher records in the students' files such data as information about the student's family, standardized test scores, reading levels, samples of written work, grades, and notes on parent–teacher conferences. At the end of a school year, the cume files are stored in the school or district office until the next year, when they are redistributed to the students' new teachers.

Obviously, these files contain much useful information for teachers to use in preliminary planning. By studying them, the teacher can make judgments about placement in reading, math, or other study groups before meeting the students. Alert teachers may discover information about a student's home environment, such as a recent divorce or remarriage, that can help them in communicating with the student. Some files may reveal little about the students; others may be overflowing with records of conferences and staffings that signal that the student has exhibited a special need or difficulty.

Yet, many teachers resist looking at their students' cume files before meeting the class. Tracy Kidder's (1989) *Among Schoolchildren* provides a realistic look at the entire school year of a fifth-grade class in upstate New York. In the opening chapter, which describes the beginning of the school year, the teacher, Chris Zajac, reflects on the value of cume files as she ponders what to do with a student named Clarence, whose negative attitudes toward school have become apparent on the first day of school.

> Chris had received the students' "cumulative" records, which were stuffed inside salmon-colored folders known as "cumes." For now she checked only addresses and phone numbers, and resisted looking into histories. It was usually better at first to let her own opinions form. But she couldn't help noticing the thickness of some cumes. "The thicker the cume, the more trouble," she told Miss Hunt. "If it looks like *War and Peace* . . . " Clarence's cume was about as thick as the Boston phone book. And Chris couldn't help having heard what some colleagues had insisted on telling her about Clarence. One teacher whom Chris trusted had described him as probably the most difficult child in all of last year's fourth-grade class. Chris wished she hadn't heard that. . . . (pp. 8–9)

While data and observations about students made by former teachers may be a valuable resource for planning, many reflective teachers, like Chris Zajac, are aware of the power of the self-fulfilling prophecy, in which their own expectations may influence the way their students behave or achieve in school. Good and Brophy (1987) define *teachers' expectations* as "inferences that teachers make about the future behavior or academic achievement of their students" and show that the *self-fulfilling prophecy* occurs when "an originally erroneous expectation leads to behavior that causes the expectation to become true" (p. 116).

When cume files contain data and descriptions of low academic achievement or misbehavior, less reflective teachers may assume that these students are unteachable or unmanageable. On the first day of school, the teacher may place them at desks set apart from the rest of the class or hand them textbooks from a lower grade. These teacher behaviors tell the students how the teacher expects them to behave and perform in this class. If these expectations are consistent over time, it is likely to affect the students' self-concepts and motivations in such a way that they achieve poorly and behave badly. By contrast, consider the possible effects of warm and encouraging teacher behavior on these students. If the teacher builds rapport with these students, includes them in all classroom activities from the first day, and works with them to establish their achievement levels and needs, it is likely that their behavior and achievement will improve during the year.

Reflective teachers who understand the great influence of their expectations on their students prefer to assess the strengths and needs of each student independently in the first few weeks of class. They may read the cume folders at the end of September to see how their assessments fit with those of the students' previous teachers.

A good case can be made for either point of view: using cume folders for preliminary planning or waiting to read them until the students are well known to you. This is an issue that you will need to consider and decide for yourself. Perhaps if you understand the power of teacher expectations, you can find a way to use the information in the files to establish positive expectations and resist the tendency to establish negative ones.

Interpreting Standardized Test Results

In many ways, the teacher's role in diagnosing students' needs is quite similar to the role of the medical doctor in diagnosing disease. Doctors get information from observing and talking with patients about their medical histories. Similarly, teachers observe and talk with their students to assess their learning histories. But some important information needed for an accurate diagnosis cannot be observed or discussed. Just as doctors may find that laboratory tests provide them with valuable information about the patient, so teachers may find that achievement tests and other assessment procedures can provide them with valuable data about their students.

Some tests, known as *criterion-referenced tests*, are created by teachers themselves. These tests are designed to fit the subject being taught. Questions and problems on the tests are drawn directly from the teacher's lessons, and criteria for success are established by the teacher. For example, after a week of geometry lessons, the teacher presents the students with a test consisting of 20 geometry problems that are similar to those studied during the week. As criteria for success, the teacher establishes a grading system of A = 90% correct, B = 80% correct, C = 70% correct, and so forth. From tests like these, teachers are able to diagnose which students have learned the lessons and which students need reteaching. Doctors may also employ self-created criterion-referenced tests to determine how well a patient is reacting to a drug or whether the patient is improving after surgery.

A second type of test that is frequently used as a diagnostic tool by teachers is the *norm-referenced* achievement test batteries given to all students in a school district once a year. These test batteries consist of reading, spelling, English, mathematics, science, and social studies exams given over a period of several days. The teacher does not write the questions or establish the criteria to fit a particular classroom. Instead, the tests are created by nationally recognized testing companies, and the items are written to approximate what is taught across the nation in each subject area at each grade level.

Just as in medicine, the information gained from such tests must be standardized to be useful as a diagnostic tool. For example, a physician who orders a test to measure the time it takes a patient's blood to clot and receives a result of 10 minutes cannot use this information to make an accurate diagnosis until it is known how this result compares to the clotting time of other individuals on the same test. Similarly, when a teacher receives a reading achievement test raw score of 62 for a student, the score is not useful for diagnosis until it is compared with the scores of other people in the same grade on the same test.

Test standardization is accomplished by identifying the population for whom the test is written and accumulating a carefully chosen sample of scores from this target population. These sample scores are then arranged from low to high, and an average is calculated. The score of 62 now can be compared with the average score of the sample to determine whether the student scored above or below the mean of students in the grade taking that test.

Other statistical calculations provide more precise information about a student's performance. The score may be translated into a percentile or a grade-equivalent score. These interpretations are done by comparing the student's raw score with the raw scores of the sample population. A *percentile rank* tells you what percentage of the people tested scored below a given score. For example, if Joe receives a percentile rank of 78, this means that 78% of the students at Joe's grade level scored lower than he did.

Grade-equivalent scores were created by test publishers especially for use in schools. The results are reported as a function of grade level. For example, if Sally receives a grade-equivalent score of 10.2, this means that her performance is similar to that of students who are in the second month of 10th grade. If Sally is in the 10th grade, her score tells the teacher that Sally is doing about as well as she is supposed to be doing. If Sally is in the seventh grade, the score tells the teacher that Sally is capable of functioning like students who are 3 years above her present grade level. But if Sally is in her senior year of high school, her score alerts the teacher that Sally is functioning like students who are 2 years below her present grade level.

There are other score reporting systems for standardized tests, such as age-equivalent scores, stanines, and standard scores. Although it is not possible to discuss all of these scores in this text, it is important for you to acquaint yourselves with the tests and scores used in your school system when you begin your first teaching assignment. It is also important for you to realize that the use of standardized tests varies widely from district to district. In some schools, they are used to diagnose learning difficulties of individuals so that corrective measures can be taken.

In other school systems, the test results are published in local newspapers to compare how well students from different schools are doing in the basic skills. This practice is a controversial issue among educators. The tests were not designed to be used as a measure of excellence among schools, but the public believes that they can be used that way. For example, in elementary schools, the average test scores on standardized reading achievement tests for each school in a district may be compared. At the high school level, the average SAT and ACT scores are often compared from school to school. These comparisons may lead the public to assume that the school with the highest average reading score is doing the best job of teaching reading and that the school with the highest average SAT score is superior to the other high schools in the local area. Educators know that these conclusions are misleading because there are many other contributing factors, such as the socioeconomic conditions of the families whose children attend each school and the degree to which the items on the test match the school's curriculum.

Another thing that achievement tests were not designed to do is to show the aptitude for learning or to predict the achievement of any student. Reflective, caring teachers recognize that the teacher's interpretation of a student's low achievement test results could contribute to a negative self-fulfilling prophecy. To avoid that problem, the reflective, caring teacher interprets the information gained on standardized achievement tests with great caution and uses the scores as only one of a number of items helpful in making a diagnosis of a student's needs.

Achievement tests were designed, and are useful, in helping you to make a general diagnosis of the current achievement level of your class so that you can plan lessons to begin at that level. These tests can help you pinpoint the students in your class who have low achievement in a certain subject so that you can prescribe a special course of action for them. These tests help you to identify the students who have mastered the basic skills in one or more subjects so that you can provide them with more challenging learning experiences.

Another form of standardized test that may be given in your school district is the *aptitude* or *ability* test. Individual assessments of ability, known as *intelligence* or *IQ* tests, that are given by a school psychologist to one student at a time. The school psychologist then interprets the results for the teacher and the student's family. Some test publishers have sought to duplicate these types of measures to accompany their achievement tests. They have created short, timed, paper-and-pencil tests that purport to test the student's innate ability, which is a very different construct from achievement in school. The scores are reported in the same format as IQ tests, with 100 as the mean and a standard deviation of approximately 15. These scores look like IQ scores, but because of their brevity and mass production scoring, many educators are reluctant to give them much credence.

> Achievement tests have been defined as measuring what the student *has* learned up to the moment of testing. Aptitude tests, on the other hand, were said to measure the student's *ability* to learn in the future. . . . Achievement and aptitude tests are not all that different. A study of the actual test would show that in format and content they are quite similar. (Wick, 1973, p. 152)

There may be cases for which it would be very useful to know whether a student is, using a cliché, "working up to his or her ability." When this information is necessary to make a decision about placing a student in a special program, retaining the student in the same grade, or identifying the student as gifted, reflective teachers are likely to insist on a full-scale individual IQ score rather than rely on the short-form, group ability test score given as part of the achievement test battery

DIAGNOSING STUDENTS' NEEDS IN SCHOOL SUBJECTS

Assessment devices such as tests, essays, reports, performances and other student products are collectively known as *tools of evaluation.* But evaluation is a very complex and multifaceted concept. When tests are given at the end of a term or unit of study, the purpose is to sum up what each student learned. For this reason, the process is termed a *summative evaluation*. Grades may be determined by such summative tests, and reports to parents are made on each student's progress. Summative evaluations are seldom used as diagnostic measures. At the end of the term, it is too late to diagnose students' needs; the lessons have all been taught. But two other forms of evaluation provide important information teachers need, when they need it, to make an accurate diagnosis and set new learning goals.

Formative evaluation is the term given to diagnostic forms of assessment. A formative evaluation may be similar in form to a summative evaluation: tests, oral or written problems to solve, essays, or oral presentations. But, in most cases, formative evaluations are not graded, and students know this. When tests are used prior to the end of the term or unit, their purpose is often to determine how well each student is progressing in the unit of study. When a formative evaluation shows a deficiency in one or more students, the teacher uses this information to plan what needs to be retaught and to whom.

At the beginning of a term or a unit of study, teachers often use *pretests* to determine what skills and knowledge pertaining to the subject students already have mastered. Pretests, also known as *readiness tests,* are designed to determine whether students have the skills and knowledge that will allow them to be successful in the new unit of study.

Some pretests and readiness tests, especially in the area of reading, are provided by textbook publishers to accompany their texts. Others are available separately through test publishers. Kindergarten and first-grade teachers frequently use reading readiness tests at the beginning of the year to determine which students are capable of succeeding in the complex task of learning to read. Certain skills, especially visual and auditory discrimination, have been shown to be essential prerequisites for learning to discriminate between letter shapes and sounds. Students who score very low on a reading readiness test may be provided with a curriculum designed to improve their visual and auditory discrimination skills before they even attempt to learn to read. Readiness tests, then, are designed to prevent students from failing by identifying those who need preliminary experiences to help them become ready for the academic curriculum.

Many textbooks, in a variety of subject areas, provide pretests that are matched to the content of the books themselves. Math textbooks may provide an initial pretest to be used at the beginning of the school year. English textbooks often provide pretests for each unit of study in the book, such as grammar, punctuation, sentences, and organization of paragraphs.

When pretests are not provided by the textbook publishers, the teacher can create them to fit virtually any unit of study. For example, prior to introducing a teacher-made unit on molecules and atoms, the teacher may write a brief pretest to determine what the students already know about this subject.

Placement Decisions

The results of standardized tests and subject matter pretests can assist the teacher's diagnosis and planning in several important ways. One decision that may be made as a result of test scores is a *placement decision.* Students with high scores may be placed in a different group from those with moderate or low scores. The groups may be taught separately, using different materials. This conventional strategy, known as *ability grouping,* is used in the teaching of reading, and sometimes math, in many schools. Three reading groups are typically identified in this way, and students are then taught the skills they have not yet mastered at a pace that suits the group of similar or homogeneous students.

Another diagnostic decision that pretests make possible is known as the *mastery learning feedback corrective approach* (Bloom, 1984, p. 7). This strategy is used by teachers who view each student as unique, rather than as part of an ability group. Pretests can be designed to show the specific skills that a student lacks, leading to an individual diagnosis and a corrective plan of action. The teacher, an aide, a classroom volunteer, or a more capable peer can then provide the student with feedback on the deficiencies and show the student how to master those skills. After mastering those skills, the student is then ready to join the class in the regular curriculum.

Studies done by Benjamin Bloom and several graduate students in the early 1980s showed the power of this diagnostic and corrective approach. In one study, Leyton (1983) worked with high school teachers to develop pretests that covered the essential prerequisites for the Algebra 2 and French 2 courses. The pretests consisted of items from the final Algebra 1 and French 1 exams that were considered to be essential for success in the advanced courses. The pretests were administered to two French 2 and two Algebra 2 classes.

Students in one French 2 and one Algebra 2 class then had an opportunity to review and relearn the specific prerequisites they lacked.

> The teacher retaught the items the majority of students had missed; small groups of students helped each other over items that had been missed; and the students reviewed items they were not sure about by referring to the designated pages in the instructional material. The corrective process involved about 3 to 4 hours of time during the first week of the course. (p. 7)

This review and reteaching was not done for the students in the other two classes. During the 10- to 12-week period of instruction, the experimental classes continued to receive formative evaluations and corrective feedback, and the control group classes received only conventional instruction. At the end of this period, all four classes took a summative test. "The average experimental student was above 95% of the control students, on this examination. There were also attitudinal differences. . . . These included positive academic self-concept, interest in the subject, and a desire to learn more in the subject field" (Bloom, 1984, p. 8).

Although this particular study was done in a high school, Bloom (1984) recommends that the process begin in the elementary school in the sequential courses, such as math, spelling, and the skills associated with decoding in reading. If this process is initiated at the beginning of a student's education and is continued in subsequent years, the student with learning difficulties is more likely to learn the material targeted for his or her grade level from that time on.

A third decision that teachers may make partly as a result of testing is the creation of cooperative teams or pairs for peer tutoring. To strengthen student motivation and interaction, many teachers employ the cooperative team concept.

Cooperative groups typically consist of three to five students who are assigned a set of tasks to complete by cooperating with and assisting one another. In some classrooms, teachers use pretest data to decide which students to assign to each team. Often, teachers use cooperative groups to promote peer coaching and interactive assistance among their students. In this case, a team of four students may consist of one student with very strong performance, two with moderate performance, and one with relatively weak performance in the subject area. Similarly, peer tutoring dyads may consist of one skilled and one less skilled student. These are simply two examples; other types of cooperative group placement decisions, for different purposes, are possible as well.

Diagnosing Underachievement

Teachers who carefully structure their classroom lessons to ensure success are frequently baffled by the tendency of some students to fail to succeed even under optimal conditions. As Sylvia Rimm (1986) observes, "Millions of children who are very capable of learning—children with average, above average, even gifted abilities, including those from middle class homes where education is supposed to be valued—are simply not performing up to their capabilities" (p. 1).

Students may underachieve in kindergarten, but most enter school as achievers and gradually or suddenly fall into an underachievement pattern. Standardized test scores may provide dramatic evidence of this decline. Percentile scores on achievement tests may be relatively stable for several years and then suddenly drop 20 or more points. If a student has had math achievement scores in the 80 percentile range for three grades and suddenly drops into the 50 percentile range, the diagnosis of underachievement may be warranted.

A comparison of intelligence (IQ) scores with achievement test scores and grades may offer more reason to suspect underachievement. When a student is tested by a school psychologist and is found to have an IQ score above the mean, but achievement test scores and grades far below the mean, it is likely that the student is underachieving.

There is no single cause for underachievement, nor is there a single cure. Also, no consistent characteristics are associated with underachievement. Some underachievers are bossy and aggressive; others are lonely and withdrawn. Some are slow and perfectionistic; others are hurried and disorganized. A few have adopted a behavior pattern of *learned helplessness* because of previous experiences in school, unusually high expectations at home, or a combination of both. These students perceive that they are certain to fail at whatever they try, so they have learned not to try.

Underachievement is a tough diagnosis to make and, once made, an even tougher condition to overcome. Rimm's *The Underachievement Syndrome: Causes and Cures* (1986) provides vivid and realistic descriptions of underachieving children that can assist the teacher in making accurate diagnoses and creating management plans to help the students and the parents overcome this self-destructive pattern.

Diagnosing the Needs of Students with High Achievement

Each school year, teachers discover one or several students in their classrooms who learn extremely easily and rapidly. Some of these students may excel in only one subject area. One student may perform brilliantly in math computation and problem-solving; another may write long and complex stories, poems, and essays that express ideas far more mature than those of other students at the same age or grade level; still another may show a strong sense of leadership and understanding of social interactions among classmates and adults.

To serve the needs of these students, many school systems have established *gifted programs.* The assumption inherent in most gifted programs is that the regular classroom curriculum cannot meet the needs of students with unusually strong ability and achievement. Educators who are specialists in gifted education have designed a number of alternative programs to serve the needs of such students.

Some gifted programs stress accelerated curricula in a subject area such as math. Students with standardized math test scores in the 95 to 99 percentile range are often placed in special programs that allow them to learn advanced mathematical concepts at a rapid pace. Other students may be placed in special enrichment classes focusing on literature and writing. Others may be placed in special programs that allow them to work with a mentor in a field such as science or government (Cox, Daniel, & Boston, 1985).

In some schools, the gifted programs are not subject-matter specific. They are pull-out programs (meaning that students are pulled out of the regular classroom) that allow students to work on independent studies or group projects that stress higher-level thinking, research skills, and creativity.

As a classroom teacher, you may be asked to assist in the identification of students for the school's gifted programs. You may be asked to nominate students you believe need the services the program has to offer. In many cases, gifted program coordinators provide a form on which you rate the recommended student's behaviors and characteristics.

Conflicts occasionally arise over the selection of students for gifted programs. Parents may perceive their child to be gifted or may simply want their children to be included in these enriched programs for the educational value they represent. Teachers have varied values and expectations about student behavior and achievement that lead to inconsistent recommendations. One teacher may see a student as clearly gifted because of creative and independent behavior, and another teacher may think that the same student is just an obnoxious troublemaker.

Careful reflection is needed in the area of recommending students for special gifted programs and services. Consider the consequences of labeling some students gifted. In an earlier book, Eby and Smutny (1990) examined the effects of gifted programs on children and concluded that "one effect of labeling a small minority of students 'gifted' is that we are also unwittingly labeling the remaining children in the family or school 'nongifted' " (p. viii). We advocate the elimination of the term *gifted student* in schools because of its negative effects.

In our book, entitled *A Thoughtful Overview of Gifted Education,* we sought methods of teaching that provide for the needs of the high-achieving and talented students in the classroom without setting them apart from their peers. Although many teachers choose the conventional ability groups described previously, reflective, caring teachers can use other alternatives to meet the needs of high-achieving students. You can provide enriched materials and activities for any students who finish their regular work. If the materials are interesting and the activities motivating, this strategy has the added advantage of serving as a genuine incentive for completing assignments.

Students with very advanced skills can be allowed to work at an accelerated pace, on suitably challenging material from higher grade levels, by providing them with texts and worksheets from the upper grades and supervising their work on an individual basis. This strategy is known as *mastery learning* because, when students master a certain skill, they are allowed to proceed at their own pace to the next level.

You can team up with your colleagues and allow high-achieving students to take their mathematics and/or reading from teachers in the upper grades. This is sometimes called *walking reading* or *walking math* because the students walk to the classroom for that one subject. It works best when the school has a uniform time for mathematics and reading.

Another strategy is to form students into cooperative groups to assist one another in learning. This strategy does not allow for acceleration, but it does enrich the high-achieving students' self-esteem by allowing them to develop their communication and leadership skills as they assist other students in academic areas. See chapter 9 for a complete discussion of cooperative group strategies.

DIAGNOSING STUDENTS' AFFECTIVE NEEDS

In conventional classrooms managed by teachers with an R-A conception of learning, much of the diagnosis that takes place centers on the students' cognitive abilities and psychomotor skills. The diagnostic tests that have been widely adopted measure reading levels, math aptitudes, visual and auditory discrimination, and other important cognitive and psychomotor prerequisites for learning. But, reflective teachers know that the affective domain of learning is important as well, even though it is more difficult to assess—and they know that it is this domain that encompasses the important concept of motivation.

Identifying Reasons for Problem Behavior

> Motivation is that which gives direction and intensity to behavior. It is of utmost concern to teachers because the lack of it seems to be a major obstacle to learning. Some students seem to be bored, others anxious, and still others hostile. Yet these same students, outside the classroom, often seem enthusiastic, calm, and friendly. Why are many students unmotivated in the classroom and yet tremendously motivated in out-of-school pursuits? (Gagné, 1985, p. 302)

Three theories have been offered to explain student motivation: behaviorist theory, cognitive theory, and Maslow's hierarchy of needs. Briefly, the *behaviorist* theory of motivation, which was derived from experimental research with animals, is that an extrinsic stimulus (e.g., a promise of a gold star or a good grade) provokes or motivates a student response (e.g., studying hard or cheating). When the student's response is reinforced (e.g., by receiving the gold star or the good grade), the student learns to repeat the behavior that was reinforced. Behaviorists believe that when such stimulus-response-reinforcement incidents are repeated, they set up a pattern of similar responses in the student's school career.

In contrast, the *cognitive* theory of motivation, derived from studies of mental processes and information processing, also begins with an initiating stimulus, but here the initial stimulus is a goal. It may be a goal suggested by a teacher (e.g., "Do research on and write an essay on transportation") or it may be self-generated (e.g., "I'd like to know how airplanes fly"). The goal stimulus may cause students to have quite varied responses. Some may begin immediately to do the research and writing, and others may put off the task. Cognitive psychologists recognize that a variety of internal responses play important roles in student motivation. Some of these include uncertainty, curiosity, memories about similar tasks, and expectations of success or failure. These thoughts and feelings contribute greatly to the actions a student takes when presented with a goal stimulus (Gagné, 1985, pp. 302–310).

Maslow's theory of motivation was derived from clinical studies of individuals undergoing psychological therapy combined with research about the physical needs of the body. Maslow believes that the stimulus for most needs is internal rather than external. He believes that humans have unconscious physical and emotional needs that must be met or satisfied before the person is able to pay attention to outside stimuli. Translated into everyday classroom situations, a hungry student's need for food must be met before the multiplication facts can be learned; a frightened student must be comforted before full attention can be given to phonics; a lonely student must have a friend before he can learn to show concern for the environment (Maslow, 1954).

You may consider any one of these theories to be the most useful, or you may find aspects of each that, when combined, offer you a more comprehensive way to understand the motivation of the students you teach. In making a diagnosis about a student's motivation, most reflective teachers rely on informal assessment strategies: observation and conferences with the student, the parents, and the student's previous teachers.

Informal assessment and diagnostic strategies are quite different from formal testing procedures. In order to be successful, the informal assessment must be handled with genuine caring and interest on the part of the teacher. Taking a student into the hall and asking, with teeth clenched and finger pointed, "What makes you act like this?" will elicit few illuminating responses. The student is likely to withdraw, lie, or rebel in this situation.

If a conference with a student or with parents is to succeed in discovering the student's underlying needs and motivations, teachers must be willing and able to listen empathetically to the student's (and the family's) fears and hopes. Sometimes a conference in the school setting is not sufficient to encourage students to talk about themselves. American teachers rarely visit students' homes, but such a visit may reveal much more about the student's needs than can be learned in a classroom. I have used, as a neutral ground, a lunchtime or after-school visit with a troubled student to a nearby hamburger stand to find out more about what makes the student behave as he or she does.

Whatever the setting, the informal assessment conference also needs some careful planning to be successful. Jot down ideas that you want to discuss, questions that you want to ask, and encouraging remarks that you want to make before you meet with the student or the parents. The conference may reveal some very surprising information, and you will need to follow the lead of the student and the family as to how much of their private lives they want to reveal to you.

On occasion, you may find that they want to reveal more than you can comfortably assimilate. Difficult issues of poverty, divorce, abandonment, and other damaging social conditions may cause you to feel overwhelmed and helpless to serve the best interests of this student. In cases of severe social and emotional problems, it is recommended that you refer the student to the school psychologist and other school personnel who can assist in making a diagnosis and recommend a treatment plan.

Assessing Students with Special Needs

Students in most classrooms present a range of differences in abilities, experiences, motivations, and needs. No class is made up entirely of homogeneous, average, well-behaved students. It is likely that at least some of the students in every classroom have handicaps or needs that are out of the ordinary. Some may have unusual patterns of behavior that cause them to underachieve academically or to rebel against authority. Others may have unusual perceptual handicaps that make it difficult for them to distinguish the sounds or symbols needed to complete school tasks successfully. Others may learn so rapidly and efficiently that they are easily bored with the regular curriculum.

Today, most students are screened for special needs in preschool or when they register for kindergarten. These needs may stem from physical challenges, emotional difficulties in the family, or social and economic circumstances that have prevented the child from having early learning experiences. Students who are identified as having special needs are believed to be at a greater risk of failure in school than other children. For this reason, such students are currently thought of by educators as *students at risk.*

Occasionally a student is not identified by preschool screenings and enters school without the benefit of special services. In this case, it takes an alert teacher to spot the difficulties and refer the student for special testing and assessment. This is an important responsibility for teachers to consider when they examine the test scores of students in their classes and when they observe a pattern of learning difficulties that no one else has noted in the student's cume file.

Until recently, students at risk were often placed in special education programs, and many were categorized and labeled as being handicapped or learning disabled. Federal Laws (Public Law [PL] 94-142 and the Americans with Disabilities Act [ADA]) require that all states provide "a continuum of alternative placements" to meet the needs of at-risk students, but that the at-risk student should be educated in "the least restrictive environment compatible with his or her educational needs." To meet these requirements, many schools are encouraging special education teachers to collaborate with regular classroom teachers in planning how to meet the needs of the at-risk students in each classroom. In many districts, special education teachers and regular classroom teachers who co-teach in the same classroom provide services to at-risk students.

A special education teacher, Rick Bailey, who teaches at West Elementary School in Crystal Lake, Illinois, describes in the following Reflection how he co-teaches with classroom teachers to meet the needs of at-risk students.

Teachers should not assume that all students in the regular classroom have been properly diagnosed. It is likely that, except for the parents, classroom teachers know the needs of the students in their classroom better than anyone. A fourth-grade teacher may be the first to observe a student's learning difficulty; a sixth-grade teacher may be the first to suspect a student of having an emotional crisis. When this occurs, the teacher's role is to refer the student to the special education personnel for further testing and assessment. When the testing is completed, the classroom teacher will be part of a group of teachers and parents who make the recommendation for treatment for this particular student.

Chris Zajac, the teacher featured in *Among Schoolchildren* (Kidder, 1989), considers the needs of her student, Pedro:

> Pedro's voice was deep out of all proportion to his size, and his voice had a garbled sound, as if his mouth were full of water, but sometimes perfect lines like that came out and made Chris wonder if Pedro really was, as she'd begun to think, mildly retarded. . . . He didn't often talk. He never misbehaved. He almost always tried to do his homework. It was as another teacher had said: "Poor Pedro. He works so hard to get his F." (p. 80)

In deciding whether to refer Pedro for a *core* assessment for possible services in special education, Chris wonders whether the special education services provided in her school will be better for Pedro than what she can provide for him in her own classroom:

> Chris thought that the wrong students often got, as the saying went, "cored" and sent to the Resource Room, students whose main problem with school seemed to be behavior, not ability. The Resource Room teacher remarked, "It's something of a dumping ground. I hate to say it, but it is." Nevertheless, a core was the only remedy available for Pedro. At least the testing might reveal whether or not Pedro really was retarded, and maybe it would give Chris some ideas about what she could do for him. But why hadn't there been a core evaluation of Pedro already? That question really bothered her. Was it because teachers had lost their faith in cores, or was it because Pedro didn't cause any trouble? Teachers had their hands full. Every class had disruptive children. It was easy enough to forget about a student like Pedro. In her time, she had forgotten some. (pp. 81–82)

The beginning teacher should be aware that the process of referring, assessing, and identifying special needs is an imperfect system. Tests and their results may be invalidated by some condition in the testing situation, or the tests themselves may be limited in their ability to predict or measure complex human needs and traits. The size and budget of the school system may limit services to only a small percentage of those who could benefit from them. Many teachers experience great frustration when they refer a student for special education testing or services and the student is placed on a long waiting list for such services.

However, there is growing concern among many educators that students may be labeled as handicapped when no such handicap exists. Most standardized tests used in the diagnosis of learning difficulties have been challenged for their

Rick Bailey
Special Education Teacher, West Elementary School, Crystal Lake, Illinois

How Special Education Teachers and Classroom Teachers Co-teach to Meet the Needs of Students at Risk

School Event

Until recently, special education teachers worked with students who had been referred to them because of special needs. Typically, the children were pulled out of the regular classroom, and the special education teacher provided an individualized program designed to meet the child's unique needs. However, research showed that the performance of those children did not significantly improve and, particularly as the children got older, there were social disadvantages because the children believed that there was a stigma attached to being required to go to the special education classroom.

Asking Questions

The question I had to address was, "How am I going to serve these children in the areas for which they have identified needs and still let them remain in the regular classroom?" Initially, I believed that my pull-out program did make a difference for my students and that it was effective in meeting their needs. Larry Glowacki, the director of special education in my district, announced that we were going to move toward a new way of delivering special education services. The special education teacher would now go into the regular classroom where special education students were assigned and co-teach with the regular classroom teacher.

The goal was that through this co-teaching partnership the needs of the special education student and the needs of the regular students would be met.

Getting Information

The primary source of information about this new type of programming was provided by consultants who came to our district to explain to all the special education teachers how we could implement a co-teaching model. We saw videotapes of classes using this method, and we read a collection of articles describing a variety of ways that special education teachers could share responsibilities with the regular teachers.

Analyzing the Information and the Situation

As we learned about the new co-teaching model, we recognized that there could be many pitfalls to success. We didn't want the special education teacher to be treated as an aide in the regular classroom, or to be seen as the person who sat by and assisted the special education student as the classroom teacher taught the whole class. In order to make this co-teaching successful, it was imperative for the classroom teacher and the special education teacher to discuss their roles thoroughly so that there was an understanding of each teacher's responsibilities.

Making a Judgment Based on Principles

Co-teaching is based on the principle of inclusion, which means that children with special

tendency to discriminate against students from minority groups. The high percentage of African-American and other minority groups in special education programs is disturbing and has caused some to suspect that they are being inaccurately labeled and placed. "The response of schools to children who are ethnically or racially different illustrates both the use of psychometric testing as a mechanism needs deserve to be included in the full range of school activities without being segregated because of their particular disability. We wanted our plan to exhibit this inclusive policy.

Considering Alternative Strategies

I met with all the classroom teachers who had special education students in their classes. We discussed the numbers and the types of children who were going to be assigned to classrooms the following year. I believed that the classroom teachers deserved to have input into how the students were assigned and how the co-teaching would be implemented. The strategies suggested by classroom teachers became very important in defining the new program.

Selecting the Best Strategy

The whole language program provided the model that allowed me to see how I could teach effectively in the regular classroom. It allows the classroom teacher and me to provide instruction that is relevant for both children with learning difficulties and their peers. It is based on the whole language principle of demonstration, which means that instruction in specific skills is modeled by the teacher as children are involved with literature and writing experiences.

Putting the Plan into Action

In the fall, I began co-teaching in five classrooms in three grade levels. The scheduling was difficult and required a lot of negotiation with the classroom teachers. I made sure that I established myself as a co-teacher in each classroom by doing a series of demonstration lessons from the Frameworks program to the entire class. Then I worked in small groups with children who needed additional teaching or extra practice. In these small groups were the children identified with learning difficulties who were assigned to that class. In these small group sessions, I made sure that the needs of my special education students were met.

Results

In the classes in which I am co-teaching, because there are two teachers, we act as a role model for each other, giving each other support, guidance, ideas, and feedback. I have had classroom teachers say to me that they have learned so much by watching me teach, and I feel the same way about watching them. To a great extent, this model is helping many of the teachers in our building develop a new spirit of collaboration.

One of the things that has been so surprising and gratifying to me is to see how well the special education students are doing in the regular classroom. I'm seeing them have a more positive attitude about themselves and about learning than I saw in the pull-out program. I'm seeing greater academic success as well. Other children in the classroom who have needs that haven't been identified are also being served by this model. Another benefit for me is that by seeing and working with children in the regular classroom, I have a clearer understanding of how all children learn than I had by working only with special education students.

for interpreting difference as deviance, and the propensity to see school failure as a problem of the child rather than the school" (Sapon-Shevin, 1989, p. 92).

This disturbing phenomenon means that classroom teachers may also need to be willing to take a role in questioning the validity of placement decisions. Teachers should be alert to the possibility that the student labeled mildly mentally retarded, learning disabled, emotionally disturbed, or behaviorally disordered, may, in fact, be a student with normal abilities but deficient learning experiences, a student who has expectations of failure due, in part, to being labeled disabled. When a reflective, caring teacher suspects that a student could function normally in a healthy classroom environment like her own, this teacher is willing to take responsibility for asking for a reassessment of the student.

Perceiving the Needs of Bilingual and Bicultural Students

When the language, culture, and values of the parents match those of the teachers in school, the student is likely to experience school as satisfying and supportive because the messages received in both settings are congruent. When these important factors are different, the student may experience school as uncomfortable and threatening because the messages may conflict.

When you become a teacher, you can expect to teach a class made up of many different cultures and ethnic groups, particularly if you choose to teach in a large urban school district. In your own schooling, you have probably witnessed teachers who attempt to remediate and prod culturally different students into adapting to the majority culture. Reflective teachers, however, need to consider how to meet the academic, social, and emotional needs of students from cultures different from their own.

At least 10% of school-age children in the United States grow up in homes in which English is the second language; these students need assistance in learning English in order to be successful in school. In urban areas, where the concentration of immigrants is highest, a school may have students who speak as many as 25 different languages (Reynolds, 1989, p. 133).

Hispanic students comprise the largest bicultural group and are expected to account for 10% of the school population by the year 2000 (Casas & Furlong, 1986). The troubling fact is that students of Hispanic origin have a 50–50 chance of dropping out of school, which suggests that the current educational practices have not had the intended academic benefits (Ford Foundation, 1984).

These current challenges need current solutions, and one advocate for change is Joan M. First, executive director of the National Coalition of Advocates for Students. She believes that solutions need to center around providing culturally diverse students with appropriate *access* to schools and school services. She finds that immigrant students are occasionally "discouraged from attending school" and that the schools they attend are "often short on resources, poorly staffed, badly maintained, and overcrowded" (First, 1988, p. 207). When they enter the school, they require access to a comprehensible education. "Estimates of the number of students with limited proficiency in English who are enrolled in U.S. public schools range from 3.5 million to 5.5 million. It is also estimated that two-thirds of them are not receiving the assistance they need to succeed in their studies" (p. 207).

Most experts in bilingual education believe that in order for bilingual students to learn, they require bilingual teachers and instruction that uses the student's primary language until the student learns enough English to function in the regular classroom. Children with *limited English proficiency (LEP)* receive instruction in special classrooms designed to teach them English as a second language and academic skills in their own language. When students attain minimal proficiency in English, they are termed *fluent English proficient* and may be gradually mainstreamed into regular classrooms (Watson, Northcutt, & Rydell, 1989, p. 59–61).

Diagnosis of the needs of culturally diverse students is very difficult for classroom teachers who do not share the same culture. But, in general, specialists in bilingual and bicultural education recommend that culturally diverse students need classroom experiences and interactions with the teacher that "stress self-concept, pride in their culture, and academic competence—the three ultimate criteria for any relevant material or curriculum" (Milne, 1982, p. 7).

Many reflective teachers recognize that the presence of bilingual and bicultural students in their classrooms offers exciting possibilities for curriculum development that celebrates and informs all students in the class about the cultural diversity of our world. Culture fairs featuring the crafts, music, food, and language of the many students in the school are excellent ways to meet the needs of students of all cultures, including the need of the white, middle-class students to become aware of the contributions and values of others.

Determining Learning Styles

When a student's cultural and developmental patterns differ from the predominant white middle class, the student's preferred learning style may also be different. This may cause additional difficulties for culturally diverse students attempting to assimilate to a different set of expectations and patterns than they are accustomed to in their homes.

Learning styles are derived in part from biological and physical characteristics, as in a preference for learning visually, auditorially, or kinesthetically. The preference, in these three cases, may be due in large part to the relative strength of the student's vision, hearing, and motor coordination. But learning styles are also strongly influenced by developmental factors. For example, students exhibit variations in preferences for working alone or working with a group. Given a complex problem to solve and a project to create, some students prefer the challenge of working alone and others prefer the experience of working with a group. This may be the result of familiar cultural tendencies to work alone or with a group.

One element of learning style is the need on the part of some individuals for physical activity. This need on the part of many school-age students can be easily misdiagnosed as a behavior disorder. For example, Fadley and Hosler (1979) found that teachers frequently referred students to psychologists for hyperactivity. The teachers complained that the students were unable to sit quietly and pay attention during lessons. The psychologists in the study reported that most of the referred students were not clinically hyperactive; they were normal students in need of movement.

Other studies found that when previously restless youngsters were reassigned to classes that did not require passivity, their behaviors were rarely noticed. Teachers report that certain students thrive in activity-oriented classrooms and others remain stationary despite frequent attempts by teachers to coax them to move (Dunn, Beaudry, & Klavas, 1989, pp. 55–56). This demonstrates the variation among students in learning style preferences.

Learning styles are like fingerprints. No two are alike. Teachers cannot identify all aspects of their students' learning styles, nor can they meet the many diverse needs these styles represent. It would be extremely frustrating to attempt to diagnose each student's learning style and provide a unique set of experiences for every student in the class. But reflective, caring teachers can respect the fact that variations in learning styles exist and be flexible enough to allow students to work in the ways that are most comfortable and productive for them.

Learning style diagnosis and treatment is probably best accomplished by allowing students to make choices. Through self-selection, students can choose to work on a project alone or with a group, read at a desk or in a bean-bag chair, view a filmstrip or listen to an audiotape, or do a measuring project involving movement or one that can be accomplished quietly in one spot. "No learning style is better or worse than another. Since each style has similar intelligence ranges, a student *cannot* be labeled or stigmatized by having any type of style. Most students can master the same content; *how* they master it is determined by their individual styles" (Dunn et al., 1989, p. 56).

Identifying Students' Needs Without Labeling

Diagnosis of students' needs certainly requires reflection on the part of teachers as they consider the many causes of low achievement and plan appropriate school programs for students. But it requires a great deal of caring as well. Sometimes, noncaring teachers view diagnosis as equivalent to labeling. A quick perusal of a cume file, a glance at a standardized test score, and a few days of classroom observation can lead a teacher to label a student a slow learner, behavior-disordered, or an underachiever, for example. These labels and others like them, when communicated to the student and parents, can have disabling effects. The implication of these labels—that the student is deficient in some important way—can lead to a self-fulfilling prophecy, as further erosion of self-concept and self-confidence leads the student to even more severe learning difficulties.

Students with excellent school performance can also suffer from labeling. Some teachers refer to their most capable and willing students as overachievers. This pseudoscientific term is attached to students whose standardized test scores are moderate, but whose grades and work habits are excellent. The implication is that these students are working beyond their capacity, and this is somehow seen as a negative characteristic by some teachers.

Students with high test scores on standardized tests, especially IQ tests, are frequently labeled *gifted* students. This label may appear to be a very positive one; certainly it is sought by many parents for their children. But careful reflection reveals that this label may be as damaging as any other. Rimm (1986) notes that "any label that unrealistically narrows prospects for performance by a student may be damaging" (p. 84). Being labeled a gifted student narrows the expectations of performance for that student to a constant state of excellence; any performance less than excellent can be interpreted by the student (and the parents) as unacceptable.

The label *gifted* has many other negative implications. When a small percentage of students (usually 2%–5%) in a school, are labeled gifted, the other 95% of students are unwittingly labeled not gifted. This has extremely negative conse-quences for those students who are siblings of those who are labeled gifted and for those who are excluded because their test scores are a few points below the cutoff score (Eby & Smutny, 1990).

Broader labels can be just as damaging. "The term *minority* itself carries with it a connotation of being less than other groups with respect to power, status, and treatment. Even in situations where a minority group outnumbers other ethnic groups in population size, it may still be relegated to minority status due to the socioeconomic and power structure of the community" (Chinn, 1982, p. 25).

Terms such as *culturally disadvantaged, culturally deprived,* and *economically underprivileged* do not serve any useful purpose and can cause unknown effects when used without regard for the feelings of students and their parents from cultures other than the white middle class. Furthermore, these terms do not recognize the intrinsic value and unique contributions of individuals or groups.

Diagnosis of students' needs can take place without reference to stereotypes and labels. Children who need assistance in learning English can be released from the classroom to work with an English as a second language (ESL) teacher or tutor. Children who need a fast-paced math course can travel to another class for math. Children who need practice in visual discrimination and organizing for learning can have this service. But they can all be welcomed back for most of the day to the regular classroom, where they can share their cultural diversity and talents with one another in a community for learning and growing.

OPPORTUNITIES FOR REFLECTION

▼ Reflective Essay: Students with Special Needs

Students will come into your classroom with a variety of cognitive, affective, and social needs. What are some of the special needs of students with physical handicaps, learning difficulties, and cultural or language differences? How will you attempt to meet their needs and provide them with opportunities to experience pride and success in your classroom?

▼ Classroom Visit: Learning Styles

Arrange to interview one student in the class you are visiting. Ask the student questions to learn about his or her preferred learning style. Sample questions are provided here, but you may want to make up your own as well.

> Do you learn easily by reading about something?
> Do you learn well by listening to a teacher explain something?
> Do you need the teacher to write examples on the board?
> Do you learn best by having somebody show you something or by working out the problem by yourself?
> Do you need a quiet room, or can you work and learn when others are talking or when the TV or radio is on?
> Does it bother you when there is movement around you?
> Do you like to sit at a desk or a table when you are studying?

You may want to add to your information by calling the student's parents to find out what they have observed about how their child learns best. From your interview, write your diagnosis of this student's learning style. Then recommend the classroom conditions that you believe to be important for this student to learn effectively. Share your written study with the classroom teacher to see how well you agree about the diagnosis and the recommendations for classroom conditions.

REFERENCES

ANDERSON, L. (1989). Learners and learning. In M. Reynolds, (Ed.), *Knowledge base for the beginning Teacher* (pp. 85–104). New York: Pergamon Press.

BLOOM, B. (1984). The search for methods of group instruction as effective as one-to-one tutoring. *Educational Leadership, 41*(8), 4–17.

CASAS, J., & FURLONG, M. (1986). In search of an understanding and a responsible resolution to the Mexican-American educational dropout problem. *California Public Schools Forum 1,* 45–53.

CHINN, P. (1982). Curriculum development for culturally different exceptional children. In C. Thomas & J. Thomas (Eds.), *Bilingual Special Education Resource Guide* (pp. 22–37). Phoenix, AZ: Oryx Press.

COX, J., DANIEL, N., & BOSTON, B. (1985). *Educating able learners.* Austin, TX: University of Texas Press.

DUNN, R., BEAUDRY, J., & KLAVAS, A. (1989). Survey of research on learning styles. *Educational Leadership, 46*(6), 50–57.

EBY, J., & SMUTNY, J. (1990). *A thoughtful overview of gifted education.* White Plains, NY: Longman.

FADLEY, J., & HOSLER, V. (1979). *Understanding the alpha child at home and at school.* Springfield, IL: Charles C Thomas.

FIRST, J. (1988). Immigrant students in U.S. public schools: Challenges and solutions. *Phi Delta Kappan, 70*(3), 205–210.

FORD FOUNDATION. (1984). *Hispanics: Challenges and opportunities.* New York: Author.

GAGNÉ, E. (1985). *The cognitive psychology of student learning.* Boston: Little, Brown.

GOOD, T., & BROPHY, J. (1987). *Looking in classrooms.* New York: Harper & Row.

KIDDER, T. (1989). *Among schoolchildren.* Boston: Houghton Mifflin.

LEYTON, F. (1983). *The extent to which group instruction supplemented by mastery of the initial cognitive prerequisites approximates the learning effectiveness of one-to-one tutorial methods.* Doctoral dissertation, University of Chicago.

MASLOW, A. (1954). *Motivation and personality.* New York: Harper & Row.

MILNE, N. (1982). Aspects of dealing with the bilingual special education student. In C. Thomas & J. Thomas (Eds.), *Bilingual special education resource guide.* (pp. 3–10). Phoenix, AZ: Oryx Press.

REYNOLDS, M. (1989). Students with special needs. In M. Reynolds, (Ed.), *Knowledge base for beginning teachers* (pp. 129–141). New York: Pergamon Press.

RIMM, S. (1986). *The underachievement syndrome: Causes and cures.* Watertown, WI: Apple Publishing.

SAPON-SHEVIN, M. (1989). Mild disabilities: In and out of special education. In D. Biklen, D. Ferguson, & A. Ford (Eds.), *Schooling and disability* (pp. 87–127). Chicago: University of Chicago Press.

WATSON, D., NORTHCUTT, L. & RYDELL, L. (1989). Teaching bilingual students successfully. *Educational Leadership, 46*(5), 59–61.

WICK, J. (1973). *Educational measurement: Where are we going and how will we know when we get there?* Columbus, OH: Merrill.

4

Long-Term Planning of School Programs

CURRICULUM DEVELOPMENT IS among the most important planning responsibilities of the professional teacher. The term *curriculum* "derives from the Latin word *currere,* meaning 'the course to be run.'" (Eisner, 1985, p. 39). Some educators think of curriculum planning very narrowly as the plan for teaching subjects such as mathematics, language arts, reading, science, and history. Others think of the school curriculum much more broadly, including all the social and emotional experiences a child has in school, as well as the academic learning experiences.

In either case, the curriculum of a school is influenced by many forces, both past and present. History and tradition are powerful influences over what is taught in schools. The 3 Rs have served as the basis for planning in American schools for more than a hundred years and will continue to do so for many more. Social and political concerns cause the curriculum to evolve as various special interest groups influence state or local school boards to include new programs. Consider the recent additions of drug education and AIDS education programs to the curricula of many schools.

HOW SCHOOL CURRICULA ARE PLANNED
Evaluation and Use of Textbooks

One group who wields an enormous influence on school curricula are the textbook authors and publishers, who decide what to include and what to exclude in the texts they distribute nationwide. Their motivation, of course, is to earn the largest possible profits, so they create textbooks that will appeal to the broadest possible market and offend no one. Some critics say that this results in texts that are dull and lifeless. If they are used as is, the curriculum of the school could then become dull and lifeless as well.

But textbooks are changing too. One of the greatest controversies regarding textbooks today is the rewriting of social studies textbooks to include multiple perspectives on history. Current textbooks are viewed by some as written from one perspective, that of a white European male. Critics of the traditional textbooks believe that history should be taught from multiple perspectives. Traditionalists believe that eliminating content from or ignoring content in the traditional textbooks will not represent accurate history and that history will become diluted in an effort to please every ethnic group. Old views are challenged as new views are discussed. For example, as this textbook is being written, even the portrayal of Christopher Columbus, a traditional hero of the social studies curriculum, has become an issue.

Teachers must be ready to discuss controversies such as that surrounding Christopher Columbus regardless of how he and other persons and events are portrayed in textbooks because students will want to know, for example, why there have been parades and protests on Columbus Day. Some teachers have little awareness of their own values or their own curriculum orientations and beliefs. They tend to avoid making decisions about the curriculum they teach. In giving up their power to do so, they just follow orders, which are most often given by a source far removed from their own local school system. The orders come from textbooks. As Eisner (1985) observes

> . . . at present the textbook holds a place of unparalleled importance in influencing what shall be taught in schools. The reasons for its importance are not difficult to

determine. Consider the range of subject matters and tasks with which elementary school teachers must deal. The typical teacher teaching, say, the fourth grade in a self-contained classroom is responsible for the following: reading, language arts, arithmetic, social studies, science, music, art, and physical education. In addition to these areas, many elementary school teachers are responsible for health education, career awareness education, human relations education, and environmental educa-tion. . . . Given the variety of these demands, is it any wonder that many teachers—perhaps most—would welcome textbooks and other kinds of workbooks that in ef-fect decide for them what students shall study, in what order, for what ends? (p. 31)

When first-year teachers move into their classrooms, the textbooks are already there, arranged in formidable rows or piled in cumbersome stacks. The novice teachers have been told about the importance of individualizing education and meeting the needs of all students in their professional preparation programs. Then reality sets in, and the new teachers realize that many of the materials they need to plan a highly creative program that meets the students' individual needs are not in the classroom. A less reflective teacher will, *without thinking*, distribute the textbooks and begin teaching on page 1, perhaps emulating former teachers, with the intent of plowing through the entire book by the end of the year.

The reflective teacher, however, is more inquisitive and more independent in the use of textbooks, and asks questions of other teachers: How long have you been using these textbooks? How were they chosen? Which parts match the school or district curriculum guides? Which parts are most interesting to the students? What other resources are available? Where do you go to get your ideas to supplement the textbook? In your first year of teaching, how did you meet the individual needs of your students when you had only textbooks available to you?

Connie Muther, director of the Textbook Adoption Advisory Service, advises teachers to examine critically the textbooks they use for redundancy of information. Textbooks are usually formatted to present information in a spiraling sequence of increasing difficulty at each grade level. But she finds that most publishers include repetitive material year after year:

> This mindless repetition exists primarily because every teacher at every grade wants to teach, or have available to teach, everything. Therefore, publishers, who usually produce what customers want, include *almost* everything in every book. What hap-pens to sequencing and spiraling when several teachers within a district begin each year on page one and proceed sequentially through the book, completing only one-half to two-thirds by June? (Muther, 1987, p. 78)

What does happen? Less reflective teachers tend to think or rationalize that the "approved" or "correct" curriculum is the one found in textbooks because it is written by "experts." They attempt to deliver the curriculum as written, without questioning its effects or attempting to adapt it to their students' needs.

Reflective teachers consider decisions about curriculum planning to be in their jurisdiction, their domain of decision making. They consult with others, but they take responsibility for deciding which parts of a textbook to use in order to meet the needs of their own particular class and to match the goals and learning outcomes set by their state and local curriculum committees.

State Curriculum Guidelines

In the United States, each state has a department of education with responsibility for establishing guidelines for curriculum development. In the 1990s, many states are revising their curriculum guidelines by inviting representative teachers and administrators to form committees with responsibility for revising the curricular goals for each major subject area. The various departments of education have published and distributed the resulting documents to all of the school districts they serve.

For example, the California State Department of Education has recently created two documents for each subject area. A *Curriculum Framework* communicates the state committee's basic goals and expectations for each subject area, and a *Model Curriculum Guide* provides details for how the frameworks can be translated into classroom experiences.

As an illustration of this curricular process, let us examine more closely one of California's Frameworks and Model Curriculum Guides. The *English–Language Arts Framework* was created by a committee of educators drawn from around the state. It was adopted by the California State Board of Education in 1986 and was published and distributed in 1987. It describes "overarching goals" of the curriculum that are

> to prepare all students to function as informed and effective citizens in our democratic society
> to prepare all students to function effectively in the world of work
> to prepare all students to realize personal fulfillment. (1987a)

The Framework then specifies eight essential elements of English–language arts programs that include (among others) these three:

> 1. integrating instruction in the language arts
> 2. establishing a literature-based program
> 3. learning to read by reading. (1987a)

The *English–Language Arts Model Curriculum Guide* interprets these goals pertaining to reading and literature in the Framework by presenting teachers with "representative enabling activities" to use in their classrooms that will accomplish the purposes defined by the state committee. For example, in the primary grades, the *Guide* suggests the following:

> Kindergarten Through Grade Three
> The teacher, with the help of a library media specialist, assembles a classroom library of literary works. . . . Groups of students select from among these works in the classroom library, and each group decides on a method for dramatizing the selected work. Methods such as readers theater, puppetry, pantomime, or choral reading might be employed. Each group presents its selection to the entire class. Some of the selections might then be presented to other classes, parents, or to other audiences, or they might be videotaped for future showings. (1988, p. 7)

As in this illustrated example, the California Frameworks and Model Curriculum Guides emphasize learning experiences that are unusually active, engaging, and creative. The *History–Social Science Framework* (1987b) emphasizes the teaching of history, geography, and democratic values through the use of "new technologies, original source documents, debates, simulations, role playing, or whatever means that will bring the students into close encounters with powerful ideas, great events, major issues, significant trends, and the contributions of important men and women" (p. vii).

The California Curriculum Frameworks encourage teachers to take a professional responsibility for creating curriculum. Some teachers find this responsibility to be overwhelming and prefer to have more specific guidelines to follow and methods and strategies to use in reaching the state goals. With a new focus on restructuring schools and empowering teachers, other teachers welcome the opportunity to take a leadership role in the development of a curriculum that meets the needs of their students and communities. When teachers work together, on formal committees or informally as colleagues, they often find that they are able to support one another in interpreting state frameworks, gathering resources, clarifying the goals, and making plans for attaining the goals.

How Curriculum Is Transformed in Practice

In response to state mandates or guidelines, school districts usually form committees of teachers, administrators, and curriculum consultants from the central office to write or revise the curriculum documents that specify goals and expectations (i.e., the approved curriculum) for each subject and grade level in that district. Often these written curriculum guides also specify textbooks and tests that teachers may use. While some people may believe that these documents are the one and only curriculum in that district, reflective teachers recognize that there are really four different curricula in any school.

The *intended curriculum* is the explicit and approved one; usually it is written in the form of curriculum guides or lesson plans. However, close observation reveals an implicit or *hidden curriculum* that is not written anywhere but is pervasive nonetheless. It varies from teacher to teacher, depending on individual values and interests. In practice, teachers can all use the same lesson plan but teach strikingly different lessons depending on their values, knowledge about the subject, interests, and the time they have allotted to the lesson.

The *null curriculum* is whatever the teacher deletes or omits because of lack of time, interest, or knowledge. This is an important issue that can't be ignored. Teachers send messages to students in subtle ways. The elementary teacher who has science as the last period of the day and never seems to get to it is telling the students that science is something to be ignored or not liked. In addition, when science is taught by reading the textbook and answering the questions at the end of the chapter, the intent of the State Frameworks to get students involved in the process of doing science is clearly not met.

Another example of the null curriculum is secondary English teachers who never get to the poetry units because this was their weakest area in high school and college. As a result, the teachers are passing along this deficiency to their students and may be making poetry a weak area for them. By specifying outcomes in science or poetry, Frameworks and curriculum guidelines can help to ensure that important areas of the curriculum are not ignored or deemphasized.

When school programs are evaluated, usually the documents that make up the intended curricula are examined. But the actual *delivered curriculum* may differ markedly from the intended, planned curriculum. This is because each teacher plans different lessons and delivers the intended curriculum in a unique way. Another transformation occurs as students receive the lessons taught by their teachers. Because each student varies in aptitude, interests, and preexisting knowledge and schema, the *experienced curriculum* is different for every student.

The classroom teacher has both the right and the responsibility to weigh carefully the various elements influencing curriculum decisions, including personal values, interests, strengths, and weaknesses and the needs of the students, in order to plan and deliver a curriculum that meets the guidelines of the state and the school district. This chapter examines the role of the classroom teacher in planning curriculum for an academic year.

Curriculum Orientations

Most schools have a written curriculum that documents and describes the learning experiences that have been planned for that school by its faculty. Within each subject area, the curriculum may describe which elements should be emphasized and which should be minimized. The curriculum may even specify the methods teachers should use to instruct their students. In some countries, where there is one nationally mandated curriculum, there may be great uniformity from school to school and classroom to classroom. There is no national curriculum in the United States; the curriculum of a school is determined locally, leading to great curricular variations among schools and classrooms.

Curriculum decisions are highly influenced by the values of those who are making the choices. When educators discuss what to include in a course or how to teach a certain subject, several different viewpoints are usually expressed, depending on each individual's values. For example, should the subject of mathematics emphasize memorization of math facts and formulas, or should it emphasize the logical processes that can be employed to discover mathematical relationships? Should schools teach the religious or the scientific theories of the development of the universe? What types of reading materials are suitable for students to read at various grade levels? These and other curriculum questions cause very heated debates because each individual has a unique *curriculum orientation.* In areas such as teaching theories about the origins of the universe, the debate is extended to parents and the school board.

Eisner (1985) describes five different curriculum orientations to provide educators with an awareness of how their personal orientations may compare with others. He believes that by knowing all five, teachers may be able to expand their options in curriculum planning. An individual's personal values, experiences, and beliefs about what is important in the world contribute greatly to the type of orientation held. In many ways, one's curriculum orientation is related to one's philosophy of education because they are both concerned with the goals of education, the relative importance of subject matter, and how teachers and students ought to interact.

Eisner (1985) labels one of the oldest and most basic orientations to curriculum *academic rationalism.* Educators with this orientation argue that the goal of education is to teach the basic fields of study and academic disciplines that have traditionally been known as a liberal education. These academic disciplines include mathematics, literature, science, and history. Within these disciplines, academic rationalists believe that the curriculum should consist of "the very best, the most powerful, the most profound, the grandest of man's intellectual works" (Eisner, 1985, p. 68). The role of the teacher is to help students acquire the content, concepts, and ideas of these classic academic disciplines.

An academic rationalist is likely to believe that the traditional subjects are important and is likely to teach them through lecture, reading, and discussion. Tests and essays are employed to measure what students have learned.

A contrasting curriculum orientation is one that values developing students' *cognitive processes.* Teachers having this orientation would not concur with academic rationalists that there is one established content for courses. Instead, their major goal is to help students "learn how to learn" (Eisner, 1985, p. 62). The content of the curriculum is selected for its potential in causing students to use their problem-solving and information-gathering abilities. The role of the teacher is to generate problematic situations for students to investigate and solve.

Teachers with a cognitive processes orientation would be likely to combine traditional courses into thematic units, where the major goal is not to teach content, but to teach students processes such as the scientific method, research and problem-solving, and communication skills. The methods this teacher might employ include experimentation, independent research, and group investigations. Although tests might be employed to measure student achievement, these teachers are likely to require students to turn in and report on projects that show what they have learned.

A third orientation is one that emphasizes *personal relevance,* meaning that the curriculum builds on the students' interests. This view is held by educators who believe that learning is a developmental process and that students will learn best from the "inside out" (Eisner, 1985, p. 70). The teacher's role is to construct educational situations that are based on the students' present experiences, interests, and needs.

Teachers who are oriented toward personal relevance are likely to provide their students with many opportunities for free choice. Students will be encouraged to select their own reading materials based on their interests. Students may negotiate with teachers about what they want to study and how they will do it. A method of evaluation that is used in this orientation is to have students work on contracts that specify what they are going to do. A completed contract is viewed as a successful school experience.

A *social perspective* in curriculum is an orientation that attempts to develop a critical consciousness among students of the major issues of society. Given this perspective, the curriculum focuses on controversial social issues and is designed to encourage students to take an active role in improving the society in which they live. The role of the teacher using this orientation is to make students aware of the important social issues of their time and culture and to prompt them to debate alternatives, make informed judgments, and act on them.

Although this orientation is rarely employed for the entire school curriculum, many teachers with this orientation find ways to incorporate social issues into the conventional curriculum. The teacher with this orientation is likely to select reading materials for their social relevance and is likely to use discussion, class meetings, role playing, and simulation activities. Evaluation is likely to center on the degree to which students show that they have developed mature understanding of social problems and are taking an active role in solving them.

A fifth orientation toward curriculum planning is concerned not with the values and content of the curriculum but with the way curriculum is constructed. A *technological* orientation stresses a scientific approach using measurable goals and objectives. The role of the teacher is to plan the curriculum in a sequential and orderly manner by specifying a list of sequential objectives with tests that demonstrate the students' mastery of each objective.

Teachers with a technological orientation are likely to emphasize sequential learning of the basic skills in mathematics, reading, grammar, and other curriculum areas. Carefully planned lessons teach new information and skills in small steps, with much opportunity for practice. Pretests and posttests are likely to be used to show how much students have gained from each learning experience.

It is unlikely that teachers have only one of these curriculum orientations. Instead, each teacher may have one that is the most preferred or dominant orientation but can see value in some of the others as well. By recognizing and clarifying your own preferences, you can understand why you make the decisions that you do about what to teach and how to teach it. A teacher must also assume the responsibility to address students' various learning styles by using an orientation that may be different from the one they prefer. In addition, if you understand that other teachers may have different orientations, it is more likely that you will be able to have productive discussions with them even when strongly held differences in values and orientations occur.

Tyler's Basic Principles of Curriculum Planning

Ralph Tyler, an educator who has won unusually high esteem for his work on curriculum planning, observed that in planning educational goals, teachers should first consider the needs of the learners, second the needs of society or what he termed "contemporary life," and then the suggestions or recommendations of subject matter specialists. Tyler (1949) observed that "many educational programs do not have clearly defined purposes" (p. 3). To improve this situation, he proposed four fundamental questions that should be considered in planning any curriculum:

1. What educational purposes should the school seek to attain?
2. What educational experiences can be provided that are likely to attain these purposes?
3. How can these educational experiences be effectively organized?
4. How can we determine whether these purposes are being attained? (p. 1)

Reflective educators are likely to use Tyler's basic principles in planning, organizing, and evaluating their programs because they are remarkably similar to the process of reflective thinking. Essentially, Tyler (1949) suggests that teachers consider a classroom event such as curriculum planning by observing the needs of students, gathering information from subject matter specialists and others, making a judgment about an educational purpose, considering strategies that are likely to attain these purposes, selecting and ordering the strategies to be used, and then beginning the process again by evaluating the effectiveness of the curriculum plan.

Although reflective teachers do not memorize these questions word for word, they do carry with them the fundamental notion of each:

1. What shall we teach?
2. How shall we teach it?
3. How can we organize it?
4. How can we evaluate it?

They ask themselves these questions each year because it is likely that there will be subtle or dramatic changes in their communities, subject matter materials, students, or themselves from year to year that cause them to reexamine their curricula. On reexamination, they may confirm that they want to continue to teach the same curriculum in the same way or that they want to modify some aspects of the curriculum. As teachers grow in experience and skills, most greet each new year as an opportunity to improve on what they accomplished the previous year. Rather than continue to teach the same subjects in the same ways year after year, reflective teachers often experiment with new ways of teaching and organizing the curriculum.

An interesting way to contrast more reflective and less reflective teachers is that after teaching for 20 years, a more reflective teacher has accumulated 20 years of experience, and a less reflective teacher has had 1 year of experience 20 times. Reflective teachers want to have an active role in the decision-making processes in their schools, and curricular decisions are the ones that count the most. They also display a very strong sense of responsibility for making good curriculum choices and decisions, ones that will ultimately result in valuable growth and learning for their students.

Bloom's Taxonomy of Educational Objectives

Benjamin Bloom, a student of Ralph Tyler's, extended Tyler's basic principles in a most useful way. Bloom and his colleagues Max Engelhart, Edward Furst, Walker Hill, and David Krathwohl (1956) attempted to respond to the first of Tyler's questions as completely as possible. In meetings with other teachers, they brainstormed and listed all the possible purposes of education, all the possible educational objectives that they could think of or had observed during many years of classroom experience. Then they attempted to organize and classify all of these possible objectives into what is now known as the *Taxonomy of Educational Objectives*. Their intent was to provide teachers with a ready source of possible objectives so that they could select ones that fit the needs of their own students and circumstances. It was also intended to help teachers clarify for themselves how to achieve their educational goals. A third purpose for the Taxonomy was to help teachers communicate more precisely with one another.

The Taxonomy first subdivides educational purposes into three domains of learning: cognitive, affective, and psychomotor. The *cognitive domain* deals with "the recall or recognition of knowledge and the development of intellectual abilities and skills"; the *affective domain* deals with "interests, attitudes, and values"; and the *psychomotor domain* concerns the development of manipulative and motor skills (Bloom, 1956, p. 7).

The cognitive domain is further subdivided into six hierarchical levels of educational objectives that have become very widely known and used as the basis for many school curriculum plans. These six levels are shown here and are described in detail in chapter 6.

Hierarchy of Educational Objectives in the Cognitive Domain

HIGHER-LEVEL OBJECTIVES

Level 6: Evaluation (make judgments, opinions)
Level 5: Synthesis (create an original product)
Level 4: Analysis (see the relationships among elements)
Level 3: Application (use concept in life situations)

LOWER-LEVEL OBJECTIVES

Level 2: Comprehension (understand the main idea)
Level 1: Knowledge (recognize and remember facts)

As Bloom intended, the Taxonomy has had a powerful effect on planning for teaching. In the 1960s and 1970s, many educators and laypeople observed that in most classrooms, the majority of learning experiences were intended to develop knowledge and comprehension, but that fewer experiences caused learners to apply, analyze, synthesize, or evaluate what they learned. Using the Taxonomy as a guide, reflective teachers have actively sought to provide learning experiences at the higher levels of the Taxonomy as well as at the lower ones. They recognize that using high-level learning experiences will better satisfy the needs of their learners to understand a subject in more depth than is possible through memorization of facts and comprehension of main ideas alone.

Writing Educational Goals

All three domains are considered to be important in the curriculum because together they support the growth and development of the whole student. In selecting goals for a school or a classroom, it is essential to consider the needs of the whole student and to create goals that are developmentally appropriate for children. The reflective teacher is one who carefully considers what is important for students to learn and writes goals accordingly.

Cognitive goals are expressed in curriculum development as goals to master content or subject matter knowledge. For example, between kindergarten and twelfth grade, students are expected to master many of the basic facts and concepts associated with content areas such as literature, mathematics, biology, physics, astronomy, American history, and world geography.

Educators also write many psychomotor goals, including many processes and skills that involve both the mind and the body in the psychomotor domain. For example, elementary students are expected to learn how to read, write, calculate, solve problems, observe, experiment, research, interpret, make maps, and create works of art, music, and other crafts.

Affective goals are viewed by most teachers as auxiliary goals, related more to the development of character than to the skills or intellect of their students. Typically, schools emphasize the affective goals of good citizenship, self-esteem, acceptance of individual and racial differences, and appreciation of art, music, and other aspects of our cultural heritage.

For long-term planning, the clarification of schoolwide goals results in a greater likelihood of accomplishing these goals successfully. This is due to the consistency of experiences that students have in every classroom and with every adult in the school. Many school districts have statements of philosophy and goals written in policy documents, but they may or may not be articulated and applied in the schools themselves. For effective change to take place, the school faculty must consider its common goals each year, articulate them together, and communicate them to the students through words and deeds.

In a classroom, each teacher has the right and the responsibility to articulate a set of educational goals for the students. Working alone or with teammates at the same grade level or subject area, the classroom teacher may want to articulate approximately two to four yearly goals in each of the three domains that are suited for that particular group of students. Tyler (1949) encourages the teacher to select a small number of highly important goals, "since time is required to change the behavior patterns of human beings. An educational program is not effective if so much is attempted that little is accomplished" (p. 33).

Educational goals vary widely from person to person and community to community. The goals of private schools affiliated with a church reflect the values of the religious community it serves. Public school goals vary depending on the philosophy of its teachers, its administrators, and the surrounding community.

The values expressed in this book are to create a learning environment and learning experiences that enhance students' intrinsic motivation and stimulate their critical and creative thinking. The following are examples of educational goals in the social sciences that fit these values in the three domains just described.

> Cognitive goal: Students will understand the differences and similarities among political and economic systems compared with those of the United States.
>
> Psychomotor goal: Students will be able to use maps and a compass to locate directions and plan a route from one location to another.
>
> Affective goal: Students will be able to express their opinions, make suggestions, and otherwise participate in democratic decision making in the classroom on social and academic concerns.

Classroom Themes to Build a Sense of Community

Prawat (1992) describes the importance of moving toward the development of *curricular themes* in order to create classrooms that function as learning communities. This is accomplished by teachers who express their educational goals in the form of a year-long theme or statement of purpose for the entire class. Occasionally, an entire school will focus on a single schoolwide theme for a year. As an illustration, the principal of a private school near Chicago introduced the new school year by challenging teachers to find creative ways to apply the theme of "caring and sharing" for a year. Banners and signs with this theme were erected in the halls. Teachers led their students in discussions of how each class could display their caring and sharing to each other, to the environment, and to the community. This theme was actually a schoolwide affective goal carried out in a highly visible way to motivate students to develop caring and sharing attitudes.

Other ways that schoolwide themes can be used successfully are to enlist the cooperation of students in developing school slogans, flags, posters, or songs that express a particular theme or otherwise represent the school in a positive, growth-enhancing manner. We learn from sports competitions that students enjoy thinking of themselves as members of a powerful or winning school, and this sense of power or strength can be developed by any school, in any setting, just by capitalizing on its strengths and building a sense of pride in its academic program as well as its sports program. The result is a schoolwide sense of community that motivates purposeful and responsible behavior among the students.

Herb Price, the principal of Woodland School in Carpentersville, Illinois, collaborated with the art teachers to select a theme for their school. For the first year, they selected a theme of "rain forests" because it was a timely topic and could be integrated well in several curricular areas, including the fine arts. Classroom teachers used literature about the rain forest, taught science concepts, discussed social studies ideas about the people of the rain forest, and did some mathematics investigations by estimating and measuring heights of trees.

Even when a school has no common theme, an individual teacher can use the same idea in the classroom. When I was teaching elementary school, I had my students give a name to our class community each year. At the beginning of each year, the class brainstormed and selected such names as Sunshine Valley, Somewhere Over the Rainbow, Prairieville, and Curiosity Corner. Aside from the name, we selected a descriptive phrase that communicated our particular sense of purpose that year. Those that correspond to the above titles were "Reaching for the sun," "Exploring the yellow brick roads of math, science, reading, and writing," "Digging until we find paydirt," and "Together we'll find out who, what, when, where, why, and how."

The use of such a unifying theme has the effect of developing a bond among all members of the class. The shared sense of purpose works to eliminate discipline problems and to promote academic motivation.

Translating Goals into Outcome Statements

As described in the discussion of Writing Educational Goals, an educational *goal* is a general long-term statement of an important aim or purpose of an educational program. For example, most schools have a goal of teaching students how to read and write, another to ensure that they understand the cultural heritage of the United States, and another to help them develop attitudes and habits of good citizenship.

But to translate goals into operational plans, it is necessary to specify what *outcomes* are expected as a consequence of being in school and taking part in the planned curriculum. Eisner (1985) alerts educators to be aware that goals express intentions but that other factors may occur that alter the intentions in the educational process. According to Eisner, "Outcomes are essentially what one ends up with, intended or not, after some form of engagement" (p. 120).

Written outcome statements are used to translate goals into actions. They describe what students will be able to do as a result of their educational program. If educators can envision what it is they want students to be able to do or know after a series of learning experiences, they can plan with that outcome in mind. Learning outcomes generally describe actions, processes and products that the student will accomplish in a given time period.

Writing Useful and Appropriate Outcome Statements

The wording of outcome statements must be general but not vague. This is a subtle but important distinction. Some school documents contain goal statements such as "to develop the full potential of each individual." What does this mean to you? Can you interpret it in a meaningful way in your classroom? Can you translate it into programs? Probably not. This goal statement is so general and vague that it cannot be put into operation, and it would be very difficult to determine whether it is being attained.

An outcome statement should be general, but it should also describe how you want your students to change over time and what you want them to be able to do at the end of the term of study. Some examples of useful cognitive outcome statements are

> Students will be able to recognize and name all the counting numbers from 1 to 20.
> Students will demonstrate that they understand how technology has changed the world by creating a time line, graph, chart, or set of models to show the effects of technology on one aspect of human life.

Examples of psychomotor (also referred to as skill or process) outcomes are

> Students will be able to weigh and measure a variety of objects using metric units of measurement.
> Students will be able to compose and edit written works on a word processor.

Examples of affective outcomes are

> Students will demonstrate that they enjoy reading by selecting books and other reading materials and spending time reading in class and at home.
> Students will demonstrate that they tolerate, accept, and prize cultural, ethnic, and other individual differences in human beings by working cooperatively and productively with students of various ethnic groups.

Yearly outcome statements can be written for only one subject or across several disciplines. Outcome statements can also be written for a shorter period, such as a term or a month. They are used as guides for planning curriculum and learning experiences for that length of time. At the end of a given time period, the teacher is responsible for assessing whether the outcome has been successfully demonstrated by the students. If not, it may be necessary to repeat the same outcome statement or modify it to ensure that it can be met.

Some outcome statements may need to be modified because they are too vague. Compare the first vague statement with the improved second statement:

Original Outcome Statement: Students will be able to demonstrate that they know the U.S. Constitution.

Improved Outcome Statement: Students will be able to describe the key concepts in the articles of the U.S. Constitution and give examples of how they are applied in American life today.

Other outcome statements may need to be modified because they are too difficult for the students. Compare these:

Original Outcome Statement: Fourth-grade students will demonstrate that they know the key concepts of the Bill of Rights by creating a time line showing how each has evolved during the past 200 years.

Improved Outcome Statement: Fourth-grade students will be able to create an illustrated mural showing pictorial representations of each of the articles in the Bill of Rights.

Some outcome statements may need to be improved by adding learning opportunities that will stimulate student interest and motivation to learn the material. Consider the following:

Original Outcome Statement: Students will be able to recite the Bill of Rights.

Improved Outcome Statement: Students will be able to work in cooperative groups to plan and perform a skit showing how the United States would differ with and without the Bill of Rights.

Outcome statements are useful guides for educational planning but must be adapted to fit the needs of a particular teacher and class. For this reason, curriculum planning is an evolving process. A curriculum is never a finished product; it is constantly being changed and improved from day to day and year to year.

CURRICULUM PLANNING IN THE SUBJECT AREAS
The Integrated Whole Language Curriculum

For both new and experienced teachers, this is an exciting time to be in the teaching profession. The trend in curriculum development is changing to encourage teachers to create new curricula that integrate several subjects into thematic units. With the emergence of restructured schools and a renewed interest in examining and revising school curricula, classroom teachers are becoming empowered to work with their colleagues to create new curriculum plans that include reading, writing, problem-solving, research, and other forms of investigation.

Until recently, the elementary curriculum contained separate subjects called *reading, English, spelling,* and *creative writing.* It was believed that if students learned how to read, spell, and use grammar and punctuation correctly, they would be literate and able to communicate effectively. However, research on the developmental learning of language has led to major changes in philosophy and practice in this subject area.

Chomsky (1969) demonstrated that children learn to speak as they engage in talk with others around them, gradually comprehending the rule systems in the process. An investigation by Sulzby and Teale (1987) of children's early writing revealed it to be a developmental process similar to learning how to speak.

Graves (1983) and Murray (1984) have provided models of teaching for young children that treat writing as a continuous process rather than as a product. The process includes stimulating prewriting experiences, first drafts, editing conferences, revising, and sharing or publishing. Teachers who use these methods report that students show increased confidence in their ability to communicate in writing. Moreover, they like to write and see it as an opportunity to express their ideas.

As a result of this research, many (but not all) schools have radically restructured their language arts curricula away from separate rule-dependent subjects of reading, spelling, grammar, and writing toward a holistic and process-oriented approach. In schools with a whole language curriculum, students listen to or read literary works, write in journals, participate in editing groups, and speak for a variety of purposes. They gradually assimilate the proper grammar, punctuation, spelling, and other conventions of the English language.

One side benefit of the whole language curriculum is that it has led teachers to share what they are doing and work together to plan whole language learning experiences. As a result, the picture of teachers coming to school, closing the doors of their classrooms, and teaching in isolation is becoming a thing of the past. It has been demonstrated that new teachers should be given support and no longer asked to teach in isolation. Districts have begun to see the need to develop support mechanisms for new teachers (Beginning Teacher Evaluation Study, 1991). For example, in curriculum planning, many districts team beginning teachers with experienced teachers to develop and share curriculum materials.

The new trend to use a whole language approach has created an environment in which teachers do not structure their curricula into separate blocks of time. As Beane (1991) points out, the fact is that when confronted with a problem, individuals do not say, "Now which part of this is science and which part of this is language arts?" Instead people address problems with a multidisciplinary approach and use whatever resources and content they need in order to resolve the problem.

When the curriculum for the year is planned in a multidisciplinary approach, a series of themes that teachers choose for their high motivational value often result. Teachers actively gather resources to plan a thematic unit for a time period that integrates all subjects. If the theme of the integrated curriculum is how things change, for example, then subtopics can include seasons, butterflies, and tadpoles. Art, science, mathematics, language arts, and other learning experiences can be designed to allow students to identify how things change and to relate it to their own experiences.

Throughout the 1989 to 1990 school year, Ginny Bailey experimented with using the whole language approach to teach reading and writing. Rather than relying on the basal readers and workbooks, she used real children's literature, in the form of library materials and paperback books, as her "texts." Judy Yount and Sandy Krakow, the other first-grade teachers in Ginny's building, worked with her to translate the State of Illinois Outcome Statements and the school district's written curriculum objectives into a form that would fit their philosophy and the particular needs of the students in their building.

> "We began our plan by deciding that we would use thematic units to accomplish the state outcomes," describes Ginny. "We quickly discovered that language arts cannot be separated from science, social studies, and mathematics when you use a unit approach so we incorporated those areas into our planning. Both of us had attended numerous classes and workshops on using thematic units and had read every book we could find on the subject of using whole language in the classroom. But now it was time to sit down and make our plan for the coming school year. We began by going through the science, mathematics, and social studies curriculum guides to familiarize ourselves with what had to be covered in those areas. We then studied the Language Arts Outcome Statements. Our plan was to teach one or two thematic units a month depending upon the length of the units."

A *year-long plan* that provides a model of a whole language integrated curriculum is presented in the following Planning for Teaching.

In his analysis of subject matter teaching, Brophy (1992) identified the importance of teaching fewer topics with more depth. This practice allows students to have a greater understanding of the topics and to have teachers emphasize higher-order applications. Brophy indicates that state curriculum guides and textbooks should be modified in order to accomplish this task, and in many cases they are being revised to include a greater emphasis on integrated curricula such as the whole language programs.

In the middle school, much energy is being focused on restructuring the curriculum. In many cases, middle school faculty are reflecting on whether to continue with the concept of the middle school as a mini–high school, where students take subject-specific courses, or whether to consider other alternative structures that combine subject matter into integrated curricula. Beane (1991) proposes a vision of the curriculum centered around themes and not abstract or artificial subject areas. He suggests that middle school curricula could be focused on such themes as *living in the future, wellness,* or *cultural diversity.*

When this integrated, thematic approach is used in a middle school, the faculty plan together to design curricula that include literature, writing, mathematics, history, science, and health instruction within the selected theme. The result is often a highly motivating set of learning experiences designed specifically for the special needs of young adolescent students. Faculty members also report increased satisfaction with their own careers when they are involved in actively restructuring the curriculum to meet the needs of their students and celebrate their own special interests and talents.

Examples of high schools using the integrated curriculum can be found as well. One such example is the Humanitas Program in the Los Angeles Unified School District. This program integrates English, social studies, and art, with some teams also including philosophy, mathematics, science, studio art, or dance. The Humanitas programs are also built around themes such as *women, race and social protest, the protestant ethic,* and the spirit of capitalism. Students take core classes in these combine forces to make a net force of zero. We examine Newton's first law of motion (an object at rest tends to remain at rest).

ACCELERATION (2 WEEKS)
Using Newton's second law of motion (Force equals mass times acceleration), we explore acceleration with ordinary objects. Students design and build a hovercraft and also spend a day measuring the mass of a car by applying a net force and measuring the resulting acceleration.

KINEMATICS (5 WEEKS)
Kinematics is the study of motion. Our students investigate the properties of motion and its relationship to time, velocity, and acceleration through racetrack games. We also study projectile motion and circular motion, which extends the study of motion to two dimensions.

WORK AND ENERGY (3 WEEKS)
We discuss all the types of energy that can be observed and learn to classify them into kinetic and potential energy.

MOMENTUM (2 WEEKS)
We explore practical applications of the concept of momentum by focusing on automobile safety, especially the use of seatbelts and air bags. We explore forces in collisions. This unit culminates in a field trip to an amusement park to explore energy conservation and circular motion. We have created a guidebook for physics experiences in an amusement park.

ELECTRICITY (2 WEEKS)
We explore electrostatic forces between stationary charges and charges in motion or current electricity and emphasize their uses in the home and the workplace.

our country and the world. Also important to the academic orientation toward social studies are the important concepts that distinguish various cultures and the basic facts about world geography. Recent critics of American schools have decried the lack of knowledge of history and geography among American young people. Televised tests and magazine quizzes have demonstrated that many young people lack knowledge about the place names and locations of geographical data. Content-oriented curriculum planners seek to improve this condition by providing history and geography courses that emphasize knowledge and comprehension objectives to teach facts and concepts.

Process-oriented curriculum planners believe that instead of memorizing facts, names, places, and dates, learners should experience the processes of acquiring information on their own. By teaching students how to do research in social studies and how to use tools such as maps, globes, atlases, charts, graphs, and other resources, they will be able to find information when the occasion demands it. The credo of this orientation toward curriculum development can be summed up in the sentence, "Give a man a fish and he will be hungry the next day; teach him to fish and he'll never go hungry again." Process-oriented teachers emphasize the higher-level objectives of Bloom's Taxonomy.

Decision making is also a key focus in the process-oriented approach to teaching social studies. Harlan Cleveland defined social studies as "the study of how citizens in a society make personal and public decisions on issues that affect their destiny" (in Bragaw & Hartoonian, 1988, p. 9). To accomplish this, Bragaw and Hartoonian suggest that the curriculum planner must make sure that students

▾ develop an information base in the social sciences
▾ think using the logic and patterns of history and the social sciences
▾ communicate with others about social science data
▾ make enlightened personal and policy decisions and participate in civic activities

To illustrate the process of creating a year-long plan in social studies, we asked an education student taking a teaching methods course much like the one you are taking to create a year-long plan in social studies. The student, Jess Johnson, who lives in Jamul, California, is interested in world history and decided to create a plan for sixth-grade social studies because it focuses on early civilizations. Jess began by consulting the California State Frameworks for History and Social Science. He also used a textbook that has been approved by the state as one of his major resources. Jess created units of study for the entire year. A year after he created this plan for a class, he was hired by the Lemon Grove School District to teach sixth grade. As this book goes to press, Jess is teaching social studies and using his year-long plan for the first time. His plan is shown in the following Planning for Teaching.

Creating Time Lines That Fit Your Goals and Outcome Statements

Time is the scarcest resource in school. Reflective teachers who organize time wisely are more successful in delivering the curriculum they have planned than teachers who fail to consider it. Teachers who simply start each subject on page 1 of every textbook and hope to finish the text by June are frequently surprised. In some cases, they finish a text early in the year, but more often the school year ends and children never get to the subjects at the back of the textbook. In mathematics, some classes never get to geometry year after year. In social studies, history after World War I is often crammed into a few short lessons at the end of the year.

Will you be satisfied if this happens in your classroom? If not, you can prevent it by preplanning the time you will give to each element or subtopic of each subject area you are going to teach. This may seem like an overwhelming task at first, but it can be less threatening if you understand that you are not required to plan every outcome and objective for every subject before the year begins. It is necessary to give the entire curriculum an overview and to determine the number of days or weeks you will allot to each element.

Begin by examining the textbooks in your classroom, looking at the way they are organized. Most books are divided into *units,* each covering a single topic or collection of related topics within the academic subject. Mathematics books are likely to contain units such as Place Value, Operations, Measuring, and Geometry. History books are divided into units on Exploration, Settling the New Frontier, Creating Government, and others. English books contain units such as Listening, Writing, and Speaking. Units are excellent planning devices because they show students how facts, skills, concepts, and application of ideas are all related. The alternative to planning with units is planning a single, continuous, year-long sequence of experiences or planning unconnected and unrelated daily experiences. Units will be used as the basis for planning throughout the rest of this book.

Decide if the units in your school's textbooks are valuable and important, whether you agree with the way they are organized and the quality of learning experiences they contain. Consider whether using the textbook will result in achieving the outcomes in your school curriculum guide. Will it result in achieving the goals and outcomes you have for your class? If the textbook learning experiences match your outcomes, you can plan the year to coincide with the sequence of units in the book. If the textbook does not coincide with your planned outcomes or if you disagree with the quality and/or the organizational pattern of the book, you have several options. You can plan to use the book but present the units in a different order. You can delete units, or you can use some units in the book as they are written but supplement with other materials for additional units not covered or inadequately covered in the book. The most adventuresome and creative teachers may even decide to use the textbook only as a resource and plan original teaching units for the subject.

In any case, you should carefully consider the amount of time you want to allot to each unit that you plan to teach. Create a time line, chart, or calendar for each subject and use it as you judge how much time to spend on each subtopic. For time-line planning, the school year can be divided into weeks, months, or quarters. For a subject such as mathematics, you may think about the year as a total of 36 weeks and allot varying numbers of weeks to each math topic you want to cover during the year. For a subject such as language arts, you might think of the school year as 8 months long and create 8 different units that involve students in listening, speaking, writing, and reading activities. You may divide the year into quarters for subjects such as science or social studies with four major units planned for the year. These examples are only suggestions. Each subject can be subdivided into any time segment, or you may combine subjects into interdisciplinary units that involve students in mathematics, science, and language arts activities under one combined topic for a period of time.

Making reasonable and professional judgments about time-line planning depends on having information about your students' prior knowledge and their history of success or failure before the year begins. The pace of your curriculum depends to some degree on the skills and knowledge your class has acquired before you meet them. But your own expectation for their success is also important. You do not want to fall into the trap of reviewing basic skills all year simply because a majority of your students have been unsuccessful in the past. If you expect them to respond to your curriculum with success and be ready to move on to new challenges, it is more likely that this will actually occur.

The time lines you create in September do not have to be rigid and unchanging. They are guidelines based on the best knowledge you have at the time. As the year progresses, you will undoubtedly have reasons to change your original time line. Student needs, interests, and success will cause you to alter the pace of the original plan. Current events in the country, your classroom, or your local community may cause you to add a new unit to your plan.

Collegial Long-Term Planning

Long-term planning is an important role for teachers working singly or collegially. If you are teaching in a self-contained classroom, you have the freedom to write your own outcomes as long as they relate to the district and state guidelines. If you are working in a team-teaching school, you will need to articulate your vision of student outcomes to your teammates and adjust yours to include their ideas as well as your own. In either case, the outcome statements you create will improve with experience. As you see the effects of your original outcome statements, you will reflect on them and find ways to improve them with each succeeding year.

Ancient empires
Ancient Egypt
Kingdom of Kush

The Foundation of Western Ideas: Ancient Hebrews and Greeks
Ancient Israelites
Old Testament
Ancient Greeks
Greek life
Greek ideals
Alexander the Great

West Meets East: The Early Civilizations of India and China
Indus Valley
Buddhism
Hinduism
China
Confucius

East Meets West: Rome
All roads lead to Rome
The Roman Empire
Roman life
Christianity
Life of Jesus
Decline of Rome

Not all teachers take the time to clarify and articulate their educational goals into outcome statements. Not all teachers write learning objectives to fit their outcome statements. Some teachers never think about planning ahead for an entire year. Those who do not use reflective, long-term planning may be reluctant to try it.

When you begin teaching, you may find that you are the one who has to suggest or lead the discussion regarding the articulation of schoolwide, team, or grade-level outcomes. You may be the one to suggest innovative ways of dividing the curriculum into units. Although your ideas may be met with skepticism or resistance from some teachers, it is quite appropriate for you to articulate them because schools rely on fresh ideas from the faculty members with the most recent college or university training to enhance the curriculum and create positive innovations and change.

OPPORTUNITIES FOR REFLECTION

▼ Reflective Essay: Clarifying Your Own Goals of Education

What are your highest-priority educational goals? Write at least one cognitive, affective, and psychomotor goal that you consider to be extremely important in the curriculum.

▼ Classroom Visit: Observe Goals and Long-Term Plans

Observe a classroom in action for a few hours and try to infer what the goals are from what you see taking place. Write down your estimates of the major affective, cognitive, and psychomotor goals in effect. Ask the teacher to describe his or her goals and to show you the long-range plans. Write a brief description of the intended curriculum and the hidden curriculum that you observed.

REFERENCES

BEANE, J. (1991). Middle school: The natural home of the integrated curriculum. *Educational Leadership, 49*(2), 9–13.

Beginning Teacher Evaluation Study. (1990). San Francisco: Far West Laboratories.

BLOOM, B., ENGLEHART, M., FURST, E., HILL, W., & KRATHWOHL, D. (1956). *Taxonomy of educational objectives: Cognitive domain.* New York: Longman.

BRAGAW, D., & HARTOONIAN, M. (1988). *Social studies: The study of people in society.* In R. Brandt (Ed.), *Content of the curriculum* (pp. 9–29). Alexandria, VA: Association for Supervision and Curriculum Development.

BROPHY, J. (1992). Probing the subtleties of subject-matter teaching. *Educational Leadership, 49*(7), 4–8.

CALIFORNIA STATE DEPARTMENT OF EDUCATION. (1987a). *English–language arts framework.* Sacramento: Bureau of Publications Sales, P.O. Box 271, Sacramento, CA 95802-0271.

CALIFORNIA STATE DEPARTMENT OF EDUCATION. (1987b). *History–social science framework.* Sacramento: Bureau of Publications Sales, P.O. Box 271, Sacramento, CA 95802-0271.

CALIFORNIA STATE DEPARTMENT OF EDUCATION. (1988). *English–language arts model curriculum guide.* Sacramento: Bureau of Publications Sales, P.O. Box 271, Sacramento, CA 95802-0271.

CALIFORNIA STATE DEPARTMENT OF EDUCATION. (1992). *Mathematics framework.* Sacramento: Bureau of Publications Sales, P.O. Box 271, Sacramento, CA 95802-0271.

CAMPBELL, P., & FEY, J. (1988). New goals for school mathematics. In R. Brandt (Ed.), *Content of the curriculum* (pp. 53–74). Alexandria, VA: Association for Supervision and Curriculum Development.

CHOMSKY, C. (1969). *The aquisition of syntax from 5 to 10.* Cambridge, MA: MIT Press.

EISNER, E. (1985). *Educational imagination* (2nd ed.). New York: Macmillan.

GRAVES, D. (1983). *Writing: Teachers and children at work.* Exeter, NH: Heinemann.

McKNIGHT, C. (1987). *The underachieving curriculum: Assessing U.S. school mathematics from an international perspective.* Champaign, IL: Stipes.

MURRAY, D. (1984). *Write to learn.* New York: Holt.

Muther, C. (1987). What do we teach and when do we teach it?. *Educational Leadership, 45*(1), 77–80.

Prawat, R. (1992). From individual differences to learning communities—our changing focus. *Educational Leadership, 49*(7), 9–13.

Reynolds, M. (Ed.). (1989). *Knowledge base for the beginning teacher.* New York: Pergamon Press.

Rutherford, F., & Ahlgren, A. (1988). Rethinking the science curriculum. In R. Brandt (Ed.). *Content of the curriculum* (pp. 75–90). Alexandria, VA: Association for Supervision and Curriculum Development.

Sulzby, E., & Teale, W. (1987). *Emergent literacy: Writing and reading.* Norwood, NJ: Ablex.

Tyler, R. (1949). *Basic principles of curriculum and instruction.* Chicago: University of Chicago Press.

Planning Motivating Curriculum Units

EDUCATORS THROUGHOUT THE COUNTRY are currently engaged in a broad-based and comprehensive reexamination of almost all educational policies, curricula, and practices. One of the most productive and practical changes occurring today is the increasingly active involvement of teachers in curriculum development at the state, district, and school levels. Just a few years ago, most teachers relied heavily on textbooks and curriculum guides prepared by distant curriculum specialists. Now state and district administrators are empowering teachers to take more professional responsibility for decisions that affect their students. Teachers are taking active roles in examining and selecting textbooks and revising district curriculum guides; they are also proposing new ways of organizing classroom experiences. In California, for example, classroom teachers have taken an active role in the development of new state-sponsored curriculum documents entitled *Curriculum Frameworks* and *Model Curriculum Guides* (Kierstead & Mentor, 1988).

At the local school district level, California teachers are encouraged to create original curriculum projects that will translate the vision of excellence described at the state level into practical classroom learning experiences. The word *vision* is carefully chosen in this example because, at the local level, teachers and principals are asked to "develop a common vision" and "shape a mental image of what they want to accomplish with students and how this might look in the various disciplines" (Kierstead & Mentor, 1988, p. 37).

Briefly, the process for creating curricula that is being used in the California school reform movement involves a local planning group in (1) defining their goals for a particular discipline, (2) describing "performance expectations" (learning outcomes) for their students, and (3) determining the skills and concepts needed to achieve these expectations. They then create a series of learning units that increase in complexity, so that by the end of the year or course, they will have achieved the expectations set out for them (Kierstead & Mentor, 1988, p. 36).

HOW TEACHERS PLAN CURRICULUM UNITS

This model of curriculum development involves teachers in an active and professional capacity in planning, teaching, and evaluating learning experiences. It appeals to reflective teachers who want to be part of the decision-making process and have a commitment to improve the curricula they are expected to teach. It also adds greatly to the responsibility of classroom teachers. As curriculum decision makers, teachers must have an excellent knowledge base about the subjects they teach so that the curricula they plan will deliver accurate information. They must also be willing to work with their colleagues to make sure that their individual plans articulate what was covered in earlier grades and what the students will learn in subsequent years.

When teachers create their own curriculum, they most frequently use a thematic unit as the means to deliver or translate curricular visions into actual classroom experiences. In this chapter, we examine how teachers decide what units to teach and how they organize the learning experiences in a curriculum unit to ensure that students gain the knowledge, skills, and processes that are intended when a unit is planned.

Deciding On Unit Topics

A single teacher can work alone or with colleagues to translate state and local curriculum outcomes into units of study. Working alone, a single teacher analyzes state and local outcome statements to be implemented at that grade level in math, science, social studies, language arts, and fine arts. The teacher also examines the curriculum materials supplied by the school district, looking for themes or topics. The teacher may choose to look for topics within a subject, such as a math unit on fractions, a science unit on magnets and electricity, or a social studies unit on the electoral process. Other units may be interdisciplinary (i.e., designed to include information and material from several subjects at one time). For example, the theme "Change" may include learning experiences in science, math, social studies, and literature.

Although many teachers choose to work alone, other teachers at the same grade level frequently work together to create units of study. When this occurs, their combined knowledge and ideas are likely to result in a much more comprehensive set of units and a greater variety of learning experiences. Whether a teacher works alone or with a team, the first step is to decide on a series of curriculum units that correspond to the major educational goals in a subject or several subjects for that grade level.

Unit topics may be suggested or recommended by the district curriculum guide and the textbooks purchased for the subject area. Teachers can decide to use the suggested topics either in the order presented or in a different order. Teachers may choose to delete or add units to those recommended in order to fulfill the needs of their students.

Teachers may decide not to use units for every subject throughout the year. Instead, they may choose to teach a subject as an unconnected series of lessons. They may use units occasionally to highlight a particular topic in the curriculum. Sometimes teachers are able to plan units that combine more than one subject area, such as language arts and social studies or math and science. No two teachers will use the same units in the same order. Teachers have much discretion in planning units that fit their own strengths and their students' needs.

When a series of units is planned for a subject, each unit within the series is then developed in planning sessions that may begin in the summer before school begins or take place in after-school meetings during the year. Often teachers plan the first unit during the summer so that it is ready for the fall. Later units are then planned during the school year. After a unit has been planned, it can be reused in subsequent years, although reflective teachers usually review their older units and revise and update them prior to teaching them a second or third time.

The Process of Creating a Curriculum Unit

When reflective teachers approach the development of a curriculum unit in a subject area, they first consider their long-term goals for that subject. They may begin with the question "What are my major social studies goals this year, and what should I include in each unit of study to accomplish these goals?" Reflective teachers are also likely to monitor each decision point by asking "Why?" or "How?" Why is it important for students to learn this content? Why am I choosing this method or process? How does it fit with my primary goals for the year?

Practically speaking, the process of developing a curriculum unit also includes the following:

1. defining the topics and subject matter to be covered in the unit
2. defining the cognitive, process, and affective goals or outcomes that tell what students will gain and be able to do as a result
3. outlining the major concepts that will be covered
4. gathering resources that can be used in planning and teaching
5. brainstorming learning activities and experiences that can be used in the unit
6. organizing the ideas and activities into a meaningful sequence
7. planning lesson plans that follow the sequence
8. planning evaluation processes that will be used to measure student achievement and satisfaction

Analysis will reveal that these statements correspond to Tyler's (1949) four questions. Items 1, 2, and 3 pertain to the question "What shall we teach?" Items 4 and 5 relate to the question "How shall we teach it?" Items 6 and 7 respond to the question "How shall we organize it?" Item 8 answers the question "How will we know if we are successful?"

When seen in print, as they are here, these steps appear to depict an orderly process, but curriculum planning is rarely such a linear activity. Instead, teachers find themselves starting at various points in this process. They skip or go back and forth between these steps as ideas occur to them. For example a team member may begin a discussion by showing a resource book with a particular learning activity that could be taught as part of the new unit. Discussions may skip from activities to goals to concepts to evaluation to organization.

Nothing is wrong with this nonlinear process as long as teachers are responsible enough to reflect on the overall plan to determine if all of Tyler's questions have been addressed fully and adequately. On a cautionary note, less reflective teachers often focus almost entirely on learning activities and materials when planning a unit. They may skip the planning of goals and outcomes in their eagerness to plan fun or practical learning activities. Their units may be nothing more than a loosely organized collection of games and worksheets, with no planned outcomes or concept development. As an evaluation, they put together a test or do a project with no real consideration for whether it measures important goals.

Sequencing Learning Experiences in Unit Plans

Unit plans vary in types of learning experiences and in the way they are organized. Some subjects, such as math, are organized very sequentially, and others are not. The type of learning experiences also vary greatly depending on the subject, the resources available, and the creativity or risk taking of the teacher.

Some guidelines to consider in the creation of your unit plans are to use the textbook or a district curriculum guide as the basis for planning and as an important resource. *Do not limit yourself, however, to a single textbook as the source of all information in planning your unit or in teaching it.* A good textbook can be a valuable resource for you as you plan and for your students as they learn about the topic, but a rich and motivating unit plan will contain many other elements.

Supplementary reading materials from libraries or bookstores might include biographies, histories, novels, short stories, plays, poetry, newspapers, magazines, how-to books, and myriad other printed materials. Other resources to consider are films, videotapes, audiotapes, and computer programs on topics that relate to your unit. Many interesting child-centered computer programs allow your students to have simulated experiences, solve problems, and make decisions as if they were involved in the event themselves. A good example is the computer game called "Oregon Trail," distributed by the Minnesota Educational Computer Consortium (MECC), in which the student travels along the Oregon Trail, making decisions about what supplies to buy, when and where to stop along the way, and how to handle emergencies. This program can enrich a unit on westward expansion by providing more problem-solving and critical-thinking experiences than can ever be provided through reading and discussion.

Many educational games also provide students with simulated experiences. Some are board games that can be purchased in a good toy or book store. Others are more specialized learning games that must be purchased through educational publishers or distributers. Your school district probably receives hundreds of catalogs from educational publishers. Locate them and find out about the many manipulative and simulation games available on your topic.

Consider field trips that will provide your students with experiences beyond the four walls of the classroom. Which museums have exhibits related to your topic? A simple walk through a neighborhood to look for evidence of pollution or to view variations in architecture can add depth to your unit. If you cannot travel, consider inviting a guest speaker to speak to your students about the topic. Sometimes parents are excellent resources and are willing to speak on their careers or other interests.

In thinking about how to organize a unit, many reflective teachers prefer to begin with a highly motivating activity such as a field trip, a guest speaker, a simulation game, a hands-on experiment, or a film. They know that when the students' initial experience with a topic is stimulating and involving, interest and curiosity are aroused. The next several lessons in the unit are frequently planned at the knowledge and comprehension levels of Bloom's Taxonomy to provide students with basic facts and concepts so that they are able to build a substantial knowledge base and understanding of the topic. After the knowledge base is established, further learning experiences can be designed at the application, analysis, synthesis, and evaluation levels to ensure that the students are able to think critically and creatively about the subject. This model of unit planning is not universal, nor is it the only logical sequence, but it can be adapted to fit many topics and subjects with excellent results.

EXAMPLES OF CURRICULUM UNITS

The following sections illustrate the processes used by teachers as they select, order, and create unit plans in several subjects from the elementary curriculum. Because each teacher has a personal curriculum orientation and philosophy, the process of decision making is more complex when teachers plan together than when they plan alone. The following examples demonstrate how teachers create their own curriculum units and what they put down on paper to record their plans for teaching. You will notice many variations in the way units are created and what they contain depending on their purposes and the philosophies and values of the teachers who create them.

Developing a Middle School Mathematics Unit

Mathematics is generally thought of as a sequentially ordered subject. For example, students learn the basic skills of addition and subtraction in first and second grade; they learn multiplication and division later. As Piaget demonstrated, mathematics is a subject that requires early experiences with concrete examples and hands-on experiences allowing students to manipulate materials in order to understand mathematical relationships. Only in the upper intermediate grades can students be expected to understand these same relationships at an abstract level, without the need to "see" them in a concrete way. A third expectation in math is that skillful computation is not sufficient as an outcome or performance expectation; it is also important that students be able to apply mathematical operations to real-life problems and tasks.

Based on these organizational principles, an effective curriculum unit in math is likely to (1) present new skills and concepts in order of difficulty; (2) initiate new learning with concrete, manipulative experiences so that students can understand the concepts involved; and (3) provide examples, tasks, and problems that call on students to apply their newly learned skills in lifelike situations.

Mathematics is an example of a *spiral curriculum.* This means that certain concepts and skills are taught every year but in an upward spiral of difficulty. Each year begins with a review of skills from previous years and then new skills and concepts are introduced. For this reason, the topics of mathematics units are likely to be similar from year to year, but the way these topics are addressed and the complexity of the concepts vary greatly. Mathematics education now emphasizes problem-solving and investigation as a means of developing mathematical power. Whenever possible, real situations and problems are becoming the basis for the curriculum.

A good example of a mathematics unit that involves students in realistic investigations and problem-solving is presented in the following Planning for Teaching. This unit, entitled "Television-Viewing Habits," was created by Pam Knight for her middle school students. She uses it during the first week of school to engage her students' interest in mathematics, help to develop a sense of confidence in their mathematical power, and show them how useful and important mathematics can be in their everyday lives.

Creating an Elementary Language Arts Unit

Units created for the language arts curriculum of an elementary classroom are likely to be very different from math units. Because language arts is a composite of the skills and creative abilities related to reading, writing, speaking, and listening, a language arts unit is likely to include a great variety of learning experiences. Expected outcomes are likely to call on students to apply basic skills in some form of creative product.

As an example of a language arts unit, let us consider the thinking and planning processes used by a fourth-grade teacher as she created a unit called "Friendship in Fiction" (one of the units shown in the second Planning for Teaching in this chapter. She decided on the topic because she observed that friendship is a very important element in the lives of her fourth-grade students. She noticed that the students in her classroom who had a number of good friends seemed to enjoy and succeed in school activities better than students with few friends. She knew that it would not be possible to order students to be friendlier to isolated students, but she believed she could influence the students in her class to become more sensitive to the friendship needs of their classmates.

This teacher's understanding of student development led her to believe that her students would have a strong interest in the topic of friendship and that they would be more than willing to spend class time reading, writing, speaking, and listening on a topic of such vital social interest to fourth graders. Therefore, she decided to blend her goals of meeting the social needs of her students with her goal of teaching students to listen, think, and read critically and to express their ideas effectively in writing and speaking. The goals and purposes for the unit plan began to take shape in her mind.

Next, she went to the school learning center and made a list of children's books with friendship as a theme. A reference book entitled *The Bookfinder* (Dreyer, 1985) provided her with a long list of books on the theme of friendship, with annotated reviews and appropriate reading levels. She also asked the learning center teacher to recommend her favorites. She purposely chose books with reading levels at, below, and above the fourth-grade level to accommodate the students in her class with varying reading levels. She found that the books themselves suggested learning experiences and activities that used reading, writing, listening, and speaking skills.

She created a list of possible activities and began to envision the unit taking place. She could see, in her mind's eye, the students role playing scenes from the books they read and writing in journals about their own views of friendship. She tried to envision the class meetings she would hold on the topic of friendship and how she would introduce the subject to the students to gain their interest and willingness to learn and grow. She silently rehearsed the words she would use to ensure that they understood what she expected of them as they read and discussed their books in cooperative groups and planned their creative products together.

She believed that, if her unit was successful, she would be able to detect an affective change or growth in her students in at least two ways: (1) a greater degree of friendliness toward classmates would occur and (2) individuals would express in their journals or in discussions that they felt more accepted and better liked by their classmates. She also believed that, if her unit was successful, there would be notable changes in the ways students used language in her classroom, including the following: (1) students would choose to read more fiction, (2) they would listen with greater accuracy and empathy, and (3) they would be able to express more clearly their ideas in writing and speaking.

During a long weekend, the teacher organized her materials, ideas, and learning experiences into a sequence of events that she could envision taking place in her classroom with her students. That sequence of events is presented in the following Planning for Teaching as an example of a language arts unit plan initiated and created by a single teacher.

A Student Creates a Social Studies Unit

Social studies in the elementary and middle school curricula combines several academic disciplines, including geography, history, economics, political science, anthropology,

TELEVISION-VIEWING HABITS

A Middle School Mathematics Unit
Pam Knight, Poway Middle School, Poway, California

DESCRIPTION

This unit functions both as a personal exploration of how students use their free time and as a mathematics investigation. Students keep a log of all the time they spend watching TV every day for a week. With parental permission, students may also log the TV viewing habits of their parents. After a week of data gathering, students carry out a variety of mathematical calculations and interpret the data they collected.

COGNITIVE AND SKILL OUTCOME STATEMENTS

Students will be able to collect and record data accurately and efficiently.

Students will be able to calculate percentages of time spent watching television and compare those with percentages of time spent doing other activities.

Students will be able to create bar and circle graphs based on the data they collected and the percentages they calculated.

Individually, students will interpret the data they collected about their own television-viewing habits.

As a class, students will combine their data with that collected by other members of the class to make interpretations and generalizations regarding TV-viewing habits of their age group.

Individually, students will write articles describing the conclusions and generalizations they reached from this study.

In small groups, students will make oral presentations on the findings of their group.

AFFECTIVE OUTCOME STATEMENT

Students will become aware of the amount of time they and their classmates spend watching television and will make value judgments about whether they want to continue spending their time in this way.

CALENDAR OF EVENTS

I plan this investigation for the first week of school. It gives me insight into the students' incoming work habits and mathematical power.

First Week of School

FRIDAY: Introduce unit and distribute data collection materials. Assign students the task of collecting data, beginning Sunday, on the amount of time they watch television. Because video games are played on a TV screen, my students also decided to count the time spent playing video games. I ask students to be as honest as possible and to keep track to the nearest quarter of an hour.

Second Week of School
MONDAY–FRIDAY: Data collection continues. Discussions in class focus on data collection problems and techniques.

Third Week of School
MONDAY: BAR GRAPHS
Individually, students create bar graphs demonstrating the amount of time they watched TV each day of the preceding week.

TUESDAY: CALCULATING PERCENTAGES AND CIRCLE GRAPHS
Individually, students calculate the amount and percentage of time they spent sleeping, in school, in after-school or weekend activities, and watching television, as well as extra time not spent watching television. They create circle graphs showing these percentages.

WEDNESDAY–FRIDAY: GROUP DATA INTERPRETATION
Cooperative groups combine class data in order to answer these questions:

1. Who watches more television—seventh or eighth graders? Explain how you came to this conclusion.
2. Which day of the week do people watch the most television? Explain how you came to this conclusion.
3. Who watches more television in general— boys or girls? Does any particular age group watch more television? How did you come to your conclusions?
4. By using data about parent viewing habits, is there any relationship between the television-viewing habits of a parent to the habits of a child?

Fourth Week of School
MONDAY: WRITING ARTICLES
Individuals are assigned to write an article about their conclusions about television-viewing habits of middle school students. They must answer the questions Who? What? When? Where? and Why? in the articles.

TUESDAY–WEDNESDAY: ORAL PRESENTATION PLANNING
Cooperative groups plan presentations on the findings of their groups. They create visual displays to show the data they collected.

THURSDAY: ORAL PRESENTATIONS
Cooperative groups present their findings to the rest of the class.

FRIDAY: UNIT EVALUATION
Students evaluate their accomplishments in this unit. Individuals participate in a teacher student conference to discuss the points each students earned in the unit. Cooperative groups discuss the processes they used in their group planning sessions, the visual displays they made, and the effectiveness of their oral presentations.

WHAT ARE FRIENDS FOR?

A Fourth-Grade Language Arts Unit

DESCRIPTION

A unit in which students read books on the theme of friendship. Discussions, writing, speeches, dramatizations, and other events are planned to allow students to express their views on what they have read.

OUTCOME STATEMENTS

Outcome 1

Students will read at least six books on friendship and demonstrate comprehension of and critical and creative thinking about the books by interacting with classmates to create an original product related to each book.

Related Projects and Performance Objectives

Students will

Read: Choose and read at least six books (at a reading level appropriate for the student) from the list provided.

Listen: In cooperative groups of students who have read the same book, each student will *listen* to the opinions and ideas of others in discussions about the book's content and meaning and to the ideas and suggestions of others about the creation of an original product related to the book.

Speak: Each student will take part in a group project to create an original product related to each book and perform or describe it to the class.

Outcome 2

Students will express their opinions, ideas, and suggestions to others in the classroom with clarity, creativity, and supportive evidence for their opinions.

Related Projects and Performance Expectations

Students will

Speak: In cooperative groups, students will create an "advertisement" to sell others on reading the book.

Write: Students will choose to write an original story, poem, play, or essay in response to at least one book.

Outcome 3

Students will demonstrate that they recognize, accept, and understand that the need for friendship is important to each member of the class and that each student has a responsibility to offer support and friendship to other students in the classroom community.

Related Projects and Performance Expectations

Students will

Read: Students will look for examples of the importance and value of friendship as they read the books they select for this unit.

Speak: Students will contribute opinions about what friendship means during classroom meetings.

Listen: Students will listen to and paraphrase opinions stated by others about what friendship means to them.

Write: Students will choose one classmate and write in a journal about the experience of offering friendship to that person.

ORGANIZATIONAL PLAN

Book Selection: Each week for 6 weeks, students select a book from a list of four titles, each with a different reading level. Students are encouraged to select titles at their own personal reading level but are allowed to select titles above or below this level if they have a strong interest in reading the book.

Sustained Silent Reading (SSR): Each day, students spend 45 minutes in sustained silent reading of the books they have selected.

Literature Circles: During (or immediately following) SSR, the teacher may call on four students to form a literature circle. The students bring their books and discuss interesting passages from them with others in the circle. The teacher shares a book in the same way (idea taken from Hanson, 1987).

Cooperative Groups: Each week, cooperative groups are formed by those who have selected a particular book. They must discuss the book, create a plan for advertising the book to the rest of the class, and perform their advertisement on Fridays.

Enrichment Plan: Individual students may select additional titles to read from the list in response to student advertisements. Individuals may work alone or with partners to create original projects in response to the book.

Classroom Meetings: Weekly classroom meetings on the topic of friendship will be led by the teacher. In these meetings, students will relate the stories they are reading to their own lives and friendships. Suggested topics for the classroom meetings include:

Week 1: What are friends for? What are some of the reasons to have friends? What can friends do together that a person cannot do alone?

Week 2: What does it feel like to move away from friends or to lose a good friend?

Week 3: Is it good to have one best friend or many friends? What happens if your best friend chooses another best friend?

Week 4: What happens when friends fight or disagree? How can you make up with a friend after a quarrel? How can you deal with conflict?

Week 5: How can you make more friends or better friends?

continued

Week 6: What can you do if you notice that someone needs a friend? How can you include them in your activities? How can a class of children make sure that everyone is included and no one is left out? Do we want to do that after all that we've learned about friendship? If so, what will we do differently?

EVALUATION PLAN

Outcome 1 will be evaluated by recording the books each child reads in a cooperative group or independently. Descriptions of the original products are also kept on the checklist. At the end of the unit, the checklist can serve as a means of communicating with the parents what the student has accomplished.

Outcome 2 will be documented by keeping a portfolio of each student's written responses to books read in the unit.

Outcome 3 will be individually recorded by having students write in their journals following each weekly classroom meeting. They will write their own views on the questions raised in the meeting. The teacher will write at the same time on the same topic.

sociology, and psychology. The curriculum is designed as an ever-widening circle of ideas, in keeping with the developmental stages of students. In the early grades, the curriculum centers on the home and the community; the middle grades focus on the states and the United States; concepts related to nations and the world are dealt with in the later grades.

Units are the ideal way to deliver a combined curriculum such as social studies. Primary teachers often create units on the community, including maps of the school neighborhood, history of the community, roles of community helpers, economics activities related to stores in the community, and other similar experiences.

Middle-grade teachers frequently create units on topics such as Native Americans, the explorers, geography of the United States, and U.S. presidents. Upper-grade teachers may offer units comparing countries of the world in terms of geography, politics, economics, and history.

As an example of how a social studies unit may be developed, consider the one created by a student in an education methods course much like the one you are taking. Jess Johnson chose to do a unit in social studies and language arts because of his interest in history and communication skills. He began by reviewing the state frameworks in these two areas. He also reviewed textbooks and district guidelines that were used in his community. He chose to focus on sixth grade because of his interest in ancient world civilizations.

Jess had already created a year-long plan for this subject (see chapter 4). For his unit plan, he selected Roman culture because he was interested in it and already owned books and materials on this subject. For example, he had a book that contained some real epitaphs of Roman citizens, which he wanted to use as examples of primary sources about the culture.

WHEN IN ROME, DO AS THE ROMANS DO

Jess Johnson, Sixth-Grade Teacher, Lemon Grove School District, Lemon Grove, California

DESCRIPTION

This unit fits the California State Framework for History–Social Science for sixth-grade. It is one of the units in my year-long plan for social studies (see the Planning for Teaching in chapter 4 entitled "Year-Long Plan in Social Studies for Sixth Grade"). It provides students with new knowledge about an important ancient culture and civilization in such a way that allows them to compare and contrast their own culture with that of the ancient Romans. It involves students in attaining and using skills in research, using primary sources, thinking critically, writing, and doing oral presentations in order to communicate what they've learned to others.

COGNITIVE GOALS

Students will know why primary sources are important for understanding an ancient culture and will be able to describe a primary source.

Students will be able to describe Roman culture in regard to class, housing, slavery, family life, roles and statuses of men, women, and children, educational processes and values, social life, entertainment, economy and occupations, religion, art, ideals, and values.

AFFECTIVE GOALS

Students will appreciate the richness of knowledge gained from primary sources and enjoy getting involved with the authors and their subjects.

Students will develop an interest in Roman history and culture and see how it is related to their lives.

PSYCHOMOTOR GOALS

Students will act out aspects of Roman life in order to gain an understanding of Roman customs, ceremonies, and rituals.

Students will improve their critical thinking and communication skills by writing and speaking about the lives of Roman citizens.

TIMELINE OF LEARNING EVENTS

Week 1: All Roads Lead to Rome

The legendary beginning of Rome	Latium
	Development of the Roman republic
Romulus and Remus	Expansion of power;
Etruscans	conquering Greece

Weeks 2–3: Friends, Romans, Countrymen, Lend Me Your Ears

The Roman Empire	Pax Romana
Julius Caesar	Government
Augustus Caesar	Justice

continued

Military   Technology
Highways   Aqueducts
Architecture

Weeks 4–5: When in Rome, Do as the Romans Do

Roman Life	Education
Class	Social life
Housing	Entertainment
Slaves	Economy
Family life	Occupations
Men's roles and responsibilities	Religion
Women's roles and responsibilities	Art
Children's roles	Ideals and values

Weeks 6–7: Crossroads

Christianity	Roman and Christian
Life of Jesus	relationships
Life of Paul	Persecution
Jewish and Christian	Rise of Christianity
relationships	

Week 8: It's All Downhill from Here

Decline of Rome	Division of the empire
Later emperors	Barbarian invaders
Constantine	Causes of the fall of Rome

Resources in the classroom for illustration and student interest

Art reproductions from the era	Pillows for reclining
Chariot model	Posters of modern Rome
Gravestone and tomb model	Posters of Roman ruins
Jewelry that approximates the era	Pottery ware
Maps of Roman world	Roman abacus
Models of Roman life, buildings,	Roman calendar
technology, and so forth	Roman coins
Musical instruments that approximate	Terra-cotta lamp
the period	Toga
Papyrus roll facsimile	Wax tablets

Evaluation Process

A two-tiered means is used to evaluate the students' mastery of "When in Rome, Do as the Romans Do."

In developing this unit plan, Jess found that he continually referred to the *California History–Social Science Framework* for guidance. It served as his compass, helping him to feel that he was going in the right direction. However, he reported that within the framework's broad guidelines, he felt free to develop his own teaching and learning experiences. The unit that Jess created is shown in the following Planning for

Tier 1: Assessing and Adjusting for the Students' Success

▼ To reinforce and review, the class will play Team Jeopardy at the end of the 2 weeks.

▼ To help me assess how they are doing with facts, I will routinely have a short time in the afternoon to ask questions that will be similar to the ones in Team Jeopardy.

▼ To help me assess how the students are learning concepts, I will routinely have a short time in the morning to ask a few questions that require thoughtful answers.

▼ To help me evaluate individual student knowledge and understanding, I will have my regular one-to-one discussions with students.

▼ To help me assess individual student understanding, I will monitor class work and homework of those students who might be struggling.

Tier 2: Determining Points for Grades

▼ Points are given for participation in class activities and projects: 10 points for each project or activity. If a student misses a day, the activities can be made up or, if that is not practical, an alternative project can be assigned.

▼ Points are given for class work and writing. (It may be revised and re- turned.) 10 points for each assignment. If a student misses an in-class as- signment, it can be made up.

▼ Points are given for homework. (It may be revised and returned.) 10 points for each assignment.

▼ Points are given for the test at the end of the 2 weeks. (Students will be allowed to use their notes, class charts and diagrams, class materials, journals, class data base, and so forth.) (50 points)

Finishing each assignment listed above will entitle the student to gold foil leaves that the students will work into the laurel wreaths to make and wear for the culminating event.

The homework for the unit, a brief description, its possible point value, and the points needed for each grade will be listed on a sheet for their notebook and will go home to their parents with additional comments and information.

CULMINATING EVENT—THE EMPEROR REQUESTS YOUR PRESENCE!

Because this unit is actually a sub unit of an 8-week unit called "East Meets West: Rome," the students will have a culminating event at the end of the 8-weeks. An invitation will go home to the parents to join the class during the day or in the evening for a trip on the class time machine back to ancient Rome. The students will present history and aspects of Roman life and culture to each other and their parents. The students will wear togas. The day will end with a party with some Roman desserts.

Teaching. After graduating from his university program and receiving his teaching credentials, Jess was hired as a sixth-grade teacher and was able to use his long-term plan and this unit during his first year of teaching. He was glad to have all the planning done ahead of time.

WAVE PHENOMENA

A High School Physics Unit
Chris Chiaverina, New Trier High School, Winnetka, Illinois
Jim Hicks, Barrington High School, Barrington, Illinois

DESCRIPTION

In this unit about wave phenomena, we study both sound and light waves. As with all our units, we begin with dramatic and puzzling demonstrations by the teacher to generate students' interest in the topic. Students then explore waves in a qualitative laboratory experience in order to observe them in action. This enables the student to construct their own meaning and understanding of the properties of waves. During class discussions, we probe students' preconceived ideas about the phenomena and help students unlearn their preconceptions in order to construct more accurate understandings. Only after students have experienced the phenomena in action do we introduce mathematical relationships. At this point, students do a quantitative laboratory experiment in which they learn to express their new understandings in a formula or mathematical expression.

OUTCOME STATEMENTS

Cognitive Outcomes:

Students will investigate wave phenomena and identify key features of light and sound waves.
Students will distinguish between energy transfer by waves and particles.

Skill and Process Outcomes:

Through kinesthetic learning experiences, students will derive the relationship between wave speed, wave length, and frequency.
Students will investigate constructive and destructive interference of waves and apply the principle of superposition.
Students will demonstrate how sound is produced and transmitted.

Affective Outcome:

Students unlearn their preconceived notions of physical phenomena and replace them with scientifically accurate observations and understandings.

TIMELINE AND CALENDAR OF EVENTS

Slinkies and Human Slinkies:

Students create and observe waves in the hallways using Slinkies. They explore their views, preconceptions, and observations of wave phenomena and examine different types of waves. Mathematical relationships are derived from students' observations. Students learn to communicate what they have observed about the speed of waves, what happens when waves meet and interfere with each other, and other basic properties of waves using mathematical expressions.

Sound Waves

We explore what happens when sound waves meet and interfere with each other. We discuss acoustics and how sound is produced and perceived. We look at the sources of sound, including musical instruments and how sound is recorded and reproduced. We make Edison record players so that students can experience the reproduction of sound.

Light and Its Properties

Using mirrors and lenses, students look at how light interacts with matter. As a culminating activity, we go to the University of Wisconsin where the students attend college classes and create their own holograms. They keep a journal of their observations on this trip.

Sound and Light Show

In the school auditorium, we use loudspeakers connected to a signal generator. Students line up in the regions in the auditorium that have no sound because of wave interference. We also explore how the walls act as acoustical mirrors. Using primary colors, we produce all the other colors of the spectrum by mixing light.

EVALUATION PLAN

Students complete both quantitative and qualitative laboratory explorations, worksheets, paper-and-pencil tests. They take notes and write reports on holograms and the sound and light show. They create acoustical and optical devices.

Tests and quizzes	50%
Laboratory experiments	25%
Homework	20%
Special projects	5%

RESOURCES

Edge, R. (1981). *String and sticky tape experiments.* College Park, MD: American Association of Physics Teachers.

Edmund Scientific Catalogue. 101 E. Gloucester Pike, Barrington, NJ 08007; (609) 547-3488.

Exploratorium science snackbook. San Francisco: Exploratorium Museum Store; 1-800-359-9899.

Freier, G., & Anderson, F. (1981). *A demonstration handbook for physics.* College Park, MD: American Association of Physics Teachers.

Hewitt, P. (1987). *Conceptual physics.* Palo Alto: Scott, Foresman.

Liem, T. (1981). *Invitations to scientific inquiry.* El Cajon, CA: Science Inquiry Enterprises.

A potpourri of physics teaching ideas. College Park, MD: American Association of Physics Teachers.

The physics teacher. American Association of Physics Teachers (AAPT). 5112 Berwyn Road, College Park, MD 20740.

The science teacher. National Science Teachers Association (NSTA). 1742 Connecticut Avenue, NW, Washington, DC 20009.

Two Colleagues Create a High School Science Unit

Chris Chiaverina and Jim Hicks are high school science teachers who believe that the world is a richer and more interesting place when people are aware of the principles of physics that operate around us. They plan their physics units to replace students' misconceptions about science as a dull and abstruse body of knowledge with a new view that science consists of exciting opportunities to satisfy their curiosity about how things work.

Working as colleagues, Jim and Chris have created a number of science units that begin with concrete explorations that encourage students to explore and investigate science phenomena. When they begin to create a new unit, they think about spectacular opening demonstrations to pique the students' interest in the topic. Jim and Chris report that they work very hard to plan and teach science units that are full of active exploration, real-life applications, and opportunities for students to experience the wonders of science. They say that the pay-offs for them and their students are well worth the effort. When a student looks at Jim with a light in her eyes, and says, "Hey, that's neat!" he knows that all the work that went into the lesson was well spent. Their unit on wave phenomena is shown in the preceding Planning for Teaching.

Creating a Multidisciplinary Unit

Some units of study cross the boundaries between subjects or disciplines such as math, science, language arts, and social studies. For example, Jess Johnson's unit on Roman life incorporated many communication and language arts skills in what was primarily a social studies unit. Curriculum plans that include learning experiences from more than one subject area are called *multidisciplinary* or *interdisciplinary* units.

To create such units, teachers frequently choose themes or topics and plan learning experiences that involve students in reading, writing, speaking, science investigations, mathematical problem-solving, music, and art. A single teacher can certainly plan and teach a multidisciplinary unit, but we've found that the units planned by two to four teachers are often more exciting because they incorporate each teacher's different perspectives and strengths. For example, at Woodland School in Carpentersville, Illinois, three first-grade teachers often plan their whole language thematic units together. Ginny Bailey, Judy Yount, and Sandra Krakow recently planned an interdisciplinary unit, "Change," highlighting the changes of butterflies and moths.

They know that teachers often have difficulty fitting in all the subjects of their busy curricula. They find that by using a thematic unit, they can teach several subjects simultaneously. To plan a unit, these teachers use a graphic organizer known as a *planning web*. They sit down with a large piece of paper and write the thematic topic in the middle of the page. They write the various disciplines they want to cover at different positions on the paper and then brainstorm learning experiences that fit the topic under the appropriate subject areas. An example of one of their planning webs is shown in the following Planning for Teaching.

Through their observations of the children they teach, the three teachers learned that, in the minds of first-grade students, reading and writing are very closely related. Their interdisciplinary thematic units allow students to read, write, and investigate interesting topics such as caterpillars, cookies, and planets. For each unit, they select appropriate topic-specific children's books of fiction, nonfiction, and poetry.

PLANNING WEB FOR A THEMATIC UNIT

Ginny Bailey, Judy Yount, and Sandra Krakow, Woodland School, Carpentersville, Illinois

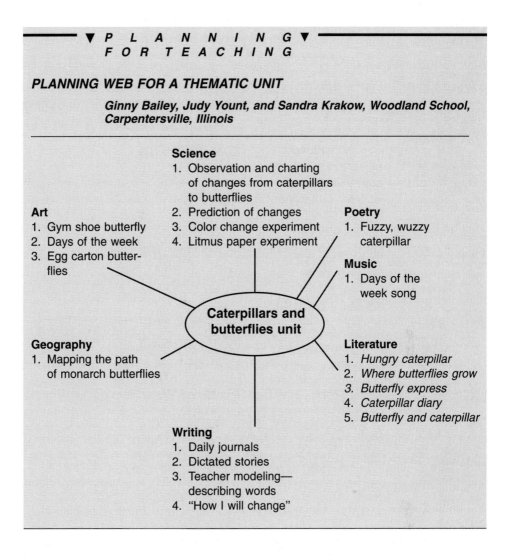

Science
1. Observation and charting of changes from caterpillars to butterflies
2. Prediction of changes
3. Color change experiment
4. Litmus paper experiment

Art
1. Gym shoe butterfly
2. Days of the week
3. Egg carton butter-flies

Poetry
1. Fuzzy, wuzzy caterpillar

Music
1. Days of the week song

Caterpillars and butterflies unit

Geography
1. Mapping the path of monarch butterflies

Literature
1. *Hungry caterpillar*
2. *Where butterflies grow*
3. *Butterfly express*
4. *Caterpillar diary*
5. *Butterfly and caterpillar*

Writing
1. Daily journals
2. Dictated stories
3. Teacher modeling—describing words
4. "How I will change"

They locate songs on the topics when possible. Skill teaching is embedded in the unit, within the context of the literature, poetry, or music. The science and social studies facts and concepts are easily mastered by students when they are presented in the context of hands-on experiments and are reinforced by illustrated stories, poems, and songs. Math concepts are introduced by counting, measuring, sequencing, and patterning games and activities appropriate to each unit. The following Planning for Teaching shows a written plan for the unit "Changes," describing some of the specific learning experiences and how the unit is evaluated.

Conclusions

The curriculum of any subject or of a combination of subjects may be subdivided into thematic units of study that are often highly motivating to students and a source of

UNIT THEME: CHANGES; SUBTOPIC: BUTTERFLIES AND MOTHS
A FIRST-GRADE UNIT PLAN

**Ginny Bailey, Judy Yount, and Sandra Krakow Woodland School,
Carpentersville, Illinois**

DESCRIPTION

This primary learning unit was planned to provide students with a set of varied learning experiences to understand the concept of change, with an emphasis on changes in the life cycle of living things.

Cognitive Goal:

Students will understand that all living things change over time.

Affective Goal:

Students will accept change as a natural part of their own lives and environment.

Psychomotor Goals:

Students will use observation skills to identify changes. They will use writing and speaking skills to report what they have learned through observation.

Nature walk: Prior to the nature walk, students are asked to imagine what they might find out about caterpillars and butterflies on their walk. During the walk, they look especially for cocoons. When they return to the classroom, they discuss their findings. They predict whether the cocoons they found will become butterflies or moths. Then they write about what they saw on their nature walk.

Observing caterpillars: Caterpillars ordered from a science supply dealer arrive in plastic jars. Students observe them climb to the top of the jar preparing to form a chrysalis. In just a few days, they begin to spin their chrysalis. They remain in this form for 3 or 4 days and then emerge as butterflies or moths.

As a follow-up activity, students are asked to illustrate the various changes they observe. A strip of 18-inch by 6-inch paper is prepared for each child. They fold the paper into fourths and draw each stage of a butterfly's development: (1) egg on a leaf, (2) caterpillar, (3) chrysalis or cocoon, and (4) butterfly or moth.

In groups of four, children evaluate their products and check the proper sequence. Each child can then tell the other children a story about his or her butterfly.

Color changes: In a learning center, students experiment to discover how colors change. Using diluted red, blue, and yellow food color, the children use an empty cup and an eye dropper to mix colors and experiment on their own to create new colors from the original primary colors.

Children's literature: A variety of picture books related to change are collected by the teacher, who will use them in this unit. Some books will be read aloud by the teacher and used as a focus for discussion. Others will be selected by the children to read on their own.

Caterpillar/butterfly art activity: Students create a wiggly caterpillar by cutting 12 cups from an egg carton. They make a small hole in the bottom of each cup, tie a knot at one end of a piece of yarn, and string the 12 cups together. Then they add paper eyes and decorate with crayon or paint.

They create a butterfly by cutting out 3 of the 12 cups from an egg carton for the body. Then they add wings and pipecleaner antennae.

Gym shoe butterfly: Each child places his gym shoes on a large pastel paper (arches on the outside) and traces the shoes into a butterfly shape. The child then cuts out the shape and adds antennae. The child can write a poem inside the butterly shape.

Days of the week: Students create a caterpillar with seven circles cut from construction paper. They then copy one name of each day of the week on each circle and glue them onto a background paper in the correct order. Afterward, they added a face, legs, and antennae. Students learn a song about the days of the week.

How people change: Students bring in pictures of themselves as babies and put them on a bulletin board. Current school pictures are also arranged on the bulletin board. Students have to try to match the baby pictures with the current pictures of their classmates. Discussions focus on how people change; observing differences in size, hair, and other physical features; and what people are able to do at different ages. As a follow-up, students write in their journals about how they have changed.

Growth charts: Charts on the students' current heights and weights are initiated during this unit. Each student measures and weighs a partner. This data is recorded on a wall graph. These charts are updated 3 times in the year.

Poetry about change: Poems about caterpillars and butterflies, seasons, and other changes are distributed frequently during the unit. Students read them, memorize and recite them, discuss them, and illustrate them. They are also used to teach language structure and vocabulary skills. A poem is projected onto a screen by an overhead projector. Students also have copies of the poem on their desks. We teach skills such as these:

1. reading from left to right
2. finding and reading individual words
3. using the context of the poem to decode words
4. learning specific phonics skills (e.g., beginning sounds, endings, rhyming words)

Art/nutrition activity: Create a caterpillar out of fruit, vegetables, and peanut butter. Eat it for a snack and discuss its nutritional value.

Unit Evaluation Activity

Provide students with a paper that has the beginning of three paragraphs (see below). Use a copy on the overhead projector and clarify for students how to begin and what is expected.

continued

Planning for Teaching Continued

Because primary students are unable to write all that they know and have observed, this evaluation can be extended by asking children from an upper elementary grade to interview the primary children and write the younger students' responses for them.

> This week, I learned about butterflies and moths. First, I learned . . .

> Next, I learned . . .

> Finally, I learned . . .

pride for the teachers who create them. Teacher-crafted curriculum units are often highly creative and original products. For teachers who choose to create them rather than rely on textbook lessons and content, units are a way of individualizing the curriculum to capitalize on the interests and talents of the teacher and the students.

OPPORTUNITIES FOR REFLECTION

▼ Reflective Essay: Selecting a Unit Topic

List several unit topics or themes that interest you. What are their strengths and weaknesses? Which topics might you be able to use during student teaching? Do you want to work on your unit alone or with a colleague? Why?

▼ Classroom Visit: School Resources

While at the school, visit the school library or media center. Locate resources that you could use in your unit if you taught in that school. Interview the librarian to ask for suggestions for other resources on that topic. Include these materials in your unit resource list.

REFERENCES

CALIFORNIA STATE DEPARTMENT OF EDUCATION (1987). *History–social science framework.* Sacramento: Bureau of Publications Sales, P.O. Box 271, Sacramento, CA 95802-0271.

DREYER, S. (1985). *The bookfinder* (Vol. 3), Circle Pines, MN: American Guidance Service.

KIERSTEAD, J., & MENTOR, S. (1988). Translating the vision into reality in California schools. *Educational Leadership, 46*(2), 35–40.

TYLER, R. (1949). *Basic principles of curriculum and instruction.* Chicago: University of Chicago Press.

6

Sequencing Objectives in Lesson Plans

EDUCATIONAL GOALS, LEARNING OUTCOMES, AND UNIT PLANS are important elements used in planning curricula to educate our young people. But they are meaningless words on paper unless they are translated into a practical set of logically ordered day-to-day learning events. Goals, outcome statements, and unit plans are only guides for the real-life classroom encounters between teacher and students. To be successful, when teachers introduce new units in class, they must have a systematic plan for what to teach on each day of the week. But, as all teachers know, these plans must be flexible enough to fit the particular needs of students in the specific classroom.

This chapter provides some guidelines for the creation of a sequence of day-to-day learning events, usually referred to by teachers as *lesson plans*. It also challenges you to consider what to do when the lesson plan goes awry, when students have insufficient skills to master the planned objectives, or when you introduce a topic and find that some students have already mastered that content or skill.

WRITING OBJECTIVES TO FIT GOALS AND OUTCOME STATEMENTS

Goals and outcome statements are the broad, long-term descriptions of how you want your students to grow and develop and what you want them to know, understand, and be able to do during a given time period. To chart your students' progress toward meeting these long-term goals, it is useful to write a series of objectives that work together to enable your students to show that they are achieving the intended outcomes.

Before we can apply curriculum theories to actual practice, it is necessary to clarify the use of the terms *objective* and *behavioral objective*. Educational *objectives* are short-term, specific descriptions of what teachers are expected to teach and/or what students are expected to learn. As described by Bloom and colleagues in *Taxonomy of Educational Objectives* (1956), they are intended to be used as an organizational framework for selecting and sequencing learning experiences. Embedded in the goal of teaching children how to read are hundreds of possible specific objectives. One teacher may have an objective of teaching students how to decode an unfamiliar word using phonics and another objective of teaching students how to decode an unfamiliar word using context clues. Another teacher may select and emphasize the objectives of decoding unfamiliar words by using syllabification or linguistic patterns.

Objectives are used to describe the *sequence* of learning events that must take place in order for an outcome statement to be realized. Objectives also allow teachers to chart the progress made by the group or by individuals. Diagnosis of students' needs and deficiencies can be done accurately if there is a guideline or chart of normal progress with which to compare each student's achievement.

Behavioral Objectives

During the past several decades, many educators have searched for ways to apply scientific principles of controlling for conditions, and measuring outcomes of educational planning. Robert Mager (1962) proposed that teachers plan their lessons by

152.21
1,148 all for CA

writing *behavioral objectives* that state very precisely what the learner will be able to do after successfully completing a learning experience.

Behavioral objectives are distinguished from other types of objectives in that they describe an observable and measurable behavior. They are written in a form that specifies the *conditions under which the learning will take place,* the *action or behavior,* and the *criteria for success.* As an example, a behavioral objective could be written as follows:

> After practice-writing the spelling words five times each, the student will write the words when dictated by the teacher, spelling 18 of the 20 words correctly.

This statement includes a description of the conditions for learning (after practice-writing the spelling words five times each), the behavior (write the words when dictated by the teacher), and the criteria for success (spelling 18 of the 20 words correctly).

Behavioral objectives can have a very positive effect on teaching effectiveness; teachers who use them become better organized and more efficient in teaching and measuring the growth of students' basic skills. When following a planned sequence of behavioral objectives, the teacher knows exactly what to do and how to judge the students' success. The teacher is also better able to explain to the students exactly what is expected and how to succeed with this system of planning.

As with any educational practice, however, overreliance on specific objectives can have a negative result. Critics of behavioral objectives believe that when curriculum planning is reduced to a rigid behavioral form, much of what is worth teaching and knowing can become trivialized. As with much in life, the use of objectives can be destructive if used in excess.

Problem-Solving Objectives

Eliott Eisner (1985) observes that when specific skills or competencies are being taught, behavioral objectives can serve as a useful way of visualizing and organizing the appropriate learning experiences. "One must be able to swim four lengths of the pool to be able to swim in the deep end" (p. 117). But, he cautions, "one should not feel compelled to abandon educational aims that cannot be reduced to measurable forms of predictable performance" (p. 114).

As an alternative form for learning outcomes that cannot be predicted and calibrated, Eisner (1985) suggests the *problem-solving objective:*

> In a problem-solving objective, the students formulate or are given a problem to solve—say, to find out how deterrents to smoking might be made more effective, how to design a paper structure that will hold two bricks sixteen inches above a table, or how the variety and quality of food served in the school cafeteria could be increased within the existing budget.
>
> In each of these examples, the problem is posed and the criteria that need to be achieved to resolve the problem are fairly clear. But the forms of its solution are virtually infinite. (pp. 117–118)

Eisner points out that behavioral objectives have "both the form and the content defined in advance. There is, after all, only one way to spell aardvaark" (p. 119).

The teacher using behavioral objectives is successful if all children display the identical behavior at the end of the instructional period. "This is not the case with problem-solving objectives. The solutions individual students or groups of students reach may be just as much a surprise for the teacher as they are for the students who created them" (p. 119). As an example, a problem-solving objective might be

> When given a battery, a light bulb, and a piece of copper wire, the student will figure out how to make the bulb light.

This objective describes the conditions and the problem that is to be solved, but the actual behaviors used by the student are not specified. The criterion for success is straightforward but is not quantifiable, and in fact, some of the most important results of this experience are only implied. The teacher's primary aim is to cause the student to experiment, hypothesize, and test methods of solving the problem. This cannot be quantified and reported as a percentage. Problem-solving objectives, then, are appropriate when teachers are planning learning events that allow and encourage students to think, make decisions, and create solutions. For this reason, they are frequently employed when teachers plan lessons that are designed to develop critical, creative thinking. They are especially valuable when teachers are planning learning events at the higher levels of Bloom's Taxonomy.

Expressive Outcomes

Some lessons are purposely designed to be open-ended experiences. In any of the fine arts, for example, lessons may be designed that have no preplanned or explicit objectives. An example of an expressive outcome is for students to listen to a symphony and draw or paint a response to the music. To expose children to new ideas and experiences, a lesson may consist of a field trip to a museum or through a forest. The teacher may have no prespecified objectives for either event, except to allow the students to discuss their observations afterward. For lessons such as these, Eisner (1985) suggests that the appropriate planning device is the *expressive outcome,* which is intended to "provide a fertile field for personal purposing and experience" (p. 120).

Expressive outcomes are also valuable for including the affective domain in lesson plans. If an affective goal of the unit is to encourage independent thought and action, lesson plans must include outcome statements that allow room for exploration and original ideas. If you have an affective goal to increase cooperation among students, lessons must be planned to allow students to work together. If you hope to encourage any form of creative expression, your lesson plans can reflect and acknowledge the importance of such creative pursuits through the use of expressive outcome statements.

Bloom's Taxonomy

Many teachers use Bloom's Taxonomy of Educational Objectives (1956) as the basis for organizing instructional objectives into coherent and connected learning experiences. The term *Bloom's Taxonomy,* commonly used by teachers, refers to the six levels of the cognitive domain described next. Any curriculum project—a year-long plan, a unit, or a lesson plan—can be enriched by the conscious planning of learning events at all six levels of the Taxonomy:

HIGHER-LEVEL	Level 6: Evaluation
OBJECTIVES	Level 5: Synthesis
	Level 4: Analysis
	Level 3: Application
LOWER-LEVEL	Level 2: Comprehension
OBJECTIVES	Level 1: Knowledge

Knowledge-level objectives can be planned to ensure that students have a knowledge base of facts, concepts, and other important data on any topic or subject. *Comprehension-level* objectives cause students to clarify and articulate the main idea of what they are learning. Behavioral objectives are very useful and appropriate at the knowledge and comprehension levels.

At the *application level,* problem-solving objectives or expressive outcomes can be written that ask students to apply what they've learned to other cases or to their lives, thereby causing them to transfer what they've learned in the classroom to other arenas. *Analysis-level* objectives and outcomes call on students to look for motives, assumptions, and relationships such as cause and effect, differences and similarities, hypotheses, and conclusions. When analysis outcomes are planned, the students are likely to be engaged in critical thinking about the subject matter. Because the *synthesis level* implies an original response, expressive outcomes are very appropriate. They offer students opportunities to use creative thinking as they combine elements in new ways, plan original experiments, and create original solutions to problems. At the *evaluation level,* students engage again in critical thinking as they make judgments using internal or external criteria and evidence. For these levels, problem-solving objectives or expressive outcomes are likely to be the most appropriate planning devices.

For example, in planning a series of learning events on metric measurement, the teacher may formulate the following objectives and outcome statements:

Knowledge-Level Behavioral Objective: When given a meter stick, students will point to the length of a meter, a decimeter, and a centimeter with no errors.

Comprehension-Level Behavioral Objective: When asked to state a purpose or use for each of the following units of measure, the student will write a short response for meter, centimeter, liter, milliliter, gram, and kilogram, with no more than one error.

Application-Level Problem-Solving Objective: Using a unit of measure of their choice, students will measure the length and width of the classroom and compute the area.

Analysis-Level Problem-Solving Objective: Students will create a chart showing five logical uses or purposes for each measuring unit in the metric family.

Synthesis-Level Expressive Outcome: A group of four students will hide a "treasure" on the playground and create a set of instructions using metric measures that will enable another group to locate the treasure.

Evaluation-Level Expressive Outcome: Students will debate their preference for metric or nonmetric measurement as a standard form of measurement.

When the six objectives and outcomes for metric measurement are reviewed,
it is clear that the first two differ from the others in that they specify exactly what
students will do or write to get a correct answer. In addition, the criteria for success are
not ambiguous. These two qualities are useful to ensure successful teaching and
learning at the knowledge and comprehension levels. After successfully completing
these first two objectives, students will have developed a knowledge base for metric
measurement that they will need to do the higher-level activities. In the problem-
solving objectives, students are given greater discretion in determining the methods
they use and the form of their final product. In the expressive outcome statements,
discretionary power is necessary if students are to be empowered to think critically and
creatively to solve problems for themselves.

Although the Taxonomy was originally envisioned as a hierarchy, and
although it was believed that students should be introduced to a topic beginning with
level 1 and working upward through level 6, most educators have found that the
objectives and learning experiences can be successfully taught in any order. For
example, in dealing with the topic of racial segregation in the United States or in South
Africa, a teacher may introduce the topic by asking students to discuss their opinions or
attitudes toward segregation (an evaluation-level objective). The teacher may then
provide the students with knowledge-level data and work back up to the evaluation
level, hoping to demonstrate the differences in attitudes that the learning experiences
have created among the students. Jane Elliott, a third-grade teacher who divided her
class by eye color to teach them to think critically about racial segregation, began with
an application-level objective. This story is described in *A Class Divided* by William
Peters (1984).

It is often desirable to begin with objectives that call on students to do, think,
find, question, or create something and thereby instill in them a desire to know more
about the topic. Knowledge- and comprehension-level objectives can then be designed
to provide the students with the facts, data, and main ideas they need to know in order
to further apply, analyze, synthesize, and evaluate the ideas they are interested in.
Figure 6–1 shows a planning device offering teachers ideas for learning events that
correspond to each level of the taxonomy.

SEQUENCING OBJECTIVES IN SCHOOL SUBJECTS
Sequencing Objectives in Mathematics

Some subjects are very sequential in nature. Mathematics is the best example because
its concepts and operations can be ordered from simple to complex quite readily.
Teachers can organize effectively the teaching of computational skills in the basic
operations of addition, subtraction, multiplication, and division. For example, Outcome

FIGURE 6–1
Lesson Planning Using Bloom's Taxonomy

Learning objectives can be planned at all levels of Bloom's Taxonomy. Behavioral objectives are best suited for knowledge and comprehension levels; problem-solving and expressive objectives are best suited for application, analysis, synthesis, and evaluation levels.

Examples of Objectives	*Appropriate Action Verbs*
Knowledge Level Can recognize and recall specific terms, facts, and symbols.	**Knowledge Level** Find, locate, identify, list, recite, memorize, recognize, name, repeat, point to, match, pick, choose, state, select, record, spell, say, show, circle, or underline.
Comprehension Level Can understand the main idea of material heard, viewed, or read. Is able to interpret or summarize the ideas in their own words.	**Comprehension Level** Explain, define, translate, relate, demonstrate, calculate, discuss, express in own words, write, review, report, paraphrase, summarize.
Application Level Is able to apply an abstract idea in a concrete situation, to solve a problem or relate it to prior experiences.	**Application Level** Change, adapt, employ, use, make, construct, demonstrate, compute, calculate, illustrate, modify, prepare, put into action, solve, do.
Analysis Level Can break down a concept or idea into its constituent parts. Is able to identify relationships among elements, cause and effect, similarities and differences.	**Analysis Level** Classify, distinguish, categorize, deduce, dissect, examine, compare, contrast, divide, catalog, inventory, question, outline, chart, survey.
Synthesis Level Is able to put together elements in new and original ways. Creates patterns or structures that were not there before.	**Synthesis Level** Combine, create, develop, design, construct, build, arrange, assemble, collect, concoct, connect, devise, hypothesize, invent, imagine, plan, generate, revise, organize, produce.
Evaluation Level Makes informed judgments about the value of ideas or materials. Uses standards and criteria to support opinions and views.	**Evaluation Level** Appraise, critique, consider, decide, assess, choose, conclude, debate, judge, editorialize, give opinion, grade, rank, prioritize, value.

Created by Judy Eby from TAXONOMY OF EDUCATIONAL OBJECTIVES: The Classification of Educational Goals: HANDBOOK I: COGNITIVE DOMAIN. By Benjamin S. Bloom, et. al. Copyright © 1956. By Longman Publishing Group. Reprinted by permission of Longman Publishing Group.

Statement 1 describes a possible sequence for teaching an essential understanding about the concept of number:

> *Mathematics Outcome Statement 1:* Primary students will be able to show how addition and subtraction are related to each other.

To accomplish this outcome, primary teachers will introduce the students to the concept of numbers and give them concrete, manipulative experiences in adding and subtracting one-digit numbers. Students may act out stories in which children are added and subtracted from a group. They may make up stories about animals or objects that are taken away and then brought back to demonstrate subtraction and addition.

Math textbooks offer a sequence of learning activities and practice of math facts, but reflective teachers find that the math textbook must be used flexibly and supplemented with other learning experiences. Prior to planning math lessons for a particular group of students, the teacher must pretest the students' entry-level knowledge and skills. Pretests will reveal that some children have already mastered some of the skills in the sequence and do not need to spend valuable time redoing what they already know. They need enriched mathematics activities to allow them to progress. Other children may not have the conceptual understanding of number relationships to succeed on the first step. For them, preliminary concrete experiences with manipulative materials are essential for success.

Sample math objectives to fit Outcome Statement 1 follow:
Students will be able to

1. use blocks to show addition of two single-digit integers
2. use blocks to show subtraction of two single-digit integers
3. use pennies and dimes to show place value of 1s and 10s
4. subtract pennies without regrouping
5. add pennies and exchange 10 pennies for a dime
6. subtract pennies by making change for a dime to show regrouping
7. tell out loud how subtraction is related to addition using coins as an example

These sample objectives are representative of the basic knowledge- and comprehension-level skills needed to accomplish the outcome statement. They can be written in the behavioral objective form, specifying what percentage of correct answers must be attained to demonstrate mastery.

These objectives emphasize basic computational skills. In keeping with the National Council of Teachers of Mathematics' recommendation to emphasize problem-solving over computation, reflective teachers are likely to plan lessons that include many additional math outcomes and objectives at the higher levels of Bloom's Taxonomy (1956) to teach students how to apply the math facts to actual problem-solving situations. However, this example does illustrate the importance of matching objectives to outcome statements in a logical sequence. Each of the objectives builds on the one before it, as in going up a series of steps on a stairway. If students master each objective, they are continually progressing toward mastering the outcome statement.

Sequencing Objectives in Language Arts

Not all subjects are as sequential as mathematics. Language arts consists of knowledge, skills, and abilities that develop children's understanding and use of language. Reading, writing, speaking, and listening are all part of the language arts curriculum, and each can and should have its own outcome statement(s). Outcome Statement 2 suggests one illustration of how the language arts curriculum is designed:

> *Language Arts Outcome Statement 2:* Students will be able to write standard English with correct spelling, accurate grammar, and well-organized meaning and form.

Again, this outcome statement will take years to accomplish, but teachers at every grade level are responsible for providing learning experiences that build toward the ultimate goal. The objectives to reach this goal may be similar each year for several years, but written in increasing levels of difficulty. This is known as a *spiral curriculum.*
Sample language arts objectives to fit Outcome Statement 2 follow:

By the end of grade 1, students will be able to

1. write a sentence containing a subject and a verb
2. use a capital letter at the beginning of a sentence
3. use a period or question mark at the end of a sentence
4. review and edit sentences for complete meaning

By the end of grade 3, students will be able to

1. write a paragraph that focuses on one central idea
2. spell common words correctly in writing samples
3. use capitalization and sentence-end punctuation correctly
4. review and edit a paragraph to improve the organization of ideas

By the end of grade 6, students will be able to

1. write several paragraphs that explain one concept or theme
2. use a dictionary to spell all words in a paper correctly
3. use correct punctuation, including end marks, comma, apostrophe, quotation marks, and colon
4. review and edit papers to correct spelling, punctuation, grammar, and organization of ideas

By the end of Grade 8, students will be able to

1. write papers with introductory paragraph, logical reasons, data to support the main idea, and a closing statement
2. use a dictionary to spell all words in a paper correctly; use a thesaurus to increase the vocabulary of the paper
3. eliminate fragments and run-on sentences
4. review and edit papers to correct misspellings, incorrect punctuation, poor grammar, bad organization of ideas, and appropriateness for the purpose

When teachers are given curriculum guidelines such as these, they must still translate the outcome statements and objectives into actual learning experiences that are appropriate and motivating for their students. To pretest how well your students can use written language when they enter your classroom, plan a writing experience in the first week. Analysis of these writing samples will allow you to plan suitably challenging activities for your students. In this example, the first-grade teacher must decide what topics to have students write about and when to limit students to copying teacher-made examples or to allow them to begin to write their own sentences. The third-grade teacher knows that students will not learn all of these skills in just one writing lesson. It is necessary to provide many interesting classroom experiences so that students will have ideas to express in their writing.

The sixth-grade teacher has to plan a series of research and writing experiences so that students will have ample opportunities to synthesize all the skills required at that grade level. The eighth-grade teacher must provide students with a variety of purposes so that they can learn to write differently for different audiences and purposes.

Curriculum planning of subjects such as language arts is a complex undertaking because it contains so many varied outcomes and objectives. The previous example illustrates only a single outcome for teaching students how to write. Teachers must also plan outcome statements and objectives for reading, listening, and speaking.

Sequencing Objectives in Science

As discussed in chapter 4, the science curriculum should inform students of the basic facts and concepts of science topics, but it should also allow students opportunities to experience how scientists work. These dual goals of the science curriculum are often expressed as *teaching both content and process.* An example of an outcome statement in science that covers both content and process follows:

> Science Outcome Statement 3: Students will be able to demonstrate how waves are produced and transmitted.

The following learning objectives show a sequence of learning experiences that allow students to discover some important properties of waves:
By the end of the unit on wave phenomena, students will be able to

1. investigate wave phenomena using Slinkies
2. investigate waves using water in plastic containers
3. write observations, analysis, and hypotheses of how waves behave
4. investigate waves using films of waves in slow motion and computer simulations of waves to discover whether the hypotheses are accurate
5. discuss observations and theories of wave phenomena as a class, with an emphasis on students articulating their own ideas
6. identify key features of waves, define wave terminology, and derive the wave equations through a kinesthetic learning experience. Under the direction of the teacher, students line up in the hall and simulate the motion of a Slinky. Wave terminology is introduced by the teacher during the experience.

This set of learning experiences, designed by Jim Hicks and Chris Chiaverina, begins with hands-on investigations allowing students to observe the wave phenomena. The students are involved in the process of science during these learning experiences because they are behaving like scientists investigating unknown phenomena. Content (wave properties and terminology) is introduced by the teachers after students are immersed in the process. Because of its emphasis on exploration, discovery, and communication of findings, the sequence of lessons in science is rarely linear, but more often circular or even a figure-eight pattern.

Chris Chiaverina and Jim Hicks find that rather than lecture about scientific phenomena, they first must use a "smorgasbord" of concrete experiences in which students interact with the scientific materials and literally begin to see the world in a new and more scientifically principled way. The concrete experiences are followed by class discussions that allow time to deal with the students' initial misconceptions about the phenomenon they are exploring. The discussions are very important, as students describe their experiences and gradually begin to construct new schemata to fit what they've observed. Jim and Chris organize a series of lessons to include qualitative demonstrations and explorations, followed by homework. The next day, there are discussions that help eliminate prior misconceptions and build new scientific schemata. During quantitative laboratory experiences, Chris and Jim rarely give formulas. Instead, they present open-ended challenges that cause students to translate what they've learned into mathematical language. Following the quantitative labs, they spend time on discussion of practical applications of what they have learned in the unit. Figure 6–2 shows the figure-eight sequence of events that Jim and Chris have developed for the science courses they teach.

FIGURE 6–2
Sequence of Science Lessons, by Jim Hicks and Chris Chiaverina

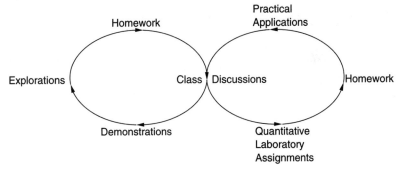

Sequencing Objectives in Social Studies

Reflective teachers can also see the need for both content and process in their social studies curriculum. They attempt to help their students build a knowledge base in history and geography, but they also give attention and time to teaching students how to acquire information on their own.

An example of an outcome statement in social studies that covers both content and process follows:

> *Social Studies Outcome Statement 4:* Students will be able to use a map and a globe to find place names and locations. They will then create a chart listing the countries, major cities, rivers, and mountain ranges in each continent.

Sample social studies objectives to meet Outcome Statement 4 follow:
The student will be able to

1. identify the seven continents on a world map and a globe
2. interpret the countries' boundaries with a map legend
3. list the countries in each continent
4. interpret the symbol for rivers on the map legend
5. list the major rivers in each continent
6. interpret the symbol for mountain ranges on the map legend
7. list the mountain ranges in each continent
8. create a chart showing the countries, cities, rivers, and mountain ranges in each continent

In this example, the teacher has planned a set of learning activities that will add to the students' knowledge base about world geography. This set of activities also equips the student to be able to find and interpet information on maps and globes. This social studies curriculum demonstrates that by employing hands-on learning experiences, students are able to learn both content and processes simultaneously and that they are active rather than passive learners throughout the entire set of activities. An oral or written pretest might consist of having students name or point to certain geographical locations and read and interpret a map legend. The information from the pretest is valuable in planning lessons that use students' existing knowledge and add to it.

Sequencing Objectives in Interdisciplinary Units

Whenever possible, many teachers enjoy enriching the curriculum units they plan by incorporating fine arts experiences into the academic subjects. Primary children are often asked to illustrate mathematics examples by drawing one pumpkin plus two pumpkins or to create 10 different pictures using a rectangle. Songs and rhymes frequently accompany learning about historical events and people. Many such events are dramatized as well. Stories and films are often used to augment many aspects of the curriculum.

In later years, there may be a diminishing emphasis on the fine arts except in special art and music classes or on special occasions and holidays. This is due, in part, to the crowded curriculum that teachers are required to deliver. Given the prevailing culture of the late 20th century, the fine arts are often deleted to make time for academic and social subjects. But each teacher must consider the place of fine arts in the curriculum. Reflective teachers are likely to consider the importance of the arts in enhancing the joy of living and to make them an integral part of every learning experience. This has the effect of increasing the active involvement, creative thinking, and inventiveness of children.

An example of an outcome statement that includes fine arts with an academic subject follows:

Fine Arts/Social Studies Outcome Statement 5: Students will be able to distinguish the important similarities and differences among world cultures by comparing their politics, economies, sports, art, music, literature, and drama.

Sample objectives to meet Outcome Statement 5 follow:
The student will be able to

1. select one country of the world to study
2. read at least three books or articles about that country
3. draw a map of the country's geographical boundaries and features
4. write a fact sheet or make a chart about the country's political and economic conditions
5. analyze how the geographical features of the country have influenced the political and economic conditions
6. draw examples of the country's art and architecture treasures
7. analyze how the political and economic conditions have influenced the art and architecture of the country
8. locate a story, poem, or piece of music from that country
9. create a drama event featuring the stories, poems, and music of all the countries

This ambitious set of learning experiences demonstrates how well the fine arts can be incorporated into an academic subject. Cognitively, children who take part in this series of experiences will learn a knowledge base of facts, ideas, and concepts about the world. They will also gain understanding and use of such processes as communication and problem-solving skills. Affectively, they will learn to appreciate and understand differences and similarities among people by sharing the cultural arts of each country.

PLANNING ASSESSMENTS THAT FIT YOUR OBJECTIVES

How does a teacher measure success? Traditionally, the methods used to assess individual achievement are written quizzes, tests, and essays. When elementary teachers want to determine whether the class as a whole has understood what was taught in a lesson, they frequently use oral responses to questions that usually begin, "Who can tell me . . . ?" These methods are useful and efficient ways to assess student achievement at the knowledge and comprehension levels of Bloom's Taxonomy, but reflective teachers are seldom satisfied with these measures alone. They look for other methods that are less frequently used but more appropriate in evaluating learning at the higher levels.

Knowledge-level objectives are tested by determining if the student can remember or recognize accurate statements or facts. Bloom et al. (1956) observed that, "probably the art of testing has been developed to the greatest extent in the measurement of knowledge. This type of behavior can be measured with great efficiency and economy" (p. 78). Multiple-choice and matching tests are the most frequently used measuring devices.

Comprehension-level objectives are often tested by asking students to define terms in their own words (only knowledge would be tested if the students are asked to write a definition from memory). Another frequently used testing device is a question requiring a short-answer response, either oral or written, that demonstrates that the student understands the main idea. Essays that ask students to summarize or interpret are also appropriate. Multiple-choice tests are also used as tests of comprehension, but the questions call on the students to do more than recall a fact from memory; they ask students to read a selection and choose the best response from among several choices.

Knowledge- and comprehension-level objectives are frequently written as behavioral objectives that specify the criteria for success in a measurable form. If the observable behavior is writing an essay, the teacher may need to describe the length, form, and content of a paper that is acceptable. For example, the criteria may be specified as follows:

> with a minimum of five paragraphs, each describing a geographical feature of the country being studied.

At the *application level,* students are usually asked to apply what was learned in a classroom to a new situation. "If the situations presented to the student to test 'application' are old ones . . . , the student does not have to 'apply' the learning. Rather, he needs merely to recall" (Bloom et al., 1956, p. 125). For that reason, application-level objectives are usually assessed by presenting an unfamiliar problem that requires the student to transfer what has been learned to the unfamiliar situation. These types of problems can seldom be quantified into minimums, maximums, or percentages. Instead, success is measured by the extent to which the problem is solved and the means employed to solve it.

To assess application, then, teachers must provide students with challenging problems to solve and a format for tendering their solutions. Essays in which students describe what they would do in the new situation can be used to assess their ability to apply what they have learned. In classrooms where students are encouraged to use manipulative materials and experiment with methods to solve problems, teachers assess the processes used by the student and the end product, such as a hand-drawn or computer-generated design of a new device, a written plan for solving a problem, or a model of a new product. These products may or may not be graded, depending on the teacher's need to quantify or qualify students' success.

Analysis-level objectives may also require that the teacher present unfamiliar material and ask the student to analyze it according to some specified criteria. "The material given for analysis in a test may be a literary passage, a description of a scientific experiment or a social situation, a set of data, an argument, a picture, or a musical selection" (Bloom et al., 1956, p. 149). In these situations, students may be asked to analyze various elements, relationships, or organizational principles, such as the way elements are categorized, differences and similarities, cause and effect, logical conclusions, or relevant and irrelevant data.

Again, essays may be used to assess analytical behavior, but the essays must do more than tell the main idea (comprehension) and describe how the student would apply previously learned knowledge. Analytical essays must clarify relationships, compare and contrast, show cause and effect, and provide evidence for conclusions. Other student products that are appropriate for assessing analysis are time lines; charts that compare, contrast, or categorize data; and a variety of graphs that show relationships.

Bloom et al. (1956) noted that there were special problems in the assessment of *synthesis-level* objectives:

> A major problem in testing for synthesis objectives is that of providing conditions favorable to creative work. . . . Perhaps the most important condition is that of free-dom. This should include freedom from excessive tension and from pressures to adopt a particular viewpoint. The student should be made to feel that the product of his efforts need not conform to the views of the instructor. . . . Time is another important condition. Many synthesis tasks require far more time than an hour or two; the product is likely to emerge only after the student spends considerable time familiarizing himself with the task, exploring different approaches, interpreting and analyzing relevant materials, and trying out various schemes of organization. (p. 173)

The types of student products that demonstrate synthesis are infinitely variable. Written work such as creative essays, stories, poems, plays, books, and articles are certainly appropriate for assessing language arts objectives. Performances are just as useful, including original speeches, drama, poems, and musical compositions. Student-created products may include original plans, blueprints, artwork, computer programs, and models of proposed inventions. Currently, student work may be collected in portfolios to demonstrate growth and achievement in a subject area.

Evaluation of the relative success of synthesis products is a very difficult matter. There may be no objective criteria for judging the value or worth of a student's original product. When student products are entered in a contest or submitted for publication, outside judges with expertise in the subject area provide feedback and may even make judgments that are impossible for the classroom teacher to make. "Checklists and rating scales should be especially useful here, but the examiner ought to insure that they do not emphasize elements of the product to the neglect of *global* qualities which, after all, may be more fundamental in any synthesis" (Bloom et al., 1956, p. 174). Many elementary teachers simply record whether a finished product was turned in by the student, rather than attempt to evaluate or grade it.

Bloom and colleagues (1956) describe two quite different forms of *evaluation-level* objectives. One type calls on students to make a judgment based on internal evidence. In this case, all the facts and data needed to make the judgment are provided in the test situation, and the student simply selects and applies them. To test a student's ability to make this type of judgment, the teacher must provide all the needed data, perhaps in the form of charts or graphs, and ask the student to draw certain conclusions from these data.

Another form of evaluation is to make judgments based on external criteria, such as rules and standards by which such works are generally judged. In this case, assessment strategies are designed in which the student is given a situation, makes a judgment, and justifies that judgment by applying the appropriate criteria. For example, students may be asked to make and justify aesthetic judgments of a work of art or to judge the validity of a political theory, stating the appropriate criteria used in making the evaluation. The types of products that students create at this level are critical essays, discussions, speeches, letters to the editor, debates, drama, videotapes, and other forms that allow students to express their points of view.

As with synthesis outcomes, evaluation outcomes and objectives are also difficult to grade. A teacher who offers students an opportunity to express their own views usually places high value on independent thinking and freedom of expression. Therefore, the teacher cannot grade a student response as "right" or "wrong." But the teacher can assess whether the student has used accurate, sufficient, and appropriate criteria in defending a personal opinion. Student work that has cited inaccurate, insufficient, or inappropriate evidence should probably be returned to the student with suggestions for revision.

Affective outcomes may be assessed by teacher observation as students work on various projects. It is also useful to involve students in self-evaluation to monitor their own affective growth in areas such as self-confidence, independence, cooperation, or creativity.

In summary, evaluation of student accomplishment should be directly linked to the lesson's objectives. To assess basic knowledge and skills, behavioral objectives are useful because they state exactly what the student will be able to do and specify the criteria for success. For higher-level objectives, problem-solving objectives may be less precise but still should describe the type of student behavior or product expected and give some general criteria for success. To assess the growth in the affective domain, expressive outcomes are planned and students can state orally or in writing what they have gained from a certain experience.

When teachers plan by writing clear behavioral, problem-solving, and expressive objectives for their lessons, they are, in effect, clarifying their expectations regarding what students will gain from the lesson and their criteria for success. The evaluation section of a lesson plan is then usually a restatement of the criteria expressed in the objectives. You will see an example of this in the sample lesson plans presented later in this chapter.

VARYING OBJECTIVES FOR STUDENTS WITH SPECIAL NEEDS

Often teachers plan their lessons with a set of objectives for the students in their class whose knowledge and skills are at grade level. The term *at grade level* means the average or typical level of understanding or skill that most children are able to achieve at that age and in that grade. Standardized achievement tests have been normed to provide teachers with information about what average learners should know and be able to do at their grade level in the basic subjects of the curriculum. As teachers gain experience teaching at a grade level, they are able to describe what the typical learner at that grade level can accomplish. Because most children in the class will have skills and knowledge near the average, it makes sense for teachers to plan lessons with difficulty levels conforming to that average.

But reflective teachers also observe that within each classroom, there are likely to be children whose skills and knowledge levels are quite different from the norm or average. *Criterion-referenced pretests* are essential tools in determining what students know and what they are ready to learn. They reveal that some children are able to work more quickly and understand more difficult material than the average child at that grade level. Pretests reveal that other students do not have the prerequisite skills and knowledge in order to master the planned objectives. They will learn successfully only if the teacher modifies the lesson to meet their needs. Individual or small-group lessons must be planned to provide them with the vocabulary and skills they lack. For some children to achieve successful growth of skills and understanding, the teacher must be willing to alter the pace of the lesson, the difficulty of the material, and the criteria for success.

For students who learn more slowly, one modification that is needed is to reduce the volume of material in a lesson. If the grade-level lesson calls for the students to complete 20 problems in one class period, the teacher may reduce this requirement to 10 or 15 problems for a student who works slowly. If 20 problems were expected of this child, there would be little chance for success, resulting in frustration for both teacher and student. When the pace is lowered, the student has an opportunity to succeed and is likely to show the increase in motivation that accompanies success.

There are a variety of reasons that a child may have missed or not learned some important basic skills in previous grades. Illness, family problems, emotional difficulties, inferior teaching, or frequent moves may have prevented a child from learning the skills that most students his or her age have attained. In the children's novel *Roosevelt Grady*, by Shotwell (1963), a child from a migrant family moves so often that he never learns what "putting into" means:

> This was his question: When you put something into something else and it doesn't come out even, what do you do with what's left over?
>
> What happened yesterday was exactly what had happened at the school where he'd first heard about putting into. The teacher came to where it seemed she must explain it the very next day. And then what? That time it was the beans that ran out. This time it was celery. . . . And same as yesterday, Roosevelt never got back to school to hear what the teacher had to say. (pp. 19–20)

For students like Roosevelt Grady, who have not attained the basic skills necessary for a grade-level task, the modification that is needed is to teach the prerequisite skills before introducing the new material. When these prerequisite skills have been successfully mastered, the student may be able to proceed at the average pace.

Some children in your classroom may have been identified as having *learning disabilities*. This label may mean that a student has one or more of a variety of learning disorders, some physical and others social or emotional in origin. When a student has been labeled learning disabled, a teacher who specializes in working with such students will be called on to create an individualized education program (IEP) for that student. The classroom teacher will receive some guidance from the IEP on how to modify lessons for that student.

In some schools, many students come from backgrounds where the primary language of the home is not English. This has implications for instruction and lesson planning. Although these students may be able to understand the content of the lessons, they may not be able to understand the delivery of the content by the teacher because of their language differences. These students are frequently served by English as a Second Language (ESL) or Sheltered English programs. When this is the case, the ESL teacher can assist teachers in assigning appropriate materials and helping students in language skills that will help them to be successful.

In addition, a classroom where language skills are deemphasized will assist students to be more successful. Therefore, lessons will need to be developed to provide context clues using props, visuals, graphs, and real objects. Input must be simplified through a slower natural speech rate with clear enunciation. Instruction must be student-centered with fewer concepts taught.

Obviously, children with hearing impairments need lessons that are modified to provide directions and instruction with visual aids. Similarly, children who are sight impaired may require extra auditory learning aids. Less obviously, there may be children in your classroom with strong auditory, visual, or kinesthetic learning style preferences. To meet the needs of these children, teachers must modify their lessons to accommodate all three types of learning styles. This is usually accomplished by providing instructions and examples using visual aids to learn, such as the chalkboard, books, and written handouts. For auditory learners, the teacher may allow students to use tape recorders to record the instructions and examples given in class. Kinesthetic learners require manipulative materials and hands-on experience in order to make sense of unfamiliar material. When a teacher provides visual, auditory, and kinesthetic learning aids and experiences, students may modify their own lessons by taking in the needed information in the modality that fits their own learning style preferences.

For students who work unusually rapidly and accurately on grade-level material, the task is to provide appropriately challenging learning experiences so that these students are able to continue to make gains even though they have mastered the grade-level requirements. There are two standard methods of meeting the needs of highly able learners: *acceleration* and *enrichment*. Although both strategies are valuable modifications, acceleration is appropriate for sequential subjects such as math, and enrichment is appropriate for other subject areas. An *inappropriate* modification is to give the child more work at the same level. For example, if 20 math problems are required of the students working at grade level, an innappropriate modification is to require the highly able learner to do 40. This practice is common, but does not serve the student's real need to be challenged to gain new skills and understanding.

Some acceleration strategies from which teachers can choose include ability grouping, curriculum compacting, and mastery learning. *Ability grouping* requires the teacher to modify the curriculum to correspond to three different groups in the classroom. High, middle, and low groups are created, with variations in material and in expectations for success. Reflective teachers must consider the possible negative consequences of lowered self-esteem and the possible positive benefits of academic fit and organizational efficiency when deciding whether or how to use ability grouping in the classroom.

In some schools, ability grouping may be organized across several grade levels. Subjects such as mathematics and language arts may be scheduled at the same time of day, allowing students who work above or below grade level to leave their classrooms and travel to other classrooms where the instruction is geared to their learning level.

Curriculum compacting can occur in a single classroom. This strategy requires the teacher to pretest students in various subject areas. Those children who demonstrate mastery at the time of the pretest are allowed to skip the subsequent lessons. In this way, the grade-level curriculum is compacted for them. Teachers then provide materials at a higher level of difficulty for these students, who typically work on their own through the more difficult material, with little assistance from the teacher, who is busy instructing the students at grade level.

Mastery learning is a highly individualized teaching strategy that is designed to allow students to work at their own pace on material at their own difficulty level. Pretests are used to place students at the appropriate difficulty level. As each new skill is learned, a posttest is used to demonstrate mastery. This technique is described in more detail in chapter 10.

Enrichment strategies vary according to the imagination of the teacher who creates them. The teacher provides students who demonstrate mastery of a basic skill with a challenging application of that skill. Objectives and learning experiences at the higher levels of Bloom's Taxonomy are often used as the basis for enrichment activities. A child who easily masters grade-level material is frequently allowed to investigate or research the topic in greater depth. As outcomes of enriched activities, students typically create an original product, perform an original skit, or teach the class something that has been learned from the research.

Modification of lessons is a continuous challenge to teachers. It is not easy to decide whether a student needs a modified lesson. Reflective teachers struggle with this decision because they know that when they lower their expectations for a student, one of the effects may be lower self-esteem, which creates the conditions for a self-fulfilling prophecy that the student cannot achieve at grade level. But they also know that when adult expectations are too high, students experience little or no success, leading to a similar downward spiral. For beginning teachers, it is wise to consult with other teachers in the school, especially teachers who specialize in working with students with learning or physical disabilities or who are gifted. Talk over your concerns with these specialists and make informed decisions about lesson modifications.

WRITING A WELL-ORGANIZED LESSON PLAN

When teachers plan for day-to-day learning experiences, they are creating lesson plans. Usually a lesson plan is created for a single subject or topic for 1 day. Elementary teachers in self-contained classrooms must devise several different lesson plans each day, one for each subject they teach. Teachers in the upper grades who work in departmentalized settings where students travel from class to class for various subjects must still create different lesson plans for each grade or group of students they teach.

In the university or college courses designed to prepare teachers, the lesson plan is an important teaching and learning device. The professor and experienced

FIGURE 6-3
Model Lesson Plan (This model may be entered and saved in your word processor.)

Title of Lesson:

Subject Area:

Grade Level:

DESCRIPTION OR OUTCOME STATEMENT:

OBJECTIVES:

1.

2.

3.

MATERIALS AND RESOURCES:

PROCEDURES (What will you be doing? What will students be doing?):

1. Motivation:

2. Statement of Purpose:

3. Teacher Modeling or Demonstration:

4. Check for Understanding:

5. Guided Practice or Activity:

6. Independent Practice or Activity:

ASSESSMENT PLAN:

classroom teachers can provide the aspiring teacher with models of good lesson plans. As students create their own, they are able to demonstrate the extent to which they understand and can apply the theories and principles they have learned about reflective thinking and planning.

For that reason, many university and college programs require students to create a number of precise and detailed lesson plans. Sometimes students observe that the classroom teachers they know do not write such extensive plans for every lesson. Instead, these teachers write their lesson plans in large weekly planning books, and a single lesson plan may consist of "Math: p. 108," "Social Studies: Review Ch. 7," or "Science: Continue Nutrition." Although experienced teachers may record their lesson plans with brief notes, novice teachers need to write lessons in great detail in order to know which resources to gather for the lesson. Writing detailed lesson plans also enables the novice teacher to visualize the procedures to be used ahead of time. In addition, by writing lesson plans, novice teachers can communicate their plans to the professor or mentor teacher, who can provide feedback on the plan before the lesson is taught.

Well-written lesson plans have another value. They can be shared. A teacher's shorthand notes that serve as a personal reminder can rarely be interpreted by an outsider. If a substitute teacher is called to replace a classroom teacher for a day or longer, it is necessary to be able to communicate the daily plans to that teacher in language that can be understood and used. Teams of teachers often write lesson plans together or for one another. In this case, it is important that they have a common understanding of the lesson objectives, procedures, evaluation, and resources.

The form may vary, but most lesson plans have a number of common elements. Three essential features of a complete, well-organized lesson plan are the objectives, procedures, and evaluation. These correspond to the four questions of curriculum planning formulated by Tyler (1949). Lesson *objectives* specify the "educational purposes" of the lesson. The *procedures* section describes both "what educational experiences can be provided" and the way they can be "effectively organized." The *evaluation* section describes the way the teacher has planned in advance to determine "whether these purposes are being attained" (Tyler, 1949, p. 1).

The *description,* another feature in a lesson plan, is used to identify it and to give the reader a quick overview of its purpose. Also, a lesson plan often contains information about the resources needed by teachers as background preparation for teaching the lesson as well as any materials that will be needed in the actual execution of the lesson.

A suggestion for teachers in this age of computers is to create a basic outline of a lesson plan on a word processor and save it on a disk. Then, whenever you want to write a lesson plan, you can put the outline on the screen and fill in the spaces. The outline for a lesson plan should contain elements such as those given in Figure 6–3. Not all these elements, especially in the procedures section, may be needed for every lesson, but this outline gives you a framework for thinking about what to include as you begin to plan your own lessons. This outline can be copied onto your computer disk for use in college and the rest of your teaching career.

On rare occasions, a teacher may create a single lesson on a topic such as fire safety, a holiday, or a news item. Usually, however, a single lesson plan does not stand alone in a classroom. It is part of a unit or a year-long plan for a subject in the curriculum. As shown earlier in this chapter, learning events are planned in a logical

Mathematics and Social Science Lesson Plan

Pam Knight, Twin Peaks Middle School, Poway, California

Title of Lesson: Television-viewing habits of students
Subject Area(s): Mathematics/social sciences
Grade Level: Middle school

DESCRIPTION:

Students will keep records of the amount of television they watch and will present this information using graphs.

OBJECTIVES:

1. Application level—students will construct bar graphs using data collected on television-viewing habits.
2. Analysis level—students will interpret and make inferences based on the analysis of the data gathered, by writing a statement that describes the data on the graph.
3. Evaluation level—students will evaluate their television-viewing habits and the television-viewing habits of the class as a whole.

MATERIALS NEEDED:

Graph paper, rulers, and pencils

PROCEDURES:

1. Motivation: The lesson begins with a discussion of the observations students have made about their own television-viewing habits. This is an open-ended discussion and students may talk about types of shows seen (MTV, movies, sports contests, etc.). Ask students: Do students watch too much television and play too many video games? How much TV do students really watch? Are there methods by which students can gather data on their television-viewing habits?

sequence of lessons designed to gradually increase student understanding and skill in the subject area. In the next three sections, sample lesson plans are described for four subjects in the elementary curriculum, showing the lesson itself and how it fits into the long-term plan for that subject.

Sample Lesson Plan in Mathematics

Students like to explore their own world. A large portion of time in the middle school student's world is devoted to watching television. In the Planning for Teaching shown above, a lesson plan is from Pam Knight's unit on television-viewing habits is shown

2. Statement of Purpose: We will learn how to gather information and data to make informed decisions about important matters in our lives.
3. Teacher Modeling and Demonstration: Teacher models data collection by surveying students on their favorite TV show. Teacher tallies these data and, with class participation, creates a bar graph of the data at the chalkboard.
4. Guided Practice: Students duplicate the teacher's tally and bar graph at their desks.
5. Check for Understanding: Ask questions to determine whether the students know the processes of recording data and constructing a bar graph.
6. Independent Study/Activity: Students gather data on their television-viewing habits for 1 week.
7. Class Discussion: At the end of the week, students choose ways to display their data using bar graphs. Examples of displaying the data could be the amount of television boys watched compared with the amount girls watched, the amount of television watched on different days of the week, or the types of programs watched. After looking at the different ways the data could be displayed, the class is divided into groups of three.
8. Group Activity: In groups of three, students construct the graph and identify an inference they could make based on their graph. They share their graph and inference and display them on a bulletin board.
9. Closure: Students discuss what they have learned about their television-viewing habits. They discuss what the results mean to them. For example, do they think they watch too much television? Do they watch more or less television than they expected? Is the bar graph an effective way to display the data they gathered?

ASSESSMENT PLAN:
Students write in their journals about the activity completed. Students' graphs are examined to see if the data has been correctly graphed. The inferences made by students are checked against the constructed bar graphs. The graphs become part of the students' mathematics and social studies portfolios.

(See chapter 5). On the surface, this appears to be a mathematics lesson. However, after analyzing the objectives and activities in it, you will see that it involves the social sciences and language arts as well.

This lesson plan requires more than one class period. One day is needed to prepare for data collection; a week is needed to collect and record the data; and a day or two are required for constructing the bar graphs and describing the findings.

Pam's lesson demonstrates how students can use mathematics in their lives. They become researchers who collect and organize data. For the data to be relevant, they must be able to analyze the data and explain what they found. Finally, the students are expected to make inferences and evaluate an important factor in their lives.

Sample Elementary Social Studies Lesson Plan

Jess Johnson, Lemon Grove School District, Lemon Grove, California

Title of Lesson: Epitaphs
Subject Area(s): Social studies and language arts
Grade Level: Elementary

DESCRIPTION:
Students will learn what an epitaph is and how to write one.

OBJECTIVES:

1. Comprehension level—after a discussion of epitaphs and reading of samples by the teacher, the students will be able to describe an epitaph and write one.
2. Analysis level—after learning about epitaphs from the discussion and the exercise of writing one, the students will read Roman epitaphs and analyze their value and their problems as sources of information about a culture.

MATERIALS AND RESOURCES NEEDED:

1. *California State Framework for History–Social Sciences*
2. *A Message of Ancient Days*—Houghton Mifflin
3. Epitaph sheets for everyone in class

PROCEDURES:

1. Motivation: Ask students the following questions: Have they ever visited a cemetery? What would they find there? What kind of literature would they find in a cemetery? Why would it be there? Who would have written it? What would the literature be like? Serious? Funny?
2. Purpose: Students will learn what an epitaph is and be able to write one.
3. Connection with Previous Learning: Students are studying history. One method of tracing history is to observe what people have written about themselves and others. Students may have read excerpts of journals, letters, and notes people have written. They may also read an epitaph.

Sample Lesson Plan in Language Arts and Social Studies

Many times a single unit contains learning events in more than one subject, and a single lesson can accomplish objectives in two or more areas at the same time. For example, students can use language skills in a social studies unit or discuss and write about social studies topics in a language arts unit.

The example of the lesson on epitaphs in this Planning for Teaching is such a lesson. It could have been an activity for social studies or language arts. The focus of

4. Model/Demonstration: Explain what an epitaph is. Use an overhead or pass out a sheet of real epitaphs. Review these with the students. Some examples follow.
   a. Elizabeth Cupper:
      Sharp was her wit, mild her nature
      A tender wife and a good humored creature
   b. George Warmington:
      'Tis my request
      My bones may rest
      Within my chest
      without molest
   c. Anne Jennings:
      Some have children
      Some have none
      Here lies the mother
      of twenty-one
   d. George Morgan:
      Say more I need not, and say less who can
      Here lies the generous, humane, honest man

   Ask students which example they liked best and why. Have them write the definition of an epitaph in their own words.
5. Guided Practice: The class will write an epitaph for a fictional or cartoon character (e.g., Mickey Mouse, Indiana Jones).
6. Independent Activity: Students will choose someone who is dead or some fictional character and write an epitaph for that person. If there is time, students will read their epitaphs to the class.
7. Closure: Students will review how history can be examined through an individual's epitaph.

ASSESSMENT PLAN:
Students' epitaphs will be read and written comments made on them. Students will be asked how an epitaph can be used to study history. Students will be asked to write in their own words what an epitaph is.

this lesson originally was to show how history can be studied by looking at gravestones in cemeteries. When I read the lesson, I remembered the first time I had visited Boston and the excitement of walking the "Freedom Trail." A major event on the walk was to visit the old cemeteries and to see the graves of people I studied and read about in the days of the American Revolution.

In terms of language arts, the lesson has an important application to the writing process. It allows students to be creative but does not require them to write

Sample High School Science Lesson Plan

Chris Chiaverina and Jim Hicks

Title of the Lesson: Wave phenomena
Subject Area: Science
Grade Level: High School physics

DESCRIPTION:

Using a variety of items that vibrate and produce sounds, students investigate wave phenomena.

OBJECTIVES:

1. Comprehension—students will become aware of their naive ideas about sound and be able to describe how sound is produced.
2. Application—students will make their own source of sound through a device called the *hummer.*
3. Knowledge—students will develop their science vocabulary by being able to define and use wave terminology appropriately.

MATERIALS NEEDED:

Tuning fork, guitar, carpet tubing, music box, 78 rpm record, needle, pencil, "talking strip," Fisher burner, aluminum rod, resin, "sound wagon" toy, rubber bands, file cards, tongue depressors, and string

PROCEDURES:

1. Motivation/Modeling/Demonstration: The teacher demonstrates a variety of common vibrating systems that produce audible sounds. For example, strike a tuning fork and have the students observe if there is a noticeable visible vibration on the fork. Strike the tuning fork and place it in

long essays. All students can be successful at such a task, regardless of previous language and writing experiences.

This lesson also makes history come alive. The characters from other times and places literally speak to the students about concerns and issues important to their lives. Discussions will naturally occur that cause students to compare their lives to the writers of the epitaphs.

Sample Lesson Plan in Science

The lesson plan for high school is taken from a science unit developed by Chris Chiaverina and Jim Hicks. Their plan is exciting because they are constantly trying to find ways to make science interesting, practical, and fun. In fact, one of the most important comments shared with us by them was, "If there isn't a common understanding of the application of a concept in science, then it isn't worth teaching." As you read a glass of water and observe what happens. The water will be stirred. The teacher plucks a guitar string and the students listen to the sound.

The teacher then demonstrates some unusual sources of sound. An old record is played with a straight pin. A carpet tube is placed over a Fisher burner, which makes a sound like a fog horn. A talking plastic strip is pulled across a fingernail and delivers a message. An aluminum rod is stroked with resin and produces a high-pitched tone.

2. Statement of Purpose: To learn how sound is produced by vibrations.
3. Connect to Previous Learning: Students have done laboratories, seen demonstrations, and watched a movie on waves. They have also done laboratories using Slinkies and a ripple tank. After students have observed the demonstration of sounds in the motivation activity, they are asked to relate their observations to the concepts learned in the previous lessons of wave phenomena, including reflection and transmission. They are also asked to relate this to the terminology of wave speed and amplitude.
4. Independent Activity: Students produce their own hummer: (1) A rubber band is stretched around a tongue depressor and acts as a vibrating object; (2) A file card is stapled to the tongue depressor and is used to amplify the vibrations; (3) A string is attached to an end of the device; (4) The hummer is spun in a circle by the string, and a sound is produced.
5. Guided Practice: Students are assigned problems on the sources and transmission of sound. These problems relate to the earlier examples as well as the hummer.
6. Closure: Students interpret this phrase: "Sound equals vibrations." They demonstrate their hummers.

ASSESSMENT PLAN:
Students create hummers and describe, in their own words, using correct wave terminology, how the hummer produces sound.

this lesson plan, remember that the philosophy of their approach to science is to use a smorgasbord of examples and demonstrations as well as a hands-on approach by their students. Their lessons clearly meet the expectations of the new science frameworks that require teachers to take an active and exploratory approach to the learning of science. See the Planning for Teaching shown above.

Conclusions

Lesson plans are scripts that teachers write so that they can present a well-organized set of learning experiences for their students. The objectives of the lesson specify the teacher's expectations for what the students will learn or be able to do as a result of the lesson. When teachers plan objectives that specify the criteria for success, they are clarifying for themselves what the students must be able to do in order to demonstrate mastery of the skill or understanding of the concepts of the lesson.

To plan the procedures of a lesson in advance, many reflective teachers visualize themselves teaching the lesson. They write what they must do to teach the lesson successfully and what the students will do in order to learn the material. Teachers who can visualize the entire process of teaching and learning can write richly detailed lesson plans. When they begin to teach the lesson, they have a supportive script to follow.

As teachers become more proficient and experienced at planning and teaching, their written lesson plans are likely to become less detailed. But for beginning teachers, a thorough, richly detailed plan is an essential element for a successful lesson.

OPPORTUNITIES FOR REFLECTION

▼ Reflective Essay 6: Adapting Lessons to Fit Individual Needs

What are your views on meeting the individual needs of students in your classroom? With mainstreaming becoming more prevalent, you are likely to have a number of students with special needs in your classroom every year. How will you provide them with appropriate learning experiences and criteria for success that are possible for them to achieve? How will you cope with the fairness issue if other children complain that they have to do more work than a student with special needs?

▼ Classroom Visit 6: Teachers' Lesson Plans

Ask the cooperating teacher to show you his or her lesson plans. How do these plans differ from the ones in this chapter? Teachers with many years of experience seldom write detailed lesson plans. Instead, they use a plan book and jot down main ideas for each lesson to be taught.

REFERENCES

BLOOM, B., ENGLEHART, M., FURST, E., HILL, W., & KRATHWOHL, D. (1956). *Taxonomy of educational objectives: cognitive domain.* New York: Longman.

EISNER, E. (1985). *Educational imagination* (2nd ed.). New York: Macmillan.

MAGER, R. (1962). *Formulating instructional objectives.* Palo Alto, CA: Fearon.

PETERS, W. (1984). *A class divided: Then and now.* New Haven, CT: Yale University Press.

SHOTWELL, L. (1963). *Roosevelt Grady.* New York: Grosset & Dunlap.

TYLER, R. (1949). *Basic principles of curriculum and instruction.* Chicago: University of Chicago Press.

OUTLINES FOR REFLECTION

▸ Reflective Essay: Adapting Lessons to Fit Individual Needs

▸ Classroom Visit 8: Teacher's Lesson Plans

REFERENCES

CHAPTER

7

Reflective Classroom Instruction

LEARNING TAKES PLACE almost continuously in our lives. Every new experience has the potential to teach us something that we didn't know before. From the day of birth, individuals learn new responses, skills, facts, and ideas. We learn at home, at the ball park, at a swimming pool, in the woods, and in school classrooms.

Teaching is also a common and natural occurrence. Small children teach each other new words, how to climb trees, and how to make block towers. As we mature, we have more occasions to teach others what we have learned from our experience. Some individuals are referred to as *born teachers.* They seem to require no textbooks or courses to instruct them how to teach; teaching appears to come naturally to them. They sense what the learner needs to know, and the language springs easily from their lips to assist the learner in understanding the new idea or the next step in a process.

As you begin to have opportunities to teach, it is likely that you will begin to develop your own conception or personal theory of how learning is best encouraged in classrooms. Your personal conception of the teaching–learning process will be drawn from your experiences as a learner, from the values and beliefs you hold about what students ought to know and how students ought to behave, and from your perceptions and reflections about the theories and practices of other classroom teachers that you observe.

CURRENT RESEARCH ON TEACHING AND LEARNING

In order to become a reflective teacher, it is also important that you are aware of the emerging research and knowledge base about teaching and learning. Gathering information from research is an important attribute of a reflective thinker and teacher.

The Cognitive-Mediational Conception of Learning

Anderson (1989a) describes two widely disparate conceptions of learning that affect teachers' perceptions and reasoning about the teaching and learning processes. "These conceptions do not correspond exactly to formal theories of learning offered in the psychological literature. They do, however, represent two types of common personal theories held by teachers and other adults" (p. 86). Anderson terms one the *receptive-accrual (R-A)* view and the other the *cognitive-mediational (C-M)* view.

Teachers who hold the R-A view believe that each student has innate, immutable individual differences in the ability to learn. Learning itself is defined as a relatively passive act of receiving information and storing it in memory without modification. In order to demonstrate achievement, the student is expected to recall information from memory and display or demonstrate that it was retained accurately. One implication of this view is that although teaching may be a very active process, learning is passive.

Because R-A teachers view learning as the gaining and storing of informa- tion, they believe that the best method to assess how much a student has learned is through the use of tests of memorized data and skills. An important derivative of this view is that success in school is believed to be due to a combination of a student's innate ability and the effort to accrue and retain knowledge. This view leads teachers to explain student failure as a result of inherent inadequacies or lack of effort. When failure occurs, teachers who have this view comfort themselves with the conviction that some students are able to learn and achieve success in school, and others can't or won't learn (Anderson, 1989a).

In contrast, teachers who hold the C-M view believe that learning is dependent on the student's cognitive activity. Learning is defined as the act of processing new information through active, selective perception, relating the new information to prior knowledge and storing it in an organized way until it is called for again.

In this view, teachers view success in school not as dependent on ability or effort but on the student's background knowledge and on knowing how to select and apply cognitive strategies appropriately. Teachers with this view explain student failure as most likely a result of the student's having inadequate prior knowledge or a need for more training in selecting and using the cognitive strategies appropriate for the task.

Which view do you hold? Your many years as a student in conventional classrooms will strongly influence your belief in the R-A theory. For many years, you were led to believe that students are smart, average, or stupid. Because you are now in a teacher education program, it is likely that you were one of the smart ones. You may have observed long-suffering teachers struggling with students in the low reading group or the low tracks in high school, and you may be convinced, as your former teachers were, that these students can't or won't learn.

The C-M viewpoint, then, will be a struggle for you to accept. From experience, you can expect some of your students to be skillful, accurate, and quick in processing new information, and others to be clumsy, erroneous, and slow. As a teacher, it is your task to diagnose the reasons for students' failure to process information efficiently and accurately. It is then your task to plan a set of learning experiences that assist students in activating their existing knowledge so that they can comprehend the new information or skill you are teaching.

In practice, the teaching methods selected by teachers with these two contrasting conceptions of learning are likely to be quite different from each other. The teacher with the R-A view is likely to assign a reading or a page of problems and then monitor students by responding to questions, but doing little else to deliberately stimulate the cognitive processes necessary for students to actively construct meaning. From this perspective, the teacher's role is simply to provide tasks and information and then to offer incentives (in the form of grades or gold stars) for students to perform these tasks. Unfortunately, the R-A teacher may believe that the actual learning of the material is "out of the teacher's power" (Anderson, 1989a, p. 87).

In contrast, a C-M teacher believes in the power to mediate in the learning process. This power is not automatic and it is not easily won, but by using the reflective teaching model, the C-M teacher observes students carefully, gathering information about what prior knowledge they possess and what they lack. This teacher observes students as they work on a problem and listens to them as they read or respond to a question. From this process of gathering information, the C-M teacher plans lessons and selects teaching strategies that will fill in the gaps in students' knowledge and helps them to organize what they know into useful patterns and structures, so that they are able to activate the appropriate knowledge and bring it to bear on new learning situations.

Teachers who understand the cognitive process of acquiring and processing information can apply their power in countless ways to the benefit of their students. They can reduce external stimuli so that the important bits of knowledge are perceived by their students' short-term memories. They can pace the delivery of new information to give students sufficient time to process one bit of knowledge in working memory before introducing another. They can phrase questions in such a way that they provide the appropriate cue to retrieve the stored information from long-term memory.

Schema Theory

The retrieval process is obviously a critical factor in being able to use stored information. Knowledge, concepts, and skills that are learned must be stored in the brain until they are needed. According to the *schema theory,* each subset of knowledge is stored in a *schema,* an outline or organized network of knowledge about a single concept or subject. It is believed that young children develop *schemata* (the plural form of *schema*) made up of visual or other sensory images, and as language increases, verbal imagery replaces the sensory images (Anderson 1989a; Anderson & Pearson, 1984; Bransford, 1983).

For example, an infant stores sensual images in the schemata for mother, bottle, bed, and bath. Later, the verbal labels are added. A schema grows, expands, or otherwise changes due to new experiences. If the infant sees and touches a large, round, blue ball, he or she can store sensory images of its size, color, rubbery feel, and softness. At a later encounter, the infant may experience it bounce and can store these images in the same schema. A year later, when the child learns to say the word *ball,* the label is acted on in working memory and stored in long-term memory within the schema for ball.

Students come to school with varied schema. Some students who have had many experiences at home, in parks, at zoos, and in museums, and in other circumstances, may enter kindergarten with complex schemata for hundreds of topics and experiences. Other students, whose experiences have been severely limited by poverty or other circumstances, are likely to have fewer schemata, and the ones they have are quite sparse. Similarly, if students come from highly verbal homes where parents talk with them frequently, their schemata are likely to contain accurate verbal labels for stored sensory experiences and phenomena. But students who are raised in less verbal homes will have fewer verbal components to their schemata. This theory complements Piaget's observations of stages of development and helps us to understand how a child's vocabulary develops.

Schemata also vary according to their organizational patterns. As children mature, each schema expands to include many more facts, ideas and examples. In cases of healthy development, the schemata are frequently clarified and reorganized. Learning new information or observing unfamiliar examples often causes a schema to be renamed or otherwise altered. For example, very young children have a schema labeled *doggy* that includes all four-legged, furry creatures. As they see new examples of animals and hear the appropriate labels for each type, the original schema of doggy is reorganized to become simply a subset of the schema *animal*. New patterns and relationships among schemata are forming every day of a child's life when the environment is full of unfamiliar concepts and experiences.

The importance of schema theory in the C-M conception of learning is that it helps to explain why some students are able to retrieve knowledge better than others. Students who have many accurately labeled schemata are more likely to have the background knowledge needed to learn an unfamiliar concept. Students whose schemata are richly detailed and well organized into patterns and hierarchies are much more likely to be able to retrieve useful information on request than are students whose schemata are vague and sparse.

There are several other important connections between the schema theory and the C-M view of learning. Teachers who believe that it is in their power to help their students improve their cognitive processing recognize that one of the best ways to do this is to stimulate students to actively create more well-developed, accurately labeled, and better-organized schemata.

At the elementary grade levels, teachers recognize that one of their most important responsibilities is to aid students in schema development with accurate verbal labels. At the earliest grades (especially kindergarten), teachers emphasize spoken labels, teaching students to recognize and be able to name objects and concepts such as numbers, letters of the alphabet, and colors. At the primary grades, teachers emphasize the recognition and decoding of written labels as an integral part of the reading program. When students exhibit difficulties in learning to read, the C-M teacher is likely to plan learning experiences that assist the student in developing schemata that are prerequisites for reading.

Students who have been raised in environments characterized by few experiences with books are likely to have an underdeveloped schema for reading and books. Reflective teachers who consider the needs of the whole individual are likely to provide their students with many opportunities to hear stories read aloud, to choose from a tempting array of books, and to write their own stories as a means of developing a rich and positive schema for the concept of reading.

Advance Organizers

When teachers want to assist students in retrieving information from their schemata, they provide verbal cues that help the students access the appropriate information efficiently. It is also possible for teachers to provide cues to assist students in accurately and efficiently processing and storing what they read, see, or hear. Ausubel (1960) proposed that learners can comprehend new material better when, in advance of the lesson, the teacher provides a clear statement about the purpose of the lesson and about the type of information they should look or listen for. This introductory statement is known as an *advance organizer*.

When we relate this theory to the information processing theory, it is apparent that the advance organizer provides the learner with an important cue as to which schema will incorporate this new knowledge. The learner can be more efficient in processing the information in working memory and transferring it to the appropriate schema in long-term memory than if no advance information was presented.

For example, consider what is likely to happen when a third-grade teacher introduces a lesson on long division with no advance organizer. Some students will simply reject the new knowledge as incomprehensible. But if the teacher tells students to listen for how division is similar to subtraction, and how it is the opposite of multiplication, the teacher is providing students with the cues they need to retrieve their subtraction and multiplication schema in advance of the new learning. In the second case, it is more likely that the new facts will be routed into working memory, where they can be processed using the subtraction and multiplication schemata as a framework.

In follow-up studies of Ausubel's hypothesis, many educational researchers designed experiments that showed the same effects. Therefore, this knowledge has been added to our growing common knowledge base about teaching and learning. In fact, this particular study demonstrates the way the knowledge base grows. The original hypothesis and study conducted by Ausubel (1960) led others to apply the principle to different types of students and environments. As the hypothesis was confirmed in subsequent studies, the knowledge was gradually accepted as a reliable principle of effective teaching. You probably experience the beneficial effects of advance organizers when your teachers tell you in advance what to listen for in a lecture or what to study for an exam. Now you can learn how to use this principle in your teaching career for the benefit of your students.

Time on Task, Active Learning

Students who are provided with suitably challenging learning experiences, and who are involved in cooperative efforts to solve problems or reinforce skills, are actively involved in learning. But active learning is not as common in classrooms as you might suppose.

A major study known as the Beginning Teacher Evaluation Study (BTES) was conducted in the 1970s by a group of researchers who wanted to identify teaching activities and classroom conditions that foster student learning in schools (Denham & Lieberman, 1980). Fifty classrooms in urban, rural, and suburban school districts were observed during mathematics and reading periods. The observers kept logs of the way the teachers taught mathematics and reading, and they interviewed both the students and the teachers to gather data for the study. They used achievement tests as outcome measures (Rosenshine, 1979, 1980).

Their findings showed dramatic differences in the amount of time that teachers allocated for mathematics and reading. Some allocated 25 minutes, and others allocated 50 minutes for one subject per day. As expected, student achievement was found to be positively related to the amount of time allocated.

But allocated time is not always time well spent. The study revealed that in some classrooms students were engaged in work on classroom tasks during the time allocated to the subject, and in other classrooms, the students did not pay attention to the task for a portion of the allocated time. Time that is actually spent on learning tasks is known by teachers as *time on task*. This is quite a different concept from allocated time, which may or may not be spent on actual work or learning by students.

Studies such as these, as well as reflective observation in their own classrooms, have caused many teachers to realize that simply allocating time to a subject does not ensure that students will be actively engaged in the task. The BTES study showed that student time on task occurred more frequently in the classrooms of teachers who had a high degree of interaction with their students during the task and gave students a good deal of academic feedback.

Other teacher behaviors found to be highly correlated to student achievement were accurate diagnosis of students' skill levels and the prescription of appropriate tasks so that the students were able to have a high success rate during the learning period. These elements suggest that it is not only allocated time or time on task that is important. It is the *active learning time*, the amount of time the students spend working at their own levels with a reasonable degree of success in learning something new, that is most important in student achievement.

Rosenshine (1980) analyzed the data from the BTES study to determine what actually occurs during the school day. The data showed that only 58% of the school day was spent on academic activities; 23% was spent on nonacademic subjects, such as music, art, and physical education; and approximately 19% was spent on other activities, such as transitions between classes and class business. Within the time teachers allocated to a subject, he found that "overall, students spent about 30% of their time in teacher-led activities and 70% of their time doing seat work" (p. 117). Since seat work is such a large part of the day in most classrooms, reflective teachers give as much serious thought to planning and managing seat work as they do to planning and managing other forms of instruction. It is important that seat work provide students with active learning opportunities rather than busy work.

PRESENTATION SKILLS THAT INCREASE CLARITY AND MOTIVATION

Teaching is more than telling. You have been on the receiving end of teachers' lectures, discussions, and other forms of lessons for many years. You know from your own experience that the way teachers teach or present material has an effect on student interest and motivation, which are both integral aspects of the classroom climate. You may have been unable to understand the beginning of a lesson taught by a teacher who failed to get the full attention of a class before speaking. You have probably experienced sinking feelings when a teacher droned on and on in a monotonous voice during a lecture. You may have experienced frustration when a teacher explained a concept once and hurried on, ignoring questions or comments from the class. Reflective teachers are not likely to be satisfied with a dull, repetitive, or unresponsive presentation style. Most of them are anxious to improve their presentation skills in order to stimulate interest and motivate student achievement.

Getting the Attention of Students

To consider systematically the way you present a lesson, think about the beginning. The introduction to a lesson is very important, whether it is the first lesson of the day or a transition from one lesson to another. As Kounin (1977) found in his study of well-functioning classrooms, transitions and lesson beginnings start with a clear, straightforward message or cue signaling that the teacher is ready to begin teaching and stating exactly what students should do to prepare themselves for the lesson. To accomplish this when you teach, it is necessary to tell your students to get ready for a certain lesson and to give you their full attention. Some teachers use a visual cue for this purpose, such as a finger on the lips or a raised arm. Others may strike a chime or turn off the lights to cue the students that it is time to listen.

It is unlikely that students will become quiet instantly. It will probably take a few moments to get the attention of every student in the class. While you are waiting, use an erect bodily carriage and direct eye contact with those who are slow to respond. Watch quietly as the students get their desks, pencils, books, and other needed materials ready for the lesson. The waiting may seem uncomfortable at first. You will be tempted to begin before they are ready because you will think that time is being wasted. Don't give in to this feeling. Wait until every voice is quiet, every chair stops scraping, every desk top stops banging, and every pencil stops tapping. Wait for a moment of pure, undisturbed silence. Then quietly begin your lesson. You will have the attention of every student.

Often teachers begin with a statement of purpose, describing how this particular lesson will help their students to make an important gain in skills or knowledge. Still others begin by doing a demonstration or distributing some interesting manipulative materials. Hunter (1982) calls this technique providing *anticipatory set,* both to gain attention and to motivate students to be interested in the lesson. She encourages teachers to use a variety of anticipatory sets appropriate to the lesson content and objective.

In contrast, less reflective teachers begin almost every lesson with, "Open your books to page _____ . David, read the first paragraph aloud." No presentation skills are employed in this example. This nonmethod relies on the material itself to whet the students' interest in the topic. Although some materials may be stimulating and appealing, most are not. The message the teacher gives to the students is "I don't care much about anything; let's just get through this." The students' motivation to learn drops to the same level as this message and can best be expressed as "Why bother?"

Teachers often display a greater degree of excitement and interest for material they enjoyed learning. Excitement about learning is passed on to the students. A teacher who reads aloud with enthusiasm conveys the message that reading is fun. A teacher who plunges into a science investigation with delight causes students to look forward to science.

After you gain your students' attention and inspire them to want to know more, you move on to the lesson itself. Presentation skills that you can learn to use systematically in your lessons include:

> enthusiasm
> clarity
> smooth transitions
> timing
> variation
> interaction
> active learning
> closure

Enthusiasm

Animation is the outward sign of a teacher's interest in the students and the subject. Enthusiasm is the inner experience. "There are at least two major aspects of enthusiasm. The first is conveying sincere interest in the subject. . . . The other aspect is vigor and dynamics," and both are related to getting and maintaining student attention (Good & Brophy, 1987, p. 479). Outwardly, the teacher displays enthusiasm by using a bright and lively voice; open, expansive gestures; and facial expressions that show interest and pleasure. It is well accepted that salespeople who use animated, enthusiastic behaviors could sell beach umbrellas in the Yukon . . . in January. Why shouldn't teachers employ these techniques as well? You can "sell" long division better with an enthusiastic voice. You can convince your students that recycling is important with a look of commitment on your face. You can encourage students' participation in a discussion with welcoming gestures and a warm smile.

Is animation something that you can control? Absolutely. You can practice presenting information on a topic with your classmates, using an animated voice and gestures. They can give you feedback, which you can use to improve your presentation. Have yourself videotaped as you make a presentation. When you view yourself, you can be your own best teacher. Redo your presentation with new gestures and a different voice. Repeat this procedure several times, if necessary. Gradually, you will notice a change in your presentation style. You will add these techniques to your growing repertoire of effective presentation skills.

Clarity

A critical factor for student success is the extent to which the teacher's presentation of lesson directions and content is clear and understandable by students. Brophy and Good (1986) listed the importance of teacher *clarity* as a consistent finding in studies of teacher effectiveness. Their review of research on teacher clarity describes negative teacher behaviors that detract from clarity. These include using vague terms, mazes, discontinuity, and saying "uh" repeatedly.

As an example of *vague terms*, Brophy and Good (1986) present the following example, with ambiguous language in italics:

> This mathematics lesson *might* enable you to understand *a little more* about *some of the things* we *usually* call number patterns. *Maybe* before we get to *probably* the main idea of the lesson, you should review *a few* prerequisite concepts. . . .
> (p. 355)

The vague terms in this example have the effect of making the teacher sound tentative and unsure of the content. As an introduction to a lesson, it is not likely to capture students' attention or interest. Clarity can be improved, in this example, by exchanging the vague terms for specific ones, resulting in a simple straightforward statement: "This mathematics lesson will enable you to understand the concept of number patterns. Before we get to the main idea of the lesson, we will review three prerequisite concepts."

Clarity is also reduced by what Brophy and Good call *mazes:* false starts or halts in the teacher's speech, redundancy, and tangled words. For example

> This mathematics lesson *will enab* _ _ , will get you to understand *number, uh,* number patterns. Before we get to the *main idea of the,* main idea of the lesson, you need to review *four conc* _ _ _ _ four prerequisite concepts.... (Brophy and Good, 1986, p. 355)

Even when students attempt to pay attention, they may be unable to decipher the meaning of the teachers' words if the presentation is characterized by the false starts in this example. It is quite obvious that the way to improve this statement is to eliminate the redundant words. This example is a very simple one. Clarity is also reduced when the teacher has begun to present a lesson and is interrupted by a student's misbehavior or a knock at the door, and then begins the lesson again. Kounin (1977) observed that the most effective teachers are able to *overlap* teaching with other classroom management actions. That is, they are able to continue with the primary task, presenting the lesson to the class, while at the same time opening the classroom door or stopping misbehavior with a glance or a touch on the shoulder. When teachers can overlap their presentations, the clarity of their lessons is greatly enhanced.

The third teacher behavior that detracts from clarity is discontinuity, "in which the teacher interrupts the flow of the lesson by interjecting irrelevant content ..." (Brophy & Good, 1986, p. 355). This is why lesson planning is so important. Without a plan, teachers may simply begin a lesson by reading from a textbook. As they or the students are reading, the teacher (or a student) may be reminded of something they find interesting. They may discuss the related topic for quite some time before returning to the original lesson. This side discussion may or may not be interesting or important, but it is likely to detract from the clarity of the original lesson.

The fourth detractor from teacher clarity noted by Brophy and Good (1986) is repeatedly saying "uh." It is also likely that other repetitive speech patterns are just as annoying, such as "you know." For the beginning teacher, it is likely that some of these teacher behaviors will occur simply as a result of nervousness or unfamiliarity with the content being taught. It would be interesting to study the hypothesis that these four detracting behaviors decrease as a result of teaching experience; in other words, as a teacher gains experience, the four detracting behaviors are reduced and clarity increases. Two teacher behaviors found to enhance clarity were an "emphasis on key aspects of the content to be learned and clear signaling of transitions between parts of lessons" (Brophy & Good, 1986, p. 355).

Smooth Transitions

Just as lesson introductions are important to gain students' attention, *smooth transitions* are essential to maintaining that attention and making the classroom a productive working environment. Transitions occur within a lesson, as the teacher guides students from one activity to another. They also occur between lessons as students put away what they were working on in one lesson and get ready for a different subject.

Knowing when to terminate a lesson is an important element of teacher withitness.

> When the group is having difficulty maintaining attention, it is better to end the lesson early than to doggedly continue. This is especially important for younger students, whose attention span for even the best lesson is limited. When lessons go on after the point where they should have been terminated, more of the teacher's time is spent compelling attention and less of the students' time is spent thinking about the material. (Good and Brophy, 1987, p. 245)

In addition to going to another classroom, transitions between activities and lessons may require that students move from place to place in the room, such as having one group come to the reading circle while another group returns to their seats. Usually students are required to exchange one set of books and materials for another. These movements and exchanges have high potential for noise in the form of banging desk tops, scraping chairs, dropped equipment, and students' voices as they move from lesson to lesson.

Jerky and chaotic transitions are often caused by incomplete directions or vague expectations about student behavior from the teacher. "Take out your math books" is incomplete in that the teacher does not first specify that the students should put away other materials they have been working with. The result may be that the students begin to work on desks cluttered with unnecessary materials.

Often, inexperienced teachers begin to give directions for a transition, and the students start to get up and move around while the teacher is speaking. When this happens, teachers may attempt to talk louder so that they can be heard over the din. A way to prevent this from occurring is to clearly inform students that they are to wait until all directions have been given before they begin to move.

Smooth transitions are characterized by clear directions from the teacher about what is to be put away and what is to be taken out, and about who is to move and where they are to go. Clear statements of behavioral expectations are also important. The same techniques for getting attention that were described previously apply to the beginning of each new lesson. After a noisy transition between lessons, it is essential for the teacher to have the students' complete attention before beginning the new lesson. Wait until all students move into their new postions and get all their materials ready before trying to introduce the lesson.

The teacher can use a signal to indicate that the new lesson is about to begin. A raised hand, lights turned off and then on, or a simple verbal statement such as, "I am ready to begin" will signal to the students that they should be ready for the next lesson. After giving the signal, the teacher should wait until the students have all complied and are silent before beginning the new lesson.

In considering strategies that result in smooth transitions, teachers do well to reflect on the students' needs for physical activity. In a junior high or high school, students can move between periods. At the elementary school or in a block period of time in the middle school, it is unrealistic to expect students to be able to sit still through one lesson after another. Some teachers take 5 to 10 minutes to lead students in singing or movement games between two working periods. Other teachers allow students to have a few moments of free time in which they may talk to friends, go to the washroom, or get a drink of water. Some transitions are good opportunities for teachers to read aloud from a story book or to challenge students to solve a brain teaser or puzzling mathematics problem. Reflective teachers find that when they allow students a respite and a change of pace during a brief transition period, the work periods are more productive and motivation to learn is enhanced.

Timing

Actors, speakers, and comedians give considerable attention to improving the timing of their presentations. Good use of timing engages the attention of an audience, is used for emphasis of major points, and sometimes creates a laugh. Teachers also work in front of an audience, and class presentations can be improved by considering timing and pacing as a means of getting attention and keeping it. Pausing for a moment of complete silence before you begin teaching is a good example of a way to incorporate timing into your presentation.

In most instances, students respond best to teachers who use a brisk pace of delivering information and instructions. Kounin's (1977) research on the most effective classroom managers demonstrated that students are best able to focus on the subject when the lesson has continuity and momentum. Interruptions result in confusion. When teachers forget to bring a prop, pause to consult a teacher's manual, or backtrack to present material that should have been presented earlier, inattention and disruptive behavior are likely to occur (Kounin, 1977). Jones (1987) found that students' attention improved when teachers gave them efficient help, allocating *20 seconds or less* to each request for individual help or reteaching. When this time was lengthened, the result was restlessness and dependency on the part of students.

However, there are times when a pause in instruction can improve your presentation. Researchers have found that it is important to present new information in small steps, with a pause after the initial explanation to check for understanding (Hunter, 1982; Rosenshine, 1979). Students may not respond immediately during this pause because they need a moment to put their thoughts into words. Wait for them to do so. Encourage questions and comments. Ask for examples or illustrations of the fact or concept being discussed. This pause allows your students to reflect on the new material and allows you to test their understanding.

One high school teacher used a timer, which he set to go off every 10 minutes as he lectured. After 10 minutes, he did a content check by asking students what they had written in their notes or what major concepts they were learning from the lecture. As he lectured, he walked around the room to examine the students' notes. If he determined that he was not clear in his lecture, he modified and restated the content until the students understood the concepts he believed were important.

Variation

Lesson variation is an essential presentation skill for teachers who want to develop a healthy, vital classroom climate. On analysis of classroom videotapes, Kounin (1977) noticed that satiation results in boredom and inattentiveness. If presentations are monotonous, students will find a way to introduce their own variation by daydreaming, sleeping, fiddling with objects, doodling, or poking their neighbors.

Planning for variation is important whenever you plan a lesson requiring 30 minutes or longer. Divide your lesson into several segments. Use lecture for only a part of the time. For example, include segments of discussion, independent practice, small-group interaction, and application activities. If you cannot break a single lesson into segments, plan to use a variety of strategies during the day. Use quiet, independent work for one subject, group interaction for another, lecture for a third, and hands-on activities for a fourth. In this way, your students will always be expectant and eager for each new lesson of the day. They will feel fresh and highly motivated to learn because of the variations in the way you choose to present material. If teachers attempt to address different learning styles in each lesson, they can't help but provide variation in the classroom. All lessons should be checked for activities that address the different learning modalities. This is discussed in more detail later in this chapter.

Interaction

Students thrive on interaction with the teacher and with their classmates. Rather than employing a traditional teacher-to-student, student-to-teacher communication pattern, open your classroom to a variety of interactive experiences. Pushing the desks into a large circle encourages open-ended discussion from all students. Arranging the desks in small groups encourages highly interactive problem-solving. Pushing the desks aside leaves a lot of space in the middle of the room for activities. Pairing the desks provides opportunities for peer teaching or partnerships of other kinds. Your presentations can include all these types of activities, and you will find that it is motivating not only to your students, but to you as well. You will feel a sense of expectant excitement as you say, "All right, students, let's rearrange the desks. . . ."

The need for interaction derives from the powerful motivational need for belonging described by Maslow (1954) and Glasser (1986). When these needs are frustrated or denied, disruptive behavior is likely to occur as a means of satisfying them. When teachers consciously plan interactive learning experiences, they allow students to satisfy their important drive for belonging and thereby prevent unnecessary discipline problems.

Active Learning Experiences

The BTES study demonstrated the important differences between time allocated for learning and the actual time students engaged in active learning. Presentations must be designed to engage the student in *active learning;* otherwise the time allocated to the learning experience may, in reality, result in passivity, rote learning, or even resistance to learning.

Presentations can include many verbal, visual, or hands-on activities and opportunities for active learning. Consider a lecture on a topic such as the closed circuit in electricity. Ho hum. Add a visual aid—a poster or an overhead projection. Students sit up in their seats to see better. Now add a demonstration. Turn off the lights. Hold up a battery, some copper wire, and a light bulb. Your students watch expectantly with a new sense of interest.

Turn on the lights again. All these techniques are adequate to teach the students a concept, but none is as valuable as a hands-on experience for in-depth learning and understanding. Picture this scene instead. After lunch the students come into their classroom to find a battery, a flashlight bulb, and a piece of copper wire on each desk. After getting their attention, the teacher simply says, "Working independently, try to get your bulb to light up." Lights go on all over the room—in children's eyes and in their minds as they struggle with this problem. The motivation to succeed is intense and it is intrinsic, not tied to any exterior reward. Each individual has a sense of power and a need to know.

Closure or Lack of Closure?

In the active learning experience example, the teacher can aid the students in comprehending what they've learned by having them share what they did that worked and didn't work. Concepts can be developed by articulating and generalizing what they learned about electricity. For this reason, a teacher-led discussion is an essential part of active, hands-on learning. It provides a sense of closure.

However, Bloom (1981) described a *lack of closure* as an element of the peak learning experiences he studied. He found that some students responded to the lack of closure with an independent effort to find out more about the subject. Each teacher must reflect on this dilemma and find a reasonable balance. To develop concepts, it is vital to lead a discussion of what the students observed and discovered in the present lesson. To stimulate further independent learning, it is possible to generate some additional unanswered questions and hypotheses at the conclusion of a lesson.

Every lesson or presentation can be improved by some thoughtful consideration given to its ending. It is important to allow time for closure. You may use this time to ask questions that check for understanding so that you will know what to plan for the lesson that follows. You may allow the students to close the lesson with their own conclusions and new insights. A few moments spent summarizing what was learned is valuable in any form. If insight is to occur, it will probably occur in this period. At the close of one lesson, you can also indicate what will follow in the next lesson so that your students know what to expect and how to prepare for it.

SYSTEMATIC CLASSROOM INSTRUCTION
Direct Instruction of New Knowledge and Skills

The curriculum contains a high proportion of basic knowledge and skills that learners must master thoroughly in order to be successful in the upper grades. Basic language concepts, such as letter recognition, phonics, decoding words, writing letters and words, and the conventions of sentence and paragraph construction, must be mastered. Basic mathematical concepts, such as number recognition, quantity, order, measurement, and the operations used in computation, must be learned.

In the 1980s, a number of experimental studies were conducted to discover the effects of various teaching methods on the achievement of basic language and mathematics skills. In these studies, student achievement was compared between untrained teachers using conventional teaching methods and teachers who were trained to use a certain sequence of instructional steps in planning, teaching, and evaluating the progress of their students. From these studies, Rosenshine and Stevens

(1986) concluded that the most effective series of instructional strategies for teaching basic, sequential knowledge or skills are

> Begin a lesson with a short review of previous, prerequisite learning.
> Begin a lesson with a short statement of goals.
> Present new material in small steps, with student practice after each step.
> Give clear and detailed instructions and explanations.
> Provide a high level of active practice for all students.
> Ask a large number of questions, check for student understanding, and obtain responses from all students.
> Guide students during initial practice.
> Provide systematic feedback and corrections.
> Provide explicit instruction and practice for seat work exercises and, where necessary, monitor students during seat work. (p. 377)

When these nine strategies are reviewed quickly, many readers may respond with reactions such as, "But isn't that what all teachers do? What is new about these methods?"

It is true that many teachers have used these strategies throughout the history of education in rural, urban, and suburban classrooms. But it is equally true that many teachers have not. We have all observed classroom teachers who take a much less active role than these nine steps describe. For teachers who foster the R-A view of teaching and learning, there are often only two steps: assigning work and correcting it.

Rosenshine and Stevens (1986) refer to the proposed sequence of strategies as *systematic teaching* because of its highly organized and sequential pattern of events. On close examination, these steps are comparable to the C-M view of teaching and learning because they describe methods that would be used by a teacher who expects all students to achieve in school if the teacher takes an active role in helping them process the new information that is being taught.

In selecting appropriate teaching methods and strategies, reflective teachers are likely to look for and discover relationships among various theories of learning and methods of teaching. One such relationship exists between the Rosenshine–Stevens model of systematic teaching and the process of thinking and learning known as *information processing*.

The first step, *Begin a lesson with a short review of previous, prerequisite learning*, is a signal to the learner to call up an existing schema that will be expanded and altered in the new lesson. Beginning a lesson with *a short statement of goals* provides the student with an advance organizer that allows the processing to take place with increased efficiency. In practice, these first two steps are often presented together and can be interchangeable with no ill effects.

Current information processing theories suggest that there are limits to the amount of new information that a learner can process effectively at one time (Gagné, 1985). When too much information is presented at one time, the working memory becomes overloaded, causing the learner to become confused, to omit data, or to process new data incorrectly. This overload can be eliminated when teachers *present new material in small steps, with student practice after each step.* "In this way, the learner does not have to process too much at one time and can concentrate his/her somewhat limited attention to processing manageable size pieces of information or skills" (Rosenshine & Stevens, 1986, p. 378).

Teachers who *give clear and detailed instructions and explanations* are likely to provide students with the support they need while they are processing new information in their working memories.

Providing students with *a high level of active practice* after each step, and again at the conclusion of a series of steps, is important because the practice enhances the likelihood that the new information will be transferred from working memory to long-term memory, where it can be stored for future use. Each time a new skill is practiced, its position in long-term memory is strengthened.

As teachers *guide students during initial practice* and *ask a large number of questions, check for student understanding,* and *obtain responses from all students,* they are also encouraging their students to process the information accurately. Learning occurs when schemata that are stored in long-term memory are expanded, enriched, and reorganized. Effective teacher questions and checks for understanding cause students to think about new ideas from a variety of perspectives and to update their existing schemata accordingly.

Providing systematic feedback and corrections and *monitoring students during seat work* also increases the likelihood that students will process the important points and practice the new skills in the most efficient manner.

Teacher Modeling and Demonstration

When teachers present new information to students, they must carefully consider the method they will use when they introduce it. For students, it is rarely sufficient for teachers to simply talk about a new idea or skill. A much more powerful method of instruction is to model or demonstrate it first and then give students an opportunity to practice the new learning themselves.

A simple example of this technique occurs in the primary grades when teachers say, "First, I will say the word; then you will say it with me." In the middle grades, the teacher may first demonstrate the procedures used in measuring with a metric ruler and then ask students to repeat them. In the upper grades, teachers may write an outline of a paragraph and then ask students to outline the next one.

Teacher demonstration and modeling is an effective instructional technique for almost every area of the curriculum. It is useful in teaching music: "Clap the same rhythm that I do." It is vital in teaching mathematics: "Watch as I do the first problem on the chalkboard." It can be easily applied to teaching creative writing: "I'll read you the poem that I wrote about this topic, and then you will write your own."

When teachers circulate throughout the classroom to monitor students as they practice or create their own work, it is efficient to use modeling and demonstration on a one-to-one basis to assist students in getting started or in correcting mistakes.

Scaffolding

Scaffolding is a variation on the technique of teaching by modeling and demonstrating a new skill. It involves a highly interactive relationship between the teacher and the student while the new learning occurs. Anderson (1989b) cites Jerome Bruner's work with mothers and children as the first reference to scaffolding. As a mother reads aloud to a toddler, she may simplify the book to meet the attention span and interests of her child, calling the child's attention to material that is appropriate and eliminating material that is beyond the child's present capacity. She is also likely to allow the child to interact with her as they read and discuss the words and pictures on each page. This flexible and simplified interaction between child and parent allows the child to connect new ideas to existing schemata at his or her own level.

Teachers can apply scaffolding in the classroom by reducing complex tasks to manageable steps, helping students concentrate on one task at a time, being explicit about what is expected and interpreting the task for the student, and coaching the student using words and actions that are familiar and supportive. When a teacher coaches the student through a difficult task, it is important to provide sufficient scaffolding through the use of hints and cues so that the student is able to succeed. As students become more and more skillful, the scaffolding can be reduced and finally eliminated entirely.

Scaffolding is a technique that is especially valuable for the primary teacher, since most young students require supportive interaction and accommodation to their existing vocabularies in order to learn new skills. But scaffolding is also appropriate for upper-level students when the tasks are complex or the students have difficulty with the language.

Some teachers do not use scaffolding techniques at any level:

> Instead of seeing themselves as supporters of students' constructions of knowledge, many teachers see themselves as presenters of content (especially facts and skills) and as orchestrators of activities that bring students in contact with that content (i.e., the receptive-accrual view described previously). One result is the predominance of the recitation mode of instruction, in which the teacher asks a question, students offer answers that the teacher confirms or disconfirms and the cycle is repeated. Teachers spend little time in the classroom encouraging students to explain how and what they are thinking, elements that are necessary for scaffolded dialogues. (Anderson, 1989b, p. 107)

For beginning teachers, scaffolding may not come naturally, because they may not have experienced scaffolded learning in their own school experiences. This technique can be learned only by reflecting on the needs of students, gathering the latest information on such techniques from reading and talking to experienced teachers who have used the techniques successfully, and gradually adding such strategies to personal repertoires.

Structuring Tasks for Success

Researchers have found that the degree of success students have on school tasks correlates highly with achievement in the subject area (Rosenshine, 1979). This supports the widely known maxim that "success breeds success." Both formal research and informal discussions with students reveal that when students experience success on a given task, they are motivated to continue working at it or to tackle another one. The number and type of successful learning experiences students have affect their self-knowledge, leading them to have expectations regarding probable success or failure in future tasks (Anderson, 1989a, p. 93).

In order to structure tasks for success, there must be a good fit between the teacher's expectations, student ability, and the difficulty of the task. Rimm (1986), who has specialized in assisting underachieving students reach their potential, describes it this way:

> Children must learn early that there is a relationship between their effort and the outcome. . . . If their schoolwork is too hard, their efforts do not lead to successful outcomes but only to failures. If their work is too easy, they learn that it takes very little to succeed. Either is inappropriate and provides a pattern which fosters underachievement. (p. 92)

When teachers select and present academic tasks to their students, it is important that they reflect continuously on how well the task fits the students' present needs and capacities.

Glasser (1969) has been committed to improving schools throughout his career. As a psychiatrist, he strongly believes that a person cannot be successful in life "until he can in some way first experience success in one important part of his life" (p. 5). Glasser recognizes that children have only two places in which to experience success: home and school. If they are lucky enough to experience success in both settings, they are likely to be successful in their adult lives. If they achieve success at home, they succeed despite a lackluster school experience. But many students come from homes and neighborhoods where failure is pervasive. For these students especially, it is critical that they experience success in school. Glasser's book, *Schools Without Failure,* offers many realistic and practical methods for teachers to develop a classroom environment that breeds success.

Matching Teaching and Learning Styles

In order to fully motivate students to learn new material, it is also important to consider each student's particular *learning style*. Dunn, Beaudry, and Klavas (1989) define a learning style as "a biologically and developmentally imposed set of personal characteristics that make the same teaching method effective for some and ineffective for others" (p. 50). In other words, each person has a particular pattern of needs for optimum learning.

Some students learn best in quiet rooms; others prefer a certain level of noise in the room. Students have individual preferences for light and dark, temperature, and seating. Learning styles in enormous variety have been described, including preferences for the structure of tasks and the best time of day for learning. Although you cannot accommodate all the needs of all your students, you will want to become aware of some of the many variations in learning styles so that when a student with an unusual sensitivity or a severe impediment to learning appears in your classroom (and this will happen), you will be able to reflect on this student's particular needs and provide a learning environment or restructure your teaching style to better match the student's learning style.

A set of learning styles based on sensory preferences is especially useful to reflective teachers. In eight studies in the 1980s, learning style preferences for *visual, auditory,* and *kinesthetic* learning were examined. It was discovered that most learners have a preference to receive information either visually (by viewing or reading), auditorially (by hearing), or kinesthetically (by touching, working with, or otherwise manipulating materials). There is a strong tendency for teachers to teach using the modality they prefer as a learning modality. Specifically, visual learners who rely on reading and viewing material to learn tend to rely on reading and other visual aids as teachers. Similarly, if you learn best by hearing, you may assume that others do also, and as a result, you may teach primarily using lecture and discussion. Kinesthetic learners who enjoy hands-on activities as students tend to provide many of these active learning materials in their own classrooms.

> When youngsters were taught with instructional resources that both matched and mismatched their preferred modalities, they achieved statistically higher test scores in modality matched, rather than modality mismatched, treatments. (Dunn et al., 1989, p. 52)

At present, there are two major approaches to solving this educational dilemma. One solution requires schoolwide cooperation. At each grade level, teachers may be identified as having visual, auditory, or kinesthetic preferences. Students are then tested and placed in the classroom with the teacher whose style matches their own. But this approach offers few opportunities for learners to improve their weaker learning modalities.

Another approach is for each teacher to conscientiously plan to teach using all three modalities. For example, when presenting a lesson, the teacher will provide visual aids in the form of pictures and reading material; auditory aids in the form of lecture, a discussion, or tape-recorded material; and kinesthetic aids in the form of models or other manipulative materials. Studies show that providing all three types of learning experiences to all students is likely to result in higher achievement than simply by matching one style. "When students were taught with multisensory resources, but *initially through their most preferred modality,* their scores increased even more" (Dunn et al., 1989, p. 52).

Conclusions

Reflective, caring teachers are likely to value the C-M view of teaching and learning, which holds that students must be active learners rather than passive recipients of knowledge. With this philosophy, reflective teachers attempt to plan varied and interesting lessons, with many opportunities for students to practice actively what they are learning.

In this chapter, we have discussed some general presentation skills that can engage the learner's interest in the lesson being taught. We have also focused on the strategies that teachers use to instruct a large group of students in the basic skills of a subject. Because the techniques of direct instruction are used frequently in classrooms, it is important for the beginning teacher to become proficient in planning and teaching lessons of this type.

Although some teachers may rely on direct instruction of the entire class as their major or only teaching strategy, reflective teachers are likely to want to be able to choose from a variety of strategies. The next three chapters offer the beginning teacher a glimpse at a range of teaching methods. From these, you may begin to build a repertoire of teaching strategies to expand your own teaching skills and increase your students' motivation for learning.

OPPORTUNITIES FOR REFLECTION

▼ Reflective Essay: A Successful Teaching Experience

Write about a time when you were very successful in teaching something to another person. It may have been an informal setting, such as a kitchen or a ski slope. What made this experience a success? How did you begin the "lesson"? How did you interact with the "student(s)"? What did you do that worked best? Do you believe that you can apply what worked in this lesson to your classroom teaching?

▼ Classroom Visit: Teaching Strategy Log

Begin to keep a log of all the teaching strategies you observe in the classroom you visit. After describing an example of a strategy, describe how you would adapt or change it to fit your own style.

REFERENCES

ANDERSON J., & PEARSON, P. (1984). A schema theoretic view of basic processes in reading. In P. Pearson (Ed.), *Handbook of reading research* (pp. 255–291). New York: Longman.

ANDERSON, L. (1989a). Learners and learning. In M. Reynolds (Ed.), *Knowledge base for the beginning teacher* (pp. 85–99). New York: Macmillan.

ANDERSON, L. (1989b). Classroom instruction. In M. Reynolds (Ed.), *Knowledge base for the beginning teacher* (pp. 101–115). New York: Macmillan.

AUSUBEL, D. P. (1960). The use of advance organizers in the learning and retention of meaningful verbal material. *Journal of Educational Psychology, 51,* 267–272.

BLOOM, B. (1981). *All our children learning.* New York: McGraw-Hill.

BRANSFORD, J. (1983). Schema activation—schema acquisition. In R. Anderson, J. Osborn, & R. Tierney (Eds.), *Learning to read in American Schools* (pp. 23–37). Hillsdale, NJ: Erlbaum.

BROPHY, J., & GOOD, T. (1986). Teacher behavior and student achievement. In M. Wittrock (Ed.), *Handbook of research on teaching* (3rd ed.) (pp. 328–375). New York: Macmillan.

DENHAM, C., & LIEBERMAN, A. (1980). *Time to learn.* Washington, DC: U.S. Department of Education.

DUNN, R., BEAUDRY, J., & KLAVAS, A. (1989). Survey of research on learning styles. *Educational Leadership, 46*(6), 50–57.

GAGNE, E. (1985). *The cognitive psychology of school learning.* Boston: Little, Brown.

GLASSER, W. (1969). *Schools without failure.* New York: Harper & Row.

GLASSER, W. (1986). *Control theory in the classroom.* New York: Harper & Row.

GOOD, T., & BROPHY, J. (1987). *Looking in classrooms,* (4th ed.). New York: Harper & Row.

HUNTER, M. (1982). *Mastery teaching.* El Segundo, CA: TIP Publications.

JONES, F. (1987). *Positive classroom discipline.* New York: McGraw-Hill.

KOUNIN, J. (1977). *Discipline and group management in classrooms.* New York: Robert E. Kreiger.

MASLOW, A. (1954). *Motivation and personality.* New York: Harper & Row.

Rosenshine, B. (1979). Content, time and direct instruction. In P. Peterson & H. Walberg (Eds.), *Research on teaching: Concepts, findings and implications* (pp. 28–56). Berkeley, CA: McCutchan.

Rosenshine, B. (1980). How time is spent in elementary classrooms. In C. Denham & A. Lieberman (Eds.), *Time to learn* (pp. 107–126). Washington, DC: U.S. Department of Education.

Rosenshine, B., & Stevens, R. (1986). Teaching functions. In M. Wittrock (Ed.), *Handbook of research on teaching* (3rd ed.) (pp. 376–391). New York: Macmillan.

CHAPTER

8

Discussion and Questioning Strategies to Promote Cognitive Engagement

"A BASIC TENET of the cognitive-mediational perspective on learning is that active processing by the learner is necessary for learning to occur" (Anderson, 1989, p. 108). Researchers in education are currently focusing considerable attention on the phenomenon known as *cognitive engagement,* which occurs when a student becomes actively and enthusiastically interested in thinking about and discussing an idea. Making cognitive engagement a classroom goal is a powerful new concept for teachers to consider when they select teaching strategies for their classrooms. It connotes the opposite of the sterile, passive classroom environment in which students attend listlessly to the lessons and carry out their seat work and homework with little real effort or interest.

When students are fully engaged in reading, listening, discussion, or creation, the classroom climate is likely to be as lively and stimulating as a thundershower. Can you recall a classroom learning experience so powerful that you have almost total recall of it many years later? When you recall the event, do you feel as if you are reliving it because the memory is still so vividly etched in your mind? Do you think of this event as life-changing? Perhaps it altered the way you think about an issue or caused you to change your career goal or provoked you into making a life-style change. These relatively rare classroom events have been described as "peak learning experiences" by Benjamin Bloom (1981, p. 193) and are related to the "peak experiences" described earlier by Maslow (1971).

TYPES OF CLASSROOM QUESTIONS AND DISCUSSIONS

Not all of the discussions that you plan will be as engaging as a peak experience, but many can approach it and many others can be satisfying and provocative when you take care to plan for full cognitive engagement on the part of your students.

In some classrooms, what passes for discussions are really dull and repetitive question-and-answer periods. Some teachers may simply read aloud a list of questions from the teachers' manual of the textbook and call on students to recite the answers. As you probably recall from your own school experiences, when this type of "discussion" occurs, many students disengage entirely. They read ahead, doodle, or do homework surreptitiously. They seldom listen to their classmates' responses, and when it is their turn to recite, they frequently cannot find their place in the list of questions.

Reflective teachers value the process of considering alternatives and debating opinions and ideas. That is how reflective teachers approach the world themselves, and they are likely to want to stimulate the same types of behavior among their students.

Educational literature abounds with terms and systems related to the promotion of high-quality and actively engaged thinking. Teachers are encouraged to promote *higher-level thinking processes* (also known as *higher-order thinking skills*), *problem-solving skills, critical thinking,* and *creative thinking* among their students. These terms and concepts can be confusing and overwhelming for the beginning teacher, because it appears that it is necessary to establish separate programs for each of them.

That is not the case. When you become more familiar with these concepts, you will find that it is possible to discover common attributes among them. You can then plan classroom discussions and other experiences that promote high-level thinking, problem-solving, and critical and creative thinking at the same time. One question may pose a problem, another may call for a creative response, a third may be analytical, and a fourth may ask students to evaluate a situation and make a critical judgment. The best (which is to say, the most highly engaging) classroom discussions do all of these in a spontaneous, nonregimented way.

In the following sections, descriptions of various thinking processes are presented along with alternatives for planning classroom discussions to promote these processes. As you read these sections, reflect on the similarities and differences; look for patterns and sequences; and consider how you would use, modify, and adapt these systems in your classroom.

Although these processes can be applied to both academic and nonacademic areas of the curriculum, we will illustrate how classroom discussions are created and managed, using the topic of racial discrimination as a common theme. In this example, the operational goal is to promote understanding of the effects of racial discrimination on the lives of human beings and to generate a sense of respect for individuals who are different from oneself.

Questions That Develop Higher-Level Thinking Processes

Bloom's Taxonomy (Bloom, Englehart, Furst, Hill & Krathwohl, 1956) is the most widely known and commonly used system for promoting the use of higher-level thinking processes. Discussion questions can be readily planned at every level of the Taxonomy, just as other learning experiences are planned. The term *higher-level* refers to the top four levels of the hierarchy:

HIGHER-LEVEL	Evaluation
THINKING	Synthesis
PROCESSES	Analysis
	Application
LOWER-LEVEL	Comprehension
THINKING PROCESSES	Knowledge

Given any topic, teachers can fashion questions to fit each of these levels. Because the Taxonomy is arranged as a hierarchy, teachers frequently ask lower-level questions first in order to develop a base of knowledge on the topic and then proceed to higher-level questions. In our example, the teacher has assigned the class to read a biography of Dr. Martin Luther King, Jr., and has planned a discussion that includes questions at all six levels:

▼ *Knowledge Level* At this level, the learners are asked to recall specific bits of information, such as terminology, facts, and details:

When and where was King born?
Who were the other members of his family?
What jobs did King's father do to earn a living?
What jobs did his mother do?
What career did Dr. King choose?

▼ *Comprehension Level*   At this level, the learners are asked to describe the main ideas in their own words:

King lived in a *ghetto.* What does this term mean?
What does prejudice mean?
How did school change King's life?
How did the church affect his life?

▼ *Application Level*   At this level, the learners are asked to apply what they have learned to their own lives or to other situations:

Give an example of prejudice that has affected you.
If Dr. King were alive today, what do you think he would be most concerned about? What do you think he would do about it?

▼ *Analysis Level*   At this level, the learners are asked to describe patterns, cause-and-effect relationships, comparisons, and contrasts:

How did Rosa Parks' decision to sit in the front of the bus change King's life? How did her decision change history?
In what ways was Dr. King a minister, a politician, and a teacher?

▼ *Synthesis Level*   At this level, the learners are asked to contribute a new and original idea on the topic:

Complete this phrase: I have a dream that one day. . . .
If there were suddenly a strong new prejudice against people that look just like you, what would you do about it?

▼ *Evaluation Level*   At this level, the learners are asked to express their own opinions or make judgments about some aspect of the topic:

What do you believe was Dr. King's greatest contribution?
Which promotes more social change: nonviolence or violence? Give a rationale or example to defend your answer.

Some teachers find that Bloom's Taxonomy is a useful and comprehensive guide for planning classroom discussion questions as well as other classroom activities. Others find that the Taxonomy is more complex than they desire and that it is difficult to discriminate between some of the levels, such as comprehension and analysis or application and synthesis. Other systems of classifying thinking processes are available. Doyle (1986) proposes that teachers plan classroom tasks in four categories that are readily applicable to classroom discussions: (1) memory tasks, (2) procedural or routine tasks, (3) comprehension tasks and (4) opinion tasks.

Classroom questions and discussion starters can be created to fit these four task levels, as follows:

▼ *Memory Questions*   Learners are asked to reproduce information they have read or heard before:

When and where was Dr. King born?
Who were the other members of his family?

▼ *Procedural or Routine Questions*   Learners are asked to supply simple answers with only one correct response:

What jobs did King's father do to earn a living?
What jobs did his mother do?
What career did Dr. King choose?

▼ *Comprehension Questions*   Learners are asked to consider known data and apply them to a new and unfamiliar context:

Dr. King lived in a *ghetto*. What does this term mean?
What does prejudice mean?
How did school change King's life?
How did the church affect his life?
How did Rosa Parks' decision to sit in the front of the bus change King's life? How did her decision change history?
In what ways was Dr. King a minister, a politician, and a teacher?

▼ *Opinion Questions*   Learners are asked to express their own point of view on an issue, with no correct answer expected:

Give an example of prejudice that has affected you.
If Dr. King were alive today, what do you think he would be most concerned about? What do you think he would do about it?
Complete this phrase: I have a dream that one day. . . .
If there were suddenly a strong new prejudice against people who look just like you, what would you do about it?
What do you believe was Dr. King's greatest contribution?
Which promotes more social change: nonviolence or violence?
Give a rationale or example to defend your answer.

You will notice that the questions in Doyle's four categories are the same as the ones listed in the Taxonomy's six levels. Questions at the comprehension and analysis levels are both contained in Doyle's comprehension category, and questions at the application, synthesis, and evaluation levels are contained in Doyle's opinion category. Both of these systems offer teachers a comprehensive framework for planning a range of thought-provoking questions. The choice of which system to use is entirely up to you.

Problem-Solving Discussions

Much is written about the need for developing students' problem-solving and decision-making abilities. This can be done by presenting students with a complex problem and providing adequate scaffolding support so that they are able to learn how to solve problems. Although some problems must be solved by paper and pencil or by a hands-on experimental approach, others can be solved through classroom discussion.

To create productive problem-solving discussions, the teacher must understand the processes involved in problem-solving and then structure the questions to guide students through that process. A problem is said to exist when "one has a goal and has not yet identified a means for reaching that goal. The problem may be wanting to answer a question, to prove a theorem, to be accepted or to get a job" (Gagné, 1985, p. 138).

According to cognitive psychologists, the framework for solving a problem consists of identifying a goal, a starting place, and all possible solution paths from the starting place to the goal. Some individuals are efficient and productive problem-solvers; others are not. An excellent classroom goal for the beginning teacher is to help students become more efficient and more productive problem-solvers.

Nonproductive problem-solvers are likely to have difficulty identifying or defining the problem. They may simply feel that a puzzling situation exists, but they may not be aware of the real nature of the problem. Students who are poor problem-solvers need experience in facing puzzling situations and defining problems. They also need experience in identifying and selecting worthwhile goals.

When a problem has been defined and a goal established, it is still possible to be either efficient or inefficient in reaching the goal. Efficiency in problem-solving can be increased when students learn how to identify the alternative strategies to reach a chosen goal and recognize which ones are likely to provide the best and quickest routes to success. This can be done by helping students to visualize the probable effects of each alternative and applying criteria to help them choose the most valuable means of solving the problem they have defined.

As in the teaching of higher-level thinking processes, several useful systems are available to teachers who want to teach students to become better problem-solvers. Osborne (1963) proposed the technique known as *brainstorming*, which includes four basic steps:

1. defining the problem
2. generating, without criticism or evaluation, as many solutions as possible
3. deciding on criteria for judging the solutions generated
4. using these criteria to select the best possible solution

Brainstorming is an excellent way to generate classroom discussion about a puzzling issue. Rather than formulating a series of questions, the teacher supplies a dilemma or puzzle, teaches the students the steps involved in brainstorming, and then leads them through the process itself.

In discussing the life of Martin Luther King, Jr., and helping students to understand the effects of racial discrimination, the teacher might use a portion of the classroom discussion to brainstorm answers to one of the most perplexing questions. For example, the teacher might choose to use brainstorming to expand the discussion on the following question,

> If Dr. King were alive today, what do you think he would be most concerned about? What do you think he would do about it?

The techniques of brainstorming call for the teacher to pose the question or problem in such a way that it engages the students' interest and motivates them to take it seriously. Because students may not be proficient at discussion of this sort, it is frequently necessary for the teacher to give additional cues and suggestions as a scaffold. In this instance, the teacher might need to pose the original question and then follow it with prompts such as these:

"What do you think he'd be concerned about in our community?"
"What has been in the news lately that might alarm him?"
"Who are the people in the world who are presently in need?"
"What about threats to our environment?"

Open-ended questions such as these will generate many more responses than if they were not used. After recording all of the students' responses on the chalkboard, the teacher leads the students through a process of selecting the most important items for further consideration. This may be done by a vote or a general consensus. When the list has been narrowed to several very important issues, the teacher must then lead the students through the process of establishing criteria for judging the items.

Because the question is related to Martin Luther King, Jr.'s values, one possible criterion is to judge whether King showed concern for the issue in his lifetime. Another criterion might be the number of people who are threatened or hurt by the problem. After judging the items by these criteria, the class makes a judgment about which items would most concern King. Then the process of brainstorming begins again, but this time the problem the class is considering is what King would be likely to do to help solve the problem. Generating responses to the first question, "If Dr. King were alive today, what would he be most concerned about?", will help students understand the many aspects of racial discrimination that exist today. By selecting one of these as the main concern and generating responses to the question, "What do you think he would do about it?", the students will reflect on their own responsibilities to other human beings and on ways to increase tolerance and brotherhood in their own community.

To moderate a brainstorming discussion, the teacher faithfully records every response generated by the students, no matter how trivial or impossible it sounds. The teacher then leads students through the process of eliminating the least important items and finally works through a process of establishing criteria to use in evaluating the best possible solutions.

Brainstorming alone does not solve problems. It merely trains students in thinking productively about problems and in considering many alternative solutions. In some classrooms, teachers may wish to extend the hypothetical discussion of possible solutions to an actual attempt to solve a problem or at least contribute to a solution.

Discussions That Promote Critical Thinking

The term *critical thinking* is not a separate and distinct concept that is different from higher-level thinking processes and problem-solving. It overlaps both of them. It is presented here in a separate section because, during the past few years, it has become a field of study with its research base and suggested classroom processes.

The field of study known as critical thinking grew out of the philosophical study of logic, which was a staple in the secondary curriculum in the mid-20th century. The principles of logical thinking were meant to train people to think about a single hypothesis deductively in order to arrive at a rationale conclusion. But in the late 1960s, de Bono (1967) observed that although logical thinkers were prepared to deal with a single issue in depth, they were not prepared to deal with unexpected evidence or ideas.

Using the analogy of digging for treasure, de Bono (1967) suggested that in thinking about a hypothesis, a logical thinker might dig a deeper and bigger hole, but if the hole is not in the right place, then no amount of digging would improve the solution. In contrast, de Bono (1967) believed that a critical thinker would be more flexible than a logical thinker, and after considering a problem or issue, the critical thinker would be able to select from a tool box of thinking skills that allows the individual to clarify where to dig, select from alternative digging methods, use a variety of procedures to analyze the contents of the hole, and judge the worth of what is excavated.

Critical thinking, then, is partially defined as a complex set of thinking skills and processes that are believed to lead to fair and useful judgments. Lipman (1988) defines it as "skillful, responsible thinking that facilitates good judgment because it (1) relies on criteria, (2) is self-correcting, and (3) is sensitive to context" (p. 39). He points out the strong association between the words *criteria* and *critical thinking*. In this way, the process obviously overlaps the problem-solving technique of brainstorming and applying criteria to select the best solution.

But critical thinking is a much more multifaceted concept than problem-solving. Ennis (1985) points out that critical thinking occurs as a result of both dispositions and abilities. "The list of dispositions includes such things as being open-minded, paying attention to the total situation, seeking reasons, and trying to be well informed" (p. 48). This implies that the teaching of critical thinking involves much more than simply training students to use a set of strategies or procedures. It also involves establishing some affective goals for students to support them in becoming more independent and open-minded.

Paul (1988), director of the Center of Critical Thinking at Sonoma State University in Rohnert Park, California, agrees. He describes affective attributes of critical thinking that include independence, avoidance of egocentricity and stereotyping, and suspending judgment until much evidence has been gathered.

Ennis (1985), Paul (1988), and other investigators have also described lists of cognitive strategies that critical thinkers can be trained to use. These include skills involving observation, focusing on a question, distinguishing facts from opinions, distinguishing relevant from irrelevant information, judging credibility of sources, recognizing contradictions, making inferences, and drawing conclusions. Because almost every specialist in critical thinking proposes a slightly different set of thinking processes and skills that comprise critical thinking, it is necessary for reflective teachers to judge for themselves which strategies to stress in their own classrooms.

Raths, Wasserman, Jonas, and Rothstein (1986) describe a set of thinking operations that they believe comprise critical thinking, and then provide a wealth of practical classroom applications at both the elementary and secondary levels. The operations they emphasize are comparing, summarizing, observing, classifying, interpreting, criticizing, looking for assumptions, imagining, collecting and organizing data, applying facts and principles in new situations, and decision making.

To systematically train students to become better thinkers, Raths et al. (1986) suggest methods using the whole class or with small groups. In classroom discussions, they recommend that the teacher select one thinking operation at a time and tell the class that they will be focusing on improving this thinking skill. The teacher then proposes a discussion topic, listens attentively to students' responses, and records them if appropriate.

In our classroom example focusing on Martin Luther King, Jr., and the effects of racial segregation, the teacher might introduce a *comparison* question such as "Compare the way African-Americans felt discriminated against when Dr. King was a boy and when he died." For a *summary* question, the teacher may ask students to summarize the class response to the first question. For an *observation* question, the teacher may propose that students observe instances of racial discrimination for 24 hours and report their observations to the class the next day. The other critical thinking operations can be treated in a similar manner.

Discussions That Enhance Creative Thinking

Can individuals learn to be creative? Perhaps the more important question is, do individuals learn to be uncreative? A century ago, William James (1890) stated his belief that education trains students to become "old fogeys" in the early grades by training them to adopt habits of convergent, conformist thinking.

Divergent thinking is the opposite of convergent thinking in that it diverges from common understanding and accepted patterns. Guilford (1967) contributed a definition of divergent thinking that is still well accepted and has become the basis for E. Paul Torrance's (1966–1984) well-known tests for creativity. Guilford describes (and Torrance's test measures) four attributes of divergent thinking: *fluency, flexibility, originality,* and *elaboration.* In other words, a divergent thinker is one who generates many ideas (fluency), is able to break with conformist or set ideas (flexibility), suggests ideas that are new in the present context (originality), and contributes details that extend or support the idea beyond a single thought (elaboration).

Classroom discussions can be designed to help students develop these four attributes of creativity. In a technique similar to brainstorming, the teacher can ask students to generate many responses to a single question as a means of helping them to become more fluent in their thinking. For example, given our topic of King's "I have a dream" speech, the teacher may begin the process with the unfinished sentence, "I have a dream that someday. . . ."

Students may be asked to write their own responses for several minutes before the actual discussion begins. This allows each student to work for fluency individually. Then the ideas on paper are shared, and other new ideas are created as a result of the discussion. To promote flexibility, the teacher may ask students to imagine making their dreams come true and suggest ways that they could do this, using flexible and original strategies rather than rigid and ordinary methods. Finally, to extend the students' elaborative thought, the teacher may select one dream and ask the entire class to focus on it and create a more detailed vision and a more in-depth plan to accomplish it.

Einstein and Infeld (1938) add a further dimension to our understanding of creative thinking:

> The formulation of a problem is often more essential than its solution, which may be merely a matter of mathematical or experimental skill. To raise new questions,

new possibilities, to regard old problems from a new angle, requires creative imagination and marks real advance in science. (p. 92)

Problem-solving, then, is related to creative thinking. It is readily apparent that the methods described for improving problem-solving involve critical thinking, and that both involve the use of higher-level thinking processes. Whatever we call it, the goal of aiding students in developing better thinking skills is an integral part of any classroom discussion.

Just as we respect Einstein's ability to pose new problems, we should respect and develop our own and our students' capacity to ask questions and suggest new ways of solving age-old problems. Certainly, the teaching profession needs people with the capability of regarding old educational problems from a new angle. Often it is the newest and youngest members of a faculty who see things from a helpful new perspective and suggest new ways of dealing with difficult school issues.

Another dimension of creativity involves the production of something useful, interesting, or otherwise valued by at least a small segment of society. Rogers (1954) defines creativity in terms of a process that results in a "novel relational product growing out of the uniqueness of the individual on the one hand and the materials, events, people, or circumstances of his life on the other" (p. 251).

In this textbook, the definition of creative thinking is a combination of the concepts described above. That is, a creative thinker is one who poses new problems, raises new questions, and then suggests solutions that are characterized by fluency, flexibility, originality, and elaboration. The solutions result in a product unique for that individual in those circumstances.

Do schools enhance or discourage these conditions and processes? Do textbooks, curriculum guides, rules, regulations and expectations support the development of creative thinking and the process needed to create a unique product? Many teachers do, and this book supports those who want to try to assist students in learning to become creative thinkers rather than 9-year-old old fogeys.

THE ROLE OF THE TEACHER IN LEADING DISCUSSIONS

Discussions that promote the use of critical thinking can be exciting classroom events for both students and teachers, but beginning teachers may find it difficult to elicit responses from students who are not used to taking part in such activities. Raths et al. (1986) asks:

> "What if you ask a wonderful question and the pupils don't respond?"
>
> There is nothing quite so demoralizing for a teacher as a lack of response from students.
>
> "Now boys and girls, how do you think the sound got onto this tape?"
>
> No response. Interminable silence. Finally the teacher leaps in to break the tension and gives the answer. Everybody, including the teacher, visibly relaxes. Whew! Let's not try that again. (p. 183)

This example of a nondiscussion is more common than is desirable. Students in your classroom may not have had opportunities to think creatively and express their own ideas. If not, they may be very reluctant to do so at first. They may believe that you expect one right answer, just as most of their teachers have in the past. Because they do not know the one right answer, they may prefer to remain quiet rather than embarrass themselves by giving a wrong answer. Your response to their silence will tell them a great deal. If you jump in with your own response, they will learn that their own responses were not really wanted after all.

Scaffolding is a necessary component of teaching critical thinking and discussion strategies to students. Be explicit about what you do expect from them in a discussion. Tell them that there are no wrong answers and that all opinions are valued. If they still hesitate, provide cues and prompts without providing answers. Simplify or rephrase the question so that they are able to answer it. If the question, "How do you think the sound got on this tape?" gets no response, rephrase it. "What sounds do you hear on this tape?" "Can you imagine how those sounds were captured on a piece of plastic like this?" "Do you think machinery was used?" "What kinds of machines are able to copy sounds?" These supporting questions provide scaffolds for thinking and talking about unknown and unfamiliar ideas.

In the following Reflection, Mary O'Donnell, a high school history teacher who has been teaching for 2 years, describes how she works to develop a classroom climate that encourages active discussion and provides a support system for reluctant participants.

Another consideration in leading discussions is to *value silence* rather than fear it. Silence can indicate that students are truly engaged in reflection. By allowing a few moments of silence, the resulting discussions may be much more creative and productive. Students need time to process the question. They need time to bring forward the necessary schema to their working memories and to consider the question in light of what they already know about the topic. Some students need more time than others to see connections between new ideas and already stored information and to generate a response of their own.

Some teachers consciously use *wait time* by requiring a short period of silence after each significant question is asked. Students are taught to listen quietly, then think quietly for several seconds and not raise their hands to respond until the wait time has passed. Rowe (1974) found that when teachers use a wait time of 3 to 5 seconds, more students were able to generate a response to the question. Without a planned wait time, the same group of fast-thinking students are likely to dominate all discussions. With the wait time, even slower-thinking students will have an opportunity to consider what it is they do believe before hearing the opinions of others.

Lyman (1989) recommends that teachers employ a system called *listen, think, pair, share* to improve both the quantity and the quality of discussion responses. This technique employs a structured wait time at two different points in the discussion. When a question is asked, wait time goes into effect while students jot down ideas and think about their responses. Students are then expected to discuss their ideas in pairs for a minute. Then a general discussion takes place. After each student makes a contribution, the remainder of the class is expected to employ a second wait time of 3 to 5 seconds to process what their classmate has said before they raise their hands to respond.

Mary O'Donnell

History Teacher, Crystal Lake South High School, Crystal Lake, Illinois

Classroom Event

In my classroom, I want to make history come alive. I use a variety of teaching strategies, including having students go out into the community to write and create their own local history. However, it isn't always possible to do such projects. So, even when we are stuck in the classroom, I want to make our discussions about historical events and issues dynamic and exciting.

Asking Questions

The questions I continually ask myself are "How do I make history relevant to my students' lives? How do I encourage lively discussions that involve as many students as possible? What can I do to help insecure students recognize that their view of history is valid and important to our class so that they will feel comfortable speaking up?"

Gathering Information

Whenever I get an opportunity to observe other teachers, I focus on their discussion strategies. Craig Pfannkuche, my cooperating teacher during student teaching, was an especially valuable resource for me. His classes always had the liveliest (and loudest) discussions of any I've ever observed. At the end of class periods, his students would often stay to continue the discussion they had started in class. I wanted to develop that same kind of climate in my classroom.

Analyzing the Information and the Situation

What I discovered from my observations was that the most successful discussions were led by teachers who had created a classroom climate that made their students feel secure. Students in these classrooms seemed to believe that their opinions were valuable not just to the teacher but to their classmates as well. There was a sense of mutual respect that made the majority of students feel comfortable contributing to the discussions. I knew then that in order to encourage lively and active discussion in my classroom, I had to create a safe and supportive emotional climate for my students.

Making a Judgment Based on Principles

One major reason that I became a history teacher is to encourage students to take an active civic role as adults in their community. Students who recognize that they have the ability to analyze historical and current events and make critical decisions and judgments about these events will be empowered to become voters, community leaders, and political leaders. Another strong belief that I hold is that each individual should respect the values and opinions of every other individual in our society. Based on these beliefs, I have tried to establish an understanding with my students that respect is the basic social rule of my classroom.

Considering Alternative Strategies

To reach my goal of having lively, diverse, and mutually respectful discussions, I considered using cooperative learning. Although I do find cooperative learning useful for small group discussions, I still find it necessary to allow the class as a whole to share the various opinions they hold on each important issue.

Early in my teaching career, I considered using wide open, unrestrained discussions in the hope that the students would take the class into all the possible realms, but I quickly found that these discussions could become chaotic and uncomfortable to manage.

Selecting the Best Strategy

To make my discussions exciting but manageable, I realized that I would have to establish some way to make sure that only one person spoke at a time. I set up a modified form of parliamentary procedure, which requires that the class recognize that the person speaking has the right to the floor until he or she is finished talking. In my classroom discussions, I take the role of parliamentarian. Sometimes I call on students to recognize their right to speak, but as the year progresses and the students show an understanding of parliamentary procedures themselves, I have been able to allow students to speak up when they want to comment without raising their hands. When a person begins to speak in my classroom, the rest of the class has learned to recognize that the speaker "has the floor" until he or she is finished, at which time, someone else can feel free to speak.

To make these discussions work, I have learned that I must be well prepared with a good list of questions that will elicit the types of student responses that I want. I design my questions to confront students with tough issues and encourage them to use critical thinking in response.

For example, in discussing Christopher Columbus, I may begin with such simple questions as "What were the names of the three ships?" Then I ask, "Why are you all able to recite these names so easily?" "Why is Columbus so important? Wasn't he just a bad navigator who happened to land on an island in the Bahamas? Does he really deserve the credit he receives?"

Putting the Plan into Action

In the first week of school, I plan discussions on interesting topics to train my students to use parliamentary rules and to encourage all of them to contribute to discussions. I tell them that we all want to hear what they have to say. I explain that when someone is speaking, they have the right to speak without interruption until they are finished. For the first few weeks of school, I have to remind students to remain quiet while a classmate is speaking. I try to call on quiet students and encourage them to say what they are thinking. I may stop the discussion for a minute and ask students to reflect on what has been said so far. Then I will ask a quiet student, "Which of the opinions that you've heard do you believe has the most historical merit?" That allows the listener to become an active participant.

Results

The most dramatic results of our discussions are evident in my students' essays and other writing assignments. In their written work, students remember and sometimes even paraphrase what they've learned from other students. I find myself using their views as well. My students enjoy our discussions so much that they frequently initiate discussions themselves. I get excited when I notice that my students are beginning to ask one another what they think. As the year progresses, the most outgoing students will call on their quieter classmates to ask them their opinions. When this happens, I believe that my principles of mutual respect for diverse opinions and equal access to knowledge are being successfully passed on to my students.

The quantity and quality of students' responses may be improved by introducing the questions early in the class period, followed by reading, a lecture, or another type of presentation and then discussion of the questions themselves. This strategy follows the principle of using the question as an advance organizer. By hearing the question prior to the presentation of new material, the students are alerted what to listen or read for and have sufficient time to process the information they receive in terms of the question. When teachers use this technique, they rarely experience a silent response.

Another strategy that promotes highly interactive discussions involves the physical setup in the classroom. To facilitate critical and creative thinking, it is important for students to be able to hear and see each other during the discussion. Arranging the chairs in a circle, rectangle, U-shape, or semicircle will ensure that each student feels like a contributing member of a group.

Meyers (1986) notes that a hospitable classroom environment is the most important factor in engaging students' attention and interest and promoting their creative responses during discussion:

> Much of the success in teaching critical thinking rests with the tone that teachers set in their classrooms. Students must be led gently into the active roles of discussing, dialoguing, and problem solving. They will watch very carefully to see how respectfully teachers field comments and will quickly pick up nonverbal cues that show how open teachers really are to student questions and contributions. (p. 67)

Reflective teachers are critical and creative thinkers themselves. They welcome opportunities to model their own thinking strategies for their students and plan experiences that encourage the development of their students' higher-level thinking processes. They are likely to make even the simplest discussion an exercise in problem-solving, reasoning, logic, and creative and independent thinking. They examine the subjects taught in the curriculum in search of ways to allow their students to learn to think and communicate their ideas. They plan discussions involving the creation and testing of hypotheses into science. They promote thinking that avoids stereotypes and egocentricity into social studies. They teach their students to suspend judgment when they lack sufficient evidence in discussions of math problems. They promote flexible and original thinking in discussions of literature. Discussions in every part of the curriculum can be crafted in ways that cause individuals to learn to think reflectively, critically, and creatively.

OPPORTUNITIES FOR REFLECTION

▼ Reflective Essay: Your Own Discussion Leading Abilities

Write about your own experiences as a participant in discussions. Do you enjoy contributing ideas? What type of support do you need from a teacher or discussion leader to encourage you to take a more active role?

Write about your own experiences in leading discussions. Are you comfortable in the role of leader? Do you tend to ask good questions spontaneously? Do you need to prepare carefully and write questions ahead of time?

▼ Classroom Visit: Leading A Discussion

Ask the classroom teacher for an opportunity to lead a classroom discussion under his or her guidance. The topic can come from the curriculum, or you can plan your own topic. Prepare the questions ahead of time and show them to the teacher for feedback before leading the discussion. Afterward, ask the teacher to provide you with feedback on the discussion itself.

REFERENCES

ANDERSON, L. (1989). Classroom instruction. in M. Reynolds (Ed.), *Knowledge base for the beginning teacher* (pp. 101–115). New York: Macmillan.

BLOOM, B., ENGLEHART, M., FURST, E., HILL, W., & KRATHWOHL, D. (1956). *Taxonomy of educational objectives: Cognitive domain.* New York: Longman.

DE BONO, E. (1967). *New think.* New York: Basic Books.

DOYLE, W. (1986). Classroom organization and management. In M. Wittrock (Ed.), *Handbook of Research on Teaching* (3rd ed.) (pp. 392–420). New York: Macmillan.

EINSTEIN, A. & INFELD, L. (1938). *The evolution of physics.* New York: Simon & Schuster.

ENNIS, R. (1985). A logical basis for measuring critical thinking skills. *Educational Leadership,* 43(2), 44–48.

GAGNÉ, E. (1985), *The cognitive phychology of school learning.* Boston: Little, Brown.

GUILFORD, J. P. (1967). *The nature of human intelligence.* New York: McGraw-Hill.

JAMES, W. (1890). *Principles of psychology.* New York: Holt.

LIPMAN, M. (1988). Critical thinking—What can it be? *Educational Leadership,* 46(1), 38–43.

LYMAN, F. (1989). Rechoreographing the middle-level minuet. *Early Adolescence Magazine,* IV(I), 22–24.

MEYERS, C. (1986). *Teaching students to think critically.* San Francisco: Jossey-Bass.

OSBORNE, P. (1963). *Applied imagination.* New York: Scribner's.

PAUL, R. (1988). *31 Principles of critical thinking.* Rohnert Park, CA: Center for Critical Thinking and Moral Critique.

RATHS, L., WASSERMAN, S., JONAS, A. & ROTHSTEIN, A. (1986). *Teaching for thinking.* New York: Teachers College Press.

ROGERS, C. (1954). Toward a theory of creativity. In S. I. Hayakawa (Ed.), *ETC: A review of general semantics* (Vol. II, no. 4, pp. 249–260). Chicago: International Society for General Semantics.

Rowe, M. (1974). Wait time and reward as instructional variables, their influence on language, logic and fate control: Part one—Wait time. *Journal of Research on Science Teaching, 11,* 81–94.

Torrance, E. (1966–1984). *Torrance tests of creative thinking.* Bensenville, IL: Scholastic Testing Service.

CHAPTER

9

Cooperative Learning Strategies

> The age of cooperation is approaching. From Alaska to California to Florida to New York, from Australia to Britain to Norway to Israel, teachers and administrators are discovering an untapped resource for accelerating students' achievement: the students themselves. There is now substantial evidence that students working together in small cooperative groups can master material presented by the teacher better than can students working on their own. (Slavin, 1987, p. 7)

MANY REFLECTIVE TEACHERS are reconsidering the traditional practices that emphasized competition over cooperation in the classroom. Teachers are reevaluating the conventional wisdom that individuals should work quietly, in isolation, hiding their findings from each other so that no cheating can occur. Instead, many teachers are experimenting with a variety of strategies that promote student interaction and encourage them to share their skills, knowledge, and understandings.

But experimentation may lead to failure if it is not based on a mature understanding of the principles and methods that successfully promote cooperative learning in the classroom. Sometimes teachers will hear about a new strategy and quickly decide that they like the idea and will use it immediately. Without taking adequate time to gather the necessary information and evaluate it carefully in light of the needs of their own students, they may simply try it out the very next day. This premature adoption of a new teaching method can have disastrous results.

Imagine, for example, that a teacher hears some general ideas about cooperative groups at a conference or reads the first few paragraphs of an article on the strategy. Thinking that it seems to be an intriguing idea, the teacher may hurry back to the classroom, divide the class into several small groups, and tell them to study the Civil War together for a test that will be held next Friday. After a few moments of discussing what they have (or have not) read about the Civil War, the groups are likely to dissolve into chaos or, at best, will evolve into groups who sit near each other and talk to each other as each person studies the text in isolation.

> Cooperation is *not* having students sit side-by-side at the same table to talk with each other as they do their individual assignments.
>   Cooperation is *not* having students do a task with instructions that whoever finishes first are to help the slower students.
>   Cooperation is *not* assigning a report to a group of students wherein one student does all the work and the others put their names on the product, as well. (Johnson & Johnson, 1984, p. 8)

Teachers who wish to become knowledgeable and proficient in the use of cooperative learning in their classrooms must take the time to seek out information from books, journals, conferences, and visits to classrooms where the techniques are being used. This chapter provides a cursory overview of the multifaceted strategy and lists some references for your own follow-up study of the subject.

MODELS OF COOPERATIVE LEARNING
Group Investigation

The strategy or model known as *group investigation* is a good place to begin the search. Dewey (1910, 1916) believed that students can only learn to live in a democratic society if their education provides them with actual experiences of democratic decision making and problem-solving. He envisioned classrooms in which students participate fully in the democratic process by investigating real problems.

Thelen (1960) adapted Dewey's educational philosophy into the *group investigation* model for the study and improvement of social issues and concerns. In this model, a class of students encounters or is presented with a puzzling situation that they are encouraged to discuss freely. It is expected that individual views will differ and that values and assumptions will clash. The teacher's role is to facilitate the discussion without being overdirective and lead the group to make a plan for studying and investigating the issue further. The larger group is divided into smaller study groups with various assignments to gather data and information to present to the larger group. An extended time period is given to the small group investigations. Finally, the small groups report their findings and suggest their ideas or solutions to the entire group. This may lead to a resolution of the problem. If it does not, the investigation continues.

An excellent example of group investigation at the middle school level occurred in Jean Malvaso-Zingaro's sixth-grade classroom (See the following Reflection). The students encountered a real problem in their neighborhood. At school the students voiced strong concerns, and their teacher encouraged the discussion and guided their investigation into the matter. She allowed students to take school time to study the matter and, in effect, built the investigation into her social studies curriculum. Guest speakers were invited, field trips were taken, and the class took an active role in proposing a solution to the City Council and defending it with data they had collected.

Sharan (1984) adapted the group investigation procedures to include opportunities for students to participate in all aspects of planning the investigation. In his model, the teacher proposes a general topic for study and asks students to organize themselves into small, academically and ethnically heterogeneous groups of students to be responsible for subtopics. The students are allowed more choice in what they study and who they study with, but they are led by the teacher to make responsible choices and ensure that the groups are heterogeneous. By sharing in this responsibility, Sharan (1984) believes that students will grow in awareness and tolerance of individual differences.

In Sharan's (1984) model, students also participate in deciding on the methods they will use in the investigation and the types of products that will be produced by the groups. In studying the human body, for example, the class may decide to produce booklets, charts, and diagrams, or entirely different products. Teacher and students negotiate together to decide on methods and products that the groups will use. When the final presentations are made, the teacher asks students to assist in evaluating the contributions made by each group to the class as a whole.

Group investigation is a relatively unstructured form of cooperative learning. The role of the teacher is fairly nondirective, and the goals of the learning situations are almost always social or affective rather than academic. Cognitive learning may take place, but it is a by-product of the investigative process into the social issue. Recently, educational researchers have been adapting the notion of cooperative learning to include more highly structured models that can be used to teach students academic material as well.

Jean Malvaso-Zingaro
Sixth-Grade Teacher, School No. 6, Rochester, New York

Community Action Unit: A Group Investigation

The curriculum must be meaningful to students. They are concerned with immediate, real problems that touch their lives. When the curriculum also includes these issues, students want to learn.

As a recent example, a historic church was going to be torn down in the inner-city neighborhood of our school. This was going to happen because it was deteriorating due to lack of maintenance.

The children in my class were alarmed. They didn't want another vacant lot where drug dealers would sell their drugs, the homeless would congregate, and garbage would be dumped. So they wrote letters voicing their concerns to the City Council. The letters were also published in the local newspaper.

The children invited speakers to come to our class to speak on both sides of the issue. Four representatives of various groups came to our school to share with us their reasons for either demolishing or preserving the church. The class also went on a walking field trip to the church to examine the architecture of the period in which it was built and to assess the extent of the damage. They compared the cost analysis of preserving the church with the estimates of the cost of tearing it down.

We began working with the Rochester Historical Society to have the church declared a landmark. The children brainstormed different ways the church could be used. Finally, the children were asked to speak in front of the City Council. The children prepared well for the event, writing and practicing their speeches. Two hundred people were at the Council meeting that night. The students spoke with pride about their neighborhood and what they foresaw for the church.

At least in part because of the efforts of my sixth-grade class, the City Council elected to preserve the church and declare it a historic landmark.

Jigsaw

Aronson, Blaney, Sikes, and Snapp (1978) propose a model known as *jigsaw* that was developed to foster understanding among students from various racial and ethnic groups. In this model, cooperative groups are made up of students from a variety of ethnic groups. Each student is given a different portion of the total task to foster mutual interdependence. Often each student is also given a different portion of the materials or information needed to complete the task.

For example, if the class is studying the human body, the teacher may form ethnically heterogeneous primary groups of five students to work together. The teacher then assigns each primary group responsibility for doing research on a different system in the body. One group studies the nervous system, another the circulatory system, another the respiratory system, another the digestive system, and another the skeletal system. After the primary groups have had sufficient time to become knowledgeable about the systems they studied, the teacher reassigns students to secondary groups, consisting of one student from each of the primary groups. In the secondary groups, the student who had previously studied the nervous system is considered the expert on that system. For example, the student who had previously been part of the circulatory system research group is now the expert on that system.

In the secondary groups, a typical assignment may be to work together to create a life-sized mural of a human body showing all the systems and major organs of the body. As they work on this mural, students take responsibility for drawing and labeling the parts of the body associated with the systems they had studied in their primary groups. Each student who has studied one system teaches the others in the group what he or she has learned. Because the final exam will cover all of the systems of the body, students are dependent on other members of their group for learning about the systems they did not study. This interdependence motivates students to listen carefully to each other and to offer assistance and encouragement to each other as needed (Stallings & Stipek, 1986, p. 749).

Learning Teams

Robert Slavin (1983, 1987) emphasizes the team concept in several variations of cooperative learning that are designed to accompany the regular academic curriculum of the school. In a model called *student teams achievement division (STAD),* the teacher presents information to the entire class in the form of lectures, discussions, and/or readings. As a follow-up, students are formed into four- or five-member heterogeneous teams to learn the new material or practice the new skills. The teacher then gives individual quizzes and tests to determine how well the material has been learned. Students are not allowed to help each other on the tests themselves, only during the practice sessions. The individual test scores are then combined to produce a team score.

As a variation on this approach, Slavin's (1983, 1987) model called *teams-games-tournaments (TGT),* tests are replaced by tournaments and groups work to prepare one another for the event. In the tournament, individuals from each team compete against others of similar ability, and the results are combined to produce a total team score. This method appeals to teachers who prefer this lively, oral assessment of learning to the written testing used in STAD.

Team-accelerated instruction (TAI) is a third model created by Slavin (1983, 1987). In this approach, cooperative learning is combined with individualized instruction. It was designed especially to teach mathematics to students in grades three through six. TAI students are given placement tests in math, and each student enters a sequential mathematics curriculum made up of many units at the appropriate starting level. Students work individually at their own rates on the math assignments in the sequence. Tutoring teams are heterogeneous, with students at all levels on a single team. Teammates check each other's work using answer sheets and help each other understand their errors and learn new concepts. On completing a unit, the student takes a unit test. Each week the teacher totals the number of units completed by all team members and gives certificates and other rewards to teams for homework, completed units, and extra points for perfect papers.

Because students are responsible for monitoring and assisting each other, the teacher is free to spend class time presenting lessons to small groups of students drawn from the various teams. For example, the teacher may call together all students in the fraction unit, present a lesson, check on their understanding, and then send them back to their teams to work on their assignments (Slavin, 1987, pp. 10–11).

Cooperative integrated reading and composition (CIRC) is designed to enrich conventional methods for teaching reading and writing in the elementary grades. Pairs of students are assigned to encourage and support each other in their reading and writing efforts. In Ginny Bailey's first-grade classroom, these pairs of students are known as *reading buddies.* While the teacher works with a reading group, pairs of students read aloud to each other, summarize stories to each other, and write and edit stories and poems.

THE PURPOSE OF COOPERATIVE LEARNING

Although many variations of cooperative learning have been proposed, Stallings and Stipek (1986) found that most models have a common set of purposes, which, in turn, are founded on certain assumptions and beliefs.

Cooperative learning is designed to encourage students to help and support their peers in a group rather than compete against them. This purpose is based on the assumption that the perceived value of academic achievement is raised when students are all working toward the same goal. Cooperative groups emphasize the notion of pride in one's "team" in much the same way that sports teams do.

Another major purpose of cooperative learning is to boost the achievement of students of all ability levels. The assumption is that when high-achieving students work with low-achieving students, they both benefit. Compared to tracking systems that separate the high achievers from the low achievers, cooperative groups are composed of students at all levels so that the low-achieving students can benefit from the modeling and interaction with their more capable peers. It is also believed that high-achieving students can learn to be more tolerant and understanding of individual differences through this type of experience than if they are separated from low achievers.

Still another point is that cooperative teams are believed to be more motivating for the majority of students because they have a greater opportunity to experience the joy of winning and success. In a competitive environment, it is likely that the same few high-achieving students will win over and over again. But, in a classroom divided into cooperative teams, each with its own high- and low-achieving students, the opportunity to succeed is more evenly distributed. To this end, the reward systems do not honor individuals, but are contingent on a group effort. As in a sports team, individual performances are encouraged because they benefit the whole team.

Selecting and Adapting Models

After researching the various models of cooperative learning that are being written about and discussed, reflective teachers must consider which model fits the goals they have established for each learning experience. Some models are most appropriate when the goal is to develop cooperation and communication skills; other models are more appropriate when the major goal is to motivate students to learn cognitive material accurately and efficiently. In many cases, reflective teachers adapt and change the models they read about to fit the unique needs of their own classes.

In *Circles of Learning,* Johnson and Johnson (1984) describe in detail how cooperative learning can be implemented in a classroom, but they do not prescribe a certain set of guidelines or steps for teachers to follow. They believe that for most teachers, prepackaged programs will not work. Creative teachers may feel too constricted by rigid rules and procedures. Instead, they propose a set of principles that reflective teachers can use as the basis for creating their own models of cooperative learning.

According to Johnson and Johnson (1984), the structure of productive and mutually beneficial cooperative groups contains four basic elements: positive interdependence, face-to-face interaction, individual accountability, and the development of interpersonal skills.

The tasks and goals assigned to the cooperative group must use the skills of all members and require that all members take an active role in completing the job. When this *positive interdependence* occurs, there is a sense that each member of the group is making a valuable contribution toward the common goal. To achieve this, it is necessary for the teacher to assign a singular role to each member, to divide the tasks among members, or to provide each member with some materials and information needed by the group. Through any or a combination of these means, the teacher engineers the group's perception of "all for one and one for all."

Individual members could conceivably complete their tasks quite separately and turn them in together. But to encourage the maximum benefit from the cooperative effort, it is necessary for the teacher to allow class time for students to work *face-to-face* with each other. When this occurs, the groups have an opportunity to increase their communication skills as well as work to achieve other academic goals.

When a well-defined group goal and an incentive are established, cooperative groups tend to resolve differences and follow through to the completion of their tasks. But in addition to the group goal, a system of *individual accountability* must be established. Individuals must each be responsible for demonstrating their own mastery of the subject matter by completing and turning in assignments or by performing well on written or oral quizzes and tests. Without a system of individual accountability, what begins as a group effort can turn into the efforts of a few carrying the rest of the group. High-achieving students may become impatient with slower classmates and want to take over the entire task. Low-achieving students may be fearful of making errors or holding the others back, so they pass off their work to be completed by others.

Whenever students are assigned to work in cooperative groups, they need guidance from the teacher in order to recognize, practice, and enhance their *interpersonal skills.* Effective listening and speaking skills must be employed to work productively together. Students need to learn how to manage conflicts and be assertive. Teachers can help by training students in these skills and designing tasks that encourage their development. When students are initially introduced to working cooperatively, the tasks may be simple so that the groups can be successful. Early experiences will require simple communication and problem-solving skills. But as groups become more experienced and mature, it is possible to increase the complexity of the tasks in such a way that the members continually enhance and develop their communication and problem-solving skills.

HOW COOPERATIVE LEARNING IS USED IN CLASSROOMS

Cooperative groups can be used in almost every part of the curriculum. Various models may be more appropriate for different subjects and grade levels. The uses and adaptations of the cooperative group strategy are limitless, depending only on the classroom teacher's imagination and style.

Some teachers may divide students into long-term cooperative groups: pairs or small groups of students who sit near each other and assist each other in all subject areas. Other teachers may prefer to create cooperative groups for a single purpose only, changing the membership of groups for each new project.

In the following examples at each grade level, a typical classroom task is described as it would be taught using conventional methods. Then it is revised to describe how the subject could be taught using cooperative group strategies.

Kindergarten Applications

A major component of the kindergarten curriculum is learning to recognize letters and the sounds that letters represent. In a conventional classroom, the day may begin with a large group meeting to discuss the day, the weather, and the season. Students may then be encouraged to share important news with each other in a "show and tell" format. The teacher may then teach the group the shape and sound of the letter *B,* and, as a follow-up exercise, ask the students to go to their desks and do phonics worksheets emphasizing this letter.

Because kindergarten classes emphasize socialization as part of their curriculum, it is natural to introduce children to cooperative groups at this early age. The lesson on the letter *B* can easily be adapted to a cooperative venture. When the large group meets in a circle for opening exercises and sharing time, the teacher may initiate a search for things in the room that have the *B* sound. The teacher can then assign students to cooperative groups, taking care to include both readers and nonreaders in each group. In their groups, students are given a stack of old magazines and are asked to work together to find and cut out pictures of objects that begin with *B* and paste them on a large piece of paper. The student with the most advanced skills can then write the name of each object as a label for each picture. Roles that can be assigned to each student in the group include finder, cutter, paster, and labeler. On successive days, these tasks can be reassigned so that all students get an opportunity to perform each task that they are capable of doing.

As a group goal, the task is to find as many objects as possible in a given time. Incorrect items do not count toward the final tally. The group reward may be a minute of free play for each item or a similar number of grapes or crackers for snack time. As a measure of individual accountability, the teacher may meet with each student individually and have each student "read" aloud the names of the objects on the poster.

First-Grade Applications

At the first-grade level, students may be studying a science lesson on nutrition that could be handled in a similar fashion. The conventional method might be to read and discuss the four food groups, followed by an activity in which individual students search for examples of foods that fit each group. To make the task more interesting, the teacher may choose to assign students to cooperative groups and tell them that each group is going to be responsible for starting a new restaurant. Their first task will be to name the restaurant. Then they must work together to plan three menus: one each for breakfast, lunch, and dinner.

Given large sheets of construction paper, the groups will create menus that include all four food groups for each meal. The division of labor can be handled by having three students per group, one responsible for each meal. When the menus are completed, the groups can interact by having students role-play the act of visiting one another's restaurants as customers and choosing a well-balanced meal. Individual accountability can be built in by giving a quiz at a later date. Groups can earn certificates of merit if their group menus are accurate and well prepared and if the individuals in their group meet a minimum criterion on the follow-up quizzes.

In an activity-centered math program or a whole language reading and writing program, pairs of learning partners are vital to the success of the programs. By pairing a high achiever with a low achiever as learning partners, the teacher can ensure that students are actively learning each new concept and will get the scaffolding necessary to understand difficult new concepts. For example, in teaching addition without learning partners, the teacher usually models the operation on the chalkboard and asks students to duplicate the process at their desks. As learning partners, students work on their problems and then check each other's work. If there is a difference between the two answers, they redo their work until they both have the correct answer.

Tim Curbo, who teaches first grade at Hawthorne School in San Francisco, California, describes in the following Reflection how he uses cooperative groups to encourage students to develop their language skills, problem-solving skills, and cooperation skills simultaneously.

Second-Grade Applications

The second-grade curriculum emphasizes the concept of community. Reflective teachers recognize that in order to truly understand the concept of community, students need to live it. Using a jigsaw approach, small groups can each study one element of a community and report their findings to the class. Using a group investigation approach, students may discover a controversy in their own community that they wish to study and then take a stand on the issue.

As an example of a cooperative learning unit on communities, the teacher may choose to begin with the local community or neighborhood if the school is located in a large city. Beginning with a walking or bus tour of the commercial area, the entire group discusses the various elements that are needed for a successful community. If possible, some teachers extend the tour to pass by the houses of each person in the

Tim Curbo

First-Grade Teacher, Hawthorne School, San Francisco, California

Cooperative Groups in First Grade

At Hawthorne School, Monday through Thursday, students move to different classes for language arts. On Friday they stay in their own classroom. I use that day for cooperative group activities.

I divide the class into groups of four. Because I have many bilingual students in my class, I make sure each group has a combination of English-speaking and Spanish-speaking children.

In each group there are four different jobs or roles for children to take. I post the roles on the bulletin board—for example:

Maria—Materials
Jed—Reporter
Carlos—Facilitator
Ana—Writer

The materials person gets all the necessary materials for the task. The facilitator makes sure everyone is participating and solves any problems that arise. The writer keeps a written record of the activity. As I teach first grade, the writer may just draw illustrations, and as I circulate through the room, I record the observations of the other members of the groups. The reporter gives a report of what the group accomplished. Children get a different role each time we do cooperative group activities.

Before the first task, we talk about the various responsibilities. I usually choose a simple task initially, such as a puzzle. All the students work together to solve the puzzle. Then the writer may draw the finished puzzle, and the reporter describes the process the group used to solve the puzzle.

One of the first tasks of the group is to select a name. This is then posted on the board. The writer's report is posted next to the group's name. Other products can also be posted in this space.

From the beginning, I turn questions and problems that arise back to the group. I encourage the facilitator to take leadership but to involve the others in trying to solve the problems. I tell them, "Four heads are better than one." I keep myself free to circulate, clarifying, extending the activity, and making encouraging remarks.

It's always noisy, and things are bumpy at first. Children aren't sure of their roles. There are personality clashes. We process or talk about all of these issues. Most issues are worked out with time. My students enjoy the spirit of cooperation that develops and the social interaction. Through repeated use of this strategy, it becomes evident that cooperation and problem-solving skills are prominent shared values in our classroom.

---

class. Given a map of the area, cooperative groups can be formed with an initial assignment of depicting on the map the important sites they observed on the tour. Each person in the group can be given the job of locating and recording an equal number of sites on the map.

Later, the same cooperative groups can select one aspect of the community to study, such as the hospital, fire station, police station, city hall, library, churches, or the school itself. With the teacher's help, each group can invite speakers to come to the class to discuss their jobs and responsibilities to the community. Each group can also prepare a short skit (including all the members of the group) that informs the rest of the class about the roles and responsibilities of the community helpers they studied.

After a thorough study of the local community, this unit can be expanded to include a study of very different communities around the world or how one community has changed with time. Again, cooperative groups can each take responsibility for researching one type of community and creating a model of it for others to see. Roles and tasks may have to be assigned to ensure that everyone in the group is included in the project. These roles could include reader, writer, builder, and painter.

Third-Grade Applications

At the third-grade level, students are expected to demonstrate mastery of the basic skills taught during the primary grades. Standardized achievement or criterion-referenced tests may be given to document the gains made by the students as a class and as individuals. For example, many third graders are expected to demonstrate that they can meet the school's criteria for computing the basic addition, subtraction, and multiplication facts. In a traditional classroom, teachers may prepare students for this assessment by providing them with daily worksheets for practicing and memorizing the math facts. In an effort to motivate students to improve their skills, conventional teachers may post charts for all to read that display the names of students who have reached the criteria and those who have not.

Although this type of competitive environment may please and motivate the high achievers, it is not likely to encourage the remainder of the class. To modify the process of learning math facts from a competitive to a cooperative experience, teachers could adapt the STAD model to fit the needs of their classrooms.

Using a STAD approach, the teacher would begin by giving a pretest of 100 math facts to the entire class. By sorting the pretests into high, medium, and low scores, the teacher can divide the class into heterogeneous groups with equivalent ability in math facts. Each group would contain one of the top scorers, one of the lowest scorers, and two in the middle range.

How the teacher sets up the conditions and expectations for this cooperative learning experience is very important. The achievement goal and the behavioral expectations must be clearly explained at the outset. For example, the teacher may state that the groups are expected to practice math facts for a given period of time each day. Worksheets, flash cards, and other materials will be provided, and the teams are free to choose the means they use to practice. The goal, in this instance, is to raise all scores from pretest levels as much as possible. A posttest will be given on a certain day, and each individual will have an improvement score, which is the difference between the correct responses on the posttest and the correct responses on the pretest. The group score will be computed by adding up the individual improvement scores. This method of scoring encourages the group to give extra energy to raise the scores of the lowest scorers because they have the most to gain. Top scorers, in fact, may not gain many points at all, because their pretests may already be near the total. Added incentives for this group may be devised, such as a certain number of points for a perfect paper.

The incentives that will be awarded for success depend a great deal on the class itself. The teacher may choose to offer one reward for the group whose scores improve the most or reward each group, depending on their gains. For example, a single reward for the most improved group may be tangible, such as a certificate of success or temporary possession of a traveling math trophy. Less tangible incentives are also important to third graders, such as the opportunity to be first in line for a week, go to the library together during a math class, or eat lunch with the teacher. To spread the incentives to all groups, the points that each group earns may be translated into an award such as 1 minute of freetime per point, or may be cashed in to "buy" special opportunities and materials.

When it is time for the standardized tests to be given, these groups are likely to take a considerable interest in assisting and supporting their members in doing well on the math portion of the test. Similar groups could operate to improve spelling, vocabulary, the mechanics of writing, or other basic skills. The members of these groups would be different because students would score differently on pretests for various subjects.

Fourth-Grade Applications

While math computation lends itself to a STAD approach, math problem-solving can be enhanced by the extra incentive of working toward participation in a tournament in the TGT model of cooperative learning. Traditional methods of teaching math problem-solving involve individual students doing pages of story problems on paper and having the papers corrected and graded. When students have difficulty with story problems, the teacher must work personally with them to help them understand the processes and operations needed to solve the problems.

Using a team approach, pretests or other measures of past performance in math problem-solving are used to form heterogeneous groups consisting of high, middle, and low achievers. Textbooks, worksheets, and other practice problems can be given to groups of students to prepare them for tournaments to be held once or twice a week. During a tournament, the groups are divided again so that each student is assigned to a table or station to compete individually against students of similar achievement levels from other teams. Problems can be presented orally or in written form during the tournaments. The difficulty of problems can be varied to match the achievement levels of students at each station.

Slavin (1983) recommends that scoring of tournaments be cumulative. The top scorer from each table receives six points, the middle scorer four points, and the low scorer two points. Team scores are then calculated by simply adding the results for the teammates. These scores are added to the team's tallies from previous sessions. Team standings are then publicized in newsletters that go home to parents.

Fifth-Grade Applications

In many classrooms, the conventional approach to teaching science centered on textbook reading, discussion, an occasional demonstration by the teacher, and written tests of understanding. But more recently, science curricula have been revised to include many more hands-on experiments and investigations. The current philosophy is that students need to learn how to *do* science rather than simply learn about it.

Hands-on science is an area of the curriculum that has a natural fit with cooperative group strategies. By participating in cooperative science investigations, students learn how scientists themselves interact to share observations, hypotheses, and methods. Although many teachers value these current science goals, they may be reluctant to try them because they are unsure of how to manage the high level of activity in the classroom when science experiments are happening. Cooperative groups can provide the support and structure that is needed to manage successful science investigation in the classroom.

When a topic or unit approach is taken for teaching science, each unit offers opportunities for cooperative learning. For example, the topic of astronomy may be studied by jigsaw groups, each of which studies one planet, creates models and charts of information about their planet, and reports their findings to others.

Investigations into the properties of simple machines, magnets, electricity, and other topics in physics can be designed by establishing a challenge or a complex goal for groups to meet by a given date. Groups may be given a set of identical materials and told to create a product that has certain characteristics and can perform a specific function. For example, given a supply of toothpicks and glue, groups are challenged to construct a bridge that can hold a pound of weight without breaking. Given a raw egg and an assortment of materials, groups work together to create ways to protect their eggs when they are dropped from a high window onto the pavement below.

Science groups can be mixed and matched frequently during the year, offering students an opportunity to work cooperatively with most other members of their class. In this way, the principles of social science are likely to be reinforced as well. As Johnson and Johnson (1984) recommend, one interpersonal skill can be learned and practiced during each academic group experience. For example, during the astronomy unit, the emphasis could be on learning how to come together as a group quickly, quietly, and efficiently when getting started on the day's project. During the bridge-building unit, the groups could practice encouraging everyone to participate, taking time to ask for opinions and suggestions from every member of the group before making an important decision. After each unit is completed, it is recommended that the groups participate in an evaluation of how they worked together and how well they demonstrated the interpersonal skill emphasized during that unit.

Sixth-Grade Applications

The sixth-grade reading curriculum is designed to introduce students to a variety of literary forms. Using conventional methods of teaching reading, three homogeneous reading groups based on ability may still be used at the sixth-grade level. Each group reads stories, essays, poems, and plays collected in a basal reader geared for their reading ability. Discussions of reading materials are led by the teacher, and seat work is assigned to be done while the teacher works with other groups.

Many upper elementary teachers, however, prefer to use literary materials in their own format rather than as collections in basal readers or anthologies. They believe that students' motivation to read will be increased if they are encouraged to choose and read whole books, novels, poetry collections, and plays. A variety of paperback books in sets of six to eight books apiece are needed to carry out this type of reading program.

At Our Lady of Mercy School in Chicago, Illinois, sixth-grade teacher Roxanne Farwick-Owens has developed a system that allows choice, maximizes cooperative efforts, and holds individuals accountable. She has woven elements of the CIRC, jigsaw, TGT, and Sharan's group investigation models into her own unique system of cooperative learning.

To maximize student motivation and enjoyment of reading, Roxanne believes that students must be allowed to choose their reading materials. Each month she provides three or four reading selections, in the form of paperback books, to the class. Students are allowed to choose the book they want to read, and groups are formed according to interest rather than ability level. Roxanne may advise students about their selections and try to steer them toward appropriate selections, but in the end, she believes that they have the right to choose for themselves what they will read, especially because she has provided only books that have inherent value for sixth graders.

During initial group meetings, students decide for themselves how much to read at a time. They assign themselves due dates for each chapter. Periodically, each group meets with Roxanne to discuss what they are reading, but most discussions are held without her leadership. Usually, the groups are held responsible for generating their own discussion on the book. To prepare for this discussion, all members are expected to prepare questions as they read. For example, each person in the group may be expected to contribute three "why" questions and two detail questions per session. Roxanne reviews the questions each day as a means of holding each individual accountable for reading the material and contributing to the group.

Another task is to plan a presentation about the books using art, music, drama, and other media to share with the rest of the class at the end of the month. In this way, books read by one group are introduced to other members of the class, who are then likely to choose them at a later date. One group made wooden puppets and a puppet stage to portray an event from Mark Twain's *Tom Sawyer.* To advertise Judy Blume's *Superfudge,* a group created a radio commercial complete with sound effects and background music. Familiar television interview shows are sometimes used as a format, as are music videos.

About once per quarter, two teams are formed to compete in a game show-type tournament. Questions about the books are separated into categories such as characters, plot, setting, authors, and miscellaneous. Each person is responsible for writing five questions and answers on index cards to prepare for the tournament. One student acts as emcee, while another keeps track of the points. The team with the most points wins the tournament.

Roxanne finds that this cooperative group structure increases her students' social skills, especially their ability to work with others and to find effective ways to handle disagreements. But the primary reason for the program is to help her students learn to see that reading can be enjoyable and that instead of being a solitary pursuit, reading can have a social aspect. It is Roxanne's belief that many of her students may become lifelong readers from this 1-year experience.

Middle School Applications

In many states, at the middle school or junior high level, students are expected to pass a test on the U.S. Constitution before they graduate to high school. In most classrooms, the study of the Constitution and memorization of key items is seen as an individual responsibility, but it can easily become a very productive cooperative group experience. Study groups can be formed that are similar to the study groups used by law students. The goal is to have everyone in the study group pass the exam and score as well as possible.

Study groups can participate in selecting incentives to work to achieve. Weekly incentives can be used to encourage members to learn enough to do well on the quizzes or tournaments. A whole class incentive can be planned, with the goal that every member of the class passes the test on the first or second try. When middle school students are invited to participate in the planning of their own learning, they are likely to show interest, energy, and responsibility in handling the task.

Laurie Mednick, of Kellogg School in Chula Vista, California, uses permanent cooperative groups in her middle school classroom. Students are assigned to a "tribe" at the beginning of the year. Tribes consist of four or five members who are expected to work on all their assignments together, supporting and teaching one another as needed. Tribes create their own names and rules for working together and assign duties to each member. As a result, Laurie's students take their work very seriously and show pride in their group's accomplishments. They have learned to solve problems without relying on adult intervention.

High School Applications

Students in cooperative groups in high school classes are generally given a great deal of responsibility for their own learning. They are asked to do their own research, solve their own problems, and support one another as they plan and carry out learning investigations.

In her global studies course that is required for freshmen at Crystal Lake South High School, Mary O'Donnell planned a jigsaw cooperative learning experience on traditional Chinese culture and civilization. After reading assigned material about the class distinctions in China, students were divided into seven small groups. Each group represented one social class and was assigned the responsibility of finding out what that social class in China experienced. One group became the peasants, and others became the merchants, government officials, scholars, gentry, scientists, and soldiers. In their small groups, the students reread the assigned material and then discussed what it meant to be a member of their assigned social class and what the life-style was like in traditional Chinese society.

Using the jigsaw approach, one student from each social class group was then reassigned to form secondary cooperative groups. Each secondary group consisted of one member from each original social class assignment. In these secondary groups, each student became the expert on their social class and assumed responsibility for teaching what they had learned to the others. They did this by role-playing the social class they had studied in their first group and introducing themselves to each other. Together, the secondary groups created skits to demonstrate the various roles and responsibilities of each social class.

In her U.S. history course, Mary used a different form of cooperative learning to encourage students to explore the concept of imperialism. She divided students into groups of three students and asked them to decide whether or not they supported the concept of U.S. imperialism. She assigned one student the role of reader. This student had the responsibility of reading and reporting on the information from their textbook. Another was a notechecker, who reviewed notes taken from previous class lectures and discussions. The third member was the recorder, who prepared the new notes and plans for this group assignment.

After studying and discussing the concept of imperialism in their groups, the students decided whether the United States should act as an imperialistic power. To support their opinions, they selected and described three historical events that supported their points of view. Each group presented their arguments and then defended their views from classmates' questions.

Science teachers typically use cooperative groups to encourage investigation and experimentation and to allow students to create their own hypotheses and test them together. Math teachers at the high school level engage their students in learning experiences that require problem-solving and communication of their findings to others.

CLASSROOM CONDITIONS THAT ENCOURAGE COOPERATION

Cooperative groups are a welcome change of pace for many students. They enjoy the opportunity to interact with their peers for part of the school day. But teachers may be hesitant to try the strategy for fear that the students will play or talk about outside interests rather than work at the task assigned. Cooperative groups can degenerate to chaotic groups if certain conditions are not met.

When the goals of the task are poorly understood by the group, the results may be unproductive and frustrating. To prevent this, it is important that the teacher clearly state the goals and expectations of each group task and provide a copy of them in writing so that the group can refer to them from time to time.

In addition to being clear, the goal or task must have some inherent value, and be perceived by the group to be worth their time and effort. When students care about the outcome, they are more likely to take each other seriously and ask each other for help in achieving the goal (Slavin, 1987).

In order to encourage high-quality effort and achievement, incentives must be perceived as meaningful and valuable by the groups. The incentives may be extrinsic, in the form of a certificate, points, grades, a pizza party, or an extra-long recess. In some cases, there may be intrinsic incentives as well, such as enhanced group pride or the good feeling that comes from having contributed to the well-being of other human beings. Each teacher and each school community has different needs and values that must be taken into account as incentives are planned and communicated to the students.

Johnson and Johnson (1984) provide the following suggestions to implement successful cooperative groups. The size of the group may vary from task to task. Generally, groups consist of two to six students, with smaller groups in the primary grades and larger groups in the upper grades. Pairs are excellent for monitoring and checking tasks. Groups of three to six are used for study teams and investigations. The shorter the period of time available, the smaller the groups should be. Small groups can be more efficient because they take less time to get organized, they operate more quickly, and there is more "air time" per member.

Assigning students to cooperative groups can be the most difficult part of the process for teachers. The philosophy of heterogeneous grouping is excellent in theory, but is difficult to achieve in a classroom where no two students are alike. There are likely to be one or two superstars in a classroom whose ability cannot be matched in some subject areas. Similarly, one or two students may have very unusual learning difficulties or behavior problems. For most types of learning situations, the teacher must simply make the best judgment about the combinations that are approximately equivalent in ability.

It is advised to put non-task-oriented students into groups with highly task-oriented teammates so that the peer pressure will work to keep them on task. This theory, however, does not always work out in the classroom. Angry or highly restless students may refuse to participate or otherwise prevent their team from succeeding. When this happens, it is believed that the group itself should be encouraged to deal with the problem as a means of learning how to cope with and resolve such occurrences in real life.

In arranging the room during cooperative group activities, it is important that each group have comfortable space together and that members be able to face one another and have eye contact with every other member of the group. Separating the groups from one another is also necessary so that they can each work undisturbed by the conversations and activities taking place in other groups.

Materials that are intended for cooperative groups may differ from those used in conventional teaching and learning situations. It is suggested that only one set of materials explaining the task and the expectations be distributed. This causes students in the group to work together from the very beginning. In some cases, each member of the group may receive different information from other members. This promotes interdependence, as each member has something important to share with the others.

Interdependence can also be encouraged by the assignment of "complementary and interconnected roles" to group members. These roles will vary with the type of learning and task, but might include discussion leader, recorder of ideas, runner for information, researcher, encourager, and observer.

Tasks that result in the creation of products, rather than participation in a test or tournament, are more likely to succeed if the group is limited to the production of one product. If more than one product is allowed, students may simply work independently on their own products. It is also suggested that members of the group be asked to sign a statement saying that they participated fully in the development of the group's product.

To ensure individual accountability, students must know that they will all be held responsible for learning and presenting what they learned. During the final presentations, the teacher may ask any member of the group to answer a question, describe an aspect of the group's final product, or present a rationale for a decision of the group.

THE EFFECTS OF COOPERATIVE LEARNING

To compare the academic achievement of students using the cooperative learning methods with other more conventional approaches, Slavin (1987) compared pre- and posttest scores for students in math, writing, reading, social studies, science, and language arts. "Of 38 studies of at least four weeks' duration comparing cooperative methods of this type to traditional control methods, 33 found significantly greater achievement for the cooperatively taught classes" (Slavin, 1987, p. 10). In addition, positive effects were found on higher-order objectives as well as on the basic skills. But perhaps the most striking effects of cooperative learning are affective rather than cognitive.

In a school setting, students learn in classes made up of their agemates, for the most part. With conventional teaching methods, the relationships among peers in a class are likely to become somewhat competitive because most students are aware of how well they are doing in relation to their classmates. Grading systems reinforce the competitive nature of school, as do standardized tests and entrance exams.

It is recognized that individual competition can enhance the motivation for high-achieving students who perceive that they have a possibility of winning or being the best. However, the public nature of competitive rewards and incentives leads to embarrassment and anxiety for students who fail to succeed. When the anxiety and embarrassment are intense, students who recognize that they are not likely to win no matter how hard they work eventually drop out of the competition in one way or another.

Even when the anxiety over competition is less intense and under control by students with average or high-average achievement, they may become preoccupied with grades to the extent that they avoid complex or challenging tasks that will risk their academic standing and grades (Doyle, 1983).

Despite these negative effects of competition, it is difficult to imagine a classroom without some type of competitive spirit or reward system, and despite its obvious flaws, competition does create an energetic response from many students. Slavin's (1984) models of cooperative group structures are designed to maintain the positive value of competition by adapting it in the form of team competition so that each student is equally capable of winning.

Team competition, then, has motivational advantages for low- and middle-achieving students that individual competition does not. Still, any competitive situation has winners and losers, and Johnson and Johnson (1984) caution that losing team members may blame one another and hold as scapegoats individual members of their team whom they believe to be responsible for the team's loss.

Reflective teachers who undertake some form of cooperative learning will need to be aware of all possible effects and observe for both positive and negative interactions among teammates. When using competitive teams, teachers should take steps to ensure that every team has an equal chance to win and that attention is focused more on the learning task than on who wins and loses. When anger or conflict arises within groups, teachers must be ready to mediate and assist students as they learn the interpersonal and communication skills necessary to learn from their team losses.

Johnson and Johnson (1984) report that when cooperative groups are well planned and managed, they "promote considerable more liking among students" than do competitive and individualistic structures. "This is true regardless of differences in ability level, sex, handicapping conditions, ethnic membership, social class differences, or task orientation. Students who collaborate on their studies develop considerable commitment and caring for each other no matter what their intitial impressions of and attitudes toward each other were" (p. 18).

Slavin (1984) and Sharan (1984) also report that cooperative groups may actually improve race relations within a classroom. When students participate in multiracial teams, studies show that they choose each other for friends more often than do students in control groups. Researchers attribute this effect to the fact that working together in a group as a part of a team causes students to promote more differentiated, dynamic, and realistic views (and therefore less stereotyped and static views) of other students (including handicapped peers and students from different ethnic groups) than do competitive and individualistic learning experiences (Johnson & Johnson, 1984).

Slavin (1984) also reports that cooperative groups have a positive influence on the successful mainstreaming of handicapped students into the regular classroom. Research on the use of cooperative groups to facilitate mainstreaming and meet the needs of remedial readers has found positive effects on both the achievement and the social acceptance of these learners. This is believed to occur because students generalize the concept of helping one another learn from the team efforts in cooperative groups to become a fundamental principle of classroom organization.

Cooperative learning experiences have also been shown to promote higher levels of self-esteem. Johnson and Johnson (1984) attribute this effect to a relationship between cooperative relationships with peers and basic, unconditional self-acceptance. In contrast, they found that competitiveness promotes conditional self-acceptance and that highly individualistic attitudes tended to be related to self-rejection.

Cooperative learning experiences also have been shown to affect student relationships with adults in the school. "Students participating in cooperative learning experiences, compared with students participating in competitive and individualistic learning experiences, like the teacher better and perceive the teacher as being more supportive and accepting academically and personally" (Johnson & Johnson, 1984, pp. 21–22).

Slavin (1987) also believes that the effects of cooperative groups can lead to the concept of a cooperative school, in which it becomes the norm for students to help each other and for teachers to coach and support one another as well. Administrators, parents, teachers, and students could work together to develop a community sense that "every student's learning is everyone's responsibility, that every student's success is everyone's success" (p. 12).

OPPORTUNITIES FOR REFLECTION

▼ Reflective Essay: Cooperative Group Experiences

Do you believe in using competition or cooperation to motivate your students to learn? In your own experience with cooperative groups, do you find them to be enjoyable and stimulating or frustrating and discouraging? What type of role do you usually take in a cooperative group? Do you get impatient with others in your group and wish you could work on the assignment by yourself? What could be done to improve the structure of the groups you have participated in? Are you likely to use cooperative groups in your classroom? Why or why not?

▼ Classroom Visit: Cooperation Versus Competition

In the classroom you are visiting, is competition or cooperation more highly valued? Give examples of classroom events or incentive structures to support your observation. How would you alter this balance to create more cooperation? Give an example of a recent classroom event that you observed and tell how you would change it.

REFERENCES

ARONSON, E., BLANEY, S., SIKES, J., & SNAPP, M. (1978). *The jigsaw classroom.* Beverly Hills: Sage.

DEWEY, J. (1910). *How we think.* Boston: Heath.

DEWEY, J. (1916). *Democracy and education.* New York: Macmillan.

DOYLE, W. (1983). Academic work. *Review of Educational Research, 53,* 159–199.

JAMES, W. (1890). *Principles of psychology.* New York: Holt.

JOHNSON, D., & JOHNSON, R. (1984). *Circles of learning.* Alexandria, VA: Association of Supervision and Curriculum Development.

SHARAN, S. (1984). *Cooperative learning in the classroom: Research in desegregated schools.* Hillsdale, NJ: Erlbaum.

SLAVIN, R. (1983). *Cooperative learning.* New York: Longman.

SLAVIN, R. (1984). Students motivating students to excel: Incentives, cooperative tasks and student achievement. *The Elementary School Journal, 85,* 53–62.

SLAVIN, R. (1987). Cooperative learning and the cooperative school. *Educational Leadership 45,*(3), 7–13.

STALLINGS, J., & STIPEK, D. (1986). Research on early childhood and elementary school teaching programs. In M. Wittrock (Ed.), *Handbook of research on teaching* (3rd ed.) (pp. 727–753). New York: Macmillan.

THELEN, H. (1960). *Education and the human quest.* New York: Harper & Row.

10

Developing a Repertoire of Teaching Strategies

SCHOOL EXPERIENCES can be enjoyable for both teachers and students. One way of heightening the enjoyment is by using a variety of teaching strategies and activities. When learning experiences are varied, students are more likely to become actively engaged in the learning process. Their intrinsic motivation to learn is also likely to be enhanced by the expectation that the skill or knowledge they are learning is presented in a novel and unusual format. To promote the enjoyment of teaching and learning, many reflective teachers are continuously searching for new methods and strategies that they can employ to motivate and engage their students in the learning process.

Developing a repertoire of teaching strategies is also necessary because students' needs and learning styles are diverse. For this reason, teachers must be ready to modify lesson plans and prepared to present information in more than one way.

The purpose of this chapter is to introduce you to a repertoire of strategies from which you can select when you teach. An overview of strategies as they relate to Bloom's Taxonomy is presented, followed by more detailed descriptions of some teaching models that are appropriate for classrooms. This book can provide only an overview of the descriptions, illustrations, and examples you will need in order to employ these methods successfully. You will need to search for more detailed descriptions of these strategies in books and journal articles, or by observing experienced teachers.

As you read about or select a strategy to try out in a laboratory or classroom, you will find that some of them work for you and others do not. You will need to reflect about what works for you and your students and why. As you think about what works for you, it is quite acceptable for you to combine, adapt, modify, and add your own unique strategies to the ones you read about or observe. Through this process of practice and reflection, you will discover, create, and refine your own unique teaching style.

TEACHING STRATEGIES THAT FIT BLOOM'S TAXONOMY

In this section, brief descriptions of some of the most frequently used teaching strategies are presented to give you an overview of the rich and varied methods that are available. They are organized within the framework of the *Taxonomy of Educational Objectives* (Bloom, Englehart, Furst, Hill, & Krathwohl, 1956) so that you can understand the relationship between planning an objective at a certain level of the Taxonomy and selecting a teaching strategy or method to accomplish that objective in the classroom. As you will see, some strategies, such as class discussion or cooperative groups can be used to achieve objectives at several levels of the Taxonomy, depending on what the class is asked to discuss or what task the group is asked to do.

Teaching Strategies That Develop a Knowledge Base

The most common teaching strategies used to help students learn a knowledge base of facts, information, and skills are reading for information and the method known as *direct instruction,* which was described in chapter 7. Many teachers also employ strategies known as *drill and practice,* which means that students repeat what they have learned in an oral recitation or in written exercises in order to reinforce their understanding of the new facts or skills and commit them to memory.

Drill, practice, lecture, reading, and recitation—are these the only strategies that teachers need to know in order to teach the basic facts and skills students must master in each content area? These were the traditional teaching strategies used in schools until educational psychologists such as Ausubel (1960) showed that meaningful learning consists of linking new bits of knowledge to already known facts and ideas gained from previous learning experiences. Reflective teachers have learned from cognitive psychology that a key to successful learning of a knowledge base is providing rich and *varied learning experiences,* not just relying on drill and practice.

The curriculum emphasizes the learning of basic facts, skills, processes, and concepts in all subject areas. As students experience the complexities of the world they inhabit, they gather many unrelated verbal and numerical symbols, facts, data, concepts, and ideas. When these bits of knowledge are successfully integrated in the brain, they can be stored and recalled on demand. Cognitive psychologists use *schema theory* to explain this process of sensing, storing, and recalling information. Each separate schema is a storehouse of images, sensations, symbols, and words that are somehow related in an individual's mind (Anderson, 1977; Bransford, 1983).

For students to develop a knowledge base on a particular subject, they need to first create a simple, rudimentary, or basic schema on that topic through direct or vicarious experience. For example, consider how students learn about animals. Many children have an experience with a dog or cat before coming to school. They store the sensations (furry, barking, wet nose and tongue, four legs, petting, tail) in a schema often labeled *doggy* or *kitty*. Images of stuffed teddy bears or goats in story books may be included in the student's schema labeled *doggy* for a time, until the child is able to differentiate among these four-legged creatures.

Children need additional experiences in school that will help them to develop richly detailed and accurate schemata on a variety of topics. Several teaching responsibilities are implied by this statement. First, the teacher must choose teaching strategies and plan learning activities that provide students with appropriate experiences so that they gain new bits of knowledge and create new schemata. Second, the teacher must assist students in ordering and classifying the knowledge they have stored so that it is readily accessible.

Teachers can use many teaching strategies to provide students with new experiences, sensations, and ideas. Very young children can gain knowledge through vicarious experiences such as listening to the teacher read aloud and older students can read for themselves. Hands-on activities are also important for schema development in the elementary grades. When children play with balls, rocket ships, measuring cups, dolls, and other objects, they develop increasingly complex schemata for these things. Middle school and high school teachers use books, lectures, films, filmstrips, videotapes, audiotapes, records, and pictures to extend their students' experience and knowledge base. Field trips are especially likely to cause students of all ages to create new schemata. Taking students out of their familiar environments to go to a zoo, museum, a play, or a concert is likely to result in the formation of new schemata.

Teachers assist students in classifying and ordering their existing schemata by planning verbal discussions and explications of what students are seeing and experiencing.

Children may develop a schema for *alphabet* by viewing *Sesame Street* or singing the "ABC song." But teachers must assist their students in making these symbols meaningful by explaining the relationship between a visual symbol and its meaning or use.

Manual tasks such as copying the letters of the alphabet help the child to differentiate among these symbols. Oral exercises make the child aware of the sound each letter represents. Matching pictures of familiar objects with the same sound as the letter help the child connect the symbol-sound-use relationship. With each new experience, the child's schema for *alphabet* becomes increasingly complex, but also much better organized and accurate.

Drill, practice, memorization, and recitation may help students to strengthen existing schemata, but they cannot replace authentic learning experiences for schema creation or development. Reflective teachers are likely to plan active, creative, hands-on lessons to teach knowledge-level objectives.

Teaching Strategies That Promote Comprehension

Is comprehension the same as decoding? "Decoding means cracking a code, and this is exactly the function of decoding processes—they crack the code of print to make print meaningful" (Gagné, 1985, p. 167). Decoding strategies include (1) instructing students to match unknown printed words to their previously learned sight word vocabularies and (2) teaching students to use phonics to sound out unfamiliar words. Although these strategies are useful in the literal comprehension of words, reflective teachers know that students need to be taught to comprehend ideas and concepts, not just single words.

To teach comprehension at the level of ideas, teachers often use a strategy known as an *advance organizer.* Ausubel (1960) demonstrated that teachers can increase student comprehension by introducing unfamiliar material with a statement showing how the new material is related to knowledge the student has already learned. This introduction allows the student to recall related schema prior to reading or hearing the new material. When the unknown ideas are encountered, the student has an existing schema in mind that makes the new idea more meaningful.

For example, when asking students to read a passage about the boundaries between nations, the teacher may describe how fences in a neighborhood are used to protect private property and maintain relationships among neighbors. This description uses language and concepts students understand. It allows the student to call up an existing schema, *fences,* and be ready to construct a new schema called *boundaries.* After the passage is read, the teacher may ask students to tell how boundaries and fences are alike. The strategy of following up the reading with a discussion that includes the advance organizer and the new material strengthens the students' understanding of the new concept.

Teachers may use questions, clues, and suggestions to alert students to look for, listen for, or search for some new, previously unknown element. Madeline Hunter (1976) encourages teachers to use a variety of introductory experiences to motivate students to want to find out more about a subject. This strategy, the use of an *anticipatory set,* creates a positive anticipation on the part of the student. For example, a teacher might preface the reading of a passage on water evaporation by wiping a wet sponge on the blackboard and drying it with a hair dryer. Students would then be asked to read the passage to discover what happened to the water.

Discussion is an important strategy that teachers use for increasing student comprehension of a new subject. As students state their ideas aloud, they are reinforcing their own understanding of the topic. When teachers respond to students' ideas by showing agreement or by giving useful feedback and clarification, the students' understanding is further enhanced. Class members who listen to their classmates' ideas and teacher's responses also may gain new perspectives and greater understanding of the subject.

One of the most frequent methods teachers use to evaluate student comprehension is to ask students to say or write the meaning of something in their own words. In the example of water evaporation, a teacher may conduct a demonstration or allow students to experiment with water properties at various temperatures and then ask students to summarize in writing how water evaporates. When students are able to do this, the teacher knows that the concept has been successfully understood. If the students are unable to state or write a summary of the concept, the teacher knows that the material must be retaught.

In order to reteach, it is necessary to present a subject differently than the first time it was taught. When descriptions and explanations of unfamiliar material do not work, many teachers find that the use of *analogies* helps students to understand a difficult new concept by building a bridge between unknown or abstract concepts and known, concrete experience. The use of the phrase *building a bridge* in the preceding sentence is itself an analogy for the abstraction known as *analogy*.

By describing how a fence is similar to an international boundary, the teacher makes an abstract concept more concrete. In a class discussion or lecture, the teacher may extend this analogy to describe how family loyalty resembles patriotism, how economies of nations are similar to the economies of families, and how the decisions about land use may vary from nation to nation as well as from family to family.

Another teaching strategy that promotes comprehension is to provide graphic examples and illustrations to assist students in interpreting new information. Just as a picture is worth a thousand words, a graph or a chart can summarize a great deal of data in a form that students can comprehend. Bar graphs show temperature comparisons much better than lists of figures do. Pie charts vividly demonstrate the amount of time or money spent on various pursuits better than paragraphs can. Reflective teachers frequently employ visual or graphic aids in their teaching. They also ask their students to create illustrations, graphs, diagrams, and charts to demonstrate that they have interpreted data or new concepts successfully.

Teaching Strategies That Allow Students to Apply What They Learn

A widely accepted principle of learning is that "if a student really comprehends something, then he can apply it" (Bloom et al., 1956, p. 120). These authors noted that the fact that most of what we learn is intended for application to problem situations in real life is indicative of the importance of application objectives in the general curriculum.

Reflective teachers are eager to offer students opportunities to apply what they've learned in most of the subjects in the curriculum. *Discussion,* as a teaching strategy, can be an occasion for application as well as for comprehension. For example, a teacher-led discussion on current events may focus on the way the news item affects the lives of the students in the class. Literary discussions are valuable for the exchange of views on how characters deal with situations and how class members might act under those circumstances.

Many teachers employ *inquiry training, dilemmas, simulations,* and *role playing* to bring the world into the classroom. These strategies are described in greater detail in this volume, but all have in common the presentation of a puzzling situation and the opportunity to discuss alternatives and generate solutions to problems. Their function is to assist students in clarifying what they know and believe about situations that they may well encounter throughout their lives. These strategies allow students to rehearse difficult decisions in the secure environment of their classroom, so that later in life they will be able to make real decisions with more confidence.

Discovery learning is another strategy that can be successfully used by classroom teachers to cause their students to apply not only what they have already learned, but also what they are currently learning, and thereby learning by doing. Instead of telling students a rule, principle, or concept, the teacher sets up conditions in the classroom so that students may discover it on their own. Math teachers frequently use this technique when they ask students to solve several equations and then state the rule or algorithm that is discovered in the process. Science processes frequently require that students discover a principle through experimentation. In both of these cases, students are applying known ideas to unknown situations and generating both solutions and insight in the process. This strategy is described in greater detail later in this chapter.

Another application strategy that reflective teachers employ is *model making,* as when students are asked to build or replicate a model of an Indian village, a simple machine, a heart that pumps simulated blood, or a volcano. Teachers also use *cooperative groups* as a strategy for having students apply communication and problem-solving skills to solve problems or do meaningful work together.

Teaching Strategies That Require Analysis

As students apply what they have learned, they often think inductively about the specific cases they are working on and make generalizations about the ideas they are applying. Analysis calls on students to do the opposite: begin with a generalization and break it down into its constituent parts, separating elements and looking for relationships and organizational principles.

Teaching strategies that stimulate analytical thinking include *discussions* that focus on identification of the elements of an argument: assumptions, hypotheses, facts, opinions, inferences, and conclusions. For example, after reading an article on a controversial topic such as the relationship between drugs and gang membership, the teacher may ask students to separate the facts from the opinions in the article and to identify the author's assumptions and hypotheses.

Expanding on the analysis of separate elements, the teacher may then guide students in recognizing how the elements relate to each other. Discussion may then focus on whether the data presented in the article are consistent with the author's original assumptions and how that affects the conclusions. Hilda Taba's (1967) strategy of *concept formation* is a way of training students to analyze concepts in order to refine their understanding. Classroom examples of Taba's method are provided in this chapter under the heading "Taba's Concept Formation Model."

Analysis of relationships also can focus on comparisons, similarities, differences, and cause and effect. A strategy other than discussion that is appropriate to this level of Bloom's Taxonomy is *independent research* to compare and contrast or show cause and effect. After the research is complete, teachers usually ask that students prepare written or oral reports on their findings. They may require students to prepare charts that classify the elements they've studied or graphs showing relationships. As an example, the teacher may assign students (individually or in cooperative groups) to investigate one of the systems of the human body. Those students researching the skeletal system will have to describe, illustrate, and analyze the bones (elements) and how they fit together (relationships). They may also prepare charts that show the cause-and-effect relationship of good and bad nutrition on bone development.

Analytical thinking has much in common with what is now known as *critical thinking*. The discussion strategies to promote critical thinking that were described in chapter 8 also help students think and communicate with one another in an analytical way.

Teaching Strategies That Encourage Synthesis

Synthesis is another word for creativity; it occurs when students express what they have learned in an original way. According to Bloom et al. (1956), synthesis involves "recombination of parts of previous experience with new material, reconstructed into a new and more or less well-integrated whole" (p. 162). Synthesis requires the creation of a unique communication or product by an individual or a group. Criteria are established by the teacher to make sure that the students' products fit the subject and demonstrate that learning has taken place.

In the classroom, synthesis is usually expressed through *art, music, creative writing, storytelling,* and *drama* activities that are related to the subject being taught. Criteria may specify that these products include a number of facts in the stories or plays, show realistic details in the drawings, or suggest new ways of solving the problems or issues in the subject being taught.

After students study the first Thanksgiving, many teachers allow them to dramatize the event with simple costumes and a real or simulated feast. In a unit on the prairie, a teacher may allow students to create a mural of the prairie along one side of the classroom. Students are allowed to draw and paint their pictures of prairie grasses, animals, and insects on the mural. After reading a story, students may be asked to write a new ending for it or to extend a book by writing a new chapter.

In middle school and high school classrooms, the use of learning experiences emphasizing synthesis is increasing. Science courses emphasize creating hypotheses, designing experiments to test them, and producing charts and graphs to communicate the findings. All of these experiences require a synthesis of what the student has learned previously combined with new and original ideas. Writing programs have increased their emphasis on journal writing, original poetry, and the production of student written dramas. History teachers are likely to involve students in active investigations of social issues, requiring them to use problem-solving skills to create new solutions to old problems.

The primary reason for including synthesis activities and products in the curriculum is because they emphasize and encourage personal expression rather than passive participation and independence of thought and action rather than dependence (Bloom et al., 1956).

Teaching Strategies That Generate Evaluation

The highest level of Bloom's Taxonomy is evaluation because it represents an "end process" in the range of cognitive behaviors in which students are asked to make judgments about some aspect of what they have studied. A key element of evaluation is that the students are expected to use criteria in making their judgments, although these criteria can be determined by the students or given to them by the teacher. It is believed that students can make the most informed judgments after experiencing all of the other levels of the taxonomy (Bloom et al., 1956). For example, a unit on economics may begin with preliminary discussions that encourage the students to give their opinions about how to spend their allowances, but it is expected that their opinions will become better informed and that they will be able to make judgments about money using criteria such as supply and demand at the end of the unit.

Teaching strategies that generate useful and valid evaluations are those that involve students in *discussion, writing, problem-solving*, debate, and any other activities in which students express their own views and opinions on a subject. In the classroom, one of the most frequently used strategies is a class discussion after reading a story or chapter in a book. Students are asked to say whether they agree or disagree with the character or the issue and to state why. Middle school and high school students take sides on issues and prepare arguments for a class debate. This may require a long-term research project to gather data and information prior to the debate. Debates such as these are likely to be connected with the science or social studies curricula.

Group problem-solving endeavors on controversial issues may cause students to clarify and articulate their attitudes and opinions about how to solve a problem. Simulations may be used to illustrate the complex nature of real-life problems. For example, students may be given roles to play in a simulation of where to locate a new city dump. They must use criteria to persuade the group to locate the dump somewhere other than their own backyards.

It is not easy for teachers to evaluate their students' evaluation activities. As free expression of opinions and judgments is expected, perhaps the only fair way to assess student products is to determine the extent to which the students use evidence and criteria to support their judgments.

ADDITIONAL TEACHING STRATEGIES

The following strategies are offered as alternatives for you to consider as you develop your own repertoire. These strategies cover a range of philosophies and styles. Not all of them will appeal to you, but many of them can be employed to provide variety and spice to your classroom curriculum. As you read these brief descriptions, keep in mind that it is necessary to look for more detailed sources of information to truly understand the model and how it can be used.

Taba's Concept Formation Model

Hilda Taba (1967) created a model of teaching social studies to students that emphasizes the formation of concepts, interpretation of data, and application of principles to explain new phenomena. The purpose of the model is teach students how to process information with accuracy and efficiency. Each concept is stored in the brain in the form of a schema. As individuals experience and learn more about the world, they add to and reconstruct their schemata. Taba believed that teachers can assist students in the development of their thought processes.

The teacher's role in this strategy is to direct students' observations and thinking about a new concept by asking questions that cause students to see relationships, identify categories, and make inferences about their experience. For example, a teacher may wish to help students differentiate their concept of animals into more specific categories, including those of domestic and wild animals.

The first strategy, known as *concept formation,* begins by listing or showing pictures of many types of animals and asking students to identify categories of animals with similarities. As an illustration, the list might include such animals as the eagle, tiger, horse, robin, rattlesnake, dog, bear, zebra, and cat. Students may identify categories based on color, number of legs, size, or habitat. When a category is identified, the teacher assists students in giving it an appropriate label, such as "birds," "four-legged animals," or "brown animals."

The second strategy, known as *interpretation of data,* includes the thinking processes of interpreting, inferring, and generalizing. To help students to form the two unfamiliar concepts of domestic and wild animals, the teacher reviews the list or pictures of the animals and directs their observations toward seeing the relationships and patterns associated with the new concepts by asking students questions such as these:

> What did you notice about the places where the animals lived?
> What did you see about how they got their food?
> Why do some animals find their own food and others get fed?
> What did you notice about their relationships with people?
> What does this mean about how they prefer to live?
> Which animals prefer to live in the wild?
> Which animals prefer to live near human beings?
> Which animals would you put in a category called *wild animals?*
> Which would you put in a category called *domestic animals?*
> What do you think *domestic* means?
> What do you think *wild* means?

The third task involved in Taba's strategy is called *application of principles.* It involves helping students make hypotheses and predictions involving the concepts they have just learned. In our example, the teacher may ask students to consider what would happen if a tiger were kept as a pet or if a pet cat were lost in a jungle. To verify their hypotheses, students may be asked to carry out research or otherwise investigate the predictions they have made. In our present example, this could lead to a visit to a zoo or an interview with a zookeeper to find out what habitat wild animals need to live.

Taba's model teaches students to think inductively, to collect information and make observations, to identify relationships, and to develop relatively sophisticated classifications and categories. It also helps them to develop a verbal vocabulary of accurate labels and improves their ability to speak about complex and abstract concepts.

Some teachers may set out to use Taba's strategy to improve students' thinking skills, and simply create a list of items and categories as a means of teaching thinking. More often the strategy is used within a content area to develop concepts and thinking about the topic itself. It can also be used as a means of developing affective concepts such as justice, fairness, and tolerance. A more complete description of this model is included in Taba's (1967) *Teacher's Handbook for Elementary Social Studies*.

Discovery Learning

In the 1960s and 1970s, a phenomenon known as the *open classroom* bloomed, mushroomed, and then faded into obscurity. The underlying philosophy of the open classroom was that students would become more active and responsible for their own learning in an environment that allowed them to make choices and encouraged them to take initiative. To this end, the rows of desks in many classrooms were rearranged to provide more space for activity and learning centers. The curriculum of the open classroom was revised to allow students to choose from among many alternatives and schedule their own time to learn what they wanted to learn when they wanted to learn it (Silberman, 1973).

One of the teaching strategies that was emphasized in the open classroom was known as *discovery learning*. The principle of discovery learning is that students learn best by doing rather than by hearing or reading about a concept. Teachers may still find this strategy to be an excellent addition to their repertoire. It can be used occasionally to provide real, rather than vicarious, experience in a classroom.

In employing discovery learning, the teacher's role is to gather and provide equipment and materials related to a concept that the teacher wants the students to learn. Sufficient materials should be available so that every student or pairs of students have immediate access to them. Materials that are unfamiliar, interesting, and stimulating are especially important to a successful discovery learning experience. After providing the materials, the teacher may ask a question or offer a challenge that causes students to discover the properties of the materials. Then, as the students begin to work, or *mess about*, with the materials, the teacher's role is to monitor and observe as the students discover the properties and relationships inherent in the materials, asking occasional questions or making suggestions that will guide the students in seeing the relationships and understanding the concepts. The period of messing about and discovery is then followed by a discussion in which students verbalize what they have observed and learned from the experience (Hawkins, 1965).

Jim Hicks and Chris Chiaverina emphasized discovery in the science unit described in chapter 5. In each new unit, they provide a smorgasbord of interactive experiences related to the concept being taught as a means of allowing students to discover the important relationships and see for themselves how scientific principles are derived.

A simple example at the primary level is the use of discovery learning to teach the concept of colors and their relationships to one another. Rather than telling students that blue and yellow make green or demonstrating that they do while students watch, the strategy of discovery learning is to provide every student with a brush and two small puddles of blue and yellow paint on white paper and allow them to discover it for themselves. In this case, the opening question may simply be, "What happens when you mix blue and yellow together?" When this relationship becomes apparent and is verbalized by the students, the teacher can then provide additional puddles of red and white paint and challenge students to "create as many different colors as you can." Experiences can be easily designed to allow students to discover how and why some things float, what makes a light bulb light, how electricity travels in circuits, and the difference between solutions and mixtures.

Math relationships also can be discovered. Beans, buttons, coins, dice, straws, and toothpicks can be sorted according to size, shape, color, and other attributes. Objects can be weighed, measured, and compared with one another. The concept of multiplication can be discovered when students make sets of objects in rows and columns. Many resources in the form of math curriculum projects involving discovery learning are presently being developed for schools because discovery is a part of the problem-solving process, a current hot topic in education.

Role Playing

When problems or issues involving human relationships are part of the curriculum, teachers may choose to use role playing to help students explore and understand the whole range of human feelings that surround any issue. This strategy is frequently used to resolve personal problems or dilemmas, but it can also be employed to gain understanding about the feelings and values of groups outside of the classroom.

For example, in order to help students understand the depth of emotions experienced by immigrants coming to a new and unfamiliar country, the teacher may ask students to role-play the interactions between family members who are separated or the dilemmas experienced by the Vietnamese boat people or others who want to emigrate to the United States but are stopped by immigration quotas.

There are two major phases to successful and meaningful role playing: the role playing itself and the subsequent discussion and evaluation period. In the first phase, the teacher's responsibility is to give students an overview of both phases of role playing, so that they know what to expect. The teacher then introduces and describes a problem or dilemma, identifies the roles to be taken, assigns the roles, and begins the action by setting the stage and describing the immediate problem that the actors must confront. Roles must be assigned carefully. Usually teachers select students who are involved in the problem to play the role. In an academic dilemma, the roles may be assigned to students who most need to expand their experience with and understanding of the issue. Those students that are not assigned roles are expected to be careful observers.

To set up the role-playing situation, the teacher can arrange some chairs to suggest the setting of the event to be played out. During the role play itself, the actors are expected to get inside the problem and "live" it spontaneously, responding realistically to one another. The role play may not flow smoothly; actors may experience uncertainty and be at a loss for words, just as they would in real life. The first time a role is played, the problem may not be solved at all. The action may simply establish the problem, which in later enactments can be probed and resolved.

To increase the effect of role playing, Leyser (1982) suggests that after a scene is played out once, the actors may exchange roles and play out the same scene so that they grow to understand the other's point of view. Actors may be allowed to select consultants to discuss and improve the roles they are playing.

In the second phase, the observers discuss the actions and words taken by the initial role players. The teacher helps the observers review what they have seen and heard, discuss the main events, and predict the consequences of actions taken by the role players. Following the initial discussion, it is likely that the teacher will decide to have new class members replay the role to show an alternative way of handling the problem. The situation can be replayed a number of times if necessary. When a role-played situation generates a useful solution or suggests an effective way of handling a problem, the situation can be adapted and subsequent role plays can focus on communication skills that will enhance or improve the situation even further.

Role playing has many applications in both the cognitive and the affective goals of the curriculum. Through role playing, students can experience history by researching the life of a public figure and taking the role in an historical interaction. Each student in the class, for example, can study the life of a U.S. president and be the president for a day. Frequently, teachers ask students to play the role of characters in books that they have read as a means of reporting their own reading and stimulating others in the class to read the book. Students can enact the feelings of slaves and slave traders, the roles of scientists as they are "doing" science, or the interaction between an author and editor as they try to perfect a piece of writing.

Students can learn new behaviors and social skills that may help them win greater peer acceptance and enhance their own self-esteem. Interpersonal conflicts that arise in the classroom can be role played as a means of helping students discover more productive and responsible ways of behaving. For example, when two students argue about taking turns with a toy in the kindergarten class, the teacher can ask the students to role play the situation in an effort to learn new ways of speaking to each other, asserting their own desires, and creating a plan for sharing the scarce resource. In a classroom, the teacher may notice that one student is isolated and treated like a scapegoat by others in the class. The dilemma can be role played with the role of the isolated student assigned to be played by some of the students who have been most critical and aggressive to the student. Through this active, vicarious experience, it is possible that the students will learn to be more tolerant and accepting of each other.

Simulation

Student drivers drive simulated vehicles before they learn to drive a real car on the highway. Airplane simulators provide a realistic but safe way for student pilots to practice flying in which mistakes lead to realistic consequences, but no lives are threatened. In many high school courses on marriage and the family, young people are offered the opportunity to simulate marriage and caring for a newborn in the form of a raw egg that they must protect and nurture for several weeks. It is believed that their experiences with the egg may lead them to carefully consider their own life choices.

Simulations usually involve some type of role playing but also includes other gamelike features, such as a set of rules, time limits, tokens, or other objects that are gained or lost through the action of the simulation, and a way of recording the results of the players' decisions and actions. Simulations almost always focus on dilemmas in which the players must make choices, take actions, and then experience feedback in the form of consequences of their actions. The purpose of simulations is primarily to allow young people to experience tough, real-life problems and learn from the consequences in the safe, controlled environment of the classroom.

Many valuable academic and social simulations can be used to enrich the classroom experience and cause students to understand the relationship among their choices, actions, and the consequences. Simulation games can be purchased or created by the teacher. A company named *Interact* publishes elementary, middle school, and secondary catalogs of simulations in all areas of the curriculum that can be purchased for a relatively small price (see the last section of this chapter for the address of this company). These kits include teacher's manuals describing the rules, time limits, and procedures to follow, and a set of student materials that may include fact sheets, game pieces, and record-keeping devices. Titles of some of the simulations they publish include "Zoo," "Dinosaur," "King Lexicon," "Shopping Spree," and "Classroom City."

The role of the teacher during a simulation is to explain the conditions, concepts to be covered, and the expectations at the outset of the event. A practice session may be held to further familiarize participants with the rules and procedures that govern the simulation. After assigning roles or creating groups that will interact, the teacher moderates, keeps time, clarifies misconceptions, and provides feedback and consequences in response to the actions of the participants. At the conclusion of the simulation, the teacher leads a discussion of what occurred and what was learned by asking students to summarize events and problems and to share their perceptions and insights with one another. At the end of the discussion, it is appropriate for the teacher to compare the simulation with its real-life counterpart and ask students to think critically about what they would do in real life as a result of having taken part in the simulation.

An example of a simulation in economics involves the creation of small companies or stores in which students decide on a product, create the product, set up the store, price and sell the products, and keep records on the transactions. The purpose, of course, is to learn about the principles of supply and demand, as well as the practical skills of exchanging money and making change. Along with the primary goals of the simulation, there are secondary learning experiences. Students are also likely to increase their capacity for critical thinking and to learn about their own actions and decisions regarding competition, cooperation, commitment to a goal, and communication.

Students may simulate the writing of the U.S. Constitution by writing a classroom constitution. After studying various countries of the world, sixth-grade students may take part in a mock United Nations simulation in which students are delegates and face daily world problems presented to them by the teacher.

In language arts, students may establish a class newspaper in order to learn how news is gathered and printed in the real world. They may even establish a number of competitive newspapers to add another dimension of reality to the simulation. Students may simulate the writing, editing, and publishing processes as they write, print, and distribute their own original books.

An excellent example of a classroom simulation that provoked students to think critically and change their views on an important human issue is described in *A Class Divided* (1984) by William Peters. Jane Elliott, a third-grade teacher in Riceland, Iowa, taught her students to think critically about racial prejudice by randomly dividing the class into two groups: those with brown eyes and those with blue eyes. She actively discriminated against the students with blue eyes for a full school day. Mimicking behaviors of people who exhibit racial prejudice, she called the blue-eyed students names, did not let them play on the swings, and criticized their work and behavior. She successfully influenced the brown-eyed students to follow her lead and convinced them to avoid social contact with their inferior blue-eyed classmates.

The next day, Jane reversed the process and discriminated against the brown-eyed students in much the same way. Blue-eyed students were now considered superior to brown-eyed students in her eyes and their own. At the conclusion of the second day, Jane led a discussion of the effects of the entire learning experience. Twenty years later, at their high school reunion, her students reported that their understanding of prejudice and their attitudes toward people of different races were radically restructured as a result of this classroom experience.

Before the experience they had not been critical thinkers about racial prejudice. They easily accepted the prevailing notion that some people are superior to others. Afterward, they had grown in empathy, had recognized points of view different from their own, and had become more self-directed or independent in their thinking than they were before the experience.

Simulations may be used to introduce a unit or as the culminating activity of a unit. They may take a few minutes or the entire year. They may be continued from week to week but played for only a specified amount of time during each session. Some may take a full day or longer. Simulations are powerful learning experiences that may change the way students view themselves and the world, as it did for the participants in the blue eyes, brown eyes experience.

Mastery Learning

Teaching strategies known as *mastery learning* derive from the philosophy that all students can learn if the task fits their aptitude and they are given sufficient time to master the new skill or concept. The theoretical model for mastery learning was inspired by Carroll's (1963) observation that students with low aptitude for a particular subject could still learn that subject, but that it would take them more time to do so. He proposed that students have different *learning rates* rather than different ability levels.

Bloom (1974) created a practical system for instruction using mastery learning based on Carroll's (1963) theoretical model. He observed that most schools are established on the assumption that learners vary in their ability to achieve. Bloom disagrees. Studies conducted under his guidance have shown that 95% of the students in our schools can achieve the educational objectives established for them, but because they learn at different rates, some students appear to be better or worse than others.

Bloom (1984) points to cases in which students are tutored to prove his point. In a controlled experiment, he demonstrated that "the average tutored student outperformed 98% of the students in the control class" (p. 5). He attributes this finding to the fact that a tutor is able to determine what each student knows in a given subject and is then able to plan an educational program that begins instruction at the student's level and proceeds at the student's own pace.

The basic structure of the mastery learning model, including adaptations known as *individually prescribed instruction (IPI)* and *continuous progress,* lend themselves best to the learning of basic skills in sequentially structured subjects. Very specific behavioral objectives are written for each unit of study. Pretests are used to assess students' prior knowledge, which then determines the placement or starting level for each student. Working individually, as students master each objective in the sequence of learning, they are able to proceed to the next one. Periodically, unit tests covering several objectives are given to check on the mastery and retention of a whole range of knowledge and skills.

The teacher's role in this process is quite different from teaching skills with a whole class approach. The teacher rarely instructs the entire class at one time. Instead, as students work independently, the teacher monitors their progress by walking around the classroom and responding to requests for assistance. In a cooperative version of mastery learning, Slavin (1987) proposes the TAI model (see chapter 9), which pairs students as monitors and assistants for each other during a mastery learning experience. This frees the teacher to work with small groups of students rather than devoting all of the time to responding to individual needs.

The value of mastery learning is that it allows students to actively learn new material and skills on a continuous basis. It is also assumed that motivation to achieve is increased because students are working at their own pace and have the prerequisite skills necessary for success. Also, because testing is done individually and opportunities are provided to repeat what they did not learn, students should suffer less embarrassment when they make mistakes. The affective goal of mastery learning programs is to help students become independent, self-directed learners.

Contracts for Independent Learning

While mastery learning is appropriate for use only in sequential subjects that require a great deal of independent practice, many teachers are searching for methods of promoting independence and self-directed learning in other subjects as well. An alternative to direct, whole class instruction is the use of independent or group academic learning contracts. A learning contract such as the one in Figure 10–1 is

FIGURE 10-1
Social Studies Learning Contract

Westward Expansion of the United States
Required Learning Activities

Date   Approval

_____ _____ Read Chapter 6 in the social studies textbook.

_____ _____ Write answers to the questions at the end of the unit.

_____ _____ Locate and read a book on the American West or the Indians.

_____ _____ Write a two- to four-page summary of the book.

_____ _____ Play the computer game "Oregon Trail" until you reach the state of Oregon.

Alternative Learning Activities

_____ _____ Imagine that you are a member of a wagon train heading west. Write a series of letters to family or friends back home describing your journey.

_____ _____ Write a play about a meeting between Indians and settlers. Find a cast for your play and be prepared to present it to the class assembly.

_____ _____ Draw or paint a large picture of a scene that you imagine took place during the westward expansion.

_____ _____ Create a song or ballad about life in the West. Be prepared to play and sing it for the assembly.

_____ _____ Create a diorama or a model of a Plains Indian village at this time in history.

_____ _____ Research the lives of the Plains Indians today. Be prepared to give a speech about the conditions in which they live now and how these are related to the westward expansion.

_____ _____ Create your own alternative plan for a learning experience on this topic.

- -

I, _____, agree to complete the following required learning activities by the date _____. In addition, I select two to five alternative activities to pursue on my own. I will present my creative work to my classmates at our assembly on _____.

_____   I have reviewed this contract and under-
        student signature   stand the work my child has agreed to
                                      do. I agree to support this effort.
_____
        teacher signature   _____
                                              parent signature

---

usually created by the teacher at the beginning of a unit of study. The contract specifies one list of required activities, such as reading a chapter in the textbook, finding a library resource and writing a summary of the topic, completing a fact sheet, and other necessary prerequisites for developing a knowledge base on the subject.

A second list of activities is offered as choices or alternatives for students to pursue. This list includes opportunities to do additional independent research or plays, stories, songs, and artwork on the topic. When learning contracts are offered to develop independence, individuals usually select the activities they want to accomplish. A variation on this strategy would be to combine the concepts of cooperative groups and learning contracts and allow each group to sign a joint contract specifying the tasks and products they will complete.

Science investigations, social studies research projects, and creative language arts activities can be presented in the form of learning contracts. The primary advantage of this strategy is that it allows individuals with various levels of ability to work on an appropriate amount and type of work during the unit of study. High-achieving students can select the maximum number of tasks and products, and lower-achieving students can select fewer tasks. The assumption is that both types of students can actively learn and experience success during the same amount of time.

Learning Centers

Learning centers or stations are areas of the classroom where students can go to do independent work on a given subject or topic. Learning centers vary enormously in the way they look, the way they are used, and the length of time for which they are set up. Teachers who use learning centers use them for a variety of purposes and with a variety of expectations.

Some centers may be informal and unstructured in their use. For example, a classroom may have a permanent Science Center containing a variety of science equipment and materials. Students are free to go to the center to do science experiments in their free time. In the same classroom, there may be a permanent Reading Center furnished with a rug, comfortable chairs, and shelves or racks of books where students can go to read quietly.

Other centers are set up for a limited amount of time and have highly structured expectations. For example, to accompany the unit on settling the western United States described in the learning contract, the teacher may have set up an area of the classroom as a Research Center. It would contain a computer, with the MECC computer program called "Oregon Trail" turned on and ready for students to use. It would also contain posters and maps of the Western United States and a variety of reading materials on the topic. When the unit is finished, the center will be redesigned; new learning materials will replace the ones in the finished unit, and the center will become the focus of a new unit of study.

In some primary classrooms, learning centers are an important adjunct to the reading and language arts program. Many teachers set up four or five learning centers or stations with different activities each week. Students in small groups travel from one station to another according to a prespecified schedule. For example, Ginny Bailey uses a weekly theme as the basis for her first-grade language arts program. Each week she sets up activities related to that theme in her five stations: art, math, writing, listening, and reading. To accompany her butterflies theme, students will find books on butterflies at the reading station, paper and directions for a writing project at the writing center, paint and brushes to create a picture at the art station, a prerecorded tape to listen to at the listening station, and a math game involving butterflies and caterpillars at the math station.

Ginny uses five centers because there are 5 days in a week, so that each group can visit each center once a week. A poster on the wall shows the schedule of groups and centers:

Learning Station Schedule

GROUP	MONDAY	TUESDAY	WEDNESDAY	THURSDAY	FRIDAY
BLUE	Art	Math	Writing	Reading	Listening
GREEN	Math	Writing	Reading	Listening	Art
RED	Writing	Reading	Listening	Art	Math
YELLOW	Reading	Listening	Art	Math	Writing
ORANGE	Listening	Art	Math	Writing	Reading

In Ginny's classroom, students can go to their stations only after completing their assignments of daily work. In her system, the stations extend the students' learning experiences on the weekly theme but are also used as an incentive system for students to complete their required work.

Computer-Aided Instruction

Although some teachers may still be reluctant, based on their fear of the unknown, to use computers in their classrooms, many others believe that having a computer in the classroom is like having another teacher. When computers were first introduced in classrooms in the 1970s, few software programs were available. The first educational goals established at that time involved teaching students about how computers function and how to write their own computer programs. This goal contributed greatly to the fear that many classroom teachers still have. Not being computer programmers, they rarely felt comfortable teaching these skills to students.

In the 1990s, the purposes of using computer technology in the classroom are very different and much more reasonable for teachers to accept. The primary computer-education goal has changed from turning students into computer programmers to helping them become efficient and creative computer operators. Operating a computer with a user-friendly software program is something teachers can master readily, and they are then confident in their ability to teach their students how to operate the computers as well.

With the growth of the computer software industry, hundreds of computer programs are now available that can be used to accomplish many useful tasks. Computer programs are now available for classroom use that can diagnose students' skill levels in math, reading, vocabulary and other basic skills and prescribe lessons at the appropriate level. In "teaching" the lessons, computers make excellent tutors because they are endlessly patient in waiting for a student response and give the appropriate feedback without emotional side effects. An excellent example is the "Write to Read" program developed by IBM, which teaches primary students how to plan, write, and edit stories and poems. Josten Laboratories is creating a package of reading and mathematics programs for the elementary school. Students are pretested on the computer in reading and math. Each student then begins to work at their level of mastery and progresses through a series of learning activities that emphasizes comprehension and problem-solving.

Some gamelike programs are useful in expanding students' experiences beyond the classroom walls into simulated journeys, laboratories, foreign countries, earlier periods of history, and the future. Many of these programs increase students' decision-making and problem-solving abilities by offering them opportunities to make choices and get immmediate feedback on the consequences of their decisions. An example is the program known as "Oregon Trail," which allows students to simulate the experience of a wagon train journey with full decision-making power over how many supplies to bring, when to stop and restock, and how to deal with emergencies along the way. Poor choices in any of these areas leads to death on the trail. It takes most students many attempts to reach Oregon alive.

Another MECC program known as "Lemonade" plunges students into the economic decision making necessary to market a product in order to make a profit. Students must decide how many lemons to buy, how many glasses to make each day, how much advertising is needed, and must establish a price based on the weather report. Good choices lead to profits, and poor choices lead to losses.

Both the "Oregon Trail" and "Lemonade" programs are available to educators through the Minnesota Educational Computers Consortium (MECC), which is available in many school districts or libraries throughout the country.

Many excellent software programs provide students with a blank slate for creating and composing original works. "Logo," and "Turtle Geometry" are frequently used in schools to allow students to create mathematical patterns and figures. Papert's (1980) *Mindstorms: Children, Computers and Powerful Ideas* and Abelson and diSessa's (1981) *Turtle Geometry: The Computer as a Medium for Exploring Mathematics* are good resources for incorporating these programs into your curriculum.

An interesting synthesis of learning material is present in the new program called "LEGO LOGO." Using Lego® building blocks wired to a computer terminal, students can create moving machines and inventions and control their actions from a computer terminal.

Word processing programs are probably the most versatile programs available for computers. Early experiences, especially in the primary grades, may be devoted to very simple writing assignments with a dual purpose: composing and learning keyboarding skills. When students master keyboarding skills, they are free to compose many types of verbal products, including letters, stories, poems, essays, reports, and plays. Studies have shown that students write longer pieces on a word processor than they do by hand. The other major benefit is that the editing and revision processes are greatly simplified on the word processor. Students' motivation to write is increased in part because of the novelty of computers, but also because the final products that are printed out are neat and relatively error-free. This provides a strong sense of pride and success related to the writing process (Moore, Moore, Cunningham, & Cunningham, 1986).

In addition to student uses, computers can be used by teachers to create classroom materials, keep records, and compute grades. Many teachers use word processing programs to create and store curriculum plans, student worksheets, quizzes, and tests. They may also use them to write reports, proposals, and newsletters. Specialized record-keeping programs are available that allow teachers to record students' achievement. Many of these will compute average grades for report cards.

The major limitations on the use of computers in the classroom are money, availability of high-quality programs, and management concerns. Because of their expense, many schools have only a few computers that must be shared by many classrooms. In some cases, computers are placed on traveling carts that are moved from room to room according to a schedule. In this case, teachers must coordinate their plans to fit the computer schedule. In other instances, the computers are all housed in a single classroom, designated as a computer lab, and teachers must arrange to bring their students to the lab when they wish to incorporate computers into their plans.

Even when there are enough computers for each classroom to have its own, locating high-quality computer software can be difficult. Most software is expensive, and much of it is of low or indifferent value. Many programs that purport to teach math or language skills are little better than workbooks. Teachers must review software carefully before purchasing it. The criteria for selecting programs vary from class to class, but at a minimum, computer programs should be selected only if they are user-friendly and easy to load, start, and understand the directions. They should also be interesting and actively engage the learner in a meaningful learning experience.

When teachers have access to computers in the classroom, they must learn to manage their use efficiently. In some cases, the computer is available for a variety of student uses, and in others, teachers may dedicate the use of the computer for a specific purpose for a period of time. Students may work singly or in pairs at a computer terminal. With 30 students, this means that each student gets to use the computer for only a short time each day.

Despite the management problems, computers are valuable tools with many uses in remediation, tutoring, and creative efforts. Additionally, when students are able to use computers frequently for a variety of purposes, they learn to accept and understand the place of computers in society and are more likely to be ready to accept further technological advances of the 21st century.

Strategies Using Audio-Video Technology

Teachers have long used films, filmstrips, and audiotapes to supplement their classroom instruction. Many of these resources can be ordered through the media center located in the school. They can be used for whole class instruction, or they can be set up at a learning center so that individuals or groups of students may listen to tapes or watch a filmstrip on their own.

With the advent of video cameras, many new teaching strategies have emerged. Video discs used along with computers have produced the capability of employing interactive video for classroom use. An interactive format means that visual images stored on the video disc can be programmed to play on a television monitor. The order of the images can be completely controlled by the teacher or the students by typing commands on the computer. If teachers wish to teach students about recent historical events, they can obtain a video disc of recorded speeches and newscasts in that time period. For example, as the teacher discusses President Truman, the monitor can display him speaking in public. When the teacher begins to describe Eisenhower, the monitor can be programmed to display a video recording of one of his speeches.

Video cameras provide the teacher with many exciting new strategies. Students' products and performances can be recorded by the teacher or an assistant for future evaluation purposes or to document that the event took place. Students can rehearse their presentations on videotape and watch the recording to see what they need to improve.

Steven Landfried (1990) describes how his students create video term papers in his contemporary political issues course. Working with equipment borrowed from the local cable television station, small groups of students identify a community issue to research. For example, one group chose to focus on school board budget cuts, and another selected local toxic waste sites to investigate. After preliminary research, students planned and conducted videotaped interviews with community officials. Each group accumulated about 8 hours of videotape during 6 weeks.

The real "writing" of the video term paper began after 8 weeks when the students reviewed all the material they'd recorded and got an overview of how the pieces of their research puzzle interrelated. Indeed, what they found was that they had too many quality pieces for a 5- to 10-minute feature. They decided to invest more time so a complete view of their findings could emerge—in a 40- to 50-minute feature.

Four months after the project began, the students were ready to share the videos with the local community. They distributed their videotapes to local news media and educational organizations. Although it is not known for sure how greatly their work influenced the community, within 2 years, the school board reversed its decision to cut budgets and three of the four toxic waste sites were added to the federal Superfund list.

Your Own Repertoire of Teaching Strategies

With a repertoire of teaching strategies from which to choose, you can expect to create a stimulating classroom that appeals to students from a range of backgrounds and with a variety of learning style preferences. You can be flexible and creative. When one teaching strategy does not work, you can select another and reteach the lesson. You can look forward to a year of varied experiences for yourself and your students.

The strategies described in this book are but the tip of the iceberg. Each one has dozens of variations, and there are many additional strategies that can be successfully employed to build a classroom environment that meets the needs of all of your students and creates new horizons and new interests that they did not have when they entered your classroom.

To continue to expand your repertoire, plan to conduct an active search for new ideas, methods, and learning activities. Consult your professors for sources of interesting learning materials. Talk to classroom teachers you admire and ask them for copies of their favorite ideas and activities. Read educational journals and magazines and clip out the best ideas. Begin now to build a file of interesting classroom materials that you can adapt and use some day.

Ask teachers or the secretary of the school you are visiting to share their catalogs of educational materials with you. Some catalogs contain unusually creative classroom materials. *Good Apple* is a catalog of materials created by classroom teachers for other teachers to use. Elementary, middle-school, and high school catalogs of simulation games are published by Interact. *Engine-Uity* is a catalog of materials that teachers can use to set up learning centers on topics ranging from literature, history, science, and multidisciplinary themes. Most of the materials are organized around the framework of Bloom's Taxonomy. The *D.O.K.* catalog is filled with materials that emphasize creative and critical thinking. *Creative Publications* contains many manipulative materials, as well as activity books geared toward problem-solving in every subject area.

> *Creative Publications Catalogue* (math manipulatives and language arts activity books)
> Toll Free: 1-800-624-0822
> *Delta Publications* (science investigations)
> Toll Free: 1-800-258-1302
> *D.O.K. Publications* (thinking skills and problem-solving)
> Toll Free: 1-800-458-7900
> *Engine-Uity, Ltd.* (learning center and literature activities)
> 8900 N. Central No. 107, Phoenix, AZ 85020; 602-997-7144.
> *Good Apple* (teacher-made materials in all subject areas)
> Toll Free: 1-800-435-7234
> *National Wildlife Federation Catalog*
> Toll Free: 1-800-432-6564
> *Project AIMS Catalog* (integrated math and science activities)
> P.O. Box 7766, Fresno, CA 93747; 209-291-1766
> *Simulations* by Interact
> Toll Free: 1-800-359-0961

OPPORTUNITIES FOR REFLECTION

▼ Reflective Essay: Teaching Strategies I Prefer

Which of the teaching strategies in this chapter are you most likely to employ in your classroom? Why? How do they fit your emerging style of teaching? Have you selected an adequate variety of strategies to motivate students with different learning styles and needs? Which strategies would you avoid using? Why?

▼ Classroom Visit: Teach a Lesson

Arrange with the classroom teacher to let you plan and teach a lesson to a small group of students. Select your teaching strategies to fit the lesson and the needs of your students. You may be able to use more than one level of Bloom's Taxonomy in your lesson. Write up a reflective evaluation of your lesson, its effects on the students, what they learned, and what you believe you could do to improve the lesson if you were to teach it again.

REFERENCES

ABELSON, H., & DISESSA, A. (1981). *Turtle geometry: The computer as a medium for exploring mathematics.* Cambridge, MA: MIT Press.

ANDERSON, R. (1977). The notion of schemata and the educational enterprise. In R. Anderson, R. Spiro, & W. Montague (Eds.), *Schooling and the acquisition of knowledge* (pp. 415–431). Hillsdale, NJ: Erlbaum.

AUSUBEL, D. P. (1960). The use of advance organizers in the learning and retention of meaningful verbal material. *Journal of Educational Psychology, 51,* 267–272.

BLOOM, B. (1974). An introduction to mastery learning theory. In J. H. Block (Ed.), *Schools, society and mastery learning* (pp. 12–21). New York: Holt, Rinehart and Winston.

BLOOM, B. (1984). The search for methods of group instruction as effective as one-to-one tutoring. *Educational Leadership, 41*(8), 4–17.

BLOOM, B., ENGLEHART, M., FURST, E., HILL, W. & KRATHWOHL, D. (1956). *Taxonomy of educational objectives: Cognitive domain.* New York: Longman.

BRANSFORD, J. (1983). Schema activation—schema acquisition. In R. Anderson, J. Osborn, & R. Tierney (Eds.), *Learning to read in American schools* (pp. 23–37). Hillsdale, NJ: Erlbaum.

CARROLL, J. (1963). A model of school learning. *Teachers College Record, 64,* 723–733.

GAGNÉ, E. (1985). *The cognitive psychology of school learning.* Boston: Little, Brown.

HAWKINS, D. (1965). Messing about in science. *Science and Children, 2*(5), 5–9.

HUNTER, M. (1976). *Improved instruction.* El Segundo, CA: TIP Publications.

LANDFRIED, S. (1990). Video term papers teach research and social responsibility. *Educational Leadership, 48*(3), 46–48, 65.

LEYSER, Y. (1982). Role playing in the classroom: A threat or a promise. *Contemporary Education, 53,* 70–74.

MOORE, D., MOORE, S., CUNNINGHAM, P., & CUNNINGHAM, J. (1986). *Developing readers and writers in the content areas.* New York: Longman.

PAPERT, S. (1980). *Mindstorms: Children, computers and powerful ideas.* New York: Basic Books.

PETERS, W. (1984). *A class divided: Then and now.* New Haven, CT: Yale University Press.

SHAFTEL, F., & SHAFTEL, G. (1982). *Role playing in the curriculum.* Englewood Cliffs, NJ: Prentice-Hall.

SILBERMAN, C. (ED.). (1973). *The open classroom reader.* New York: Vintage Books.

SLAVIN, R. (1987). Cooperative learning and the cooperative school. *Educational Leadership, 45*(3), 7–13.

TABA, H. (1967). *Teacher's handbook for elementary social studies.* Reading, MA: Addison-Wesley.

CHAPTER

11

Assessing Student Accomplishment

IT IS PERHAPS UNFORTUNATE that the chapters devoted to assessment of students' many and varied accomplishments are at the end of this book. The implication from this physical placement is that assessment and evaluation take place at the end of the learning process, after all the planning and teaching have occurred.

Nothing could be further from the truth.

In order to be able to evaluate what students have achieved from a learning experience, the teacher must have fully thought out the assessment process prior to teaching the lesson. In fact, assessment methods are described frequently in earlier chapters of this book. In chapter 3, which describes the processes teachers use to diagnose the needs of their students prior to teaching, many assessment devices are described. Cumulative files of information about students' past performance, standardized test scores describing levels of present achievement, and placement exams are methods of assessing student accomplishments and are part of the reflective teacher's continuous process of evaluation.

In chapter 4, long-term goals and outcome statements are described. These serve as the basis for later evaluation of what students gained from their school experience. Assessment of student accomplishment is primarily concerned with measuring how much students gained and comparing the actual gain with the original goal or outcome statement.

Chapters 5 and 6 described the creation of learning objectives that specify what teachers *expect* their students to gain during short-term learning events such as a single lesson or a short sequence of lessons. To evaluate student accomplishment in these areas, the teacher must measure what students actually gained during the lesson and compare that gain with the criterion established for each objective.

Chapters 7 through 10 described methods that teachers select for instructing students or facilitating their learning. These methods have an impact on the amount and type of accomplishment that students are able to achieve. Therefore, reflective teachers are continuously assessing student progress and achievement during every learning experience to verify that the teaching strategy they have selected is working or to alter it if they find that students are not accomplishing the objective for that lesson.

So, even though these final chapters on assessment and reporting on student achievement are at the end of this book, this is due only to books' linear nature. In order to genuinely understand what students have accomplished in a given school year, reflective teachers employ a systematic process of evaluation that includes observations, testing, collecting samples of students' typical work, and collecting portfolios of their best work. This process begins prior to the first day of school and continues until the last dismissal bell rings.

ASSESSMENT TERMINOLOGY

The terms used in discussing student assessment can be confusing. This brief set of definitions is provided to make it easier to comprehend what each term means in this text.

To begin, there is a subtle difference among measurement, assessment, and evaluation. In this textbook, *measurement* is a broad term referring to the process of obtaining a number of correct responses or a raw score for a student on any type of assessment device. A *criterion* is a preestablished number or score that a teacher believes will demonstrate mastery of the planned objective (*criteria* is the plural form of *criterion*). The teacher makes an *assessment* by comparing the student's raw score with the criterion score and determining whether the student successfully accomplished the objective. *Evaluation,* in this text, is the reflective process of gathering objective and subjective data on a student and making a decision about how best to help that student succeed.

In this text, the term *student achievement* is used to desribe the degree to which a student has demonstrated mastery of a subject or objective (usually paper-and-pencil) tests. *Student accomplishment* is meant to be a more inclusive term that indicates the degree to which a student has completed or demonstrated knowledge or skill on a variety of assessment devices, including tests, products, projects, oral presentations, performances, and creative works.

As described in chapter 3, *criterion-referenced tests* are those created by teachers themselves in which the test items match the specific objectives they plan to teach. Scores on criterion-referenced tests can be used to assess how well students did in relation to the criterion for success on the planned objectives. In contrast, *norm-referenced tests* are written by professional test writers and are published widely. The items may or may not match the curriculum of the school. Scores on norm-referenced tests tell teachers how much a student achieved in relationship to other students of the same age or grade throughout the country.

Many types of tests are used in an educational program. *Diagnostic tests* are used prior to teaching in order to inform the teacher about students' prior learning, especially to identify the gaps in their prior learning that must be addressed. *Placement tests* are a form of diagnostic test that are used to help teachers make decisions about the level of difficulty of material that will best match the student's present knowledge level.

A significant distinction exists between formative tests and summative tests. Although these two tests may look exactly alike, the difference between them is in the way they are used. *Formative tests* are used to measure the student's progress during a set of lessons or learning experiences so that the teacher can provide appropriate feedback and help the student correct errors in understanding or skill. They are *not* graded and are *not* used to make final judgments or evaluations of student achievement.

Summative tests are used at the end of a set of learning experiences in order to measure the progress made by a student over time. They *are* usually graded and *are* used to make final judgments or evaluations about student achievement.

Pretests are given prior to teaching a new unit or set of skills or knowledge. *Posttests* are given directly after teaching the new set of skills. The comparison of posttest and pretest scores can be an important way for teachers to learn how much their students gained from a specific lesson, sequence of lessons or unit of study. Pre- and posttests are often used in research to demonstrate gains students make under a certain set of conditions. Reflective teachers are likely to use pre- and posttests just as researchers do—as a means of gathering data about the value of various teaching strategies or sets of learning materials.

Nontest measures of student achievement and accomplishment also exist. These include informal observation, student products, presentations, and portfolios. Teachers continuously use informal observation of their students' efforts and accomplishments. It may be planned or unplanned. Teachers may observe a single student or a group of students as they work together. Although it is difficult to measure any specific achievement during an informal observation, the technique does provide subjective data that teachers need in order to understand the objective data gathered using other assessment devices.

In this text, a *student product* includes any form of written work, such as essays, stories, reports, poems, and plays that are handed in to be assessed and evaluated by the teacher. There are also a variety of student products that are not written but are completed works of art, music, models, machines, or other student-created items. A student product can be assessed by comparing it against a criterion or a set of criteria that fit that product type.

A *portfolio* denotes a collection of student products designed to show a progression of accomplishment from early undertakings to more recent and advanced efforts. By gathering portfolios of students' work, teachers may assess the accomplishments made over time in a given type of endeavor. There may be portfolios of drawings, showing increasing attention to detail and craftsmanship, or portfolios of student writing, showing growth in letter formation or use of grammatical conventions.

A *student performance* is a demonstration of effort and accomplishment that is presented to the public. It may be a speech given for classmates or a recital given for the entire school. It may be an individual effort or a group presentation such as a dramatization of an historical event. Student performances must be captured on audio- or videotape to preserve for in-depth assessment and evaluation.

Objective measures imply that no matter who scores the assessment device, they will all get the same score. This occurs only on tests with items that have clear-cut right and wrong answers. *Subjective measures* are those that will be scored differently by different scorers, depending on their own interpretations and values. These include essays, artwork, and any other creative products or performances.

Reliability is related to objectivity. Reliable tests are those that consistently measure the same thing time after time. *Validity* means that a test is appropriate for the subject and contains items that will provide useful information about student achievement in that content area. Both test and nontest assessment devices should be constructed in such a way that reliability and validity are taken into account. When assessment devices are reliable and valid for their purpose, the information they provide can be used with confidence to make decisions about children's school experiences.

PUBLIC INTEREST IN STUDENT ACHIEVEMENT

Who cares about the accomplishments of students in public schools? Who wants to know the difference between achievement of students in the suburbs and students in the inner cities? Why is so much energy, time, and money spent on assessment procedures in public education today? The answer is that we all care, and we all want to know at every level of society: national, state, local community, family, and individual.

At the national level, we care because we have seen signs that students educated in the United States are falling behind students from other industrialized nations. In 1983, the National Commission on Excellence in Education was commissioned to study American education. They reported

> Our Nation is at risk. Our once unchallenged prominence in commerce, industry, science and technological innovation is being overtaken by competitors throughout the world. . . . What was unimaginable a generation ago has begun to occur—others are matching and surpassing our educational attainments. (p. 1)

The Commission, which wrote *A Nation at Risk*, recommended that academic tests could be used to improve education by (a) certify[ing] the student's credentials; (b) identify[ing] the need for remedial intervention; and (c) identify[ing] the opportunity for advanced work" (p. 28).

The National Assessment of Education Progress (NAEP) provides a measure of the academic achievement of students in the basic skills in elementary, junior high, and high schools. These statistics are not reported to students or their parents. They are collected for the purpose of comparing achievement of American students from year to year. Reports are made to the public and to policymakers about the level of achievement of various age groups, the changes over time, and differences in achievement in gender and racial and ethnic groups. The NAEP uses the results of these tests to spot trends and make forecasts and predictions about future needs of American schools.

State governments are also vitally interested in assessing the achievement of students within their boundaries. As was described in chapter 4, each state government has established a state department of education that is responsible for providing guidance and standards to local school districts in the development of curriculum. The state departments are also responsible for holding school districts *accountable* for achieving the curriculum standards. *Minimum competency tests* are used by many state governments to measure whether districts are accomplishing the state guidelines.

Minimum competency tests are administered in schools by the classroom teachers on a specified date. Average scores are computed for various subjects and grade levels for each school district. In some states, these average scores are ranked and reported to the public in what is known as a *school district report card*. Districts with scores that are above the state mean are believed to be doing a better job of educating their students than are school districts with scores below the mean. The purpose of this practice is to strengthen the feelings of accountability on the part of school district administrators.

In some school districts, administrators choose to rank and report the results of the test by schools. In this way, they hold the principal and faculty of each school accountable for the school's educational program.

There are many unanswered questions about the value of the minimum competency tests and the practice of using the results to label schools and districts poor, good, better, and best. Some educators question whether the tests measure important student accomplishments or simply discrete, unconnected bits of knowledge. Others question whether the practice of reporting results is a valid measure of educational programming because the socioeconomic status of each school is also believed to have an effect on test scores.

Standardized norm-referenced tests of achievement in the basic skills are a fact of life in most school districts today, and teachers must learn how to interpret and use productively the information they provide. But at the same time that tests are gaining prominence in measuring and comparing achievement among school districts and states, they are also being severely criticized by many educators. Critics charge that testing takes too much time away from the curriculum. From 1 to 2 weeks of a 30-week school year may be given over to district, state, and national achievement testing.

Another criticism is that norm-referenced tests may measure only limited aspects of what the students have learned during the school year. Because they are written and distributed nationally by test publishers, the items on the tests are generic rather than specifically written to match what was taught in a particular school. Many items on a test may be unfamiliar to students because the material was not part of the curriculum of their school.

A further criticism of standardized tests is that they cause students to be labeled and categorized unfairly and unrealistically. There is great concern, for example, that generic achievement tests have a built-in bias against students who are members of racial minorities. Critics point to items, pictures, and language in early editions of such tests that were geared to the vocabulary and culture of the white middle class. Although test manufacturers now employ test writers who represent various racial and ethnic minorities to develop fairer tests, the concern remains that students from minority groups may have less opportunity to learn the content of the tests, which causes them to earn unrealistically low scores.

Test results must be interpreted with caution, and compared with other measures of student achievement. It is a serious breach of ethics when school districts misuse the data from standardized tests to classify students as learning disabled or gifted. Neither diagnosis can be made from the limited information of a generic test of basic skills. In fact, no serious educational decision should be made using only the data from standardized, norm-referenced tests of basic skills. When test scores are overemphasized and generalizations are made about them, this practice is likely to damage students' self-concepts and may even create self-fulfilling prophecies (Gronlund & Linn, 1990).

The emphasis given to standardized test scores varies from state to state and district to district. In some states and some districts, standardized achievement tests are given enormous weight in labeling students gifted or low achieving, in determining children's placement in special programs, and in determining who wins awards for merit. Reflective teachers who work in schools using these practices are likely to experience discomfort. It is important, then, to challenge such practices and encourage the use of a more balanced assessment and evaluation system.

In some states, school districts are encouraged to build evaluation systems that highlight the creative accomplishments of their students as being of equal or greater importance than tests of discrete skills. For example, the State of Illinois publishes curriculum guidelines in the form of outcome statements that describe achievement in terms of changes in behavior and productivity. For example, in the subject area of science, one of the four outcome statements is that "students will have a working knowledge of the principles of scientific research and their application in simple research projects" (Illinois State Board of Education, 1986, p. v).

The Illinois guidelines also provide specific objectives that must be attained by students in third, sixth, and tenth grades to demonstrate that they have accomplished each outcome. At the end of sixth grade, students in every school district in Illinois are expected to have worked in a laboratory group with other students; be able to distinguish between relevant and irrelevant information; convey accurately the findings and conclusions of their investigations; and organize their data into tables, charts, and graphs.

Translated into action, this outcome statement and set of objectives holds principals and teachers accountable for providing their students with laboratory experiences and opportunities to do scientific investigations and report their findings. No test of minimal competency can successfully evaluate an outcome statement of this type. Instead, each school district is expected to create a means of reporting how it has provided this experience and how well the students in the district accomplished this outcome.

Similarly, the outcome statements in the State of California's Frameworks and Model Curriculum Guides call for the active construction of meaning in relation to the students and their various cultures. School districts are encouraged to interpret the Frameworks in ways that are meaningful to their own communities. There has been a purposeful shift of emphasis from mastering basic skills to understanding concepts and ideas thoroughly. With this shift in curriculum emphasis has come a shift in emphasis of assessment devices, as shown in the *English-Language Arts Model Curriculum Guide* (California State Department of Education, 1988):

> Guideline 21. Educators, recognizing the limitations of standardized and objective testing, augment the use of such testing and emphasize informal and subjective measures for diagnosis and assessment. (p. 31)

This guideline encourages school districts in California to be accountable to themselves and their local communities in the establishment of assessment procedures that measure student accomplishment. The state does provide representative informal and subjective assessment activities that districts can use for this purpose. In the area of reading and the language arts, for example, the California *Model Curriculum Guide* suggests these informal assessment techniques for primary students:

> Kindergarten through Grade Three
> Each student reads aloud to the teacher on an individualized basis. The teacher determines the level of each student's decoding and comprehension skills by listening carefully and by asking appropriate questions.

> Grades Three through Six
> After the entire class completes the reading of a work of fiction or non-fiction or a chapter in a social studies book, the students write at least two paragraphs in which they summarize the content of the literary work or the chapter in the book. Using predetermined and previously taught editing techniques, students work in read-around peer-group evaluating teams. . . . (pp. 31–32)

HOW TEACHERS SELECT AND USE
METHODS OF ASSESSMENT

It is the responsibility of educators in state departments of education to create a balanced method of assessing whether students are meeting the state's standards. District administrators are responsible for creating a fair and useful collection of data about the achievment of students in the schools they serve. The principal of a single school provides guidance to classroom teachers in determining methods for evaluating the progress of the students in that school. But even with all of the direction and guidance provided by administrators and supervisors, there is still a great deal of leeway for individual classroom teachers in the area of student assessment.

Individual classroom teachers have varied philosophies of life and related curriculum orientations. Just as teachers' philosophies and curriculum orientations influence their methods of teaching, these values also greatly influence the types of assessment procedures teachers select and the weight they give to various measures of student accomplishment.

Teachers with an R-A philosophy of education are likely to employ assessment methods that will reinforce their views that some students have the ability to learn, and others do not. They will employ summative tests early and often, recording the results in their gradebooks as evidence of how each student's achievement matches the ability or IQ tests recorded in the student's cumulative file. Teachers with an R-A philosophy of education are, in many ways, very susceptible to the practice of making and carrying out self-fulfilling prophecies about their students.

Teachers with a C-M conception of learning are likely to employ many formative evaluation procedures in their effort to identify students' gaps of learning and cognitive processing errors. Through the application of a variety of formative evaluation strategies, these teachers provide the scaffolding necessary for students to achieve mastery and feel success in their classroom endeavors. If it has not been made obvious beforehand, it should be evident by now that the reflective teacher is likely to be one with a C-M view of teaching and learning. For the reflective teacher, evaluation is an integral part of the learning process.

Imagine that you are a teacher planning a unit on astronomy for your classroom. You have gathered together some very interesting learning materials, including filmstrips on the solar system, National Aeronautics and Space Administration (NASA) material on the space shuttles and telescope, and many exciting books with vivid illustrations. You've planned a field trip to an observatory and invited an astronomer to visit the classroom. You have worked out a time line for several weeks worth of individual and group investigations and projects.

But now it is time to think about evaluation. How will you know what students have learned at the end of this unit? What do you expect them to learn? What techniques will you use to find out whether they have learned what you expect? What about the possibility that they may learn something different from what you expect or even that some students who become very actively engaged in the study may learn more than you expect? How will you know what they learned? How will you assign students science grades at the end of this unit? How will you communicate to the students' parents what each has gained from it?

In the following sections, a variety of assessment devices are described. Each has a variety of uses and applications. Each provides answers to different questions teachers have about evaluation. To illustrate how they compare and how they complement one another, each will be applied to the astronomy unit described previously.

Reflective teachers will consider each alternative and decide whether and how to use them in their own classrooms. Recognizing that this introductory text can only provide minimal information about each assessment method, the reflective teacher will want to search actively for more information about certain methods in order to fully understand their value and use before incorporating them into a program that affects children's lives.

Informal Observations

Teachers use informal observation intuitively from the first moment the students enter the classroom at the beginning of the term. They watch groups to see how students relate to each other; they watch individuals to spot patterns of behavior that are either unusually disruptive or extremely productive. In order to manage a classroom effectively, teachers with withitness are alert to observe the overt and covert actions of their students at all times.

Informal observations also have academic implications. Teachers who observe their students while teaching a lesson are able to evaluate their understanding. Spotting a blank look, a nervous pencil tapping, or a grimace of discomfort on a student's face, the teacher can stop the lesson, check for understanding, and reteach the material in order to meet the needs of the students who didn't understand.

As students read aloud, primary teachers observe and listen for patterns of errors in decoding words. They may also listen to the expression in the student's voice in order to determine whether the student is comprehending the material or simply saying words aloud. They listen for signs that indicate whether the student is interested or bored with the material. An additional tool in informal observation is asking the student pertinent questions to check for understanding and understand the student's thought processes. This one-to-one interaction provides data and information not measureable on any paper-and-pencil test.

By observing the student read, asking a few questions, and comparing the results with other students of the same grade or age, the teacher is able to assess many things, including (1) the extent to which the student is able to use phonics and context clues to decode reading material, (2) the student's approximate reading level in terms of sight vocabulary, and (3) the student's comprehension level. In addition, the reflective teacher uses the informal observation to gather information about the affective qualities of the student, including the confidence level, the student's interest in the subject or in reading itself, the amount of effort the student is willing to give to the task, and the expectations the student has about success or failure in the subject.

By observing as students write or by reading what they have written, teachers can gather similar data about children's writing abilities, interests, and expectations. As students work out unfamiliar math problems, teachers are careful to observe who works quickly and who is struggling. Then they can gather the struggling students together for an extra tutoring session.

In the astronomy unit, the teacher may observe as students take part in discussions to determine the extent to which various students understand the concepts. When students are visiting the observatory, the teacher will watch them to learn about their interests in various aspects of the topic. When an astronomer visits the classroom, the teacher will listen to the students' questions to assess the depth of understanding they have achieved.

Informal observations are one of the most powerful assessment devices the teacher can use to gather new information about children's learning patterns and needs. Teachers may gather data about a student from academic and psychological tests, but in the end, it is the informal observation that most teachers rely on in order to understand the test data and make a final evaluation about the appropriate placement or grade value of a student's work.

Mastery of Behavioral Objectives

In contrast to informal evaluations, which provide useful subjective information, behavioral objectives are relatively formal and provide useful objective data about what students have learned. Do not assume that teachers choose one or the other of these two devices. Many reflective teachers know that it is valuable to gather both objective and subjective data. They may choose behavioral objectives as a means of gathering hard data about what students have achieved during classroom learning experiences and compare those data with the subjective information they have gathered during their informal observations.

To plan an assessment system using behavioral objectives, it is necessary to begin before the lesson is taught. By preplanning a lesson with behavioral objectives, the teacher specifies the skills that students should be able to demonstrate at the conclusion of the lesson and the criterion for success. After each objective has been taught and students have had an opportunity to practice the new skill, there is a quiz or worksheet that calls on students to demonstrate that they have mastered the new skill and can perform it with few errors.

The teaching strategies that are most often used to help students master a series of objectives are direct instruction or mastery learning. When direct instruction of the whole class is used, each lesson planned by the teacher is based on one or more behavioral objectives with a prespecified criterion for success. The criterion for success is usually specified as a percentage or as a minimum number of correct responses. For example, the following behavioral objective specifies 80% (or 16 of the 20 possible items) as the acceptable demonstration of mastery of this objective:

> *SPELLING OBJECTIVE:* When the teacher reads the list of 20 spelling words aloud, students will write 80% of the words, using correct spelling and legible handwriting.

In the whole class method, teachers provide a period of direct instruction and then students are given assignments of seat work or homework that allows them to practice the new skills. A criterion-referenced test such as the weekly spelling test common in many classrooms demonstrates whether the students have mastered the new skill. To record student achievement, teachers may write the percentage of correct responses that each student attained in a grade book. These records are later used as the basis for computing report card grades (see chapter 12).

Some teachers prefer to use the teaching strategy of mastery learning to motivate students to learn a sequence of skills. In mastery learning, individual students work through a series of learning experiences at their own pace and demonstrate mastery as they complete each objective. In this case, the daily or weekly measures of mastery are usually formative rather than summative in that the teacher uses the information gained on the tests to provide helpful feedback and reteaching rather than as a record of achievement. Summative evaluations occur only at the end of a unit of study, when students are expected to demonstrate mastery of a whole sequence or unit of learning. These summative grades of unit tests are recorded and become the basis for determining the grades students have earned.

In the astronomy unit, the teacher may have written a number of objectives, such as these:

> After viewing the filmstrip on the solar system, the students will be able to match pictures of each planet with its name, with no more than one error.

> Students will be able to draw and label an illustration of the solar system with the sun and nine planets in their respective orbits, with 100% accuracy.

Together these two objectives will inform the teacher whether students have learned the names, distinctive visual elements, and locations of the planets in the solar system. To measure whether the students have mastered this content, the teacher simply carries out the tasks described in the objectives after students have had sufficient opportunity to learn the material. The teacher prepares a matching quiz with a column of nine names and another column of nine pictures of the planets. For those who do not achieve the criterion of eight correct answers, the teacher can provide a reteaching experience or require students to do additional reading on their own. They can be retested until they achieve the criterion.

On another occasion, the teacher distributes blank paper and asks students to draw and label the solar system. From these two objectives and others like them, the teacher can begin to answer the question, "How will I know what they have learned?" Also, the data gathered from this assessment system are more readily translated into letter grades than is the data from informal observations.

Criterion-referenced Quizzes and Tests

Quizzes, such as the matching quiz just described, are frequently used with behavioral objectives to determine whether students are successfully gaining each new skill or bit of knowledge in a unit of study. Quizzes are generally short, consisting of only a few questions or items, and are thought of as formative assessments, providing teachers with a way to know whether the students are learning the material day by day.

Tests, however, may be made of many items and are generally thought of as summative assessments. Tests are often given at the end of a unit and contain a variety of items that measure students' achievement of content and skills that have been taught during a period of time.

In both cases, the term *criterion-referenced* refers directly to the criterion established for each behavioral objective. Each item on a criterion-reference test should match a preestablished criterion. Criterion-referencing provides objective data about material that all students in the class have had an equal opportunity to learn.

Objective tests may take a variety of forms. The most common are matching, true-false, multiple-choice, and short answer or completion forms.

Matching items are those that provide both the question and response. Students have only to recognize the correct response for each item and draw a line to connect the two. These tests are created by writing the items in a column on one side of the paper and the responses in a different order on the other side. In terms of Bloom's Taxonomy, matching items are an excellent way of measuring knowledge-level objectives that require students to recognize correct responses. An example of a matching quiz related to the astronomy unit might look like this:

Jupiter	Planet with rings and many moons
Earth	Planet closest to the sun
Mercury	Planet that is $\frac{3}{5}$ water on surface
Saturn	Largest planet

To construct fair matching items, it is important that each right-hand response be clearly identified with only one item on the left. In our astronomy test, for example, it is necessary that the descriptions of the planets contain unambiguous elements so that only one matches each planet. If several responses are vaguely correct, the reliability and therefore the objectivity of the test are diminished.

True-false items are also knowledge-level items, consisting of a statement that students must recognize as either true or false. These items are difficult to write, as they must be factual and objective in order to provide useful data. If items contain unsupported opinions or generalizations the students must guess what the teacher intended.

For our astronomy unit, we might construct a quiz with statements such as these:

True	False	The sun orbits Earth.
True	False	Venus is smaller than Jupiter.
True	False	Mars is closer to the sun than Neptune.

These items are reliable in that the correct responses are not likely to change in our lifetime. They are also valid because every item is an element that is directly related to our objective of teaching students about the physical characteristics of the solar system.

As examples of less reliable and less valid items, consider these:

True	False	Venus is a more interesting planet than Uranus.
True	False	The sun will never stop shining on the Earth.

Multiple-choice items also measure knowledge-level objectives because they call for recognition of a fact or idea on the part of the student. A multiple-choice item contains a question, problem, or unfinished statement followed by several responses. The directions tell the student to mark the one correct answer. While college admission tests may contain several near-right responses and students are expected to use reasoning to determine which one is best, classroom tests should probably be constructed with only one correct response. As in other objective measures, reliability and validity of each item must be considered.

To fit the astronomy unit, two valid and reliable items are these:

1. Which planet is known as the red planet?
   a. Venus
   b. Orion
   c. Mars
   d. Jupiter

2. It would take longest to travel from Earth to
   a. Neptune
   b. Mercury
   c. Venus
   d. Saturn

Short-answer or *completion* items supply a question or an unfinished statement, and students are expected to supply a word, phrase, number, or symbol. These items are used primarily to test students' knowledge of specific facts and terminology. In our astronomy unit, two examples are these:

1. The planet Saturn has _____ rings around it.
2. Which planet has the most moons?

The advantage of the four types of objective items, which comprise most criterion-referenced tests, is that they provide objective measures of students' knowledge of the basic content of a subject. They can be written to match directly the criteria of the teacher's objectives for the lessons. They are also relatively easy to correct, and the scores are easily recorded and can be averaged together to provide the basis for report card grades.

The disadvantage of such items is that they only measure students' understanding of basic knowledge-level content and skills. They do not provide information about what students comprehend, how they would apply the knowledge they've gained, what they would create, or how they analyze and evaluate the ideas they've learned.

Essays

Essays have the exact opposite advantages and disadvantages of criterion-referenced tests. They are subjective rather than objective. Two or more teachers rarely evaluate an essay the same way because each teacher has a unique set of criteria for a successful essay. They are also time-consuming to read and mark.

However, essays provide teachers with an excellent means of knowing what students comprehend, how they would apply their new learning, and how they analyze and evaluate the ideas and concepts. Essays also provide students with opportunities to be creative by asking them to synthesize a number of previously unrelated notions into an original expression of their own. Essays can answer the question, "How much more have they learned than what I taught in this unit?"

In form, essays may have either a restricted or an extended response question. The *restricted essay* usually limits the topic with specific parameters and may even specify the response. For example, in the astronomy unit, the teacher may want to assess whether students can describe the concept of outer space in their own words. This will provide information about how much students truly comprehend about the subject rather than what they simply remember. In the lesson plan, it can be written in the form of a behavioral objective with criteria for success:

> Students will be able to write a two-paragraph essay in their own words comparing the earth's atmosphere with space and telling why humans cannot live in outer space without life support.

The essay directions can be written as follows:

> In the first paragraph of the essay, describe in your own words how space differs from the Earth's atmosphere. Tell what is in space that is not in the atmosphere and what is in the atmosphere that is not in space.
>
> In the second paragraph, describe why humans can live in the Earth's atmosphere but cannot live in space without life support systems.

The directions are fairly explicit in terms of both length and content. For these reasons, this form of essay is relatively objective. Two or more teachers are likely to be looking for similar elements when correcting the papers. This form is especially useful for assessing students' levels of comprehension on a topic. It also provides an opportunity for students to demonstrate their ability to analyze the topic, but limits their use of synthesis and evaluation.

The *extended-response essay* gives students more freedom to express ideas and opinions and to use synthesis-level thinking skills to transform knowledge into a creative new idea. In the astronomy unit, the teacher may hope that students will gain a sense of responsibility for the Earth after studying it's place in the universe. This affective goal for the unit may also be expressed as a series of problem-solving or expressive objectives. For example

> At the end of the unit, students will write an essay entitled, "The Big Blue Marble," in which they express their own hopes and fears for the future of the Earth. The essays will be edited, rewritten, illustrated, and hung up for parents to view on parent's night.

This extended-response essay calls on students to integrate all that they have learned in this unit and combine it with previous learning from geography and social studies units. Their individual experiences and outside readings are likely to affect their responses as well. Objectivity in marking this essay is very low. It is quite likely that teachers will view the responses very differently from each other. Nevertheless, within a single classroom, a teacher can say or state a set of criteria or expectations that can lead students to write a successful essay. In this instance, as stated in the objective, students will have an opportunity to receive critical feedback and make corrections on their essays before the final products are displayed.

Despite the lack of objectivity of extended-response essays, there is good reason to include them in an educational program. They provide invaluable information about the creativity, values, philosophy, and maturity of our students. Moreover, they encourage students to become more creative and give them practice in making difficult judgments.

Oral Reports and Examinations

Like essays, *oral reports* can be restricted or unrestricted depending on the type of assessment the teacher wants to generate. Examples of *restricted* oral reports include book reports in which students are expected to describe the main characters, the setting, the plot, and their favorite part of the story. In a restricted oral examination, teachers may ask questions that students must answer within specified parameters. In the astronomy unit, an oral examination may be scheduled for a certain day. Students are told to prepare for it by reading material supplied by NASA on America's space program. In the examination, teachers ask questions taken from the reading material, and students are expected to respond in their own words. For example

Tell how the astronauts prepared for weightlessness.
Describe the food astronauts eat in space.

As teachers listen to the students' responses, it is possible to make a judgment about whether their answers are right or wrong. It is also possible to assess whether the students have a poor, average, or unusually good understanding of the ideas they speak about. The teacher's evalution of the students' responses can be recorded in some form, to be shared with the student later.

Unrestricted oral reports allow students more opportunities to speak about matters of great interest and importance to them. They encourage students to use their imagination to generate synthesis-level responses or to be persuasive about a matter of opinion or judgment. For example

Describe the space journey you'd like to take.
Tell what you think should be NASA's next big undertaking.

Debate is a form of oral examination in that it provides students with an opportunity to prepare to speak about a subject by learning a great deal of content and evidence for opinions prior to the event. During the debate, teachers can assess the students' energy and effort used in gathering information, as well as their understanding of the topic.

In evaluating oral presentations, teachers may write comments as they listen, or they may videotape the presentations so that they can evaluate them more comprehensively later. Students may be involved in self-evaluation of their own efforts as well. They can view the videotapes and discuss with the teacher what they did well and what they need to improve.

Tests of Inquiry and Higher-Level Thinking Skills

It is possible to construct written or oral examinations designed to measure the higher-level thinking skills of analysis and evaluation, as well as critical thinking skills of observation and inference and problem-solving strategies such as the creation and testing of hypotheses. These tests can be constructed as paper-and-pencil exams in which a situation or dilemma is printed and students are asked to respond to it in various ways. Such a test may consist of a passage to be read that describes a problem or dilemma. Maps, charts, graphs, or other forms of data might also be available on the test. The test items then consist of questions that allow the student to observe, infer, formulate a hypothesis, design methods of testing the hypothesis, and speculate about the possible outcome.

For example, in the astronomy unit, students may be presented with reprints from journals and magazines describing various theories about the evolution of the universe. From these articles, students are asked to respond to the following questions, citing evidence from the articles to support their answers:

1. Approximately how old is the universe?
2. Describe the contents of the universe, including the matter that resides between the planets and stars.
3. In your opinion, will the universe continue to expand indefinitely, or will it reach a maximum size and begin to collapse?

This test may appear to be very difficult, but its scoring does not depend on whether the students have knowledge about the actual contents of the universe. Instead, the scoring should reflect the accuracy of their observations of the data presented to them and whether their inferences can be supported by their observations.

For intermediate students, a simpler test may focus on the orbit of the Earth around the sun and its relationship to the seasons of the year. A diagram of Earth's orbit would be displayed along with a chart about the dates of the four seasons in the Northern Hemisphere and questions such as these:

1. What do you *see* about the path the Earth takes around the sun?
2. What do you *see* on the chart about when seasons begin?
3. What connection do you think there is between the beginning of summer and the Earth's position in its orbit?
4. What other connections do you see?
5. What do you think the tilt of the Earth has to do with seasons?

Even primary students can be tested for their inquiry skills, although it is probable that the tests will have to be oral rather than written. The teacher may ask students to observe a demonstration of the rotation of the Earth on its axis, using a flashlight on a beachball in a dark room. After the demonstration, students can be asked to describe their observations, make inferences, and then respond to the unfinished questions, "What if. . . ?"

Checklists and Rating Scales

When teachers wish to assess students' products or presentations, they can tell the students their reactions in a conference or write comments on a piece of paper and give these comments to the students. These methods suffice for informing the students, in

FIGURE 11-1
Astronomy Unit Checklist of Research and Study Skills

NAME _____ GRADE _____

This is a record of research and study skills demonstrated by this student. The teacher's initials and date indicate when the skill was successfully demonstrated.

Date	Initials	Skill Area
_____	_____	A. Located a book on astronomy in the card catalog
_____	_____	B. Located a book on astronomy on the library shelves
_____	_____	C. Used the table of contents to find a topic
_____	_____	D. Used the index to find a subtopic
_____	_____	E. Orally interpreted a graph or chart
_____	_____	F. Took notes on a chapter in a book on astronomy
_____	_____	G. Summarized the chapter from notes
_____	_____	H. Wrote the bibliography for the book

a general way, whether they have met the teacher's expectations in the product, and they may be adequate for evaluating an unrestricted product or presentation.

When the criteria for a product or presentation have been prespecified by the teacher and there are several important elements that must be included, teachers may choose to create a *checklist* to use for notation when listening, for example, to the speech. This is frequently done when the objective is for students to use effective speaking skills in a presentation. In preparing the students for the speech, it is likely that the teacher will specify several important elements that the students should incorporate, such as maintaining eye contact with the audience, using appropriate volume to be heard by everyone in the room, and speaking rather than reading during the presentation. By preparing a simple checklist with these items on it, the teacher can quickly and accurately record whether each student used these skills in their presentations.

Checklists may be used to record mastery of many basic skills in the primary grades. Each item on the checklist can correspond directly to a behavioral objective. Together the items on a checklist provide an overview of a sequence of objectives. Kindergarten teachers frequently employ checklists to record the letter recognition of each pupil, letter by letter. Primary teachers use checklists to record mastery of basic math operations. Intermediate and middle school teachers may use checklists to record whether students have demonstrated fundamental research skills. In our astronomy unit, for example, the teacher may combine a goal of developing research and study skills with the goal of content mastery. To record the accomplishment of these skills, the teacher may use a checklist such as the one in Figure 11-1.

Checklists provide useful and efficient means of recording information about the accomplishments of individual students. They are also valuable during a student–teacher conference. Both teacher and student can quickly see what has been achieved and what still lies ahead. Checklists are also valuable when teachers confer with parents about the student's progress along a set of learning objectives.

Rating scales are used in circumstances similar to those of checklists. They provide additional information, however, in the form of a rating of how well the student achieved each element or skill on the list. They are used when it is useful to provide students with feedback that rates their performance on an objective. In the astronomy unit, for example, students' products may be turned in and evaluated by the teacher, using a rating scale of important elements. In many classrooms, teachers involve the student in their own evaluation of the product and the efforts expended in creating them. In Figure 11–2, a rating scale is structured so that both the student and the teacher rate the finished product.

Products of Individual Investigation and Research

The rating scale just described is used to evaluate the product of a student's independent research. A common method of assessing student's learning is to encourage them to do independent research on one aspect of a unit theme and to create a product that shows what they have learned. This method allows students to demonstrate their knowledge, comprehension, and all four of the higher-level thinking skills on a topic.

This assessment technique is appropriate for every area of the curriculum. Students can do independent research or make an independent investigation in math, science, social studies, literature, music, or art. This method lends itself especially well to interdisciplinary units.

The strategy is for the teacher to introduce a unit or theme and provide some teacher-centered instruction on it at the outset. Readings may be assigned, and quizzes and worksheets may be used to assess the extent to which the student is developing a knowledge base about the topic. Essays or oral presentations may be assigned to assess whether students comprehend the main ideas and concepts of the topic. Finally, each

FIGURE 11–2
Astronomy Unit Rating Scale of the Solar System Model

NAME _____GRADE _____

To the Student: Please evaluate your own product, using the following scale:
O = OUTSTANDING; one of my best efforts
S = SATISFACTORY; I accomplished what I set out to do
N = NEEDS IMPROVEMENT; I need to revise and improve this element

Student's Rating	Skill Area	Teacher's Rating
_____	Did adequate research and information gathering	_____
_____	Elements of the model are accurate in shape	_____
_____	Elements of the model are accurate in scale (except for orbits of planets)	_____
_____	Labeling is accurate and legible	_____
_____	Legend is accurate and legible	_____
_____	Model is visually interesting and pleasing	_____

student selects one aspect of the main topic on the basis of individual preference or interest and begins to research that subtopic independently. Each student decides on a final product that will demonstrate what has been learned and achieved during the independent study.

The types of products that might be created by students as a result of this type of investigation are limitless. Many teachers prefer to plan their evaluations of student accomplishment to correspond with Bloom's Taxonomy. There are student products that are appropriate for learning objectives at all six levels. A sample of them can be found in Figure 11–3.

Evaluation of these student products may be accomplished by using a checklist or rating scale. Reflective teachers who wish to encourage critical thinking and reflectiveness among their students are also very likely to involve the students in the self-evaluation of their own products. When students evaluate their work critically, they are learning how to become more independent and responsible for revising and improving their work without the need for an outside evaluator.

Learning Contracts

A learning contract is a device that can be thought of both as a teaching strategy and a means of assessment. The learning contract described in chapter 10 listed several required activities and a number of options for the unit on settling the western United States. Teachers using this strategy meet with individual students to agree on a suitable number and type of optional activities. The activities on the contract then provide the structure for daily learning experiences. When the unit is completed, the contract is used as the basis for assessing what each student has accomplished. Just as in adult life, students are held accountable for meeting the terms of their contracts. If they succeed, they can expect a positive evaluation. If they have not met the terms of their contract, they can expect to have to explain why and describe what they will do to honor their contract.

Learning contracts can take several forms and can even be structured so that the student makes a contract to receive a certain grade for a specified amount of work. A point system can be employed to allow students to select from among options and earn the grade they desire. For example, in the astronomy unit, a learning contract with a built-in point system for earning a grade is shown in Figure 11–4.

Learning contracts also serve as the basis for recording accomplishments. In the sample learning contract for the astronomy unit, the parent is also required to sign the contract, agreeing to support the student's efforts. This strategy is a very efficient way to communicate with parents about the goals and expectations of the class. Later, during parent–teacher conferences, the parent can see the work that was accomplished. If a student did not complete the contract, the parent can see what was left undone.

Portfolios of Student Products

Portfolios are collections of work samples designed to illustrate a person's accomplishments in a talent area. Photographers collect portfolios of their best photos; artists collect their artwork; composers collect their compositions. Assessment portfolios are

FIGURE 11–3
Student Products Related to Bloom's Taxonomy

Characteristics of Each Level	*Products Associated with Each Level*
Knowledge Level Can recognize and recall specific terms, facts, and symbols.	**Knowledge Level** Worksheet, Label a given diagram, Memorize poem or song, List, Quiz Recognition of math symbols, Spelling Bee, Response to Flashcard.
Comprehension Level Can understand the main idea of material heard, viewed, or read. Is able to interpret or summarize the ideas in their own words.	**Comprehension Level** Written paragraph or summary of main idea, Oral retelling of story, Use of math symbols and numbers in simple calculations, Report.
Application Level Is able to apply an abstract idea in a concrete situation, to solve a problem or relate it to prior experiences.	**Application Level** Diagram, Map, Model, Illustration, Analogy, Mental problem solving, Action plan, Teaches others, Diorama, Costume, Diary, Journal.
Analysis Level Can break down a concept or idea into its constituent parts. Is able to identify relationships among elements, cause and effect, similarities and differences.	**Analysis Level** Graph, Survey, Chart, Diagram, Report showing cause and effect, differences and similarities, comparisons and contrasts.
Synthesis Level Is able to put together elements in new and original ways. Creates patterns or structures that were not there before.	**Synthesis Level** Artwork, Story, Play, Skit, Poetry, Invention, Song, Composition, Game Collection, Hypothesis, Essay, Speech Videotape, Film, Computer program.
Evaluation Level Makes informed judgments about the value of ideas or materials. Uses standards and criteria to support opinions and views.	**Evaluation Level** Debate, Discussion, Recommendation, Letter to editor, Court trial, Panel, Chart showing hierarchies, rank order, or priorities.

Created by Judy Eby from: TAXONOMY OF EDUCATIONAL OBJECTIVES: Handbook I: Cognitive Domain by Benjamin S. Bloom et al. Copyright © 1956, 1984 by Longman Publishing Group.

used to document what a student has achieved in school. To use this technique, teachers collect samples of each student's work and put them in a file folder with that student's name on it. Some teachers collect many types of work in a single portfolio; others have writing portfolios that contain only writing samples, math portfolios filled with worksheets and tests, and others for other subject areas.

Teachers may collect only samples of a student's very best work in a portfolio in order to demonstrate the maximum performance of that student. However, an

FIGURE 11-4
Sample Learning Contract

ASTRONOMY UNIT LEARNING CONTRACT

I, _____ , a student in the fifth grade at Otis School, do hereby contract to complete the following tasks during my investigation of the solar system.

Furthermore, I agree to complete these tasks by _____ .

I understand that I am agreeing to earn _____ points, which will earn a grade of _____ if my work is evaluated to be acceptable. I understand that the point values listed below are the maximum number that can be earned for each task and that fewer points may be awarded.

POINTS NEEDED TO EARN SPECIFIC GRADES

> 90 = A	> 80 = B	> 70 = C	> 60 = D	< 60 = F

_____ 10 pts Read chapter 7 in the science text. Do exercises, pp. 145–146.
_____ 10 pts Matching quiz
_____ 10 pts True-false quiz
_____ 10 pts Multiple-choice quiz
_____ 10 pts Short-answer quiz
_____ 15 pts Drawing of the solar system, labeled correctly
_____ 20 pts Model of the solar system, labeled and scaled to size
_____ 10 pts Essay on Earth's atmosphere and outer space
_____ 10 pts Essay on "The Big Blue Marble"
_____ 05 pts per answer on NASA oral exam
_____ 10 pts Oral report on "A Space Journey I'd Like to Take"
_____ 10 pts Finished Checklist on Research Skills

Signed this day _____ 19 _____ at _____ School.

---

student signature	teacher signature

---

parent signature	witness signature

argument can be made for the collection of samples of ordinary or typical work as well. These samples demonstrate how well the individual is performing on a day-to-day basis.

Portfolios may be kept for a long or short period of time. Many teachers collect writing samples in the first week of school, and then periodically throughout the school year. In some cases, the teacher may assign a writing topic during the first week and then assign the very same topic during the last week of school. When the two samples on the same topic are compared, the growth and development of the students' writing abilities is plain for everyone to see.

Pam Knight

Math Teacher, Twin Peaks Middle School, Poway, California

Classroom Event

For a long time, I have been concerned about the assessment techniques in my math classes. I often see student class work that shows clear understanding and mastery and sometimes I hear a student explain a process to another student, but then not do as well on the math test as the person he or she was helping. I have also observed a student who does no homework, shows little work on math problems, and is often absent from class score high on tests that require only replication of algorithms from the textbook.

Asking Questions

Are students such as those in the second instance superior at math just because they do well on tests? If I were in a position to hire a student, which would I prefer to employ? Which exhibits traits that will make him or her successful in the future? If I grade only on tests, the second student always comes out ahead, but I think that the other type of student possesses many valuable skills that will contribute to future success. How do I structure an assessment system that will show the many facets of a successful mathematics student?

Gathering Information

These questions stayed in my subconscious for a number of years. However, when I returned to school to work on an advanced degree, I began to read about newer methods of assessment that I had not known about. I discovered the term *authentic assessment.* The key element of authentic assessment is to gather representative examples of each student's work for a portfolio that will demonstrate the student's real capabilities.

Because little had been done about portfolio assessments in mathematics, I gained most of my information by researching the portfolio work being done in the field of language arts. I joined a portfolio network at the San Diego County Office of Education that met monthly for support and idea sharing.

Analyzing the Information and the Situation

In my quest, I discovered that the few efforts in mathematics portfolios involved folders of collected homework and tests or portfolios that were collections of weekly problem-solving activities. I wanted something that assessed what I covered in my mathematics class: long-term, situational problem-solving; scale drawing; experiments; and math problems from the text.

Making a Judgment Based on Principles

For many years, I have believed that a student's work ethic often determines success in life. I encourage my students to develop a positive work ethic. To do this, I believe that it is important for students to complete their homework, show their work in computation, attend

A short-term portfolio may be collected for the duration of a learning unit. For example, in the astronomy unit, all of the student's work, including quizzes, essays, pictures, and photos of the model solar system can be collected in a portfolio to document that student's accomplishment during the unit. If a contract was used during the unit, the contract will be included in the portfolio along with the work samples.

Portfolios may be used at all grade levels and for any subject or course a student takes. In the above Reflection, Pam Knight describes the process she used to adapt the idea of portfolios to her mathematics program at a middle school.

class regularly, work successfully in group activities, and communicate their knowledge both in written and oral forms. I believe that each of these skills is important for the future. Based on this belief, I decided to create a plan that would assess these skills. I believed that it would be most valuable if the assessment was completed first by the student and then by the teacher.

Considering Alternative Strategies

From my research, I found that journals are a popular method of self-evaluation in language arts. Could they be applied to mathematics? I also knew that I had to create more situational problems that could be used in an assessment plan.

Selecting the Best Strategy

My goal was to have the students create a mathematics portfolio with all the projects, journals, notes, and investigations from the year. These portfolios would show the next year's teacher more about the student's skills, attitudes, and knowledge of mathematics than test scores ever could.

Putting the Plan into Action

In the first year, for each quarter my portfolio assessment plan included a situational, long-term problem that included some type of project. Most of the projects involved the collection of data, some work analyzing the data using mathematical processes, and a written conclusion. At the end of the year, students wrote reflective statements about the value of the work they had done. They also included their best and worst tests in their portfolio.

Results

I was proud and amazed at the diversity, creativity, and excellence the portfolios displayed. As I expected, the portfolios often had little relationship to the students' average test scores. Is this a problem? Should these two types of assessment concur? Students who were experts on the computer produced portfolios that were visual treats. These portfolios had so much glitz that it was difficult for me to assess the actual content. To solve the credibility problem of my first portfolios, I began the entire reflective process again. The second year, I added both a skills assessment that included test score averages and an attitude assessment to be filled out by the student and verified by me, their teacher.

I wrote an article about my portfolio assessment plan for *Educational Leadership*. This article was published in May 1992. I have also presented my plan at several conferences and institutes. From each of these efforts, I have received valuable feedback from other teachers wrestling with similar endeavors. Where do I go from here? The next step is to organize a group of teachers willing to do some classroom research. We need to try to establish a model of portfolio assessment that fits the field of mathematics.

When portfolios are meant to be used to document student accomplishment, they must be organized in such a way that they reveal the development of a skill or the growing understanding of a set of ideas. Three collection strategies that are likely to demonstrate growth and change is to collect what Wolf (1989) calls "biographies of works, a range of works and reflections" (p. 37).

The biography of a work consists of several drafts of a work, showing the student's initial conception of the project, the first attempts, and the final product. By collecting these items, the teacher is able to document the growth and development that has occurred for this student. Wolf (1989) further recommends that after this collection is complete, the teacher may ask the student to reexamine all the stages of the work and reflect on the process and the products from beginning to end. The student's reflection may be done in writing or captured on audiotape (and later transcribed onto paper), and should then be included in the portfolio itself. This self-evaluation is valuable in helping the student develop metacognitive abilities that then can be applied to future projects.

Wolf (1989) suggests that teachers deliberately collect a range of works, meaning a diverse collection, consisting of journals, essays, poems, drawings, charts, graphs, letters, tests, and samples of daily work. When using the portfolios as a basis for a parent–teacher conference, this range allows the teacher to discuss and document many different aspects of the student's school accomplishments.

Primary teachers must take the responsibility for collecting and filing all items in students' portfolios. At the upper grades, however, students may be asked to keep their own. The teacher may suggest items to be included, and the student may decide on others. At the end of a people and nature unit, for example, each student may have a portfolio containing the tests, lab reports, essays, creative writing, and charts they created for the unit.

At the end of a unit or term, the teacher can collect the portfolios, examine them, ask for reflections on certain items or sets of items, and arrange the materials in chronological order in preparation for parent–teacher conferences. Teachers often ask students to create covers for their portfolios, which are then on display during parent open house visits or conferences.

Portfolios of student work are an excellent way to communicate with parents about a student's accomplishments. When the parent and teacher look at the writing sample together, they can both understand what the student's strengths and weaknesses are at a glance. When a parent sees the signed contract and the completed work, both parent and teacher see the same evidence to support the resulting grades.

The transition from traditional grade reports to portfolio assessment is not easy. Interpretation of student work is subjective and value-based. Challenges, such as questions about validity, and gender and racial equity in portfolios, are likely to emerge. But those who support the move to portfolio assessment believe that it offers real hope for creating assessment systems that promote high-quality work, critical thinking, and success motivation rather than simply labeling past achievements.

Videotape Records

When the purpose of evaluation is to record the accomplishment of a student so that the work can be analyzed and evaluated more comprehensively later, a videotape is an excellent way to capture and store a variety of learning events. Speeches can be videotaped easily. So can dramas, skits, presentations, and displays of students' products.

Videos are also excellent ways to communicate to parents about the accomplishments of a student or the entire class. They allow all interested parties to view the final products or performances of a unit of study. Teachers can store on tape a whole year's worth of accomplishments.

Video recordings also provide teachers with data they need to evaluate their own plans. By reviewing a video of a classroom learning event, reflective teachers are able to gain new understandings about what students need from their learning environment in order to be successful.

Cooperative Group Projects and Products

Many of the assessment methods described in this chapter can be adapted for cooperative groups. Evaluation of cooperative group efforts should include an assessment of both a task that requires a group effort to complete and an assessment of individual efforts to ensure that each member of the group takes responsibility for doing personal reading and preparation.

As an illustration of how to adapt ordinary lessons and units into cooperative lessons and units, consider the astronomy unit. To adapt this unit for use by cooperative groups, each group can function as a study team with directions to assist each other in reading and preparing for the quizzes. Group scores can be computed and recorded for each quiz at the same time that individual scores are recorded.

Rather than 30 individual models of the solar system, there will be 5 or 6 for each group in the class. The oral examination can be undertaken as a team effort, as proposed by Slavin's (1987) TGT model of cooperative learning. Essays and written reports can be combined as a group report.

The contract system works very well with cooperative groups. When used in this way, there is one contract per group instead of per individual. Each group negotiates what they will accomplish together. Evaluations can include peer assessments, with members of the group providing critical feedback for each other.

Conclusion

The assessment of student accomplishment is a complex and multifaceted undertaking. There is no one best way to assess what students have learned or accomplished in school. Some methods work better than others at various grade levels. Some work better than others with different individuals. This chapter has provided you with a number of different methods of assessment so that you can develop a repertoire of assessment devices to use as the basis for making judgments about the accomplishments of your students.

OPPORTUNITIES FOR REFLECTION

▼ Reflective Essay: Assessment in Your Class

What assessment devices are you most likely to use in your classroom? Why do you prefer them? What methods are you least likely to choose? Why?

▼ Classroom Visit: Assessment Methods

Ask the classroom teacher to discuss the methods he or she uses to assess learning in this classroom. Is one method used more than others or are a variety of methods used? Which methods are used that you would like to use in your own classroom? Which methods would you change?

REFERENCES

CALIFORNIA STATE DEPARTMENT OF EDUCATION. (1988). *English-language arts model curriculum guide.* Sacramento: Bureau of Publications Sales, P.O. Box 271, Sacramento, California 95802-0271.

GRONLUND, N., & LINN, R. (1990). *Measurement and evaluation in teaching.* New York: Macmillan.

ILLINOIS STATE BOARD OF EDUCATION. (1986). *Illinois outcome statements and model learning objectives for biological and physical sciences.* Springfield, IL: State Board of Education.

KNIGHT, P. (1992). How I use portfolios in mathematics. *Educational Leadership, 49*(8), 71–72.

NATIONAL COMMISSION ON EXCELLENCE IN EDUCATION. (1983). *A nation at risk: The imperative for educational reform.* Washington, DC: U.S. Government Printing Office.

SLAVIN, R. (1987). Cooperative learning and the cooperative school. *Educational Leadership, 45*(3), 7–13.

WOLF, D. (1989). Portfolio assessment: Sampling student work. *Educational Leadership, 46*(7), 35–39.

12

Recording and Grading Student Accomplishments

REPORT CARDS. These two words are likely to bring a number of memories filled with anxiety and a variety of other conflicting emotions to most people.

In your many years of schooling, you have probably received more than 50 report cards. You probably viewed many with relief and happiness and proudly displayed them to your parents; others may have caused torment and disbelief. On occasion, you may have questioned the teacher's fairness or integrity; you may have questioned whether the teacher really got to know you or understood the effort you put into your work. Perhaps you have even approached a teacher and challenged the grade you received, showing evidence of why the assigned grade was unjustified.

Eight or 9 weeks into your first school year, you will be faced with the task of deciding on and recording report card grades for your students. For many first-year teachers, the responsibility is considered one of their most difficult challenges. Experienced teachers often report that the task doesn't seem to get easier as the years pass. In fact, many reflective teachers find that the more they know about grades and about children, the more difficult it is to sum up the work and efforts of a student in a single letter grade.

In *Among Schoolchildren*, Tracy Kidder (1989) describes a year in a fifth-grade classroom. The teacher, Chris Zajac, takes a group of social studies tests home to grade:°

> A stack of social studies tests lay before her on the table, slippery sheets of ditto paper, the questions in purple ink—fill in the blank questions that asked for definitions of terms such as "Tory." The test closed, as always, with an essay question; the students had to describe briefly a Famous Patriot. She stared at the stack of tests for a moment. "Do I want to?" she murmured to herself, and took the first test, Arabella's, off the pile. Chris's pen made a one-part scratching sound, inscribing red C's down most of the page, and she began to smile.
>
> "84 = B," Chris wrote across the top of Arabella's test. . . . (pp. 72–73)

Although Arabella's paper proves to be a pleasure to grade, Chris later encounters the test turned in by Jimmy:

> Chris stared at Jimmy's test. He had not tried to answer more than half the questions, and had not written an essay. Jimmy was the sleepiest boy Chris had encountered in years, also one of the stubbornest when it came to evading work that required thought. . . .
>
> Chris would explain an assignment. Jimmy would say, "I don't understand." Chris would explain again. Jimmy would say, "I don't understand." Of course, he was waiting for her to do it for him. . . .
>
> Chris stared at the window. Maybe tomorrow, she thought, she'd make Jimmy take this test again. She went back to the pile. (p. 76)

Still later in the evening:

> Chris sat down again at the table. Pedro's test lay on top of the pile. She read,
>
> Tory. Like a grup of sogrs.

°Excerpts from AMONG SCHOOLCHILDREN by Tracy Kidder. Copyright © 1989 by John Tracy Kidder. Reprinted by permission of Houghton Mifflin Co. All rights reserved.

Chris placed her hand like a visor on her forehead. She stared at the blackened window across the room and slowly shook her head. "Poor kid."

. . . He didn't often talk. He never misbehaved. He almost always tried to do his homework. It was as another teacher had said, "Poor Pedro. He works so hard to get an F." His situation had seemed intolerable to Chris the very first day when, after assigning some simple classwork, she stopped to look over Pedro's shoulder, and he looked up at her and asked, "Did I do good, Mrs. Zajac?" (pp. 79–80)

"36 = F," Chris wrote on Pedro's social studies test. If she was not honest, she would never have the tangible evidence of progress or decline. (p. 85)

In carefully correcting and grading these tests, Chris Zajac is performing an important part of her job. She is holding students accountable for learning what they have been taught in her classroom. She is also providing them with feedback so that they can understand what they have accomplished and what they still need to work on. She is also contributing data to a growing record kept on each student so that assistance and special educational opportunities can be provided if necessary. But the task of grading is an arduous and time-consuming one, and the teacher may feel as emotional about giving grades to students as the students feel about receiving them.

VARIED PERSPECTIVES ABOUT THE PURPOSE OF EVALUATION

As described in chapter 11, many people want to know about student achievement in the elementary schools. Although the state and federal governments and school district administrators are interested in data about the average achievement levels of all students in a given grade, it is the student's parents and teachers who are most interested in the achievement of an individual student.

Teachers want to know what the student has gained from each learning event as a means of planning further experiences and as a measure of their own teaching methods. Parents want three very different types of information from an evaluation:

1. What has my child learned?
2. How well is my child doing in school?
3. What about my child's future? (Oakes & Lipton, 1990)

The question of what each student has learned focuses on an individual. It does not ask for comparisons among students and assigns no value on the student's achievement. To evaluate what a student has learned, teachers select from a variety of assessment methods such as those described in chapter 11. From informal observations, checklists of accomplishments, and data from tests and other assessment devices, it is possible to describe what a student knows about each subject in the curriculum and what skills the student has mastered. Compiling an accurate record of what each student has learned is an important part of the teacher's responsibility to the student and the parents. The record of what each student has achieved at each grade level is also valuable because it certifies whether the student has accomplished the expectations for that grade.

Reports of what a student has learned can be given through oral descriptions during a conference, accompanied by a portfolio of work samples, or it can be provided in written reports called *anecdotal records* that describe what the student has learned during a specific time period. An anecdotal record might read as follows:

> In kindergarten, this student mastered letter recognition of all 26 capital letters of the alphabet. He has almost mastered the recognition of small letters, but at present he still confuses *b, d,* and *p.* He can give an example of a word that starts with each letter of the alphabet.

Another example might read as follows:

> Third Grade, Second Quarter Report:
> Although she is still quite shy with other students, she has participated actively in her writing group. She writes full and complete sentences with interesting and detailed descriptions. She recently wrote a paragraph on dinosaurs and read it aloud to her group. They responded with much interest and enthusiasm to her vivid descriptions of various types of dinosaurs. She accepted suggestions from the group and incorporated their ideas into her revision of the work.

Such reports are valuable because they allow the parents to understand the objectives of the school and whether their child is achieving the intended learning outcomes. When parents understand the school's objectives, they are better able to join with school personnel in supporting their child's learning and affective development. Also, having accurate information about their child's achievements, failures, strengths, and weaknesses enables the parents to give their child the support and encouragement he or she needs to be successful in school (Gronlund & Linn, 1990, p. 429).

School evaluation would be a relatively simple endeavor if it only concerned the question of how much each student has learned during a given period of time. Unfortunately, few parents are satisfied with that descriptive evaluation alone. Parents often ask teachers, "How is my child doing in school?" This question could mean, "in relation to the curriculum" or "compared to his (or her) achievement at the beginning of the year." In response, teachers must be able to respond to the question, "How much of what I taught did this student learn?" (Oakes & Lipton, 1990, p. 136).

To answer this question accurately, the teacher must be able to compare the achievement of a student with a standard or criterion for success. This is the reason for the current strong interest in assessment by behavioral objectives. Each objective is written with a built-in criterion. Students who meet the criterion can be recorded to have passed or mastered the material. Students who did not meet the criterion are recorded to have failed or to be deficient in this learning task. Students who exceed the criterion can be reported to have excelled.

For example, consider the objective that students will apply recently learned math skills to calculate the answers to 100 problems, and the criterion for success is 90 of 100 correct. If Joan gets 91 correct, she is reported to have met the criterion and passed. If Sam gets 74 correct, he is reported to have failed, and if Greg gets 98 correct, he is reported to have done excellent work.

A second way to interpret the question, "How is my child doing?" reflects a strong parental interest in knowing how the student is doing *compared to others* of the same age or grade. This is the question that causes evaluations to become competitive. In recording or reporting this information to parents, the teacher must not only tell how the student did in relation to the objective criterion, but also how the student's performance compared to others in the class.

Using the same example, imagine that of the class of 30 students, 5 got scores of 95 or above, 15 got scores of 90 to 95, and 10 got scores below 90. Then the report on each student may contain the information that allows the parents to see how well the student is doing compared to the rest of the class. Joan met the criterion, but so did half the class, so her performance is reported to be near the mean or average. Sam got only 74 correct, but six other students made even more errors than he did. This means that Sam is in the bottom half of the class but above those who are in the bottom fifth. Greg, with his score of 98, was also the top scorer in the class, which may please his parents even more than knowing that he exceeded the criterion.

Standardized achievement test data can also be interpreted to inform parents where their child stands in relation to students in the same grade throughout the United States. In most elementary schools, the classroom teacher must be able to interpret the data from classroom events and from achievement tests for the parents, so that they understand how well the student is doing compared to others at the same grade level.

The third question that parents ask in many school evaluations is, "What about my child's future?" This really means, "What does the present performance tell us about this child's future?" In other words, "Is my child college material?" "Is it likely that my child will be able to earn a good living?" These questions call for more than simple descriptions or comparisons. The teacher is expected to be a forecaster, predicting the future achievements of the student based on the present school performance. This is not as difficult as it may sound, at least as far as the prediction of future success in school is concerned. Studies show that present performance in school is a fairly accurate predictor of future performance in school (Bloom, 1982).

Teachers are not usually required to speculate about future performance in their records or reports of student achievement. But many do so informally. They predict success or failure to other teachers in the school as in, "Oh, you have Greg this year? I had him last year. He's a straight A student." They may also offer conjectures to the parents, such as, "If we don't get this kid's behavior straightened out now, I'm afraid he'll end up behind bars."

Teachers' predictions are often made as recommendations for special gifted or enrichment programs, college-bound or vocational curricula, and ability tracks when the student leaves the elementary school for junior and senior high school. These predictions may contribute to a self-fulfilling prophecy. It is certainly true that the students who are recommended for enriched educational opportunities are more likely to succeed in school than their classmates. But some reflective teachers wonder which comes first, the enriched opportunity or the success. They'd like to see how well average students would do if they were offered the types of enriched learning experiences that are available to students selected for elementary gifted programs.

PHILOSOPHIES UNDERLYING VARIOUS EVALUATION SYSTEMS

Reflective teachers struggle with many conflicting ideas, thoughts, and concerns when they confront existing evaluation systems. Prevailing systems seem highly related to the

R-A view of teaching and learning, which is based on the assumption that students vary in ability and that they acquire learning by passively receiving knowledge from the teacher. From this assumption, it is logical to conclude that students should be evaluated by determining what they have learned and how this compares to other students of the same age. Categorizing and rank ordering of students is the next step and is done by assigning letter grades to label respective categories of ability. Teachers with this perspective can be overheard saying "John is an A student, and Sally is a C student."

Teachers with a C-M view of teaching are often very uncomfortable with such statements. They recognize the complex mix of environmental, nutritional, genetic, and experiential factors that contribute to each student's success or lack of success in school. Moreover, according to their view of teaching and learning, it is the teachers' responsibility to diagnose the students' needs and then plan a series of learning experiences and the scaffolding that is necessary for each student to experience success. The competitive nature of letter grades contrasts sharply with this philosophy.

How Curriculum Orientations Influence Evaluation

In addition to having a general overarching philosophy of teaching and learning, each teacher may prefer one or more of the five curriculum orientations described by Eisner (1985). Just as a teacher's curriculum orientation influences the learning activities that take place in that classroom, it also influences the assessment methods used to evaluate what students have learned and how well they have learned it. A teacher with only one strongly held curriculum orientation is likely to use similar methods of assessment day after day in every subject of the curriculum. For example, a teacher with a strong academic rationalism orientation will use tests and restricted essays as the preferred method of evaluating student performance.

Students who do well on that type of assessment are likely to be perceived as being successful by that teacher. They will get A's in that class. Students who do less well on that type of assessment will get lower grades. The teacher will predict the students' future success based on this strongly held curriculum orientation. Teachers who do not know or understand the variations in curriculum orientations may assume that their own perspective is the only way or the best way to view schooling.

Many teachers have more than one curriulum orientation. They may combine several or have one orientation for one school subject and a different orientation for the arts or another academic area. These teachers are likely to select a variety of assessment devices because their vision of the curriculum is multifaceted. Students in their classrooms may do well on one type of assessment and poorly on another. This varied performance will be recorded and reported.

The purpose of describing how a teacher's curriculum orientation affects the types of assessment methods chosen and the evaluation is to allow you to begin to clarify your own curriculum orientation(s) and to help you see how your orientation(s) can influence your choice of assessment methods and your vision of how well a student is achieving in your classroom. It can also help you to interpret the judgments and recommendations about your students made by other teachers.

How Various Orientations Affect Teachers' Observations

Teachers with all curriculum orientations use informal observations as a means of evaluating what students know and what they need to know. Teachers oriented to the use of curriculum technology plan their curriculum with behavioral objectives. As they observe and listen to their students, they are assessing whether the student is reaching the criterion established for the lesson.

Academic rationalists are interested in assessing what has recently been termed *cultural literacy* (Hirsch, 1987). They assume that there is a body of traditional knowledge that all students should learn in school. As they listen to students discuss the content and ideas expressed in a classic text or literary work, they assess whether students have a mature understanding of the ideas or whether they require greater explication and perhaps a rereading of the text in order to gain the desirable degree of understanding.

Teachers with a social perspective plan a curriculum that emphasizes social awareness and responsibility. As they observe their students working, they are likely to be assessing the degree to which the students interact cooperatively or the extent to which a student is taking an active role in solving a social dilemma.

Teachers with a cognitive processes orientation emphasize the learning of processes over the mastery of content. As students work on problems, the teacher is likely to interrupt their independent practice to ask them to describe how they are attempting to solve the problem. As the students describe their thinking processes, the teacher assesses whether they are using an appropriate process. The teacher also makes a judgment about whether their thinking is efficient and likely to lead to a correct solution or whether the teacher should provide the students with scaffolding that will lead to a more strategic problem-solving process.

Teachers with a personal relevance orientation emphasize the affective domain over the cognitive domain. They are interested in helping students develop positive self-esteem and intrinsic interest in learning. Their observations monitor student interest and engagement in the learning events.

How Curriculum Orientations Relate to Test Construction

Teachers with all five curriculum orientations are likely to use occasional short-answer quizzes and tests. However, academic rationalists and curriculum technologists are likely to use more of them than teachers with the other three orientations.

The type of tests used by curriculum technologists has been fairly well described in the section on mastery of learning objectives in chapter 11. These teachers create both formative and summative quizzes and tests that are designed, item by item, to be related to their preplanned behavioral objectives.

Academic rationalists are likely to use summative tests to assess whether their students have gained knowledge about the identity of the world's great thinkers and the contributions each has made to our culture. For example, tests that ask students to match the author with an idea or a title would be created by a teacher with an academic rationalist orientation.

Teachers with a cognitive processing orientation are likely to use tests in which students solve problems. They are also likely to ask students to show their work rather than simply provide an answer. This is because these teachers are primarily concerned with assessing how students think, and they can evaluate that more accurately if they can see the steps used by the student in thinking through a problem.

Teachers with a social perspective design tests to assess whether their students are able to understand and solve difficult social problems. Tests and quizzes would likely consist of some short-answer items designed to test the student's knowledge base on each subject, but most items would probably ask students to apply this knowledge to social concerns.

Teachers with a personal relevance orientation may include a few short answer knowledge base questions, but most items will ask students to apply the new information to their own lives or give their opinions about the ideas they've read. It is also likely that these teachers would write the test in such a way that students are free to choose to answer some items and omit others that in which they are less interested. Directions for tests given by this type of teacher usually include "Choose three of the five questions."

How Curriclum Orientations Affect the Selection and Use of Other Assessment Devices

Aside from informal observations and tests, teachers with a curriculum technology orientation are likely to use checklists and rating scales describing the mastery of skills. They are less likely to use essays, as these are less objective than a curriculum technologist prefers. They may use learning contracts, but these would resemble checklists of skills and would simply be used as a reminder to students of where they are in the sequence of objectives that must be mastered. They are very unlikely to use tests of inquiry, creative products, or performances as a means of evaluating student progress. Portfolios of student products would contain primarily worksheets and formative and summative tests.

Academic rationalists emphasize the assessment of students' knowledge and comprehension of a large body of content in classic literature and subject areas. They are quite likely to use essays as a means of assessing the students' comprehension of historically valued information, principles, and works of art and literature that make up the bulk of their curriculum. Oral presentations and debates are also likely to be employed for the same reason. They are less likely to use checklists and rating scales because these typically emphasize skills rather than content. The portfolios kept by academic rationalists would contain mainly tests and essays.

In contrast, teachers with a cognitive processes orientation are more interested in process than content. When they evaluate essays, they are more likely to look for evidence of the students' application of ideas, research skills, and hypothesis testing than the content itself. Oral presentations would also be evaluated more on process than on content. Tests of inquiry are likely to be used more frequently than objective tests because these teachers believe in teaching students how to use inquiry and critical thinking skills to gain knowledge. Individual creative products and performances are likely to be assigned and evaluated with an emphasis on how well the students are progressing in the processing information through the use of research, investigations, experiments, and reporting of findings. Portfolios are likely to contain "before" and "after" work samples and a variety of students' products to demonstrate how each student's skill in cognitive processing is growing and developing with time.

Teachers with a social perspective are likely to emphasize cooperative group projects and products over individual ones. Group learning contracts may be employed to assess cooperative efforts. In assessing individual work, these teachers are likely to use many expressive essays and oral presentations on social topics and problems to evaluate the extent to which each individual is growing in awareness of social needs and taking responsibility for creating solutions. Tests of inquiry into social concerns are also likely to be given. Portfolios are likely to contain these essays, letters to the editor, political cartoons, and other work that shows evidence of social awareness and concern.

Teachers with a personal relevance orientation are most likely to use learning contracts with many options for self-selection as a measure of student accomplishment. These teachers believe that it is important to match the interests and individual needs of students with the topic being learned, and that self-selection encourages intrinsic interest and motivation in completing school assignments. Essays are likely to be quite open-ended and expressive in nature. Students are encouraged to create individual products and performances, and these are likely to be prized by the teacher as evidence of student acccomplishment and achievement. Portfolios of creative efforts and videotapes of performances are likely to be used to display students' accomplishments to others.

Conventional methods of assessing students' accomplishments have stressed the use of objective tests and content-oriented essays. That is probably due to the strong orientation toward academic rationalism that was the basis of the first schools in the United States and exerts a strong influence up to the present day. The second major orientation in this country is curriculum technology, which also stresses the use of objective tests and checklists.

Although Dewey (1933) exhibited a combined orientation toward cognitive processing, social perspectives, and personal relevance, his influence did not fundamentally change the orientation of school personnel in the early 20th century. Since the 1960s these three orientations have grown in strength, number, and influence. When you enter the teaching profession, you will see and hear evidence of all five orientations any time that teachers meet to discuss curriculum concerns. You will also see and hear the philosophies of all five orientations being debated when teachers get together to discuss how to assess student learning. It will serve you well to clarify which of these orientations you hold so that you can assert your own views on the appropriate assessment methods to use to evaluate the accomplishments of your students.

METHODS OF REPORTING STUDENT ACCOMPLISHMENT

Due to the time-consuming nature of the task of correcting students' work and the complexities of the evaluation processes described previously, it is easy to see why school personnel have resorted to a form of shorthand to record and report student progress. Most teachers have too many students and too little time to hold discussions with each student's parents or to write extensive narratives of each student's learning on a regular basis. Schools use standardized shorthand methods known as *grades* and *test scores* to communicate with parents, future teachers, college admission personnel, and future employers (Oakes & Lipton, 1990).

The practice of awarding letter grades as measures of individual achievement has been part of the American educational scene for many decades. In the 1960s and 1970s, personnel in some school districts attempted to replace conventional report cards with detailed anecdotal records, describing what each student had accomplished in each subject area during the course or term. But these attempts to change the prevailing evaluation system met with opposition from parents, who insisted on a return to the letter grade system with which they had grown up. Parents were not satisfied with a description of their own child's achievements. They wanted to know how their child compared with other students. They expressed concern that these records would not be accepted at the most prestigious colleges.

In response to these debates, school boards and administrators in most school districts arrived at a compromise. While they reestablished the letter grade report cards for the intermediate and upper elementary grades, they retained the use of anecdotal report cards for the primary grades. This is the prevailing practice today. That means that if you are planning to teach at the primary grades (kindergarten through the second or third grade), you will be expected to write anecdotal report cards describing and documenting what each student in your classroom has learned. If you are planning to teach at the intermediate grades (second or third grades through sixth grade) or the middle school (fifth grade through eighth grade) or at a junior high school (sixth or seventh grade through eighth or ninth grade), you will be expected to compute letter grades every quarter for the students' report cards.

Combining Evaluation Data

There is no formula that beginning teachers can learn from experienced teachers to guide them in selecting appropriate assessment devices and combining the data into a rationale for a grade. That is because no two teachers have the same philosophies or combination of curriculum orientations. Consider what would happen, for example, if Mary, an experienced teacher who holds an R-A view of learning and a strong academic rationalist curriculum orientation, tells Pam, a beginning teacher with a C-M view of learning and a mix of curriculum orientations how to compute grades for report cards. Their conversation might sound like this:

PAM: Mary, can you tell me how to figure my report card grades.

MARY: Sure. Here are the tests I use. They are fill-in-the-blank and short essay items. I use a straight percentage to figure my grades. Ninety percent and above is an A, eighty is a B, and so on. Then, for report cards, I just average the results of the tests.

PAM: But, how do you count in projects like the models my students made of the Indian villages during colonial times?

MARY: I don't count those at all, except maybe for extra credit. If a student is on the borderline, I might give him the higher grade if he did a nice project.

PAM: Well, then what do you do about students who try very hard, but don't do well on the tests?

MARY: I just give them what they earn. That's what grades are supposed to do—communicate whether students learned what we taught them.

PAM: But what if they cooperated very well with their groups and helped to put on a great dramatic skit about the Pilgrims and the Indians but still did not retain the facts and dates on these tests? How can I give that student a flunking grade?

MARY: That's easy. You don't need to do so many of those *extra* projects. They just confuse you and the students. Spend more time on reading, recitation, and worksheets, and they'll do better on the tests. Grades are supposed to reflect knowledge of content, not fluff like group projects, models, and plays.

Pam is likely to come away from this exchange discouraged and more confused than ever. Mary makes it sound so easy. She seems to have an efficient system for deciding on grades, but it just does not seem to fit Pam's curriculum or her philosophy that every student can accomplish something valuable in school, although not all students can be expected to learn in the same way or accomplish the same goals. In an attempt to gather more useful information, Pam may consult a second experienced teacher named Tom, who is known for his creative projects and highly interactive relationships with his students. "I like the way he teaches," Pam thinks. "Perhaps his system of grading will work for me too."

PAM: Can you tell me how you figure your report card grades?

TOM: Oh, I wish you hadn't asked me that. Its not something I feel very sure about.

PAM: But you've been teaching for several years. How have you figured your grades up to now?

TOM: Well, I mostly go with student effort. If a student is willing to work and takes an active part in our class projects, I give her an A.

PAM: What kinds of tests do you give? How do you record what students have learned?

TOM: That's why I wish you hadn't asked. I use my gradebook for attendance only. If I had to show evidence of why a student got a certain grade, I'd be in trouble.

PAM: Well, don't you have to show that kind of data to the parents during the conferences?

TOM: So far, I've avoided it. They're usually so happy with the high grades their kids are getting that they don't ask me for too many details.

If you are like Pam, you are probably not satisfied with either of these explanations. You probably feel a need for answers to such questions as these:

1. What should be included in a letter grade?
2. How should achievement data be combined in assigning letter grades?
3. What frame of reference should be used in grading?
4. How should distribution of grades be determined? (Gronlund & Linn, 1990, p. 437).

Gronlund and Linn's (1990) textbook, *Measurement and Evaluation in Teaching* is an excellent resource for teachers who want to know more about this important subject than can be presented in this text. A brief summary of their response to each of these questions follows.°

What Should Be Included in a Letter Grade?

Traditionally, there are five letter grades (A, B, C, D, F), although some schools reduce this number to three (E = Excellent, S = Satisfactory, U = Unsatisfactory). According to Gronlund and Linn (1990) letter grades are efficient systems for communicating student achievement to parents and students when they are used for evaluation of academic achievement only. When extraneous factors such as behavior and effort are combined with achievement data, letter grades lose their meaning. For example, if effort and achievement are combined in the teacher's mind, a grade of C may mean excellent achievement combined with little or no effort, or it could mean excellent effort combined with very low achievement, or it could mean a moderate amount of effort and achievement. Therefore, the first recommendation is to use separate systems for communicating student behavior and effort, and to compute the letter grades on achievement data alone.

Second, "if letter grades are to serve as valid indicators of achievement, they must be based on valid measures of achievement" (Gronlund & Linn, 1990, p. 437). This means that the assessment devices selected or created by the teacher need to fit the objectives of the learning experience.

How Should Achievement Data Be Combined?

The emphasis given to tests, essays, ratings, and other measures of achievement should be guided by the type of objectives that were planned and covered in the course or term. The more important the objective in the curriculum, the greater weight it should receive in the final grade.

Teachers with various curriculum orientations are likely to establish different objectives for their classrooms or give varying weights to the same type of item. The variation among teachers cannot be eliminated, but each teacher must be able to define the learning objectives he or she has established for the subject area and to base the letter grade on a reasonable combination of all of these objectives.

Combining data is difficult because various assessment measures are often different from each other. Some tests may contain 100 items, and others contain only 25. If two measures are not equivalent, the grades on each one should be given different weights.

For example, if a student receives an A on the 100-item test and a C on the 25-item test, what grade does he or she deserve when the two items are combined? The average of an A and a C is typically a B, but that is only if the tests were equivalent. In this case, the 100-item test is worth four times as much as the 25-item test. That can be taken into account in at least two ways. One way is to multiply the value of the 100 item test times four when combining it with the 25-item test. That means that it is worth four As. Four As and one C will compute to a final grade of A.

°Excerpts from MEASUREMENT AND EVALUATION IN TEACHING, Sixth Edition by Norman E. Gronlund and Robert L. Linn. Reprinted by permission of Macmillan Publishing Company. Copyright © 1990 by Macmillan Publishing Company.

What Frame of Reference Should Be Used in Grading?

Gronlund and Linn (1990) suggest that three typical frames of reference are used in grading decisions:

1. Performance in relations to other groups (relative grading)
2. Performance in relationship to prespecified standards (absolute grading)
3. Performance in relation to learning ability or amount of improvement. (p. 439)

Relative grading involves determining grades by comparing one student's achievement with the achievement of the other members of the class. An individual's grade is influenced by both the student's performance and the performance of the group. A student is likely to receive a better grade in a low-achieving group than in a high-achieving group.

Absolute grading is the method of establishing a standard for mastery and awarding grades according to the extent of mastery each student achieves. The most common system of this type used in elementary schools is the percentage system.

The system of grading performance *in relation to learning ability* or amount of improvement is used fairly widely in elementary schools, but, as employed, it is seldom a reliable assessment. Reliable measures of growth or improvement are difficult to achieve with or without tests. Teachers may use the system in order to motivate low-achieving students, but Gronlund and Linn (1990) believe that the available measures are so undependable that achievement should be reported using one of the other two frames of reference and that improvement should be reported as a secondary or supplemental grade.

How Should the Distribution of Grades Be Determined?

Relative grading has become known as *grading on the curve.* This is because it was developed to coincide with the normal curve of distribution, but this is not a reasonable possibility in a group the size of a single class. Instead, Gronlund and Linn (1990) suggest that a reasonable distribution may be in the following ranges:

A = 10 to 20% of the pupils
B = 20 to 30% of the pupils
C = 30 to 50% of the pupils
D = 10 to 20% of the pupils
F = 0 to 10% of the pupils (pp. 441–442)

These ranges are not scientifically determined, but they represent a general target for this type of grading. Final decisions regarding the actual distribution should take into account the school's philosophy, the population served, and the purpose of the grades. One element that distinguishes this distribution from the normal curve is that it does not require some students to fail because they are at the bottom of the distribution.

Using an absolute grading system, Gronlund and Linn (1990) recommend the following distribution ranges:

A = 95 to 100% correct
B = 85 to 94% correct

C = 75 to 84% correct
D = 65 to 74% correct
F = below 65% correct (p. 443)

Elementary teachers may prefer to alter these ranges in order to create more opportunities for earning the highest grade. With absolute grading systems such as this, the distribution of grades is not dependent on the achievement of others. If all pupils demonstrate a high level of mastery, they can all receive high grades. Gronlund and Linn (1990) argue that whether students pass or fail a course should depend not on their ranking within the class but on their absolute level of learning. If all low-ranking students have mastered the material sufficiently, they should all pass (p. 442).

A Grading System That Encourages Success

A major reason for failure in elementary schools is that often the students do not know what they are expected to do in order to succeed. In some classrooms, the teacher's expectations may be vague and unclear. The students know only that they are supposed to work hard and do well on all of the classwork and tests that come their way. But some students may not be good at guessing what the teacher's real priorities are. This may be because the teacher has not sorted out these priorities either.

No two grading systems are alike. Teachers have different expectations due to their philosophies and views of how students learn. They have widely different priorities because of their curriculum orientations. They also have many other personality traits, interests, and values that influence their expectations for their students.

How can students be expected to adapt to so many different teachers with such a variety of expectations? It appears that most students can and do adapt if they are clearly and precisely informed about the expectations in each class. On entering a class for the first time, students want to know what the rules and expectations are in *this* class. Just as a clear statement of behavior rules and procedures is important, so is a clear statement of how to get a good grade on each project, paper, or test.

To be able to describe clearly to your students what you expect, it is essential that you first clarify your expectations for yourself. A synthesis of research on effective evaluation suggests that you are most likely to clarify your own expectations and communicate them effectively to your students if you use the following steps for each subject area that you are grading:

1. Plan a set of educational objectives.
2. Decide which of the objectives are most important. Plan how you will weight them when you combine their data.
3. Plan learning experiences for each objective.
4. Select a suitable assessment device to measure the students' accomplishments for each objective.
5. Create a clear criterion for success for each objective, that is also appropriate for the assessment device you selected.
6. At the beginning of each learning event, *inform students* about
   a. the goal or purpose of the learning activity.
   b. the criterion for success.

    c. what you will be looking for when you correct their work and precisely how you will *score* their work.

    d. what they may do if their first attempt is not acceptable.

7. When you correct and mark students' work, provide adequate feedback on what was done correctly and what needs to be improved. Give suggestions for improvement. Encourage students to confer with you about how to improve their work.

8. Well before report card grades are due, *inform students* about:

    a. what work will count toward the report card grade.

    b. what work will be given the greatest weight for the report card.

    c. what students may do to improve work for a higher grade.

9. When report cards are distributed, have a conference with each student and explain the reason for each grade. Describe the good work that resulted in good grades and describe the unacceptable work that resulted in poor grades. Help student to see how to make improvements in the unacceptable work during the next term.

Although some of these nine steps are commonly used in elementary classrooms, many are not. Most teachers do plan learning objectives, but many do not consider which ones are most important. Often teachers treat all objectives as if they are equal, at least on paper. They may have priorities, but these priorities are not well communicated to their students. Few teachers have clarified the weight they plan to give to each type of work and each objective. This situation was illustrated by Pam's dilemma. She had carefully planned a stimulating set of learning activities, but had given no thought to how she would combine and weigh the outcomes until the last moment.

Another rarity in elementary classrooms is the practice of telling students how each piece of work will be scored and graded. Some teachers, exemplified by Tom, don't appear to know what they are really looking for in student work, apart from enthusiasm and participation. Others may have a much clearer understanding of this issue, but they do not believe that students need to know their conclusions.

Teachers with a C-M view of the teaching and learning processes believe otherwise. Rather than keeping the evaluation process a mystery, these teachers believe strongly that students *need to know* exactly how to succeed and what is expected of them. If they know these things, they can learn to take an active role in monitoring and evaluating their own work. One of the cognitive processes that these teachers want students to learn is known as *metacognition,* the capacity to monitor and regulate their own work. They plan learning activities that promote independence and personal responsibility. They are also likely to organize their evaluation system around the principle of helping students gain more control over the quality of their work (Anderson, 1989, p. 92).

Informing students of exactly what is expected, how each piece of work will be scored and graded, and how various assignments and assessments will be weighed in determining the final grade gives students the information they need in order to regulate their own work. With this knowledge, they can make well-informed decisions about how much time and energy to spend on each assignment or task. They can learn to recognize when they should revise and improve a piece of work before turning it in or when to revise their work further after the first attempt.

Teachers who plan their evaluation systems to assist students in the development of metacognition need to recognize that the capacity for self-regulation entails the use of a very complex set of cognitive processes, such as recognition of whether they comprehend an idea or whether the learning strategy they are using is appropriate. The development of metacognition takes time. It also takes many learning experiences in which it is used and practiced by students. In the elementary grades, students need a great deal of scaffolding to help them gain these skills. Clear statements of what is expected and how to succeed, examples of what a good piece of work contains and what a poor piece of work looks like, precise and detailed feedback, and suggestions for improvement are all scaffolds that students need at this age.

An Illustration of a C-M Evaluation System

Imagine that all the seventh-grade teachers in a middle school collaborate to plan a 9-week interdisciplinary unit on people and their environment. The cognitive goal of the unit is to inform students about the present dangers to the natural environment. The affective goal is to create in each student a sense of responsibility toward the environment. The psychomotor goal stresses how to live in the environment, using it wisely.

The primary learning activities of this unit will include 4 weeks devoted to developing a knowledge base and understanding the basic concepts related to environmental concerns. Readings are assigned, discussions planned, guest lecturers invited, and films ordered. During the fifth week, the entire group is scheduled to spend a week at an outdoor education site learning how to use natural products, how to test for environmental hazards, and to create artworks and write poems, stories, essays, and dramas about the relationship of people to their environment. During the final 4 weeks, students will work in cooperative groups to investigate one environmental problem and present their findings and solutions to their peers in a science exhibit at the conclusion of the unit.

The primary objectives of this unit, with the criteria for success underlined in each, are listed below. The number of asterisks (*) next to each objective indicates the importance of that objective and the weight that will be given to its product in the final determination of grades.

Knowledge-Level Objective

*1. On a matching test, students will be able to *identify 7 out of 10 sites* of environmental pollution and connect them with the type of hazard that exists at that site.

Grade Equivalents: A = 10 correct
                    B = 9 correct
                    C = 8 correct
                    D = 7 correct
                    F = less than 7 correct

Comprehension-Level Objective

°2. On a short-answer test, students will be able to write the definitions of *10 terms* related to the environment, *with no more than two errors.*

Grade Equivalents: A = 10 correct
 B = 9 correct
 C = 8 correct
 D = 7 correct
 F = less than 7 correct

Application-Level Objectives

°°3. Students will conduct *two tests* for water and air pollution during the outdoor education experience. They will write laboratory reports worth *10 points each* that include their observations, hypotheses, tests, and the results of their tests.

Grade Equivalents: A = 20 points
 B = 18 points
 C = 16 points
 D = 14 points
 F = less than 14 points

°4. Students will demonstrate that they can find food, and create a safe shelter in the natural environment. They will *identify at least 10 edible foods, for 0.5 points each, and draw a picture, worth 5 points,* of the shelter they would create of natural materials.

Grade Equivalents: A = 10 points
 B = 9 points
 C = 8 points
 D = 7 points
 F = less than 7 correct

Analysis-Level Objective

°5. Students will create a chart showing cause and effect or a comparison between environmentally safe and hazardous practices for their cooperative group display at the science fair. The chart will contain *at least 10 comparison or cause-and-effect elements.*

Grade Equivalents: A = 10 or more points
 B = 9 points
 C = 8 points
 D = less than 7 points
 F = not done or not handed in

Synthesis-Level Objective

°6. Students will create a song, poem, story, essay, play, or skit to read aloud or perform at an assembly during the outdoor education week. Each work will contain a description of how people interact with nature and stress the importance of good ecology. *Criteria: Each work will receive 0,*

1, or 2 points for each of the following three elements: Fits Topic, Clarity, Interest, Length, and Originality

Grade Equivalents: A = 9–10 points

B = 7– 8 points

C = 5– 6 points

D = 3– 4 points

F = not done or not handed in

Evaluation-Level Objective

°°°7. Students will write a three-page essay giving their opinions of the most serious concern related to the environment. The essay will contain *at least five elements* as supporting evidence for this evaluation and will suggest *at least three ways* people can solve the problem and alleviate the hazard. *Criteria: 1 point for each element stated above. In addition, each essay will receive 0, 1, or 2 points for the writing elements of clarity and originality, for a possible total of 12 points.*

Grade Equivalents: A = 10 points

B = 8 points

C = 6 points

D = 4 points

F = not done or not handed in

Note that these seven assessment methods have a total of 10 asterisks. That means that each asterisk symbolizes a value worth 10% of the final grade. Most objectives are each worth 10%; the set of experiments is worth 20%; and the final essay is worth 30% of the final grade. The teachers planned their unit in this way so that they could easily weigh the value of each assessment in determining the students' final grades for the unit. They plan to distribute a list of all of the requirements, with their criteria for grades and the weight of each grade to the students on the first day of the unit so that the students will know at the outset what is expected of them and how they can succeed.

When they correct each of the seven assignments, the teachers plan to provide adequate feedback in their written comments or in a conference with the students so that they know what they did that was successful and what did not meet the criteria. Then the students will have 1 week to make revisions and improvements on all assignments except the two objective tests if they wish to raise their grades.

At the end of the unit, the grades may be recorded in the teachers' grade books as shown in Figure 12–1.

Computation of Grades

The computation of the final grades for the unit is shown in Figure 12–2. It involves a straightforward computation of an average grade by awarding numerical equivalents to each letter grade, multiplying each grade times its weighted value, adding the seven items, and dividing the total score by 10. Note that although there are 7 items, the average score is computed by a factor of 10 in order to take into account the greater weight placed on two of the items.

FIGURE 12–1

Teacher's Grade Book Showing the Grades Recorded for the Objectives
of the People and Their Environment Unit

	Graded Objectives						
Name of Student	*1	*2	**3	*4	*5	*6	***7
Jane	A	B	B	A	C	A	B
Bill	B	C	A	B	C	C	B
Gary	D	C	A	C	B	F	C

An alternative method for computing grades is to award points for each assessment product, add up the points, and compare the total to a predetermined scale. In this unit, each of the seven assessments could be assigned a certain point value. Refer back to the objectives with their point values. Notice that objectives 1, 2, 4, 5, and 6 are each worth 10 points. Objective 3, which is considered to be twice as important as the others has a point count that is also double in value. Only objective 7 must be weighted to reflect its relative value. The logical method for calculating a student's total points for the unit, then, is to record the raw score or points in the grade book, multiplying objective 7 by three before recording it. This produces a total of 100 points for all the assessments in the unit. Using 10% increments, the grades can be assigned as follows:

A = >90 points
B = >80 points
C = >70 points
D = >60 points
F = <60 points

The rationale for using this system instead of the first one is that it diminishes the focus on grades during the unit itself. Rather than receiving a C on a paper, the student receives a certain number of points. With appropriate critical feedback, students may be able to revise their first attempts to earn more points. When students are allowed and encouraged to revise and return their work, they are able to monitor their own progress. By keeping track of how many points they have earned to date, they can decide for themselves whether they need to revise and return their work for additional points. Deadlines for revisions, such as 1 week from receiving the corrected paper, can be used to hold students accountable for timely efforts on their own behalf. This system fits very well with the R-A philosophy of encouraging students to use metacognitive skills in evaluating and taking control of their own school achievements.

Whatever method you choose for determining grades, after they are computed they are recorded in the student's cumulative folder and on the report cards that are sent home to parents. Intermediate report cards are likely to use letter grades to sum up the student's achievement in each academic subject. Some report cards, such as the one in Figure 12–3, may also provide checklists of subskills beneath the letter

FIGURE 12–2
Teacher's Computations of Grades for the People and Their Environment Unit

Name	*1	*2	**3	*4	*5	*6	***7	Final Grade
				Value of Grade ($\times$) Weight (*)				
Jane	A	B	B	A	C	A	A	
	4×1	3×1	3×2	4×1	2×1	4×1	4×3	
								35/10 =
	4	+ 3	+ 6	+ 4	+ 2	+ 4	+ 12	3.5 = A
Bill	B	C	A	B	C	C	B	
	3×1	2×1	4×2	3×1	2×1	2×1	3×3	
								29/10 =
	3	+ 2	+ 8	+ 3	+ 2	+ 2	+ 9	2.9 = B
Gary	D	C	A	C	B	F	C	
	1×1	2×1	4×2	2×1	3×1	0×1	2×3	
								22/10 =
	1	+ 2	+ 8	+ 2	+ 3	+ 0	+ 6	2.2 = C

Values of Grades for Computation Purposes

A = 4.0   B = 3.0   C = 2.0   D = 1.0   F = 0.0

Final Grade Point Averages Equivalent to Final Letter Grade

A = 3.5–4.0   B = 2.5–3.4   C = 1.5–2.4   D = 0.5–1.4   F = 0.0–0.4

grade as a means of explaining to parents how the letter grade was determined. Because few report cards have categories for interdisciplinary units such as the one on people and the environment, it is likely that the teachers in this example would record the grade under Science or Social Studies and explain in an accompanying note what the grade represents.

Within this unit, there are many learning experiences planned, but only these seven products will be assessed as a means of determining a final grade. The teachers who created this unit are very proud of the way these assessments evaluate learning at all six levels of Bloom's Taxonomy. They are also pleased that the assessments allow students with different learning styles to demonstrate what they have learned.

They have agreed that they will inform students of exactly what is expected at each stage of the learning process. During the first 4 weeks, when the students are reading and doing assignments to establish a knowledge base, the teachers will inform

FIGURE 12–3
Intermediate Report Card

Name _____

Explanation of Marks

A—Excellent Progress
B—Very Good Progress
C—Satisfactory Progress
D—Minimal Progress
U—Unsatisfactory Progress

Sub Skills

/ / Meeting expectations
/ √ / Needs Improvement
/ + / Exceeding Expectations

GENERAL STUDY SKILLS

Listens Attentively
Is Prepared for Class
Works Independently
Completes Work on Time
Uses Time Well
Cooperates in Group Work
Follows Directions
Works Accurately
Uses Assignment Notebook
Works Neatly

PERSONAL AND SOCIAL GROWTH

Accepts & Respects Authority
Practices Self Control
Respects Rights, Opinions
  and Property of Others
Works Accurately
Assumes Responsibility
  for Own Actions

Level of Materials

1—Above Grade Level
2—At Grade Level
3—Below Grade Level

1st	2nd	3rd	4th

LANGUAGE ARTS

1st	2nd	3rd	4th

READING

Level of Materials
Effort
Comprehends What is Read
Understands Vocabulary
Uses Word Analysis Skills
Applies Reference/Study Skills
Reads for Pleasure

WRITING

Effort
Organizes Ideas
Uses Correct Grammar
Uses Proper Mechanics
Proofreads
Expresses Ideas

SPELLING

Effort
Applies Spelling Skills
Knows Assigned Words

HANDWRITING

Effort
Legibility

SPEAKING

Expresses Ideas Clearly
Uses Correct Grammar
Projects Voice

1st	2nd	3rd	4th

MATHEMATICS

Level of Materials
Effort
Knows Basic Facts (+,−,×,÷)
Understands Concepts
Computes Accurately
Uses Problem Solving Strategies
Understands Geometry

SCIENCE

Effort
Understands Concepts
Draws Conclusions
Makes Observations and
  Comparisons
Participates in Activities

SOCIAL STUDIES

Effort
Understands Concepts
Applies Graph, Chart and
  Map Skills
Is Aware of Current Events
Participates in Activities

From Glenview School District No. 34, Glenview, Illinois. Reprinted with permission.

them of the nature of the two objective tests and provide them with samples of the items on the test.

When the classes go to the outdoor education site, the teachers will inform the students which activities are to be graded and how much each grade is worth. They will provide examples of well-written lab reports and will demonstrate the difference between a creative writing product that fits the topic and has clarity and originality and one that misses the topic and lacks clarity and originality (for example, one that borrows heavily from an existing nursery rhyme or song).

Back in the classroom, as students begin their individual investigations, the teachers will show examples of well-researched charts and give examples of evaluation essays that contain all of the important elements. At all stages of the evaluation process, the teachers will encourage their students to revise and return their first attempts so that they can experience the good feelings of being in control of their own success in school.

Writing Anecdotal Records

In most school districts, teachers are responsible for writing three or four report cards per year. These contain descriptions of each student's current level of accomplishment in each of the major areas of the curriculum, plus a summary of the student's work habits and social adjustment to school and peers. At the primary grades, report cards usually consist of either anecdotal records or checklists of skills rather than letter grades. Some school districts may use both (see Figures 12–4 and 12–5).

The advantage to this double format is that it allows the teachers to describe and report their direct observations of a student's actual behaviors and accomplishments with sufficient detail so that parents understand the student's strengths and deficiencies. This is especially useful for such skill areas as listening, speaking, writing, study habits, social skills, and interests (Gronlund & Linn, 1990).

In the upper elementary grades, anecdotal records are used less often in report cards. But when a concern about a student arises, the teacher's daily observations of the student's work habits or social interactions can be important sources of data to help parents or other school personnel understand the particular needs and strengths of the student. These observations may be augmented by the use of written anecdotal records of what the teacher observes. For example, if a student comes to school late, appears tired, and has difficulty sitting still in her desk, the teacher may want to document these observations by keeping a short anecdotal record for a week, recording how late the student is every morning and describing episodes of falling asleep or inattentiveness. When this written record is shown to the parents, it is more likely to enlist their cooperation with the teacher in seeking answers to the problem than if the teacher simply reports orally that the student is "always late and too tired to work."

To be used to their best advantage, anecdotal records should be limited to observations of specific skills, social problems, or behavioral concerns. If a teacher sets out to record every behavior and event in a student's school day, the process will become too tiring and difficult to be feasible. Instead, when a student is exhibiting a

FIGURE 12–4
Primary Report Card (Checklist of Skills)

Name: _____ School: _____ Teacher: _____ Year: _____

The marks on this page reflect your child's performance. If your child is working significantly above or below grade level, that information is noted in the comment sections.

Explanation of Marks

+ - applies appropriate grade level skills on consistent basis

√ - has been introduced to skills

√ - needs further practice on appropriate grade level skills

No mark indicates that your child has not been introduced to this skill at the present time.

READING

	1	2	3
has concept of word			
identifies consonant sounds			
recognizes sight words			
uses pictures and context clues			
recognizes word family patterns			
applies phonic skills to attack new words			
recognizes long and short vowels			
comprehends material read			
can retell story in sequence			
predicts outcomes			

LANGUAGE ARTS

	1	2	3
expresses thoughts orally			
writes words			
writes sentences			
writes stories			
spelling			
handwriting			
recognizes capitalization			
recognizes punctuation			

MATHEMATICS

	1	2	3
sorts and classifies			
identifies patterns			
demonstrates concept of number			
recognizes numbers			
writes numbers in sequence			
addition			
subtraction			
uses problem solving strategies			
place value			
time			
money			
graphing			

SCIENCE

Present Unit

	1	2	3
participates in activities			
understands concepts			

SOCIAL STUDIES

Present Unit

	1	2	3
participates in activities			
understands concepts			

+ - indicates appropriate behavior

√ - indicates need for improvement in this area

CITIZENSHIP AND WORK HABITS

	1	2	3
has positive attitude			
practices self-control			
assumes responsibility			
respects rules			
respects property/materials			
respects people			
uses good manners			
cooperates with others			
puts forth effort			
has pride in schoolwork			
listens attentively			
follows directions			
uses organizational skills			
makes good use of time			
completes assignments on time			
works well independently			
works well in group activities			

From Glenview School District No. 34, Glenview, Illinois. Reprinted with permission.

FIGURE 12-5
Primary Report Card (Anecdotal Record)

Date: _____   **Name:** _____

COMMENTS ON READING DEVELOPMENT

COMMENTS ON SCIENCE/SOCIAL STUDIES

COMMENTS ON LANGUAGE ARTS DEVELOPMENT

COMMENTS ON PERSONAL AND SOCIAL SKILLS

COMMENTS ON MATHEMATICS DEVELOPMENT

COMMENTS ON STUDY SKILLS

SUGGESTIONS

From Glenview School District No. 34, Glenview, Illinois. Reprinted with permission.

particular behavior or deficiency in a skill area, the teacher can focus on daily descriptions of that one area and be successful in producing a useful document.

The major limitation or disadvantage of the anecdotal record is the tendency of teachers to project their own value judgments into the description of a student's behavior or accomplishment. This is due, in part, to the tendency to observe what fits one's preconceived notions. "For example, they will tend to notice more desirable qualities in those pupils they like best and more undesirable qualities in those they like least" (Gronlund & Linn, 1990, p. 380). The recommended way to avoid this tendency is to keep descriptions of observed incidents separate from your interpretation. First, state exactly what happened in nonjudgmental words. Then, if you wish to add your interpretation of the event, do so in a separate paragraph and label it as such (Gronlund & Linn, 1990).

In general, a single observation is seldom as meaningful as a series of events in understanding a student's behavior. Therefore, anecdotal records should contain brief descriptions of related incidents over a period of time to provide a reliable picture of a student's behavior.

Organizing Portfolios to Document Accomplishments

Portfolios are among the newest methods of documenting student accomplishment. They provide an excellent source of data when accompanied by an anecdotal record. As mentioned in chaper 11, they may contain work samples in one subject area alone or reflect the student's work across the entire curriculum. Teachers who tend to think of the curriculum as a number of separate subjects are likely to use separate portfolios of work, and teachers who think of the curriculum as multidimensional are likely to include all relevant work samples in one portfolio. Some teachers may create portfolio categories such as *verbal work, technical work,* and *artistic work.*

At the middle school and high school level, portfolios may be maintained for each subject the student is taking. The Performance Assessment Collaborative for Education (PACE), directed by Dennie Wolf at the Harvard Graduate School of Education, has been investigating portfolio assessment as a tool for reforming schools. In collaboration with a number of school districts across the country, they have created a vision of what a school that uses performance tasks and portfolios would look like (Wolf, LeMahieu, & Eresh, 1992).

Students in the PACE school are expected to become responsible partners in documenting their own learning. In every class, a student puts together a folder that contains classwork, journals, and projects. At the end of the first 9-week marking period, an *initial portfolio* is created by students in every class. These portfolios replace or supplement quarterly tests that may be given in the course, but also do more than that. Students gain reflective awareness of how much progress they have made as they gather and evaluate the material for their portfolios. Teachers use the portfolios as the basis for computing grades and communicating with parents about what the students have accomplished. Grades and written reports are sent to parents accompanied by some items from the portfolios. Parents are asked to respond in writing or by telephone.

Nine weeks later, it is time for students and teachers to collect the material for their *semester portfolios.* At the visionary PACE school, a *portfolio week* is held instead of a finals week. During this week, students attend at least one *conference* with an adult advisor to discuss past accomplishments and future goals the student has for the second half of the year. At this conference a *letter to parents* is written by the student and advisor. This letter is sent home with the student's report card.

At the end of the school year, a *year-end portfolio* is created as students draw on all of their best work of the year to provide current evidence of their progress on the essential learning tasks. In addition, the PACE school envisions holding *portfolio exhibitions* in which students can display their finest accomplishments and committees composed of teachers, other students, and family members can ask questions about their work.

When it is evident to the teacher and other readers that a student's portfolio contains incomplete or unsuccessful work, the consequences may include assignment to summer school courses or placement in special programs or courses for the following year.

To establish reasonably consistent standards throughout the school district, the PACE school recommnds that teachers *cross read* portfolios from other teachers' classes. For example, the science teacher at one school reads four portfolios from another school. The four portfolios selected for this cross reading could include one from a superstar, one created by a low achiever, one average portfolio, and one puzzling one. Teachers who cross read must become fair and honest critics of one another, asking whether the curriculum is challenging enough, whether teachers are providing enough commentary and feedback to students, and whether substantial learning appears to be occurring.

Recognizing that portfolio assessment is new and untried and that if it is going to replace other tried and true assessments, PACE (Wolf et al., 1992) also envisions a process of auditing by external readers. A communitywide audit committee made up of business people, educators from neighboring districts, and subject matter experts may examine a sample of portfolios from each school. They will look at the quality of work, skills of teacher responses, appropriateness of grades awarded, and whether all students had access to the type of learning they needed. The committee will then report its findings to the community and make recommendations to the school board to suggest planning, budgeting, and other changes and improvements.

As you enter the field of education, the debate about portfolio assessment procedures will undoubtedly continue. Challenges and questions about portfolio validity will be raised and conflicts about benefits and deficiencies will occur within schools and school districts. Reflective teachers will rise to this challenge by becoming well informed about both standardized and portfolio assessment procedures so that they can make fair and principled judgments about which to use and how to adapt and create new models of assessment that combine the best of both methods.

Involving Students in Evaluation Procedures

For C-M teachers, the natural extension of the teaching process is the interactive evaluation process that encourages students to become active evaluators of their own efforts and products. The current writing programs organized around periodic student–teacher conferences and the grouping of students who edit one another's work is an excellent example of this type of evaluation. In classrooms that feature such writing programs, the teacher's role in evaluation is to confer with the students about their current writing projects and to ask questions that engage the students in analyzing what they have written.

Teachers may use open-ended questions designed to gather information on what the student has intended to do in a piece of writing. When the teacher has a sufficient understanding of the student's goal, the teacher and student may begin to zero in on ways to improve the quality of the writing so that it more nearly matches the student's purpose. This may mean correcting the mechanics of the writing so that it can be understood by others, or it may mean guiding the student to rethink the way a passage is written and to consider new ways of stating the ideas.

The editing groups used in such writing programs encourage students to learn how to listen to and respect the work being created by their peers. Students in a group, typically, each read aloud from a current piece of writing and then answer questions about the content from the other students in the group. Through this type of interactive evaluation, students may be learning how to work cooperatively, accept critical feedback, and write better at the same time.

This interactive evaluation system can be used in other parts of the curriculum as well. "What did you learn? should form the core of the classroom evaluation. The more often this question is asked, the easier it is for students to identify and receive the help they need. It is a question children can learn to ask themselves (Oakes & Lipton, 1990, p. 132).

Interactive evaluation procedures are the benchmark of the C-M teaching philosophy. The purpose of the R-A evaluation system is simply to sum up and communicate what each student has gained and how the achievement of one student relates to the others in the class. But a C-M evaluation system is designed to breed success and enhance students' metacognitive capacities. It is as much a part of the *learning process* as it is a part of the assessment process. In fact, the long-term goals of C-M teachers are likely to emphasize the development of independence, self-responsibility, self-discipline, and self-evaluation as important affective goals of education. These goals are achieved through the development of metacognitive processes as children learn to understand how to succeed in any learning environment.

OPPORTUNITIES FOR REFLECTION

▼ Reflective Essay: What Grades Mean to You

Did you get good grades in elementary school? Do you believe that the grades you received were an accurate reflection of your effort and achievement? How will you determine grades in your classroom?

▼ Classroom Visit: Ask to View the Classroom Teacher's Gradebook

What system does this teacher use for recording grades? Are there elements of this system that seem useful to you? Does the teacher use an absolute or a relative frame of reference? Which would you use? Do the students appear to understand the teacher's grading policies and expectations? What would you do to improve their understanding?

REFERENCES

ANDERSON, L. (1989). Learners and learning. In M. Reynolds (Ed.), *Knowledge Base for the Beginning Teacher (KBBT)* (pp. 85–104). New York: Pergamon.

BLOOM, B. (1982). *Human characteristics and school learning.* New York: McGraw-Hill.

DEWEY, J. (1933). *How we think* (rev. ed.). Lexington, MA: D.C. Heath.

EISNER, E. (1985). *Educational imagination* (2nd ed.). New York: Macmillan.

GRONLUND, N., & LINN, R. (1990). *Measurement and evaluation in teaching.* New York: Macmillan.

HIRSCH, E. (1987). *Cultural literacy: What every American needs to know.* Boston: Houghton Mifflin.

KIDDER, T. (1989). *Among schoolchildren.* Boston: Houghton Mifflin.

OAKES, J., & LIPTON, M. (1990). *Making the best of schools.* New Haven, CT: Yale University Press.

WOLF, D., LeMAHIEU, P., & ERESH, J. (1992). Good measure: Assessment as a tool for educational reform. *Educational Leadership, 49*(8), 8–13.

CHAPTER

13

Reflective Teachers and the School Community

AT THE BEGINNING of chapter 1, Lori Shoults described the many thoughts, feelings, and decisions she had to make on her first day of teaching. In the week prior to that first day, Lori spent a lot of time in her classroom setting up bulletin boards and learning centers. As she worked that week, many of her new students and their parents who had come to the school for registration stopped by her classroom to see the "new teacher." Some stood outside her door looking in quietly until she approached them and introduced herself. Others came into the room and looked around, exclaiming over the brightly decorated walls. The children were all interested in trying to discern whether the new teacher was "nice" and whether they thought they would be happy in her class.

Their visits, before the first day of school had even arrived, alerted Lori to the fact that she had more than the needs of 28 students to consider. She also had to be aware of and concerned with the needs of their parents.

Some parents of primary children may be especially reluctant to see the beginning of school because, for them, it marks an end to an important phase in their lives. For 5 years, they've had complete jurisdiction over the lives of their children. Now they recognize that the teacher may have almost as much influence over their children as they have. I have observed the parent of a first grader, for example, standing outside the school after dropping off the child saying tearfully, "But we've had lunch together every day of his life."

For the majority of parents, many of whom work outside of the home and whose children have gone to day care centers and preschools, this leavetaking may not be so abrupt, but it is still a significant event in their own lives, as well as those of their children. Many parents feel a strong interest in, and responsibility for, determining whether this particular classroom is a healthy and welcoming environment for their children. For this reason, parents of primary children are likely to come to school, on one pretext or another, in the first days of school, just to see for themselves that their children are in good hands.

Beginning teachers may feel somewhat overwhelmed by these visits. All of their available energy has gone into planning the curriculum, moving furniture, decorating the classroom, and meeting and becoming acquainted with other teachers in the school. When a parent suddenly shows up, unannounced, it can be unsettling, especially if the parent wants to ask questions when the students are present. When this occurs, it is necessary for the teacher to suggest, politely but assertively, another time for this impromptu conference: "I'm sorry, Mrs. Jones, but all of my attention is needed in the class right now. Would you prefer to talk about this after school or tomorrow morning at 8:15?"

Throughout the school year, there are many occasions in which the teacher is expected to communicate with parents, either singly or in large groups. In addition, many classroom teachers invite parents to become involved in the life of the classroom. This chapter describes some methods of establishing a manageable and mutually beneficial two-way communication pattern with parents and other members of the community.

TWO-WAY COMMUNICATION WITH PARENTS

Before discussing two-way communication with parents, it is important to recognize that the traditional conference of a teacher with a student's mother and father is not the norm. Students come from single-parent families, blended families in which divorced parents have remarried and have children with previous and current spouses, foster parents, and guardians. Teachers meet students who do not have the same last names as their parents. There are many possible home situations; only a few are mentioned. Teachers must recognize that the home lives they may have experienced may be different from those of their students. When parents are mentioned in this chapter, we refer to the people who are being contacted or are meeting with the teacher.

Fall Open House

When parents come to visit the classroom early in the year, one method of deflecting their concerns is to suggest that they will be able to have many of their questions answered within a few weeks at the annual Fall Open House (sometimes called Back to School Night). This event is planned especially for that purpose in many school districts.

The Fall Open House is usually held on an evening in late September. To prepare for the event, teachers are asked to be ready to describe their goals for the year and give an overall picture of the school's curriculum at that grade level. The event usually begins in the school auditorium or other large meeting room, where the principal welcomes everyone to the school and describes the important events that the entire school has planned for the coming year. The teachers, counselors, other administrators, and sometimes the president of the parent–teacher organization are introduced. Special attention is given to introducing any new teachers on the faculty. At the conclusion of this general meeting, the teachers are released to go to their classrooms and make themselves ready for the Open House. After a few minutes, the visitors are dismissed from the general meeting to find their children's classrooms.

When the parents assemble in the classroom, the teacher makes a short presentation to the entire group, describing what is planned for the year. A time for questions and answers of interest to the entire group is also likely to occur. Because most school districts intend the Fall Open House to be a time for general discussions of goals and curriculum, there is no planned opportunity for individual parents to ask teachers for specific information about their child's achievement or behavior. If parents approach the teacher and begin to discuss personal concerns, it is expected that the teacher will suggest an alternate time and place for an individual conference.

In the middle and senior high school, parents often rotate from teacher to teacher following their children's class schedules. It is recommended that teachers have handouts or use the overhead projector to prepare a mini-presentation for parents describing the rules and academic expectations for their students. The Fall Open House is often the first opportunity to make a positive impression on parents. It is true that you don't get a second chance to make a first impression.

Parent–Teacher Conferences

Conferences between individual parents and teachers vary greatly in purpose. Some are primarily used for the diagnosis of a problem or concern, and others are set up to report to the parents about a child's progress in school. Diagnostic conferences were described in chapter 3, but are discussed briefly in this context as well because they are such a valuable means of entire evaluation.

If either the teacher or the parent has a serious concern about a child, one or the other may arrange a conference in the first weeks of school. When teachers, for example, observe unusually aggressive, passive, depressed, or antisocial behavior in a child, they are wise to call home immediately and set up a conference right away to gain information about the nature of the child's problems. This is especially true when a child's behavior disrupts other students in the class.

Setting up a conference sends an important signal to a student who is exhibiting unusual or unacceptable behavior. It tells the student that the teacher has withitness and is going to take action to correct the problem rather than let it go. It allows the teacher to seek information about the underlying reasons for the observed behavior. In a conference of this type, it is recommended that the student attend with the parents in order to gain a better understanding of the adults' views of the behavior.

When the conference takes place, the teacher should describe the behavior and, if possible, supplement the oral description with written anecdotal reports of examples of the behavior. The teacher should express concern about the behavior and then ask both the student and the parents to explain why it is occurring.

"Students usually cannot explain fully why they act as they do, and teachers should not expect them to be able to do this. If the students had such insight, they probably would not be behaving symptomatically in the first place. Instead, the hope is that clues or helpful information will emerge from the discussion" (Good & Brophy, 1987, p. 293).

When the parents discuss their own views of the child's problem, the teacher may gain significant insight by learning about the home environment. For example, the parents may agree that they have observed the same behavior at home and that it seems to be related to a crisis the family is dealing with, such as a death, divorce, drugs, lost job, or move. When the teacher, the child, and the parents confront this matter together, they can begin to put together a workable plan to help support the student during this difficult period and, at the same time, help the child gain awareness about the effects of the behavior on others.

Conferences don't always result in such harmonious cooperation. Parents may not present much useful information. On occasion, they may become very defensive or resentful of the suggestion that their child's behavior is unacceptable. In their family, this behavior may be okay. For example, a fifth-grade teacher was alarmed to see a boy walk into her class on the first day of school wearing a T-shirt that read, "Born to Raise Hell!" True to the message on the shirt, the child fought with other children at least once a day. When the parents were called in for a conference and the teacher described this behavior to them, the father replied, "So what? I tell my kids not to let anyone get the best of them." From the words and the father's tone of voice, the teacher learned that fighting was an acceptable behavior in that family. No happy resolution was discovered in this conference, but it did give the teacher some additional insight into the source and the depth of the boy's difficulties in social interactions with his peers.

At times, it may be necessary to involve others in the conference. Counselors may need to be present to suggest alternative ways of dealing with problems. If the teacher, parents, and counselor cannot effectively address a problem with the student, additional professional help may need to be offered to the parents. There are times when parents admit that they cannot even handle their child at home.

Conferences designed for reporting on student progress rather than for diagnostic purposes usually take place in the late fall to coincide with the end of the first marking period and the first report card. In many districts, the parents are asked to come to the school for a conference with the teacher shortly after report cards are sent home. This gives the parents an opportunity to look at the report card and think about the questions and concerns they may want to raise at the conference. Some school districts require parents to come to the school to pick up the child's report card and have a conference with the teacher. In this case, the teacher explains the grades and observations to the parent as the parent views the report card for the first time. This second strategy is used primarily to make sure that parents do attend the conference.

Report card conferences are generally 15 to 30 minutes in length. They may be offered during the day and at night so that parents who work during the day may choose a night conference. Usually 1 or 2 school days are used for the fall conferences. In some school districts, the entire process is repeated in the spring. In the elementary school, a schedule of 30 conferences during a period of 1 or 2 days is a very tiring experience for most teachers. In the secondary schools, teachers have the potential of talking to as many as 150 parents or guardians. Teachers may find that conference days are more exhausting than regular teaching days. This is due primarily to the tension caused by the teachers' recognition that they are responsible for the smooth flow of conversation and information. When this feeling of responsibility is multiplied by a factor of 30 or more in a few short days, it is easy to see how draining it can be.

To minimize the tension, it is extremely important that teachers plan each conference very carefully. Prior to the event, reflective teachers often write a page of notes about each student, highlighting the accomplishments and the matters of concern that the teacher wants to discuss with the parents. It is important for the teacher to be able to properly identify the child in the conference. Teachers have mentioned embarrassing moments when parents have a puzzled look on their faces only to discover that the teacher was talking about another student and not their child.

In addition to planning what you want to say about each child, it is recommended that you make a general plan for how you will conduct your conferences. The primary purpose of the report card conferences is for you to inform the parents about the child's progress in your class. But the conference is also designed to elicit information from the parents that may help you to help the child. The parents may also have concerns that they wish to discuss. To accomplish all of these things in 20 minutes is very difficult. To do so, you must act as the timekeeper and allot a reasonable amount of time to each purpose. The parent will not be concerned about going overtime, but you will because you will be aware that the next set of parents is waiting outside the door for their appointment with you.

Gronlund and Linn (1990) suggest that you consider the following elements when you plan your conferences:

1. Make plans for each conference. For each child, make a list of the points you want to cover and the questions you want to ask.

2. Begin the conference in a positive manner. Making a positive statement about the child, such as "Betty really enjoys helping others" or "Derek is an expert on dinosaurs," is likely to create a cooperative and friendly atmosphere.

3. Present the student's strong points before describing areas needing improvement. Present samples of work and focus on what the child can do and what he or she still has to learn.

4. Encourage parents to participate and share information. You must be willing to listen as well as talk. They may have questions and concerns about the school and about their child's behavior that need to be brought out into the open before constructive, cooperative action can take place.

5. Plan a course of action cooperatively. Guide the discussion toward a series of steps that can be taken by the teacher and the parents to assist the child. At the end of the conference, review these steps with the parents.

6. End the conference with a positive comment. Thank the parents for coming and say something positive about the student such as, "Erik has a good sense of humor and I enjoy having him in my class" (pp. 445–446).

The regularly scheduled report card conferences may be the only time you will meet with the parents of most of your students. But for others, those whose behavior or learning problems are quite serious, it is necessary to continue to contact the parents by telephone or in follow-up conferences in order to monitor whether the cooperative plan of action is being implemented and what effects it is having.

Effective two-way communication with parents is essential for assisting students with severe problems. In working with children whose behavior interferes with their learning in school, an excellent resource for both teachers and parents is Rimm's (1986) *The Underachievement Syndrome: Causes and Cures.* This book describes many of the most feared behavior problems that teachers must face: hyperactivity, passiveness, perfectionism, rebellion, bullying, and manipulative behaviors. Rimm believes that these behaviors cause children to achieve much less than they are capable of achieving in school. In her studies of underachievement, Rimm has discovered that most of these behaviors were learned by children in response to some elements of their home environment. Changing the behavior takes a concerted effort by the parents to isolate the causes and create new procedures to help children learn healthier, more productive behavior patterns that can lead to success.

Often it is the teacher who spots the self-defeating behavior. Parents have been living with the child for so long that they may not see that the child's behavior is unusual, and they may not be able to recognize how it affects the child's school achievement. Some examples of home situations that may lead to underachievement include the following:

▼ *The Overwelcome Child:* Although it has long been recognized that an unwelcome or rejected child is likely to have problems in life, it is also likely that excessive attention can cause achievement and emotional problems. When parents overprotect and overindulge, the child may develop a pattern of not taking initiative and of waiting for others to do the child's bidding.

▼ *Early Health Problems:* When children are born with allergies, birth defects, or other disabilities and parents respond by investing themselves almost totally in the child's well-being, a set of behaviors similar to those of the overwelcome child can develop.

▼ *Particular Sibling Combinations:* Birth order and sibling rivalry affect all children, but some combinations may be particularly damaging to a child's achievement. A student who is the sibling of a child with severe health problems or is considered to be extremely gifted may feel left out or inadequate in comparison to the sibling. This can lead to the development of attention-getting behavior patterns such as clowning or mischief-making, which may prevent the child from achieving fully.

▼ *Specific Marital Problems:* A single parent may develop a very close relationship with the child as a result of seeing the child as the only purpose for living. The parent may treat the child more like a spouse or a partner than a child, thus giving the child too much power. The child may learn to expect power and may not be willing to give it up to conform to the requirements of school (Rimm, 1990, pp. 24–32).

These are only four of many possible situations that can cause children to learn to develop behaviors that may prevent them from achieving well in school. When a teacher spots a child who is exhibiting overly dependent or overly aggressive behaviors, it is important to confer with the child's parents, to report the problem, and to learn how the behavior first developed and how the parents are responding to it. The first step toward a positive behavior change is for the teacher to describe and give examples of the behavior and its effects on the child's achievement. The parents may deny that the behavior exists or that it is serious, but if the teacher is successful in establishing a cooperative two-way dialogue with the parents, it may lead to new insights for all of them.

If parents do acknowledge the behavior, the next step is for you to describe the changes you are going to make at school to support the development of new, more positive behavior patterns and to suggest modifications that the parents may make at home. Together with the parents, set some reasonable goals for the child in terms of both behaviors and grades. Discuss methods of helping the child reach these goals and agree on a plan that fits the child and the situation. Then specify the ways that you plan to continue your communication with the parents about your joint goals and plan of action, such as daily reports (Figure 13–1), weekly reports (Figure 13–2), or frequent telephone conferences (Rimm, 1986).

Rimm cautions that children will not change their behavior just because the adults in their lives want them to do so. The child must want to break the underachieving patterns and substitute them for behaviors that lead to success. Both the teacher and the parents must also confer with the child, describing the behaviors and their effects in words the child can understand and accept. When the teacher, parent, and child all have the same goal and are working together on a plan of action tailored to fit the needs of the child, it is quite possible that the child will succeed.

FIGURE 13–1
Daily Evaluation Form

STUDENT   TEACHER NAME_____ NAME_____ DATE_____
Assignments Completed: _____ All _____ Most _____ Half _____ Less than Half
Quality of general class work: _____ Excellent _____ Satisfactory   _____ Fair   _____ Unsatisfactory
Behavior: _____ Excellent _____ Satisfactory _____ Fair   _____ Unsatisfactory
Comments: _____ _____ _____ _____
Thank you very much for your help.

From *The Underachievement Syndrome: Causes and Cures* (p. 172) by S. Rimm, 1986. Watertown, WI: Apple Publishing. Copyright 1986 by Apple Publishing. Reprinted by permission.

Independent contracts are also useful support systems for helping children change behavior. A contract can specify work that is to be done with deadlines and expectations for success. It can also be used to specify behavioral expectations as well. When the teacher negotiates the contract with the child ahead of time, there is an intrinsic incentive for the child to complete it—after all, the child helped to create it and decide what would be required. A sense of ownership is likely to increase the likelihood of the contract being fulfilled.

Additional extrinsic incentives may be employed if the teacher believes that these are useful in a given circumstance. Either the parents can provide the rewards, such as the new bicycle in Figure 13–3, or the teacher can provide rewards in exchange for earning points for successful completion of items on the contract. It is most often recommended that students receive a reward that supports academics. For example, a student could earn points toward additional time at a learning activity or game. The major point is that the reward is something a student really would like to receive. Some things a teacher thinks would be rewarding are not rewarding to students. The types of rewards would vary by grade level.

The contract in Figure 13–3 exemplifies the type of plan that may be created as a result of a successful parent–teacher conference. In this case, the behavior observed by the teacher was that the child was not turning in homework. Alerting the parents to this concern resulted in a discussion of probable causes. The parents were able to accept the reality of the problem and its negative consequences for their child's

FIGURE 13–2
Weekly Evaluation Form

STUDENT
NAME_____   TEACHER
NAME_____   DATE_____

Subject: _____

Approximate grade for week: _____

Assignments Completed: _____ All _____ Most _____ Half _____ Less than Half

Behavior: _____ Excellent _____ Satisfactory _____ Fair
            _____ Unsatisfactory

Comments and missing assignments: _____

_____

_____

_____

From *The Underachievement Syndrome: Causes and Cures* (p. 173) by S. Rimm, 1986. Watertown, WI: Apple Publishing. Copyright 1986 by Apple Publishing. Reprinted by permission.

achievement. They were also able to suggest that the major cause might be the fact that the child and his family watch a great deal of television, beginning right after school and continuing up to bedtime. When the teacher alerted the parents to the problem, they expressed a willingness to do their part to help change the child's behavior and together they drafted this contract. Daily reports can be written by the teacher for a while to

FIGURE 13–3
Sample Study Plan Contract

Troy, his mom, dad, and Mrs. Norbert agree that Troy will spend at least one hour each day, five days a week, studying and doing his homework independently at his desk in his room. He will do this before he watches TV and there will be no radio, stereo, or TV on in his room during study time. After his work is complete his dad will review his materials and together award him points which Troy will save up toward the purchase of a bicycle. Troy's mom and dad will not remind him to study and he will take the initiative independently. This agreement may be changed only by mutual agreement of the undersigned.

                    Troy
                    Mom
                    Dad
                    Teacher

From *The Underachievement Syndrome: Causes and Cures* (p. 211) by S. Rimm, 1986. Watertown, WI: Apple Publishing. Copyright 1986 by Apple Publishing. Reprinted by permission.

inform parents whether the homework is actually being turned in. Knowing that these daily reports are going to be written is likely to help everyone remember the commitment they have made.

One final caution about conducting parent–teacher conferences: Occasionally, participants in the conference may reveal a family problem that is unusual and extremely serious. Revelations of extreme poverty, desertion, or physical or sexual abuse can be made to a teacher by the student or the parents as a desperate attempt to get help. If this happens, the classroom teacher is well advised not to try to deal with this problem alone. If this happens to you, ask the parent to allow you to discuss this matter with the social services personnel in the school, and immediately contact the principal, school psychologist, social worker, and other members of the crisis team to assist in the matter.

Teaching in a Multicultural Community

When the language, culture, and values of the parents match those of the teachers in the child's school, communication is likely to be relatively clear and agreements not too difficult to achieve. When the culture of the child's home differs significantly from the culture of the teacher, the teacher must be especially willing to listen as well as talk during parent–teacher conferences.

Prior to the *Brown v. Board of Education* Supreme Court decision in 1954, children who were racially different from the "white majority" were often segregated in separate (and inferior) schools. Since that time, federal mandates have required school systems to integrate both the student bodies and the faculties of their schools. But federal laws have not been able to mitigate the subtler forms of racism that still exist in some educational settings.

Although America is known as a nation of immigrants, a melting pot of cultures, there has also been a traditionally accepted cultural norm that mirrors the philosophy of the white Anglo-Saxon majority. Other cultures have been known as *minority cultures*. The prevailing belief is that children from minority cultures must be taught the language and habits of the majority. Researchers have found that "to the extent that the home culture's practices and values are not acknowledged or incorporated by the school, parents may find that they are not able to support children in their academic pursuits even when it is their fervent wish to do so" (Florio-Ruane, 1989, p. 169).

Reflective teachers are aware that their own values and expectations may vary considerably from those of the families in their school community. But rather than assume that the children and their parents should be taught to mimic the language, behavior, and norms of the teacher's own culture, reflective teachers strive to gain a better understanding of the various cultures that make up the school community and to celebrate these differences by incorporating them into the curriculum.

In parent–teacher conferences, the reflective teacher is likely to ask with great interest about the home environment and the cultural values of the parents as a means of gaining a better understanding of the various cultures and of conveying respect to the parents. When parents sense this respect from the teacher, they are more likely to return it and to feel that the teacher shares their own concerns for their child.

It may be necessary for the teacher to be especially encouraging to parents of other cultures, urging them to share their own concerns and ask questions. People from many cultures were not raised to ask questions of teachers and may be very reluctant to do so. But if the teacher encourages them to ask questions or make suggestions for the child's benefit, they may feel comfortable enough to do so. This two-way communication and mutual understanding can lead to a more productive arrangement to work together to support the child's achievement at home and at school.

The needs of children and their parents who have emigrated to the United States are especially important, as First (1988) found when she interviewed them:

> Immigrant children and adolescents, many of whom have survived wars, political oppression, and economic deprivation, find that their problems are not over when they enter American schools. Confronted with hatred, prejudice, and violence in U.S. schools, many newcomers are left asking what they have done to deserve such treatment. One Vietnamese student spoke for many when he said, "I like school here. But I wish there would be more friendships among immigrants and American students." (p. 210)

A Spanish child revealed the following:

> I came upon a world unknown to me, a language I did not understand, and a school administration which made ugly faces at me every time I spoke Spanish. Many teachers referred to us as animals. Believe me, maintaining a half-decent image of yourself wasn't an easy thing. . . . I had enough strength of character to withstand the many school personnel who tried to destroy my motivation. But many of my classmates didn't make it. (p. 210)

The classroom teacher must demonstrate a willingness to assist culturally different children and their parents as they make the difficult transition from one land to another. One of the best ways to accomplish this is to show sensitivity and respect for the various cultures of all the children in the class. Each year, the teacher may plan a special unit of study on the contribution of the cultures represented by the members of the class. The parents of the students can be invited to participate in the learning experience by visiting the classroom and sharing with children the crafts and food of their countries. They can teach the children the songs and games of their homelands. First (1988) believes that when teachers involve the parents in the education of their children, they send a powerful message that the school cares about them.

However, a teacher must not feel offended if the parent does not want to be involved. This could be viewed as disinterest. However, in some cultures parents have been taught that the school is responsible for their youngster's education, and they should not be involved in the process on the school campus.

Visits to Students' Homes

When teachers care sufficiently about understanding the particular home and cultural environments that surround their students, one way to seek information is to visit the children and their families in their homes. This may be done by sending home a newsletter early in the year, with the announcement that the teacher would enjoy meeting the parents and seeing the children in their homes, and that invitations to do so will be gladly received. This allows the parents to invite the teacher when it is a good time for them.

The visit will probably take place after school or during the evening meal. No agendas need to be established for such a visit; in fact, doing so would be counterproductive. The visit is not a structured parent–teacher conference at all. It is simply an opportunity for the teacher to understand more fully the conditions in which the child lives. As the teacher shares the family's meal, looks at their photographs, and hears some of their family stories, it greatly enhances the feelings of the child and the parents that they are respected members of the school community.

On occasion, it may become necessary for school personnel to make a more structured visit with an agenda. This may occur if a child is having extremely serious problems and is referred for special services and a psychological evaluation. In that case, the school social worker or psychologist may visit the home to determine what factor in the home environment may be causing the child's problems.

Newsletters and Notes

Many elementary teachers communicate with parents by sending home handwritten notes describing a particular behavior or accomplishment of their child. In some classrooms, a note from the teacher signifies only bad news that is sent home when the teacher wants to describe an incident or pattern of misbehavior, a poor test result, or excessive tardiness. More recently, many reflective teachers have considered how to use the note home to encourage good behavior and reward achievement. Many teachers now send home notes describing a special accomplishment, an improvement in classwork, or an act of friendliness or generosity shown by the child.

To ensure that all children benefit from this system, the teacher may send a note of good news home to a certain number of children per week until every child has had one. Others prefer not to use a schedule, but send a note whenever they observe a child doing something especially well. Without a schedule, however, it is important that teachers be careful not to favor some children over others.

In some classrooms, teachers prepare and send home classroom newsletters describing the important events planned for that week or month. The newsletter may contain items describing completed projects and new ones just getting underway. In the newsletter, the teacher can request parent volunteers for various projects and write notes of appreciation to parents who have recently helped out in some way.

In primary classrooms, the teacher generally takes full responsibility for creating the newsletter. But in intermediate and upper elementary classrooms, many teachers allow students to help write the items. They may use a computer program designed for creating newspaperlike formats. In this case, the production of the newsletter becomes more than just a method of communicating with parents. It becomes an enriching learning experience as well. In the secondary schools, a school newsletter is usually sent to parents.

Parent Support of Educational Activities

If teachers are able to communicate the classroom goals for that year of school and are able to supply parents with regular newsletters or other reports of student progress, this increases the likelihood that the parents will support the school's educational goals at home.

Parents can support their child's education and increase the chances for the child's success in school if they understand what they can do to help and are capable of giving that help at home. Becker and Epstein (1982) report that teachers vary considerably in what they ask parents to do to support their children's education. The variation seems to be linked to the different expectations teachers have about what parents are capable of and willing to do. When asked what they request parents to do to support the child's achievement in school, many teachers have reported that they ask parents to read aloud to their children or allow the child to read aloud to them. To support this request, many teachers said that they were willing to loan school books and other materials to parents to use at home.

Many teachers have also reported that they frequently asked parents to take their children to the library. Many also suggest that parents ask their children what they did that day in school and discuss it with them. Teachers also occasionally suggest activities and games that can be used at home to support the educational goals of the class (Becker and Epstein, 1982).

Many parents welcome the opportunity to support their children in school-related activities. Teachers who regularly report to parents on classroom events and ask parents to participate by doing parallel activities in the home are likely to develop very productive two-way relationships with parents that can increase the child's self-esteem and achievement and, at the same time, add to the teacher's understanding of the student's home environment.

Telephone Calls

The telephone provides an important link between school and home. Teachers often call students' homes for the same reasons as they write notes. Some use a telephone call to report a child's misbehavior and poor achievement in order to enlist the support and assistance of parents in correcting problems. Other teachers try to call home to report both positive and negative news. They may make their first call to report a problem or concern and follow up several days later with a second telephone call to report that the student is making progress in solving the problem.

Teachers are often on the receiving end of telephone calls from students' parents as well. Parents may call to clarify something about an assignment or an announcement that they cannot understand from their child's description. If parents hear confusing stories about something that happened during the school day, they may call the teacher to find out what really occurred. Responding to these promptly and in an open and informative manner promotes a positive pattern of communication between home and school.

Occasionally parents call in anger or frustration. They may disagree with the contents of the curriculum, the way a test was graded, or the way a classroom incident was handled. When a teacher receives one of these calls, it is very easy to become defensive and angry too. Dealing effectively with these calls takes mature, well-developed communication skills. It is difficult, but very important, to listen empathetically to what the parent says. Even when the instinctive reaction of most teachers is to break into the parent's statements and present their own side of the situation, it is more productive if the teacher's initial responses encourage the parent to describe the problem in more detail and express personal feelings.

After the parent has had an opportunity to fully describe the reason for the telephone call, the teacher's side of the story can be presented in a quiet, nonthreatening, and nondefensive voice. In a situation such as this, the teacher has the responsibility for attempting to resolve the conflict and creating a mutually acceptable solution.

For example, suppose that there is a fight in the classroom during the day and John is punched in the face by Dean, a much stronger boy. Because his lip is bleeding, the teacher decides to send John to the nurse. She then tries to talk to Dean to find out what prompted the fight. Dean claims he was provoked by John's name calling, and many children in the class support that claim. When John returns from the nurse, the teacher tells him that both he and Dean will have to stay in for recess for fighting. John seethes with anger for the rest of the day.

After school, the teacher is called to the telephone to find John's very angry parent on the other end. "Why did you keep my son in for recess when he got hit by that bully? And why didn't you call me immediately when he got hit? Did you know he was bleeding? I'm going to come in right now and talk to your principal about this matter, and you will be sorry you treated my son this way!"

The instinctive reaction for most teachers is to jump in and explain after the first few words are spoken. If the parent continues to question the teacher's judgment, the teacher may soon feel as angry as the parent does. But reflective teachers recognize that there will be days like this in a classroom with 30 students and one adult. They will try to keep their feelings in control and say something to soothe the parent's hurt pride and upset feelings.

"I'm glad you called, Mrs. Jones. I can understand how you feel. Tell me how John's lip is now." This type of comment will help the teacher gather information and gain time to formulate a good response. Not all such problems can be readily resolved. Perhaps the teacher and the parent will continue to have different points of view no matter how much they discuss it. If this is the case, it is necessary to acknowledge it and end the conversation with a comment such as, "I recognize how you feel about this situation. I'm sorry John got hurt today, and I'll do my best to see that he is not involved in any more fights this year."

The key point of this section is expressed in the phrase, "reflective teachers recognize that there will be days like this." There are days like this in every school year. There are incidents where values clash and feelings are hurt. The beginning teacher may be shocked the first time this happens and overreact by feeling angry, guilty, or defensive. If possible, when incidents such as these occur in your classroom, remember that every teacher experiences conflict. Conflict is unavoidable in this career, and the first step in learning how to handle it is learning to expect and accept it as part of the job.

Spring Open House and Other Special Events

In the fall, the purpose of most conferences and open house events is to allow parents and teachers to get to know each other, communicate their goals for their children (students), and make plans for accomplishing these goals. As the year goes by, the focus of most meetings between parents and teachers is for the teacher to demonstrate to the parents how these goals are being met.

Many classroom teachers invite parents frequently, perhaps as often as once a month, to attend exhibits, plays, assemblies, or other occasions for students to display what they are learning and what they have accomplished. Some of these events may be schoolwide assemblies, such as Thanksgiving plays, concerts, and feasts, winter pageants, midwinter cultural fairs, and spring open houses in which collections of student work are displayed throughout the school.

Individual teachers may also invite their students' parents to school to view the performances or an exhibit of products resulting from a unit of study. These events are usually highly prized by students and parents, and are an excellent way for the teacher to interact and communicate continually with parents.

Consider, though, how some parents might feel if they attend a spring open house and find that their own child's work is not displayed. In some competitive classrooms, teachers tend to display only the papers with "100%" written across the top. For those children who rarely get perfect papers, this can be a discouraging experience; for their parents, it is likely to be equally discouraging. If classroom displays include examples of students' work, it is important to display the best works of every student in approximately equal numbers.

To avoid creating a competitive environment, you may want to display students' work inside their portfolios on their desks so that each parent can view the work done by his or her child alone. General classroom displays can consist of group projects and murals so that every child and parent can take equal pride in the classroom.

COMMUNITY INVOLVEMENT IN CLASSROOM ACTIVITIES

Parents as Volunteers

Parents volunteer to do many things in schools to benefit their children and the larger community. Many parents enjoy being members of an all-school organization known as the *Parent Teacher Association (PTA)* or *Parent Teacher Organization (PTO)*. These organizations have regularly scheduled meetings and yearly fundraising events to serve the needs of the school. In most cases, parents do the greatest part of the work on the committees, although teachers are usually represented as well.

In many elementary schools, parents are encouraged to volunteer their time during the school day to assist teachers in educational or extracurricular programs. Parents can serve as coaches, assistant coaches, or referees for some sports events such as all-school field day events. They often serve as helpers on class field trips, accompanying the class on the bus ride and throughout the day. Usually, teachers ask each adult to be responsible for a small group of children during the trip, reducing the adult : child ratio from 28 : 1 down to 4 : 1 or 5 : 1.

In high schools, parents become Booster Club Members and raise funds for sports and other extra-curricular activities. They sell hot dogs and soda at sporting events. They meet teachers at these events and often have an on-the-fly meeting with the teachers. They fix up the gym for dances and other fun activities. They might be asked to chaperone an event. Most parents are willing to be involved if asked.

In the classroom, many primary teachers invite parent volunteers to serve as assistants in the reading and language arts program. A parent can work with one small group while the teacher works with another, or with the rest of the class. In this way, parents can serve many important functions. They can read aloud to a group of children or listen to an individual or a small group of children read aloud to them. Parents can write the words as a child dictates a story or edit a piece of writing done by a child. Parents can listen to book reports and keep records of the number and type of books read by each child.

With the advent of computers in the classroom, many teachers have enjoyed having parents who are knowledgeable about computers volunteer to work with groups of children as they learn to operate a computer or to monitor students' progress as they work with tutorial or problem-solving computer programs.

During individualized mathematics or spelling programs, or those structured on a mastery learning model, parents can serve as assistants who correct formative tests and provide feedback to students. They can also help to organize the large amounts of paperwork, filing, and record keeping that often accompany individualized instructional programs.

There are many benefits to having parents volunteer to work in your classroom, and often there are knowledgable and experienced parents who enjoy this type of work. There are many parents who have interrupted their own careers during their child-raising years who enjoy having a regular volunteer job to look forward to.

Not all teachers, however, enjoy having parent volunteers in their classrooms. Some teachers are reluctant to have parents view the ups and downs that occur in any school day. Other teachers are not comfortable with parent volunteers because the teacher must be ready with activities and materials whenever the parent arrives. For some teachers, this is a burden that outweighs the benefit of having the extra help. It is true that working with parent volunteers means greater responsibility for the teacher, who must manage the other adults as well as the students in the class.

Whether you want to use parents as volunteers in your classroom is one of those issues that you will need to reflect on, considering the benefits against the costs. One of the best ways to gather information about the efficacy of this practice in your classroom is to try it out with one subject area and a knowledgable, experienced parent volunteer in order to find out if it is a system you want to employ.

To increase the likelihood that the practice will work in your room, it is important that you and the parent volunteer discuss in advance what you expect the parent to do and agree on the times the parent will visit. Usually parents do only routine tasks or monitor students as they work on a program that is planned by you and your co-workers. When these matters are clarified, you will probably find the volunteer effort to be very productive, allowing you to reduce the amount of time you spend on routine tasks.

Community Resources

Parents with special interests, abilities, careers, and accomplishments can also enrich your program by visiting to speak to the class about their specialties. A unit on community helpers can certainly benefit from the visits of parents who are nurses, police officers, fire fighters, and others who perform community services. Parents who are manufacturers or waste haulers can provide their input during a unit on ecology. When the class is studying economics, parents who work as merchants can describe the theory of supply and demand to the class.

During the first parent–teacher conference in the fall, you may be able to discover what talents your students' parents possess and create a community resource file to draw on throughout the year. In some schools, these files are kept schoolwide, and parents in the file are happy to come to any classroom in the school to share their knowledge and experience with the children. The file may also contain names of adults in the community who are not parents of children attending the school but who are willing to visit as a service to the community.

Moral Education Programs

The interaction between home and school becomes more complex and controversial when the school's objective changes from supporting the child's academic development to supporting the child's moral development. Nevertheless, schools in the 1990s and the 21st century are likely to be at the center of a growing concern about the need for greater emphasis on moral education. This concern grows out of an awareness that schools must take more responsibility for countering the influence of drugs, violence on television and other media, the fragmentation of the family, and the publicity about questionable ethical practices in business and industry (ASCD, 1988, p. 4).

A panel of educators met in the summer of 1988 to discuss the schools' role in teaching values. The educators agreed that due to the enormous temptations and distractions facing children today, the schools must take an active role in teaching children about the nature of right and wrong. Although the panel recognized that the increasing social, religious, and ethnic diversity of the schools makes it difficult to agree on one set of values, a few common themes appear in almost every culture. The panel recommends that schools develop community-supported programs centering on at least these four themes: *justice, altruism, diligence,* and *respect for human dignity.*

Lickona (1988) recommends that each school should recruit local parents to serve on a school–parent support group to (1) arrive at a consensus of the moral values most important to that community and (2) write a moral education curriculum that will be taught both at school and in the home at the same time (p. 36).

Mary Ellen Saterlie (1988), a school administrator in Baltimore, Maryland, illustrates how such a parent–school partnership can be formed and what it can produce. She describes the Baltimore public schools' experience, in which school administrators created a community task force to participate in an open dialogue on community values. They purposely invited people with very different religious and political beliefs to serve on the task force. After extensive reading and debate, the task force was able to agree upon a "common core" of values appropriate for a democratic and pluralistic society. They are the following:

> compassion, courtesy, critical inquiry, due process, equality of opportunity, freedom of thought and action, honesty, human worth and dignity, integrity, justice, knowledge, loyalty, objectivity, order, patriotism, rational consent, reasoned argument, respect for others' rights, responsible citizenship, rule of law, self-respect, tolerance and truth. (Saterlie, 1988, pp. 46–47)

Following the identification of these community-acknowledged values, the task force wrote outcome statements for the development of these moral values. Their report was then discussed and ratified by the Board of Education. The PTA developed a brochure on the values education program which they distributed to all parents in the system.

The method of implementation of this program allowed each of the 148 schools in the district to appoint its own values committee, which was encouraged to select certain of the task force–identified values to emphasize in its own school projects. This encouraged a creative response from most schools. Some addressed additional values such as computer ethics or academic honesty, as well as those identified by the task force. The Baltimore model linked parents, schools, and the community in a unified examination of moral and ethical issues in order to "strengthen the character of our students, which in turn will contribute to strengthening our free society" (p. 47).

As a beginning teacher, you may find that your school district is taking similar measures, and you may wish to become an active part of the task force that identifies the moral values of your community and creates school programs to educate students in these values. If you find that your school district has not yet considered such a challenge, perhaps you can be the one who initiates the idea. Reflective individuals who are committed to upholding the moral values of the community can serve as important role models for the students they teach.

THE REFLECTIVE TEACHER AS A MEMBER OF THE EDUCATIONAL COMMUNITY

Teacher Empowerment

The focus of the current research on educational reform and the restructuring of schools centers on the teacher, indicating why the role of the teacher is growing in responsibility and respect. Some use the term *teacher empowerment* to describe the new role of the teacher. Teachers are gaining power by showing a growing willingness to take responsibility for all aspects of planning, teaching, and evaluation.

Prior to the 1990s, teachers were viewed by many as the weak links in the educational system. The publishers of textbooks, for example, seemed to assume that the role of the teacher was simply a technical one, and in many schools districts, teachers were encouraged or required simply to follow the texts, workbooks, and elaborately detailed teacher's manuals, without much opportunity to exercise creativity or judgment.

During the 1980s considerable lip service was given to creating excellence in the schools, but at the same time, many states established restrictive mandates and required extensive new assessment procedures that purported to raise the achievement level of students in the basic skills but, in reality, caused many teachers to simply teach to the test.

In contrast, in the 1990s there is growing evidence that this is a time of change and school improvement from the bottom up. "A survey last year by the National Governor's Association found that 21 states offered school districts the chance to apply for waivers to impeding regulations as part of their restructuring initiatives, and several others were considering doing so" (O'Neil, 1990, p.9).

State curricula such as the California Frameworks are designed to encourage classroom teachers to generate creative learning experiences that fit the needs of their own students. They are challenging textbook publishers to provide materials that enhance, rather than limit, teachers' use of a variety of instructional strategies. School districts are being restructured to encourage teachers to contribute innovative proposals for change. Methods of assessing student achievement have changed in several states, including Connecticut, California, and Vermont, where portolios are replacing multiple-choice tests (O'Neil, 1990, p. 9). These methods of assessment empower teachers to make more and better choices about how to meet the needs of their students and design school programs that encourage success.

Teacher empowerment means that teachers have more opportunities to make choices and decisions, a necessary ingredient for reflectiveness. For without the right and responsibility to make decisions, reflecting on the way to improve one's teaching and improve the lives of one's students would be fruitless.

Teachers Mentoring Each Other

One of the most exhilarating changes in teaching today are opportunities that classroom teachers have to take part in the education and support of college and university students and beginning teachers. In Glenview, Illinois, for example, many classroom teachers have contributed to the development of an innovative teacher education program in which De Paul University students are hired as teacher interns at the same time that they take their methods courses in education. The classroom teachers work with university personnel in designing and teaching these methods courses, many of which take place in the school itself. These teachers enjoy the sense of collegiality that they share with each other, the university teachers, and the students. It gives them a sense of passing on the best of what they know to the next generation of teachers.

A few years ago, only the school principal was responsible for observing and evaluating teachers' classroom performance. But in many school systems today, teachers are sharing their own perspectives with each other as part of the evaluation process. Experienced classroom teachers, sometimes called *coaches* or *mentor teachers,* observe less experienced teachers as they work with children in their classrooms. Afterward, the two teachers discuss the observed classroom events. This practice allows the mentor teacher to provide critical feedback and to share personal knowledge with colleagues. It also encourages the beginning teachers to reflect on what they do, the effects of their actions, and decisions and ways to improve their teaching.

Conclusions

At the center of all of this change is the teacher, and the growing power, responsibility and respect the teacher has earned. Porter and Brophy (1988) report that since the early 1970s there has been a surge of activity in research on teaching. Much of it has been predicated on a deceptively simple thesis: Effective school learning requires good teaching, and good teachers are those who exercise good judgment in constructing the education of their students (p. 74). In other words, as described in chapter 1 of this text, good teachers are those who use reflective thinking, based on moral principles, in making judgments about classroom events. There is a strong, undeniable link between *reflective* and *effective* teachers.

As discussed in chapter 2, research shows that the most effective teachers are good classroom managers. This management skill grows directly out of reflective, empathetic, and democratic leadership from the first day of school. As shown in chapter 3, the role of the teacher includes the responsibility for making accurate diagnoses, which occurs when teachers use formal and informal sources of information as a means of making reflective judgments about appropriate placements of students in the curriculum so that they can achieve success.

Throughout the research on effective teaching and effective schools the attribute of *teacher clarity* surfaces again and again. "Effective teachers are clear about what they intend to accomplish through their instruction, and they keep these goals in mind both in designing instruction and in communicating its purposes to the students" (Porter and Brophy, 1988, p. 81). Clarity of goal setting requires the reflective planning practices described in chapter 4.

It is also becoming apparent that it is very effective to combine or integrate subjects into multidisciplinary units of study, as described in chapters 5 and 6. Rather than being textbook technicians, reflective teachers prefer to create their own learning experiences, either individually or with teammates. They frequently focus on interesting themes or topics in which students use and develop their reading, writing, and research skills as they gain new knowledge about a variety of subjects.

Another common element identified throughout the literature on effective teaching is that effective teachers create learning experiences in which students are not simply passive recipients of fact-based knowledge; instead, they teach their students how to use many *cognitive processes*, how to organize information in new ways, and how to solve problems for themselves. It takes a reflective teacher, with a C-M view of learning to recognize and select the appropriate teaching strategies that will engage students in active learning, as described in chapters 7, 8, 9, and 10.

Reflective teachers are willing to use a variety of assessment techniques, such as those described in chapter 11, rather than rely on one objective method. This is an especially effective practice because it allows students with a variety of learning styles to demonstrate their accomplishments and experience success. Effective practitioners are also talented at providing students with useful, timely, and detailed *critical feedback* so that students know what is expected and what they must do in order to succeed. But we now know that simply being a good evaluator is not enough; the most effective teachers are those described in chapter 12, who cause their students to take an active role in the evaluation of their own learning by teaching them how to apply *metacogni-*

tive strategies in order to become independent and self-reliant, able to monitor and regulate their own learning.

In addition to their responsibilities to their students, effective teachers are able to communicate well with the parents and other members of the school community in order to support the moral development of students.

The role of the teacher in the educational community is changing. Teaching shows considerable promise of becoming a highly respected profession in the United States during the 21st century. This is largely due to the efforts of reflective teachers who are asking the important questions about how they can improve classroom events and children's lives. Alone or in collaboration, reflective teachers are seeking out new alternatives and selecting the ones they believe might improve their teaching. They are taking responsibility for evaluating their classroom practices by gathering data from their own observations and from the current research and knowledge base on teaching and learning. They are disseminating what works for them in faculty meetings, workshops, conferences, and articles in professional journals.

Classroom teachers, such as Lori Shoults, Ginny Bailey, Tim Curbo, Jim Hicks, Chris Chiaverina, Pam Knight, Mary Catherine Swanson, Rick Bailey, Laurie Mednick, and Jean Malvaso-Zingaro are wonderful examples of what this profession can become if new teachers like you are willing to take risks and the responsibility that comes with them.

If you follow in Lori's footsteps, you are likely to create a classroom environment that is nurturing and stimulating. If you are like Ginny, you will view yourself as a learner throughout your career. If you are like Tim, you will take initiative for seeking out new and better ways of teaching. If you are like Mary Catherine, you may reflect deeply about what you can do to do what must be done. If you are like Jean, you will show caring and take responsibility for helping your students make meaningful contributions to society. If you are like Chris and Jim, you will work overtime to create exciting hands-on lessons. If you are like Pam, you will pioneer a new way of assessing learning and write about your own classroom experiences for educational journals. If you begin your teaching experience with the commitment and energy that Mary O'Donnell gives her students, they will grow strong and confident. If you are willing to do these things, you will contribute to the profession of teaching and win the respect of your students and the entire educational community.

OPPORTUNITIES FOR REFLECTION

▼ Reflective Essay: Teacher Empowerment

Are you a person who is comfortable or uncomfortable with decision-making power? If you work in a school district that encourages teachers to take responsibility for many important decisions, will you welcome this as an opportunity or look on it as a burden? Would you prefer to make decisions about your own classroom independently, or would you rather share the power and the responsibility with your teammates?

▼ Classroom Visit: Teacher Empowerment

In your observations of this classroom and school during the past several weeks, what have you noticed about the decision-making power? Does the power reside completely in the hands of school administrators, or is it shared? What are some examples of teacher empowerment that you have observed? Ask your cooperating teacher to discuss the changes in teacher power that have occurred in the past few years. What are the major impediments to teacher empowerment in this school or district?

REFERENCES

ASSOCIATION OF SUPERVISION AND CURRICULUM DEVELOPMENT (ASCD). (1988). Moral education in the life of the school. *Educational Leadership, 45*(8), 4–8.

BECKER, H., & EPSTEIN, J. (1982). Parent involvement: A survey of teacher practices. *Elementary School Journal, 83,* 85–102.

FIRST, J., (1988). Immigrant students in U.S. public schools: Challenges with solutions. *Phi Delta Kappan, 70*(3), 205–210.

FLORIO-RUANE, S. (1989). Social organization of classes and schools. In M. Reynolds (Ed.), *Knowledge base for beginning teachers* (pp. 163–172). Oxford: Pergamon.

GOOD, T., & BROPHY, J. (1987). *Looking in classrooms* (4th ed.). New York: Harper & Row.

GRONLUND, N. & LINN, R. (1990). *Measurement and evaluation in teaching.* New York: Macmillan.

LICKONA, T. (1988). How parents and schools can work together to raise moral children. *Educational Leadership, 45*(8), 36–38.

OAKES, J., & LIPTON, M. (1990). *Making the best of schools. New Haven, CT: Yale University Press.*

O'NEIL, J. (1990). Piecing together the restructuring puzzle. *Educational Leadership, 47*(7), 4–10.

PORTER, A., & BROPHY, J. (1988). Synthesis of research on good teaching. *Educational Leadership, 45,* 74–85.

RIMM, S. (1986). *Underachievement syndrome: Causes and cures.* Watertown, WI: Apple Publishing.

SATERLIE, M. (1988). Developing a community consensus for teaching values. *Educational Leadership, 45*(8), 44–47.

SUBJECT INDEX

ABOUT THE AUTHORS

JUDY EBY AND ED KUJAWA are teacher educators at the University of San Diego.

Judy began her teaching career in Head Start in San Diego in the 1960s. This experience awakened a life-long passion for improving the lives of children through school experiences. She spent 8 years as an elementary classroom teacher in Elgin, and Crystal Lake, Illinois, then became a gifted program coordinator and teacher in Barrington, Illinois.

In 1984, Judy had the opportunity to study with Benjamin S. Bloom at Northwestern University. She received her Ph.D. there in 1986 and became a teacher educator first at De Paul University in Chicago and now at U.S.D. She is also involved in volunteer programs with San Diego schoolchildren. She is assisting Robert Condon in developing a program called *Rolling Readers* that brings adult readers into schools, day care centers, and housing projects to read to children.

This is Judy's third book. She wrote *A Thoughtful Overview of Gifted Education* with Joan Smutny in 1990 and *Reflective Planning, Teaching, and Evaluation for the Elementary School* in 1992.

Ed received his Ph.D. from the University of Michigan. He began his teaching career in the Toledo, Ohio, public schools as a mathematics teacher. He piloted a federally funded program in mathematics and was involved in training teachers in the Teacher Corp. Program. He is currently the coordinator of the Elementary Teacher Education program at the University of San Diego.